PROPERTY, TERRITORY, GLOBALIZATION

Struggles over Autonomy

Edited by William D. Coleman

UBCPress · Vancouver · Toronto

21 20 19 18 17 16 15 14 13 12 11   5 4 3 2 1

Printed in Canada on FSC-certified ancient-forest-free paper (100% post-consumer recycled) that is processed chlorine- and acid-free.

Library and Archives Canada Cataloguing in Publication

Property, territory, globalization : struggles over autonomy / edited by William D. Coleman.

(Globalization and autonomy, 1913-7494)
Includes bibliographical references and index.
ISBN 978-0-7748-2017-2 (bound); ISBN 978-0-7748-2018-9 (pbk.)

1. Globalization – Political aspects. 2. Law and globalization. 3. Autonomy. 4. Intellectual property. 5. Indigenous peoples – Land tenure. I. Coleman, William D. (William Donald). II. Series: Globalization and autonomy

JZ1318.P76 2011   327.1   C2011-900998-6

---

e-book ISBNs: ISBN 978-0-7748-2019-6 (epdf); ISBN 978-0-7748-2020-2 (epub)

Canadä

UBC Press gratefully acknowledges the financial support for our publishing program of the Government of Canada (through the Canada Book Fund), the Canada Council for the Arts, and the British Columbia Arts Council.

Research for this volume was supported by the Social Sciences and Humanities Research Council of Canada through its Major Collaborative Research Initiatives Program, Grant No. 421-2001-1000, and by the Canada Research Chairs Program.

Printed and bound in Canada by Friesens
Set in Syntax and Bembo by Artegraphica Design Co. Ltd.
Text design: George Kirkpatrick
Copy editor: Lesley Erickson
Indexer: Annette Lorek

UBC Press
The University of British Columbia
2029 West Mall
Vancouver, BC V6T 1Z2
www.ubcpress.ca

Contents

Preface

The Globalization and Autonomy Series: Dialectical Relationships in the Contemporary World

THE VOLUMES IN THE Globalization and Autonomy series offer the results from an interdisciplinary Major Collaborative Research Initiative (MCRI) funded by the Social Sciences and Humanities Research Council of Canada (SSHRC). SSHRC set up the MCRI program to provide a vehicle to support larger projects with research objectives requiring collaboration among researchers from different universities and across a range of disciplines. The MCRI on Globalization and Autonomy began in April 2002. The research team involved forty co-investigators from twelve universities across Canada and another twenty academic contributors from outside Canada, including scholars from Australia, Brazil, China, Denmark, France, Germany, Slovenia, Taiwan, the United Kingdom, and the United States. Drawing on additional funding from the International Development Research Centre (IDRC), the project became affiliated with a separate interdisciplinary research team of twenty-eight scholars, the Groupe d'Études et de Recherches Interdisciplinaires sur la Méditerranée (GERIM). GERIM is based in Tunisia and includes members from France, Spain, Jordan, and Lebanon as well. Scholars from the following disciplines participated in the project: anthropology, comparative literature, cultural studies, economics, English literature, geography, history, music, philosophy, political science, and sociology.

The project was conceived, designed, and implemented to carry out interdisciplinary research. We endeavoured to put disciplinary-based theories and conceptual frameworks into dialogue with one another, with a view to developing new theories and understandings of human societies. Four conditions needed to be met if research was to be done in this way. First, we brought humanities and social science disciplines into a relationship of mutual influence, where perspectives were integrated without subordinating one to another. To achieve this integration, the team agreed on a set of core research objectives informed by existing writings on globalization and autonomy. Members developed a number of research questions designed to address these objectives and a research plan that would permit them to address these questions in a focused, systematic way. Second, team members individually were encouraged to think inside disciplines other than their own and to respect differences across disciplines in terms of how the object of knowledge is constructed. Third, team members were selected to ensure that the research was carried out using multiple methodologies. Finally, faced with researching the complex relationships involved in globalization, an interdisciplinary approach meant that our work would be necessarily pluri-theoretical. We held to the view that theories would be most effective when, in addition to applying ideas rigorously, their proponents acknowledged the limitations of any particular theoretical perspective and consciously set out to cross boundaries and use other, sometimes seemingly incommensurable, perspectives.

To ensure intellectual integration from the start, team members agreed on this approach at the first full meeting of the project and committed to the following core objective: *to investigate the relationship between globalization and the processes of securing and building autonomy.* To this end, we sought to refine understanding of these concepts and of the historical evolution of the processes inherent in both of them, given the contested character of their content, meaning, and symbolic status. Given that *globalization* is the term currently employed to describe the contemporary moment, we attempted to:

- determine the opportunities globalization might create and the constraints globalization might place on individuals and communities seeking to secure and build autonomy
- evaluate the extent to which individuals and communities might be able to exploit these opportunities and to overcome these constraints
- assess the opportunities for empowerment that globalization might create for individuals and communities seeking to secure and to build autonomy

- determine how the autonomy available to individuals and communities might permit them to contest, reshape, or engage globalization.

In seeking to address the core objectives for the project, we moved our research in three interrelated directions. First, we accepted that globalization and autonomy have deep historical roots. What is happening today in the world is in many ways continuous with what has taken place in the past. Thus, the burden of a contemporary examination of globalization and autonomy is to assess what is new and what has changed. Second, the dynamics of the relationship between globalization and autonomy are related to a series of important changes in the locations of power and authority. Finally, the globalization-autonomy dynamic plays out in the construction and reconstruction of identities, the nature and value of community, and the articulation of autonomy in and through cultures and discrete institutions. In each of these three areas, the team developed and agreed to answer core questions to provide clear direction for the research. The full text of the questions is available at http://globalization.mcmaster.ca/ga/ga81.htm.

Over successive annual meetings of the team, our research coalesced around the following themes: institutions and global ordering; democracy and legitimacy; continuity and rupture in the history of globalization and autonomy; history, property regimes and capitalism; community; culture; the situation and struggles of indigenous peoples; and the Mediterranean region as a microcosm of North-South relations. The researchers addressing these themes tended to be drawn from several disciplines, leading to interdisciplinary dialogue within each thematic group. The themes then crystallized into separate research problems, which came to be addressed by the volumes in the series. While these volumes were taking form, the project team also developed an online publication, the *Globalization and Autonomy Online Compendium* (see next page), which makes our findings available to the general public through research summaries; a glossary of key concepts, organizations, people, events, and places; and a comprehensive bibliography. The ultimate objective of all of these publications is to produce an integrated corpus of outstanding research that provides an in-depth study of the varying relationships between globalization and autonomy.

Globalization and Autonomy Online Compendium

Readers of this volume may also be interested in the *Globalization and Autonomy Online Compendium* (available at www.globalautonomy.ca). The *Compendium* is a collective publication by the team of Canadian and international scholars who have been part of the SSHRC Major Collaborative Research Initiative that gave rise to the volumes in the Globalization and Autonomy series. Through the *Compendium,* the team is making the results of their research available to a wide public audience. Team members have prepared a glossary of hundreds of short articles on relevant persons, places, organizations, events, and key concepts and have compiled an extensive searchable bibliographical database. Short summaries of the chapters in other volumes of the Globalization and Autonomy series can also be found in the *Compendium,* along with position papers and peer-reviewed research articles on globalization and autonomy issues.

Acknowledgments

The editor would like to express his immense gratitude to Nancy Johnson, the project editor for the MCRI on Globalization and Autonomy, for her excellent work, support, and committed professionalism. I am also grateful to Jennifer Clark, Sara Mayo, and Cassandra Pohl for administrative support throughout the project. I acknowledge that the research for my contributions to the book was undertaken, in part, thanks to funding from the Canada Research Chairs Program. The editor and volume authors would also like to thank the peer reviewers of this book for their helpful and insightful comments and suggestions. And the excellence of these peer reviewers would not have been possible if it were not for the efforts of Emily Andrew, senior editor of UBC Press. For this book, and for all others in the series, she has been an insightful, compassionate, and highly professional guide. I am indeed fortunate to have had the opportunity to work with her over the years, as well as with her colleagues at the Press, Melissa Pitts and Holly Keller.

Property, Territory, Globalization

chapter 1

Introduction: Property, Autonomy, Territory, and Globalization

Scott Prudham and William D. Coleman

THIS VOLUME EXAMINES THE complex relationships among property, globalization, and autonomy. The contributors explore how the development of particular property regimes has reinforced, constituted, and disrupted dynamics of globalization, as we have come to understand them, and how autonomies of various kinds have been expressed, enhanced, and hindered through property relations. These issues, in turn, reflect a common belief among the editors and authors that property is central to understanding globalization as we define it, particularly in linking the past with the present. We take as a point of departure that property regimes are particularly (though by no means only) central to understanding the nexus of globalization, autonomy, and the political economy of international capitalism.

This book contributes to expanding research in globalization studies by looking at the growing importance of international and global law, on the one hand, and place-based resistance to the effects of such legal developments, on the other. The volume focuses on property regimes at crisis points and uses these crises as key holes for examining globalizing processes and their interactions with autonomies. Property regimes at crisis points are sites of friction, conflict, and resistance in which global capitalism and international authority supported by global law are engaged by local actors through a politics of place. Some scholars of globalization such as Anthony Giddens (1990) and Manuel Castells (1999) have been criticized for overemphasizing the importance of space, while failing to seriously consider the possibility of place as a site of resistance and a source of alternative globalizations. For example, Castells distinguishes between spaces of flows and spaces of places and seems to leave little room for agency in the latter. Giddens (1990) sees globalizing processes as those that involve the "radicalization of modernity" and its implantation everywhere on the planet. He draws on an extensive discussion of time and space but offers virtually no theoretical treatment of place.

This book joins others in challenging these lines of argument and points to examples of place-based politics that engage with capital, defend both alternative modernities and alternatives to modernity, and resist global and national constitutions of property. The book therefore builds on an earlier one in this series, *Renegotiating Community,* which draws place into discussions of communities and change in a global era (Brydon and Coleman 2008). Crises in property regimes highlight how a politics of place can challenge existing globalizing processes, build new bases for autonomy, and articulate alternative ways of living.

Arturo Escobar (2001, 140) defines place as "the experience of a particular location with some measure of groundedness (however unstable), sense of boundaries (however permeable), and connection to everyday life." The politics of place is an "emergent form of politics" that "asserts a logic of difference and possibility that builds on the multiplicity of actions at the level of everyday life" (Escobar 2008, 67). In this respect, places are sites of dynamic cultures, ecologies, and economies and not simply nodes in global capitalism. They are important sources of culture, identity, and autonomy. Despite the deterritorialization and disembedding from place associated with globalization, there remains an "embodiment and emplacement to human life that cannot be denied" (ibid., 7).

When we formulated the agenda for the Globalization and Autonomy project, we realized that we could not study any kind of representative sample of place-based politics. Given our expertise, we concentrated, in particular, on cultural minorities and indigenous peoples. The case studies in this book reflect this focus by emphasizing crises in property regimes involving indigenous peoples. This volume therefore links to another in the series, *Indigenous Peoples and Autonomy: Insights for a Global Age,* which examines the absences and emergences of indigenous peoples and their struggles for autonomy (Blaser et al. 2010). Property regime crises provide an additional window on changing identities, including those of indigenous peoples, which Castells (2003) has explored at length in his book *The Power of Identity.* Writing of responses by indigenous peoples and Afro-Colombians on the Pacific Coast, Escobar (2008, 217) defines identity as a "complex form of self-understanding improvised from the cultural resources at hand in a historical background." The cracks in modernity revealed by crises over property have opened new possibilities for indigenous peoples to reaffirm identity and change the form of that identity as a particular re-articulation of differences, including the addition of a global indigenous identity in some instances (Niezen 2003). Indigenous identities are often built on conceptions of rights to land or territory, which means that the imposition of new property regimes raises deep challenges to established ways of living.

In summary, this book contributes to a broader understanding of globalization by focusing on changes in autonomy aspired to or acted upon by people in places where the property regime is in crisis. It thus emphasizes the continuing importance of place in struggles against newly globalized capitalism. It sketches out some key changes in global law that support capitalism and continuing enclosures of both land and intellectual creations arising from the knowledge, culture, and symbols and healing practices of indigenous and traditional peoples. It demonstrates that both space and place are central to understanding globalization and that viewing globalization as the radicalization of modernity, as a second modernity, or as high modernity overlooks the resistance to such a future by many peoples around the world.

Globalization

In 2000 and 2001, when the program of research for the Globalization and Autonomy project was being drawn up in an application for financial support from the Social Sciences and Humanities Research Council of Canada, participants came face to face with the question, what is globalization? At the outset, the answers varied. As the project proceeded, team members, including the contributors to this book, developed certain commonalities in their understanding of the term. They understood the word *global* as a reference to scale and to phenomena that are somehow transplanetary, to use Jan Aart Scholte's (2005) phrase. They also understood that the spread of transplanetary phenomena is not confined to the economic realm (as is often assumed in popular discourse) but includes political, cultural, military, legal, and non-human aspects as well. They recognized that the growth of transplanetary relationships was uneven, that their density and speed of growth were more pronounced in wealthier countries than in poorer ones and articulated spatially in different ways within all countries.

In 2000, most participants also believed that there was nothing inevitable about globalizing processes. That has not changed. If anything, doubts about claims to inevitability or uni-directionality in transplanetary integration have been renewed by the financial and economic crises of 2008 and 2009. Global historians, including some who have contributed to another volume in this series, *Empires and Autonomy,* note the growth and retraction of transplanetary phenomena over several centuries. A simple glance over the past 150 years suggests, for instance, that these phenomena became more pronounced between 1870 and 1914 but then receded considerably until the late 1970s (Streeter, Weaver, and Coleman 2009).

Most of the authors in this book and the participants in the project more generally entered into these discussions because they had questions about the character and implications of transplanetary connections in the period following the Second World War, particularly since the late 1970s. Most recognize that these connections have accelerated in number, intensity, and extensity. There are varying explanations for this apparent acceleration. At the heart of most explanations is the dynamic transformation of capitalism, propelled in substantial measure by the rapid growth of international financial markets and financial integration. The explosion of international finance and the financialization of capitalism (Arrighi 1994) have shaped the global order in ways not seen before (Castells 1999). Capitalism is global, Castells argues, in that, for the first time in history, it shapes social relationships around the whole planet. Through the use of information and communications technologies, capital "works globally as a unit in real time; and it is realized, invested, and accumulated mainly in the sphere of circulation, that is, as finance capital" (ibid., 471).

The particularly global form of contemporary capitalism is linked in complex ways with innovations in information and communications technologies that have permitted transplanetary connections to become supraterritorial. These connections are less bound by physical location or nation-state boundaries than at any time since the collapse of the highly integrated international economic order in 1914. Indeed, technology has likely made connections less restricted by the traditional territorial powers of states than ever before. Latham and Sassen (2005, 2) amplify this point when they write: "What has tended to operate or be nested at local scales can now move to global scales, and global relations and domains can now, in turn, more easily become directly articulated with thick local settings. In both types of dynamics, the rescaling can bypass the administrative and institutional apparatus of the national level, still the most developed scalar condition. As a result of the growing presence and use of these [information and communications] technologies, an increasing range of social relations and domains have become de facto transboundary." These technologies have permitted more connections to become planet-wide, and these global connections have intruded into the daily lives of more people than ever before (taking into account the caveats about inequalities in distribution noted above). The project came together around a set of questions that focused on the relationships among these globalizing processes and the ways in which these processes have reflected, reinforced, and constrained the autonomy of individuals and collectivities.

Autonomy

In the Globalization and Autonomy project, researchers work with the concepts of both individual and collective autonomy. Specifically, we see these concepts as emerging in tandem with modernity and with particular practices informed by ideas of individualism. Writing over a century ago, Georg Simmel (1971, 219) argued that the oppressiveness of medieval institutions gave rise to the idea of the pure freedom of the individual based on "natural" equality. This eighteenth-century idea of individualism, he added, was complemented by another version of individuality in the nineteenth century — that of the particular and irreplaceable person. These ideas have been translated into notions of autonomy that emphasize that people have "a right to choose for themselves their own pattern of life, to decide in conscience what convictions to espouse, to determine the shape of their lives in a whole host of ways that their ancestors could not control" (Taylor 1991, 2).

Yet Western ideals of individualism have taken different forms in different societies, both within and outside the West. Consequently, the performance of autonomy now varies from one place to another. *Autonomy,* as we define it, refers to the situations of individual persons or communities and to their capacity to shape the conditions under which they live (Held 1995). In part, their capacity to shape those conditions depends on the kinds of conditions in which they find themselves. As Anthony Kwame Appiah (2005, 30) notes: "To have autonomy, we must have acceptable choices." The concept thus can have a communal connotation that suggests self-government or self-determination when it is associated with collective bodies — nation-states, minority groups within states, place-based communities, indigenous peoples, social movements, and religious groups being common examples.

Scholars have critically examined these notions of autonomy. Feminists have argued that unrestrained individual autonomy reflects the dominance of social structures that favour the self-reliant male. They also note the powerful association between this conception of individual autonomy and neoliberal thinking in capitalist social formations (Code 2000). Some believe we should adopt the concept of relational autonomy. In this formulation, autonomy emerges out of the social relationships among persons. Relational autonomy is a central focus of the volume in this series that addresses the research problematic of the project through the experiences and thoughts of indigenous peoples (Blaser et al. 2010). It also underlies several chapters in this volume (see Mollett; Preston; Mackey; and Habib). Scholars in the humanities stress that autonomy is not only a practice, it also exists as a value, often cast as a universal. As Marilyn Friedman (2003, 189) notes, "The ideal of autonomy is a debatable requirement for a good human life." She finds that some groups explicitly reject this value while others implicitly value collective autonomy and refuse to recognize the need for personal autonomy.

In the volume *Unsettled Legitimacy* in this series, we examine the relationship between individual autonomy and collective autonomy in democratic theory (Bernstein and Coleman 2009). Theorists postulate that when decisions arise from the exercise of collective autonomy by individuals who themselves possess individual autonomy, they are highly likely to be accepted and, thus, legitimate. The condition that all members of a given political community must have an equal right to participate in decision making anchors the exercise of collective autonomy. How they exercise that right will vary from person to person as each exercises her or his individual autonomy.

Habermas (1996, 122) suggests that collective autonomy and individual autonomy can be seen as co-original: together, they form the basis of democracy and, thus, of the legitimacy of authoritative decisions by the state. He writes that the "idea of self-legislation *by citizens,* that is, requires that those subject to law as its addressees can at the same time understand themselves as authors of law" (ibid., 120). This idea is also consistent in certain respects with Foucault's concept of governmentality as complex administrative rule in which political subjects are actively enrolled in their own governance, in part through a cultural politics of legitimacy (Foucault 1991; Li 2007). Yet co-originality also rests on assumptions that may be called into question by globalization. Decisions affecting the lives of individuals are generally located in a geographically limited legal territory, where there is socially delimited community, where citizenship rights are shared more or less equally by all members of that community, and where there are clear jurisdictional boundaries. And behind this reasoning lies the assumption that the given polity makes the primary decisions for that community. These conditions are often not met by contemporary institutions in a world characterized by the wide social and political disparities of uneven development.

This volume is particularly concerned with the role of property at the nexus of globalization and autonomy. As is indicated below, notions of individual autonomy are associated with particular social constructions and institutionalizations of property and property regimes. At the same time, the exercise of collective autonomy, particularly by "modern" nation-states, often serves to protect and to reconstruct these same property regimes in times of crisis, thereby affecting individuals' autonomy in both positive and negative ways. Although cast as universal ideas, these notions of autonomy generate considerable friction (Tsing 2005) when they are introduced into societies, particularly indigenous ones, with cultures that have histories of colonialism and resistance to Euro-American domination.

What Is Property?

The immense scholarship on property spans multiple academic disciplines and stretches back far in time. It cannot be reviewed here. But some general comments regarding the approach to property reflected in this volume are warranted. The contributors to this volume accept the commonly held position that although property is often seen as a thing or object unto itself, the concept more correctly refers to a set of social relationships among people and how these relationships govern the relative allocation of rights, responsibilities, and access to particular things. Specifically, John Weaver defines a right to property as "a relationship between a person and other persons respecting access to material resources" (Weaver 2003, 49) (to which we might also add symbolic resources, for example, copyrights).

As C.B. Macpherson (1978) argues, a reification of historical property arrangements — specifically, increasingly comprehensive rights governing the disposal of land in emerging capitalist market economies — has given rise to increasingly common-sense (but problematic) notions. The first of these is the aforementioned mistaken impression that *property* refers strictly to things and thus that property is itself a thing rather than a social relation. Second, he notes the common equation of the term *property* with what Robert Gordon (1996) calls individual absolute dominion, that is, individualistic and highly separable absolute or monopoly (unrestricted and unconstrained) freehold rights over ownership and disposal, including exchange (on this slippage, see also Blomley 2005). Following the likes of Macpherson and Gordon, as well as critical sociological perspectives on property more generally, the essays in this volume approach property as *relational* sets of rights distributed among individuals and groups in ways that make existing property regimes and claims specific, limited and, frequently, shared.[1] We therefore view the assertion of property claims by individuals or groups as being central to notions of autonomy.

Recognition of the overlapping or shared character of property rights to particular elements of the landscape, or what Vandergeest and Peluso (2001) in the context of forest access regimes call species rights, is commonplace in much of the literature dealing with non-Western and non-capitalist contexts.[2] One finds, for instance, in studies of agrarian and peasant societies and in the broad literature on political ecology widespread recognition of typically complex and overlapping rights to particular land parcels, including separate rights to specific crops and/or trees on the same parcel (e.g., Peluso 1992, 1995; Schroeder 1993; Tsing 2005). Moreover, these rights are often tied to and help define social identities, including gender, race, age, and class or caste (see Mackey; Mollett; and Preston, this volume). By contrast, more individuated and exclusive rights, including not only monopoly territorial rights to land ownership but also patent rights that prescribe exclusive rights to inventions, are associated with capitalist social relations and tied closely to the formation of more and more inter-regional and global relations of market exchange. There are certainly good reasons to note such general tendencies. Indeed, dynamics of capitalist commodification and market formation tend towards more exclusive forms of enclosure that enable less restricted disposition and sale.

Nevertheless, an important insight from the literature is that property in many settings remains relational, specific in certain respects, and also bounded or limited. This situation is particularly apparent when we move from abstract generalizations about property to more fine-grained engagements with the specific forms of existing property rights and regimes. Even in full-blown capitalist market economies, the extreme form of Gordon's (1996) characterization of individual absolute dominion is exceedingly rare and the stuff (as Gordon is at pains to argue) of ideological reification. For instance, when we look closely at the suite of restrictions that place important constraints on rights to land and home ownership even in ostensibly free market economies, we gain a sense of how rare such pure forms are (Blomley 2004). Discrete or partial rights are also typical in many commercial resource extraction or harvesting settings, including, perhaps most evidently, instances involving lands (or waters) that remain in important respects under state control. Securing access rights to ground water, for instance, is typically a complicated affair, and water for irrigation is often subject to complex entitlements that may not be transferable. Commercial harvesting rights to federal (public) lands in the national forest system of the United States are also an example. Here, access rights for timber extraction even for the largest of multinationals are almost exclusively characterized by one-time-only private logging or gathering rights and no enduring claims to the land per se. In short, property regimes vary immensely, but they are seldom, if ever, simple or absolute. The contributors to this volume generally reflect this observation by attending to the relational specificity of particular property regimes in both their formal and informal guises.

We also emphasize that property regimes are social institutions, made in the crucible of human action, culture, and power relations. They are not pre-given or universal. This emphasis is true even though for several centuries the thrust of development in law in many jurisdictions around the world has been towards tighter definitions of formal rights and the introduction of measures meant to ease the transfer of rights. Our historicist view contrasts in this respect with much classical liberal scholarship on property. This scholarship is epitomized by the paradigmatic writings of John Locke (1952 [1690]), which construct property in terms of universal or natural rights independent of particular historical or geographical contexts. In this tradition, a pervasive naturalism represents particular social orderings as pre-given or teleological outcomes of human social development. For Thomas Malthus (Malthus and Gilbert 1993 [1798]), for example, benevolence would eventually and inevitably give way to greed as a higher form of human development and, with it, collective property would give way to more private, exclusive forms:

> It appears that a society constituted according to the most beautiful form that imagination can conceive, with benevolence for its moving principle, instead of self-love, and with every evil disposition in all its members corrected by reason and not force, would, from the

> inevitable laws of nature, and not from any original depravity of man, in a very short period degenerate into a society constructed upon a plan not essentially different from that which prevails in every known state at present; I mean, a society divided into a class of proprietors, and a class of labourers, and with *self-love* the main-spring of the great machine. (Ibid., 64-65, emphasis added)

This kind of thinking is no mere relic. A similar tack, for example, is evident in Garret Hardin's (1968) famous endorsement of privatization or coercive state intervention in the name of natural resource and land conservation. Following his better known and more familiar argument based on incentives and common-pool decision making, Hardin proceeds in the latter part of his essay to dismiss benevolent behaviour as a solution because, he argues, selfish genes in humans eventually win out (in an evolutionary sense) anyway.[3] In short, for Hardin, social policies aimed at individuation and privatization of land would only follow the so-called natural order of things.

A tight coupling of commerce, capitalism, and property relations in this genealogy is certainly no accident. Indeed, for Jeremy Bentham, as for Locke, freedom (i.e., political autonomy) is defined in substantial measure by rights to property.[4] The institutionalization of this ideal helped to underpin a particularly British-led wave of global economic integration during the nineteenth century (Polanyi 1944). The notion of freedom as a set of rights governing the acquisition and disposition of material property is also deeply ingrained in US ideals of political emancipation. Moreover, this ethos has been strengthened more recently by neoliberal discourses and projects that reassert political freedom as the absence of collective or social (usually state-based) constraints on individual rights to the disposition (including market exchange) of material property (Jessop 2002; Harvey 2005; Andreasson 2006).

In this volume, we do not engage critically with this ethos per se, although some of the contributors do take up this project directly. Rather, the volume reflects our collective recognition of the importance of property rights (particularly, though by no means only, individual, exclusive forms of property rights) to liberal and neoliberal notions of freedom. We are especially interested in how such notions of freedom and their expressions via property regimes articulate capitalism with governance and political rationality (Brown 2006). These articulations are pivotal to defining and coming to terms with US-led globalization, an issue addressed in several chapters in *Empires and Autonomy,* another volume in this series (Streeter, Weaver, and Coleman 2009). Our perspective emphasizes this period as a thoroughly *social* production characterized and punctuated by specific historical geographies, a perspective we bring to bear on the formation of significant regimes of property and their relationships to globalizing tendencies.

We also approach property as a set of rights that are at once both formal and informal. By *formal rights* we mean those that are codified in some fashion or socially understood as binding. In general terms, the expansion of global connections under colonial and postcolonial power relations has involved a transition from less to more formal property regimes (Benton 2002; Weaver 2003). Certainly, the territorialization of formal administrative regimes governing property represented a singular front in the more widespread introduction of the rule of law under European-led colonialism, one that has been largely continued in many postcolonial contexts and strengthened by neoliberal reforms. In many instances, as Vandergeest and Peluso (2001) discuss in the specific context of Southeast Asia, this shift constituted, and in significant measure produced, the colonial state. Similarly, the international integration and harmonization of formal property norms is a key front in the US-led post–Bretton Woods era of globalization, energized in no small measure by the wave of privatization introduced as part of the World Bank and the International Monetary Fund brokered structural adjustment programs. By no means do we see this broad shift from informal to formal rights as a process innocent of coercion, violence, and active dispossession. Indeed, the instantiation of the rule of law is necessarily propelled by uneven power relations, not least the coercive power of states to create and enforce property rights.

At the same time, we recognize that the institutionalization of formal property law, although propelled by uneven power relations, cannot be conceptualized entirely as a break from the past: it is frequently an incomplete project. For example, an increasing formalism in property regimes has often involved (selective) codification of pre-existing informal rights and customs (Thompson 1975; Peluso 1995). In such instances, formalization does not so much extinguish or replace informal property norms as rework them into hybrids of new and old. Moreover, even in a world of ostensibly formal and clear property rights, norms of formal and informal property circulate in everyday discourse and practise in complex and sometimes contradictory ways. Seemingly clear boundaries of private and public spaces become blurred (Blomley 2004). This collection recognizes the complex character of actually existing property regimes, even as the contributors attempt to track the broader institutionalization of international property norms pivotal to the delineation of contending autonomies in a globalizing world. Capturing some of the resulting friction between the universal and the specific, the abstract and the concrete, the formal and the informal is one of our goals.

Why Property?

Property regimes help to define, reflect, and reinforce the character and trajectory of competing autonomies and thus constitute a key lens through which to view the relationship between these autonomies and globalizing tendencies. These processes are most obvious in the ways in which material and semiotic norms of property are geographically diffused as universals in the forging of global connections as individuals, corporations, and the states supporting them extend and deepen their geographic reach. The result is not uniformity but rather a proliferation of institutional, discursive, cultural, and material "frontiers" in the power-laden crucible of making and remaking property relations. And in this remaking, universals are actively reshaped, taking particular hybrid forms (Canclini 2005). Tsing (2005, 3) uses the term *friction* to characterize the "awkward, uneven, unstable, and creative qualities of interconnection across difference" that result. Each encounter takes on its own particular form as the grip of the universal meets the ways of being, knowing, and living in a particular place. The friction that comes with the introduction of universals into a frontier means the outcome is not the same from one place to another. All parts of the world do not end up looking the same or having identical laws. More generally, the globalization of modernity itself, of which property rights are a part, differs from place to place (Dirlik 2007). The "encounters across difference" involved are messy and surprising (Tsing 2005, 4), even if certain tendencies are evident (including, importantly, more and more formalism and individuation in property regimes). And, as most of the chapters in this volume show, these encounters are often protracted and violent, understandings are frequently unstable, and law can sometimes be turned on its head as global connections take new forms. Tsing (ibid., 9) concludes that the resulting "actually existing universalisms are hybrid, transient, and involved in constant reformulation through dialogue."

These encounters provide fundamental dynamics that shape geographically uneven development in and through globalization. Property norms are thus not only one of the ways in which the extensive logic of globalization is expressed and the dynamics of autonomy are played out but also one of the mechanisms through which disparate places and peoples commingle with one another. Attempts to standardize international intellectual property regulation under the Agreement on Trade-Related Aspects of Intellectual Property Rights (TRIPS) of the World Trade Organization represent a recent example of these dynamics, and they are discussed in this volume by A. Claire Cutler and Daniel Gorman. Though different in significant ways from overt imperialism, these globalizing tendencies nevertheless share in common with colonialism the territorialization of power relations and governance. By *territorialization,* we mean the spatial expression of power relations in general and the more specific expression of property rights and their administration in the delineation of particular spaces. Not all property claims are claims to land or parcels of space, but the territorializing dynamic of property regimes in a globalizing world includes the expanding geographic scope of property regimes to be sure, whether the specific things administered by these regimes are spatially explicit or not. We are also interested, following Vandergeest and Peluso (1995), in the notion of territorialization as the filling out or deepening development of administrative power within prescribed geographic boundaries. One of the merits of this perspective, particularly vis-à-vis globalization, is that it links the spatial dynamics of what goes on *between* states with what goes on *within* states.

We also view the delineation and administration of property rights as forms of governmentality (see, e.g., Vandergeest and Peluso 2001). In the broadest terms, *governmentality* refers to particular forms of power relations and political rationalities involved in administering the well-being of populations within a particular territorial setting. It refers to a way of governing relations among "men and things" within a modern, complex administrative setting and typically, but by no means only, in reference to the institutional and discursive apparatus of the liberal nation-state (Foucault 1991; Braun 2000; Li 2007). Governmentality is a conceptualization of political rationality and power that operates through consent (in contrast with more coercive forms of the exercise of sovereignty) and features more diffuse technologies of governance. Through governmentality, populations actively embody their own governance by virtue of a cultural politics of consent whose logic and rationale in significant measure decentres and depoliticizes sovereignty within regimes of ostensibly objective truth, proper conduct, and correct orderings. According to Watts (2003, 10, emphasis added), "modern governmentality is rendered distinctive by the specific forms in which the population and the economy are administered" and by "how sovereignty comes to be *articulated through* the populations and the processes that constitute them." Through these processes, the development of the administrative apparatus is thickened geographically via its expression through relations among "men" and "things" within territorial boundaries (Braun 2000).

Although *governmentality* is Foucault's term, a rich literature interpreting, debating, and extending its meaning has emerged, cutting across academic disciplines and attempting to understand the interplay of state power, political economy, rational administration, and forms of political subjectivities (individual and collective). Specifically modern forms of property are a central concern here, not least because of the location of many property regimes at the interface of governance and territorial administration on the one hand and commerce on the other. Of particular concern to this volume is the twofold process by which property regimes lead to the geographic extension of social relations and institutions and to geographic integration via the articulation of disparate places under more or less common (though by no means homogeneous) modes of governance.

Although never static and certainly not linear in their development over time, property regimes direct our attention to the ways in which issues of access to and control over assets and resources of various kinds, by individuals and communities, are structured by formal and informal norms. The differential allocation of property is both a (partial) cause and a consequence of globalizing tendencies and, at the same time, it is constitutive of autonomy. Property is an important lens through which to study the articulation of contending autonomies (as relational capacities) in a globalizing world. After all, property regimes in significant ways delineate, institutionalize, legitimate, and (often but not always) territorialize autonomy. They prescribe — formally and otherwise — the rights and obligations individuals or groups have in relation to others, as mediated through the various things (including geographical spaces and cultural creations) to which property rights apply.

Property regimes are also crucial because they represent key sites of struggle, knowledge production, and identity formation. They often track the exercise of hegemonic power. In this respect, property regimes are always more than rights to assets: they are constitutive of the production of subjectivities — individual and collective — among rights holders (Ribot and Peluso 2003; Tsing 2005; Redclift 2006; Vasudevan, McFarlane, and Jeffrey 2008). In short, property helps make us who we are in a globalizing world increasingly articulated through the exercise of power relations among states, international institutions, and capitalist firms.

Globalist Moments: Our Approach

Any study attempting to connect property with globalization and autonomy will likely invite the criticism that struggles over property rights vary significantly in form, depending on the socio-cultural and political context in which these struggles take place. As many studies of property have shown, encounters at the frontiers of contending property regimes are singular, often violent, and usually protracted (see Weaver 2003). Our goal is not so much to add to these studies. Rather, our objective is to use property as a lens through which to gain some understanding of the complex dynamic between globalization and autonomy, the overall goal of the Globalization and Autonomy series. Although we focus, in particular, on contemporary globalization, we note that earlier periods of intensifying global connections have influenced how struggles for self-determination and individual and collective autonomy take place.

We emphasize the ways in which property regimes have been shaped by defining moments or ruptures, significant breaks or punctuation points from which a history of the globalizing present becomes more discernable. We call these ruptures globalist moments. These moments represent interwoven material and semiotic ruptures in space and time from which it becomes possible to discern trajectories. This volume is premised on the idea that significant moments in the making of enduring property regimes are critical in the demarcation of coherent periods *(longues durées)* of global integration, disintegration, and hegemony (Braudel 1980; Arrighi 1994).

With this focus in mind, each contribution in the volume features a particular struggle over property regimes to provide a window on the globalization-autonomy dynamic. We hope that these moments reveal the dialectic between globalization and autonomy and the friction that results. Again, turning to Tsing (2005, 6), "Friction makes global connection powerful and effective. Meanwhile, without even trying, friction gets in the way of the smooth operation of global power. Difference can disrupt, causing everyday malfunctions as well as unexpected cataclysms. Friction refuses the lie that global power operates as a well-oiled machine. Furthermore, difference sometimes inspires insurrection. Friction can be the fly in the elephant's nose." And yet, despite these frictions, patterns emerge, and the contributors seek to lay them bare.

The identification and strict delineation of such moments is always subjective, not to mention methodologically and epistemologically fraught. We do not pretend to suggest otherwise. Nevertheless, we feel there is sufficient reason to focus on important junctures — on frontier encounters between past and present, present and future, and here and there, on periods when one set of property norms and customs collides with another, creating new or extended norms, conventions, and institutions. Examples include the infamous *Diamond v. Chakrabarty* decision of the US Supreme Court in 1980, a precedent-setting case that extended patent rights over living organisms. This moment illuminates our approach in several respects. Certainly, in the eyes of many scholars and activists, the case marked a radical break from an institutional and discursive past, from a period when life was considered outside the scope of invention and, thus, conventional patents. Subsequent US-led efforts to export exclusive intellectual property regimes covering genes and genetically modified organisms have been successful in substantial measure, though they have certainly met with resistance (see McAfee 2003; Prudham 2007; and Gorman and Coleman and Reed, this volume), building in important ways on *Diamond v. Chakrabarty*.

Nonetheless, this particular moment cannot be understood strictly in isolation. There were important precursors in US plant patent legislation and critical developments in the political economy of biotechnologies more generally (Kloppenburg 2004). Moreover, subsequent developments and decisions in the realm of US patent law during the 1980s have also proved important in consolidating the trajectory (Kevles 1998). One must also consider the longer-term discursive and epistemic historical trajectory by which life has come to be seen increasingly in terms of discrete and separable bits of information or code (Kay 2000). And at the broadest level, the *Diamond v. Chakrabarty* decision must be understood in relation to a more long-standing US patent doctrine regarding the delineation of rights for sole inventors and entrepreneurs that dates to the late eighteenth century, together with more than 125 years of international relations mediated through patent treaties since the 1883 Paris Convention for the Protection of Industrial Property. In short, this example strongly supports arguments in favour of decentring a strictly event-focused gaze.

What this collection does, in part, is use significant events in the development and consolidation of property regimes to invoke *exactly* these kinds of debates. This court case can serve as both a narrative and analytical device to focus attention on a set of influences that converged in the moment and on subsequent developments that have defined a trajectory in the regulation of property claims over life forms. One could perhaps choose instead the period between 1980 and 1987, punctuated by the US Patent Office decision to allow the oncomouse patent, as a sort of extended moment. The point is to draw attention to important political, economic, discursive, and institutional tendencies in property regimes that are crystallized in key moments and to the ways in which these moments act as foundations for shaping and constraining the dynamics of globalizing tendencies and autonomies in their wake.

Enclosures: From Bretton Woods to the Neoliberal Washington Consensus

In the volume, we focus on a period that dates from the middle of the twentieth century, when the United States emerged as the world's greatest geopolitical power, and extends through the Washington Consensus era of neoliberal international political and economic integration.[5] The rise of the United States was characterized by important, albeit complex and sometimes highly contradictory, shifts in the expression of geopolitical power relationships and their territorialization. During the period, many former colonized societies also found that "independence" did not entirely mean the end of coloniality (Mignolo 2000, 2005). In areas of knowledge and culture, the world had not yet decentred; the power to enunciate remained largely with the West (Santos 2005, 2007). Accordingly, this shift ushered in a distinctly postcolonial era of enclosures tightly interwoven with reworked modes of geographical knowledge and representation.

What can be said about this most recent era of enclosures? This volume's case studies offer a rich substantive and theoretical diversity that in no way seeks to diminish or oversimplify. We can, however, offer some general observations on property, power relations, autonomy, and spatiality in a globalizing world. It is clear, for instance, that enclosures, as forms of what Marx called primitive accumulation, should by no means be understood exclusively as features of the pre-history of capitalism. Making this exact point, David Harvey discusses and extends Marx's conceptualization of primitive accumulation, arguing that his recasting of Marx's concept as accumulation by dispossession is a necessary and ongoing expression of the expansionary and crisis-prone tendencies of capital accumulation (Harvey 2003, 2007).[6] As the Retort Collective (2006, 194, emphasis added) puts it, "Capitalism ... is rooted in the continual *disembedding* of basic elements of the [human] species' life-world from the extraordinary matrix of social relations which had been the [prior] central creation of humanity's long history."

Without question, we recognize that the dynamics of enclosures are central to contemporary globalization in that globalization is understood (in part) as the extension of capitalist social relations of production and exchange.[7] In this context, there are several reasons for tightly coupling enclosures and capital accumulation. Most important to us in this volume, property rights and the efficiency of exchange and commerce are linked, particularly (but not only) when the delineation of exclusive property rights tends towards individual freehold that approximates individual absolute dominion. This is one of the few things upon which critics and champions of liberalized trading regimes and privatization schemes can agree. Commodity circulation requires alienating discrete things from their social and ecological context (Castree 2003). Processes of alienation are, we stress, not only material but also semiotic in both cause and consequence.[8] The alienation or dissociation of people and things facilitates commodification (as the proliferation of commodities), which is propelled by the expanding geographic scope of capitalist social relations (including relations of commodity exchange). In addition, it encourages the deepening of capitalism as more and more discrete entities are produced and exchanged as commodities (Bonefeld 2001; Lysandrou 2005). This is certainly not to say that a crude and functional economism should prevail in explanations of the complex social processes involved in delineating exclusive and enforceable property rights (for recent discussions, see Bakker 2005; Prudham 2007) or the dynamics of enclosure. It is to say, however, that commodification and the delineation of clear, enforceable, and exclusive property rights are closely linked. A world of increasingly far-flung and integrated commodity production and exchange thereby operates through structures that reflect and reinforce power relations and shape the allocation of benefits.

Yet recognizing the interwoven history of enclosure and commerce and commodity circulation is only the first step towards acknowledging the complexity of the issue. Even a relatively narrow focus on the relationship between exchangeable rights in the form of individual absolute dominion (to use Gordon's phrase) and commodity production and exchange reveals a deeply contradictory tension between what may be called movement and fixity. That is, although clearly delineated and exclusive property regimes facilitate fluid movement via exchange, they are also one of the primary institutional means that fix social relations among people. As a result, access to specific things and territory becomes fixed in ways that can hinder circulation and exchange. This is one of the contradictory tensions that shape what Harvey calls the development of spatio-temporal fixes in capitalist social formations (see Harvey 1982, 1989, 2001a; Schoenberger 2004; Jessop 2006). It is a dynamic that Scott Prudham explores in this volume in his chapter on the emergence of modern forest tenure and regulation in British Columbia. But a debate about the tension between fixing exclusive rights and enabling exchange and use has also long characterized mainstream and critical discussions about patent rights, particularly the issue of how all-encompassing and enduring they should be as monopoly rights to inventors (see, e.g., Gilbert and Newberry 1982; Eisenberg 1992; Carolan 2009). This debate has flared up in recent years in the context of arguments for or against strong patent rights over pharmaceuticals and germplasm and in discussions about how these decisions will shape the dynamics of social justice and technology transfer in poorer countries (Pogge 2005). In this volume, Daniel Gorman and William Coleman and Austina Reed discuss these themes in the more general realm of intellectual property regulation. These dynamics remind us that strong, exclusive property rights can both enable and impede globalization (as a form of integration). They can also enhance or compromise autonomy and a politics of place, depending on the context and the particular configuration of power and interests involved.

It is also important to note in the context of a discussion about the relationship between enclosure, alienation, and exchange that not all forms of enclosure take the form of individual freehold title. Rather, exclusive property regimes can and do develop in the guise of collective and communal enclosures, typically referred to as common property or common pool resource arrangements. A rich and substantial literature documents the important role of communal property regimes in human history and in many different cultures, including in the contemporary period (Ostrom 1990; Feeny et al. 1990). An important thrust of this literature is to differentiate communal from open access regimes, particularly given debates about the shortcomings of the latter when it comes to reconciling usage rights with responsibilities for stewardship (Ciriacy-Wantrup and Bishop 1975).[9] And as scholars of common property regimes have repeatedly emphasized, examples abound in which collective rights and institutions have successfully addressed such tensions in order to balance exploitation with conservation of communally governed resources (Cox 1985; Berkes et al. 1989; Ostrom et al. 1999; Agrawal 2001).

Recognition of the important role and defining features of common property regimes is an important counter to the rush to secure individual freehold rights as a singular alternative to problems posed by externalities and improper incentives (Ostrom 1990). But this recognition does not obviate so much as complicate the connection between enclosure and exchange. That is, commodity circulation and exchange are facilitated by the clear delineation of property rights, whether individual freehold or collective, in so much as clarity and social sanction (including enforceability) of exclusive property regimes reduce social frictions that might otherwise inhibit transfer of ownership.

That being the case, many actually existing common property regimes explicitly restrict or strictly delineate rights of exchange, thus excluding those outside the community in which title is vested. For example, many contemporary community resource tenure regimes allow for commodity production and exchange from resource extraction but prohibit or restrict alienation of the underlying rights to land. Similar restrictions are a noted feature of many traditional or indigenous property regimes (Berkes et al. 1998; Berkes and IUCNNR 1999). This only reinforces the importance of focusing on actually existing property regimes and enclosures to interrogate connections between autonomy, globalization, and property, even when globalization is understood more narrowly as the development of far-flung relations of commodity circulation.

When we think about the connections between force, on the one hand, and freedom and autonomy, on the other, the complexities and nuances of property relations likewise become apparent. Harvey's conceptualization of the contemporary dynamics of accumulation by dispossession explicitly develops these dynamics as contending geopolitical logics of power. On the one hand, there is overt territorial domination, associated most closely with the era of colonialism, but by no means absent from the contemporary world and the Pax Americana. On the other hand, there is the more familiar and celebrated face of geopolitical liberalism, in which access to far-flung spaces is sought through negotiated integration of financial and commodity markets (Harvey 2003). The ebb and flow of these geopolitical strategies, backed up by a global network of military bases, is a central dynamic of US-led hegemony (see also Glassman 2005) and, thus, of postwar globalization. Throughout the Bretton Woods era, each expansion of markets is present as a US-led strategy of international engagement. International relations under US geopolitical hegemony, when framed against a global network of some seven hundred military bases in over ninety countries (Johnson 2004), are bound to an underlying logic of coercive enforcement. And the periodic assertion of more direct forms of territorial domination (including post-9/11 invasions, however justified), particularly when petroleum resources are present, serves as a reminder that property as a set of enforceable claims stands at the uneasy and contradictory intersection of the invisible hand and the iron fist (Watts 1994). In short, enforceable, exclusive property claims, though packaged as vehicles of freedom, are inextricably bound up with violence, real or implied (Blomley 2003).

Acknowledging the centrality of violence to enclosures and the administration of exclusive forms of property, whether individual or communal, is not the same as arguing that formal exclusive property regimes are merely a technology of elite rule. Indeed, to situate property regimes in relation to governmentality, we must understand power and hegemony in ways that take consent seriously, particularly when property regimes appear and are maintained via political rationalities of social inclusion (however conceptualized). In his classic study of the transformation of rights to land in Hanoverian England, *Whigs and Hunters,* E.P. Thompson (1975) makes this argument to devastating effect vis-à-vis the rise of the rule of law (including in the administration of property claims). Thompson argues that English enclosures, which entailed a shift from informal customary and manorial land rights to freehold and formal rights, were indeed much less credible and universal as forms of emancipation than their Whig and subsequent liberal defenders would argue. For Thompson (and others, it must be said), political and material assets were allocated via enclosure in profoundly unequal ways and often by naked coercion. However, Thompson also argues that the emergence of formal means of defining and defending property rights, as part of a wider move to the rule of law in England, was not merely (as some have argued) a step towards dispossessing the peasantry. Thompson asks, if the ruling class was all powerful, why would it require such a ruse (i.e., the rule of law)? The question can be applied equally well to conceptualizations of power, violence, governmentality, and property in complex societies (see also Hall 1988).

Thompson's question provides an important insight into the discursive and ideological lure of exclusive, individuated, and increasingly freehold forms of property, one that arguably goes to the heart of the logic of American hegemony. It speaks directly to the political rationality that binds together coercion and consent when it comes to accumulation by dispossession. Such accumulation, defined by Harvey, involves the familiar liberal "promise" of freedom, defined as the right to freehold possessions and their universal defence by the modern state. From this perspective, although unquestionably exclusive, property in the form of Gordon's "absolute individual dominion" is also, somewhat paradoxically, a site of inclusion and social cohesion in liberal capitalist societies.

This conclusion points, in turn, to an additional dimension of property, namely, that property regimes are always simultaneously material and semiotic. Property rights are, in important respects, constituted by the material *and* semiotic properties of the things to which property rights refer. Consider, for instance, complex debates about the limits of access rights to fugitive resources such as commercial fisheries and the ways in which the rights themselves are shaped by the material properties of the resource (McEvoy 1986). At the same time, in the age of biotechnology, in debates about the delineation of property rights to genes and genetically modified organisms, the meaning of life itself (e.g., is life merely the sum of its parts, analogous to a machine, or something else?) has been repeatedly invoked, even by Supreme Court judges seeking to defend arguments about life patents (whether strictly prohibited, limited to gene constructs alone, or extended to whole organisms). In this context, the politics of making life into a commodity are tied inseparably to a politics of meaning vis-à-vis life (Prudham 2007). Moreover, if the alienation of discrete things to which exclusive property rights apply is caught up in an ontology of object and subject, then debates about property rights will inevitably become embroiled in such difficult binaries as nature and culture, human and nonhuman, us and them (Star and Griesemer 1989; Latour 1993, 1999). In short, property relations are also relations of meaning.

In related fashion, the delineation and legitimation of property regimes relies on what may be called moral economies of use (or non-use). That is, property rights are almost always accompanied by discourses of rights (in the ethical sense of the term, e.g., right versus wrong) and notions of correct practices that have their own genealogies. As Macpherson (1978) notes, some sort of moral narrative of legitimacy *always* circulates with enclosures (see also Prudham, this volume) that are in any way exclusive.[10] For Locke, for instance, the narrative of agronomic improvement serves as a powerful legitimating device to justify the displacement of some social claims to land in favour of others. Purely at face value, this argument is about efficiency, the idea being that enclosed land will be more productive land, that enclosure will be in the social interest (assuming, of course, that society more generally benefits from increased output). But Locke also bases his idea of efficient land use on distinctly English agronomic practices that make "improvement" legible. As a consequence, his argument renders land subject to Aboriginal and other "unfamiliar" regimes of practices in the colonies or future colonies empty *(terra nullius)* and wasted, and thus open to (colonial) enclosure. Implicit, then, is a social and racialized ordering based (rather remarkably) on prevailing cultivation regimes in England.

Doctrines of improvement act as powerful narratives that underpin land policy and the politics of privatization in all manner of contexts and in ways that supposedly depoliticize the practice of politics and administration. And, as in Locke, improvement doctrines in diverse contemporary settings carry utopian projects of emancipation based on increasing material prosperity and "development." Such discourses are always accompanied by affects and assumptions that help to constitute particular kinds of cultural and political subjects. When these discourses and practices are deployed in former colonial settings in ways that draw on and at the same time rework salvation and improvement narratives (see, e.g., Mollett's chapter in this volume), they lend contemporary development-as-globalization a decidedly Orientalist and postcolonial flavour (Gregory 2004; Li 2007). Our central point is that considerable cultural work is tied to the delineation and enclosure of property regimes; therefore, we have one more reason to interrogate the nexus of globalization and autonomy through the lens of property.

This Volume

The chapters are grouped roughly in temporal order based upon the globalist moments chosen by the authors. The book opens with a chapter by A. Claire Cutler that provides background on the historical development of international law, commodification, autonomy, and property. The chapter offers a legal context for most of the chapters that follow, particularly those relating to indigenous peoples. Cutler argues that, notwithstanding the growing diversity of claims to identity and subjectivity under international law, there is a singular logic to the globalization of international law in the commodity form that tends to flatten out differences, integrating disparate places and peoples. The globalization of international law is an important element of a new imperialism that is knitting the world together into a network of governance arrangements that are disciplining peoples and things through a neoliberal economic logic and a neoconservative politico-strategic logic. Cutler's first globalist moment is the articulation of state sovereignty and the analytical foundations of international law through solidification of the doctrine and practice of international legal personality. The doctrine of international legal personality took shape in the nineteenth century, establishing the ontology of international law and the foundational distinction between subjects and objects of the law and recognizing states as the original subjects of the international legal order.

Cutler's second defining moment occurred in the mid-1990s, when contemporary systems of rule were being delocalized and deterritorialized. During this period, international law took on a transnational dimension that was "both extensive (it broadened its substantive and geographic scopes) and intensive (it deepened its discipline under the new constitutionalism)." The intensive reach of instruments such as TRIPS and the General Agreement on Trade in Services (GATS) into local politico-legal orders has created new forms of enclosure by privatizing and commodifying more dimensions of existence. The statist focus of the analytical foundations of international law remains doctrinally intact, but non-state challenges to the primacy of states are emanating from aspiring identities, including (of particular relevance to this volume) indigenous peoples and transnational corporations. These aspirants for sovereignty often compete for recognition and for access to the benefits that flow from legal subjectivity. Cutler argues that these aspirations are giving rise to tensions between the goal of further globalizing a universalizing and homogenizing international law and commitments to enhancing the local autonomy of states and peoples.

Like Cutler, Susan Preston adopts a historical approach to consider the role of colonial resource exploitation companies in the renegotiation of traditional meanings and the emergence of new ways of thinking about land. Preston demonstrates that an interest in converting the physical elements of the Cree life world into extractable capital drove the colonial fur trade from the seventeenth century. Over time, these extractions increased in intensity, culminating in mining and logging in the twentieth century, especially hydroelectric developments since the 1970s, Preston's globalist moment. She proposes that, during the postwar era, a concept of land as property emerged alongside variations of traditional Cree understandings in response to — at least partly — these impositions and their associated policies. The coexistence over time of Cree understandings and Western notions of property and development, a form of improvement, reflects the

Crees' attempt to guard autonomy in the face of different waves of globalization. Preston explores a relational notion of autonomy and considers it at multiple scales across time, from the individual to the hunting group and from the extended family to the political entity of the First Nation. She considers the relevance of autonomy and how that relevance can change as a result of struggles to resist the loss or desecration of traditional lands. Accordingly, autonomy at the cultural level, over much of the past half century, has meant the right to choose how to live and how to shape a field of acceptable choices.

Scott Prudham's chapter explores a globalist moment when the precursors of contemporary property rights governing private, exclusive access to public forests in British Columbia were established. Specifically, he examines the adoption of private forest tenures and sustained yield regulation in British Columbia during the 1940s and 1950s, the time of the first two provincial royal commissions on forestry. Prudham shows that the Sloan Commissions opted for the creation of secure, private, excludable, and ultimately transferable private — and increasingly corporate — rights to so-called public forests. In doing so, he suggests, the commissions justified their recommendations by emphasizing the exchange value of forests. This emphasis on exchange value was legitimized further by developing a doctrine of forest improvement built around the *Normalbaum* (normal forest). Both of these emphases foreshadowed a new corporate globalization anchored in transnational corporations. The enclosures that resulted overwhelmed alternative, more collective, property regimes that might have provided more autonomy to workers and to indigenous peoples seeking to adapt traditional ways of living.

Sharlene Mollett's chapter questions a long-established communal property regime in Honduras by examining another globalist moment — the establishment of UNESCO's Man and the Biosphere Programme in 1980. By designating the biosphere as a United Nations world heritage site, the program created openings for more global connections to enter the region. Mollett argues that such reserves rely on a set of globalized norms that transform their situations into mainstream acts of conservation or common-sense understandings over time. Critics of global environmentalism argue that hegemonic norms transform the natural resources of poorer countries into a global commons, both discursively and materially. The "environment" becomes a significant site upon which a myriad of contests take place, many of them involving non-indigenous challenges to indigenous lands and resources. Mollett demonstrates that, in Honduras, decisions about the environment made at the global level put into question the Miskito people's long-term struggle for recognition of communal property rights, which were indigenous to the designated area of the biosphere. The goals of the Miskito were not only undermined; rather, their very territories were also opened up by the state to incursions by *colonos* in search of natural resources, further threatening the Miskito's struggle for collective autonomy. Here again, the state drew on global environmental norms, specifically the idea of sustainable development, to thwart the claims of the Miskito.

As the struggle over resources and lands outlined by Preston and Mollett played out, the issue of enclosing life forms was increasingly being debated. Daniel Gorman's chapter highlights the significance of the moment when an American scientist, Ananda Chakrabarty, invented a genetically engineered microorganism that could break down crude oil and sought to patent the life form. Gorman demonstrates the globalist nature of this moment by reviewing the global regulation of intellectual property. He traces the emergence of the various institutions in this regulatory system and describes how international cooperation began to develop in the nineteenth century. He follows this review with an examination of the emergence of two key international institutions: the Patent Cooperation Treaty and the World Intellectual Property Organization. He then factors into the analysis TRIPS, which was part of the 1994 agreement setting up the World Trade Organization. Gorman concludes that the potential ownership of human beings, the quintessential question of autonomy, is now on the horizon.

The globalist moment examined in Eva Mackey's chapter occurred in 1998 and 2002, respectively, when two Aboriginal communities, the Cayuga in New York State and the Caldwell First Nation in southern Ontario, won land claim awards and sought to use these funds to purchase land to secure their collective autonomy. She shows how these indigenous communities' attempts to buy land in conventional real estate markets ran into stout and bitter resistance from non-indigenous citizens in Canada and the United States who lived adjacent to these communities. Although these conflicts were acted out, sometimes violently, at local and national levels, Mackey argues that they were deeply embedded in global processes. These communities' material conditions of possibility, based as they were on earlier moments of global colonial power relations, were and are legitimated and enabled by global, supposedly universal, property ideologies. This argument is developed at length by Cutler in her chapter. Mackey concludes on a hopeful note by introducing the concept of relational autonomy as a new way to think about land that incorporates the understandings of the Cayuga Indian Nation.

William Coleman and Austina Reed focus on the 2001 adoption of the International Treaty on Plant Genetic Resources for Food and Agriculture. This particular global moment brought the concept of farmers' rights formally into international law. These rights are aimed at protecting collective intellectual property associated with traditional farming practices: the planting and saving of seeds to improve yields, strengthen welcome characteristics of plants, and eliminate other characteristics deemed less useful, if not harmful, by farmers. The treaty therefore puts into play a concept that challenges some of the aspects of enclosure in other global treaties, particularly TRIPS. The chapter examines the tension between farmers' rights and the international intellectual property regime and assesses the potential of the concept of farmer rights for securing the collective intellectual property of traditional and indigenous farmers. Coleman and Reed draw on a case study of the implementation of farmers' rights in India to demonstrate both the obstacles and the possibilities available to states on these issues.

Anna Greenspan's moment occurred when she stepped out of her apartment in contemporary Shanghai and surveyed the many small shops selling pirated DVDs. She argues that any attempt to enclose intellectual creations like the ones at issue in TRIPS and in international intellectual property regulation more generally cannot succeed fully. She questions those who view globalization as the movement towards a kind of world order. Globalizing processes, she suggests, have always been hybrid ones. A legal world of regulation has always, perhaps necessarily, coexisted with a shadowy world of copying, stealing, and improving on what has been taken. She argues that a history of property rights should show such hybridity as an essential characteristic of globalization. Hybridity in the future will result when the owners of property rights and their agents settle for some returns and claim social capital as benefactors. Perhaps this process of negotiation is already occurring.

A coda in music is a passage of more or less independent character that is introduced after the completion of the essential parts of a movement to form a more definite and satisfactory conclusion. Jasmin Habib's chapter performs this function in our volume. Titled "Property Rites," the chapter examines the appeal to the right to autonomy through property in its collective — that is, cultural or communitarian — form. Habib locates this appeal through an exploration of the poetry of dispossessed Palestinians. She examines the degree to which theories of and about globalization too quickly embrace the logic of the failure to modernize, focused as they are on economic processes. She suggests that such accounts cannot fully appreciate or account for land-based resistance that is neither productivist nor anti-capitalist. By doing so, she puts the foregoing chapters into a broader, more complicated context that highlights the deep emotions that lie behind many of the kinds of conflicts discussed in this book.

chapter 2

The Globalization of International Law, Indigenous Identity, and the New Constitutionalism

A. Claire Cutler

THIS CHAPTER FOCUSES ON the globalization of international law as an emergent form of governance that conditions conceptions and practices of sovereignty, with profound implications for claims to identity and autonomy in international affairs. The analysis seeks to isolate the specificity of the relationship between international law and global capitalism by showing how the so-called new constitutionalism gives rise to legal forms and institutions that define what sovereignty means and thus who or what may legitimately lay claim to identity and autonomy. The new constitutionalism involves the creation of politico-juridical and constitutional frameworks that operate regionally, nationally, and globally to establish rules that govern local and global political economies and societies (Gill 2008; Cutler 2003). It is taking shape in the uneven emergence of de facto constitutional governance structures for the global political economy and coincides with recent expansions, both intensively and extensively, of global capitalism and private property rights (Schneiderman 2010). This form of governance highlights proprietary conceptions of sovereignty, identity, and autonomy that are rooted in the historical development of international law. I argue that the new constitutionalism advances an increasingly commodified notion of governance. International legal forms constitute and set limits on identity and autonomy according to a market-friendly and economistic logic that is forming the template for global citizenship (see Bowden and Seabrooke 2006; Baxi 2005). While states constitute an important location of political authority under this logic, mediating the terms under which non-state entities are recognized as subjects with autonomous identities, transnational business corporations also exercise considerable authority.

Implicit in this analysis is the belief that law is a fundamental constitutive axis of modern social life; law is not only an institution, it is also constitutive of all social relations, including relations of domination:

> If we understand law as a state-sponsored field which grounds the conditions of possibility for actionable rights and legitimate social claims, then law is "deeply imbricated" in the very organization of modern society. Put differently, law is productive or generative of subjectivity in the nation-state. Understood in this way, law is a dimension (at least) of all modern social relations, since all social relations presume a ground of rights and legitimate claims. It is not possible to think of subjectivity within modern society without seeing law — and the rights it allows or summons into existence — as one of the basic, constitutive axes of social self and other. (Biolsi 1995, 543)

Biosli refers to the constitutive role of national law in a domestic setting.[1] However, the analysis applies with equal force to international law and its fundamental role in the constitution of contemporary subjectivities (see Cutler 2003, 2009). The commodity form theory of international law is proposed as the theory that captures the materiality and normativity of international law's increasingly global reach and its intensive penetration into domestic politico-legal orders, where it defines and regulates the terms of political engagement and contestation. The commodity form of international law facilitates the expansion of global capitalism by conditioning local political economies and societies according to what Stephen Gill (2008, 137) refers to as neoliberal discipline and the subordination of local social relations to the demands of global trade, investment, and financial markets. Although more will be said later about the commodity form of law, its operation is evident in a number of areas of transnational economic law (see Cutler 2008b). The analysis in this chapter highlights its impact on the claims to autonomy and identity under international law of non-state entities, such as indigenous peoples.

As noted in the Introduction, property rights mediate the relationship between peoples and things. International law and the property rights it recognizes mediate the relationship between peoples and things through a statist framework that confers subjectivity, identity, and autonomy on some, but not on others. International law articulates the conditions of international legal identity and autonomy, substituting "juridical persons for real people" and presenting social relations as "a product of legal institutions, dependent on enforcement of an authoritative (legal) discourse, rather than as inherent in 'natural' existence" (D'Errico 1996-97, 107). Law and the state are foundational in constituting entities that are accorded status as citizens and in ensuring the protection and enforcement of their rights (Yeatman 2004). Legal forms and the instrumentality of the state thus mediate identity, but this centrality is obscured by the naturalization of certain entities as legitimate, autonomous legal subjects or persons. International law creates, recognizes, and enforces rights that provide the conditions of possibility for the recognition of subjectivities and identities, according highly differentiated legal rights to non-state entities, including indigenous peoples, individuals, and transnational business corporations. Although the terms *international legal personality, subjects,* and *objects* will be defined more fully later in the discussion, states emerge as fully sovereign, legal subjects or persons capable of possessing rights and enforcing claims under international law. As will become apparent, sovereignty and autonomy, as embodied in the right to self-determination under international law, are shaped by legal doctrines that accord these rights to *states* as rights of *national* self-determination. Non-state entities claiming recognition as legal subjects fare differently. Individuals and transnational corporations figure as objectified categories. Although they are not accorded the status of subjects, they are objects capable of having rights and duties bestowed upon them by states. So, too, indigenous peoples emerge as objectified identities, but their recognition also reflects the operation of racialized legal categories that are historically contingent on practices of exclusion and inclusion that give rise to both oppressive and emancipatory conditions and possibilities.

This chapter presents the argument that, notwithstanding the growing diversity of claims to identity and subjectivity under international law, there is a singular logic to the globalization of international law in the commodity form that tends to flatten out differences, integrating disparate places and peoples. The globalization of international law is an important element of a new imperialism that is knitting the world together into a network of governance arrangements that is disciplining peoples and things through a neoliberal economic logic and a neoconservative politico-strategic logic (Harvey 2003). In the commodity form, international law gives rise to contradictory impulses and dialectical tensions between subjects and objects of legality, localized and delocalized social relations, territorialized and deterritorialized systems of rule, and hard and soft forms of regulation. These impulses go to the heart of the relationship between the globalization of international law and the autonomy of states and peoples, reflecting sites of contestation and struggle, as well as emancipatory aspirations.

There are two defining global moments in this analysis, although they are perhaps better conceptualized as historical developments than as discrete moments. Historically, the first global moment involved the articulation of state sovereignty and the analytical foundations of international law through solidification of the doctrine and practice of international legal personality. The doctrine of international legal personality took shape in the nineteenth century, establishing the ontology of international law and the foundational distinction between subjects and objects of the law and recognizing states as the original subjects and sovereigns of the international legal order. This doctrine also articulated the so-called sources of the law, framing a positivist epistemology that limited the creation and recognition of international law to sovereign states and their delegates. At this time, the sovereign control of territory was a defining characteristic of the right to rule, and international law formed a statist legal order moving out from western Europe to embrace ever more parts of the globe. Non-state entities formed the periphery in both theory and practice.

The second defining moment or development involves contemporary transformations to delocalized and deterritorialized systems of rule, as international law takes on a transnational dimension that is both extensive (it broadens its substantive and geographic scopes) and intensive (it deepens its discipline under the new constitutionalism). The intensive reach into local politico-legal orders of instruments such as the World Trade Organization's Agreement on Trade-Related Aspects of Intellectual Property Rights (TRIPS) and its General Agreement on Trade in Services (GATS) creates new forms of enclosure by privatizing and commodifying more dimensions of existence. The statist focus of the analytical foundations of international law remains doctrinally intact, but non-state challenges to the primacy of states are emanating from aspiring identities, including indigenous peoples, individuals, transnational corporations, and private associations who often compete for recognition and for access to the benefits that flow from legal subjectivity (Cutler 2001). These aspirations are giving rise to tensions between the goal of further globalizing an international law that is both universalizing and homogenizing and commitments to enhancing the local autonomies of states and peoples.

International Law and the Expansion of International Society

From its inception, international law has been an imperial project in the sense of facilitating the material and cultural expansion of capitalism (Pashukanis 1980; Said 1993). From the framing of the legal principle of sovereignty in the sixteenth century in a way that enabled Spanish conquest and dispossession in the Americas (Marks 2003) to the articulation of the principle of freedom of the high seas by Hugo Grotius in the seventeenth century to facilitate Dutch challenges to the Portuguese Indian maritime trade monopoly (Miéville 2005) to the nineteenth-century definition of international law as the law of "civilized" nations (Anghie 1999; Gong 1984), international law has been about constituting empire through the contestation, acquisition, and dispossession of property. Although during the early years of colonial expansion the great trading companies were the engines of colonial growth and were granted significant powers, these powers were gradually framed as appropriate only to states, which were emerging as the dominant form of politico-legal authority. The doctrine of international legal personality forms the analytical core of the nascent statist ontology. This doctrine identifies who or what is a subject of the law and, hence, who is politically authoritative as possessing "rights and duties enforceable at law" (Brownlie 2008, 57). The doctrine of international legal personality over time came to determine the entities that can declare war; enter into treaties; claim legal equality, autonomy, and territorial independence; become a member of international organizations; and make legal claims before international courts and tribunals. International legal personality thus determines who or what is a legal person or subject of international law.

Non-state entities — such as individuals or peoples and, eventually, transnational corporations — were, in contrast, recognized as objects of international law. They were regarded as possessing no original rights or liabilities, save for those granted to or bestowed upon them, derivatively, by states. As objects they are devoid of subjectivity: "that is to say, they are like 'boundaries,' or 'rivers,' or 'territory' or any of the other chapter headings found in traditional textbooks" (Higgins 1985, 478). The identification of states as the proper subjects of international law is generally associated with the theory of legal positivism, which attributes the binding force of international law to states and state consent. Legal positivism developed along with the emergence of the modern state system and through the work of theorists such as Hans Kelsen. Legal positivism provided the legal equivalent of statist political theories advanced by Jean Bodin and Thomas Hobbes (Beck, Arend, and Vander Lugt 1996). It informed the expansion of European society through colonialism at the end of the nineteenth century and the conquest of non-European peoples for economic and political advantage, which brought virtually all the territories of Asia, Africa, and the Pacific under the control of European states.

Initially framed as *jus gentium,* or principles of law common to all peoples, international law came to be circumscribed by doctrines that reflected the growing significance of state sovereignty. Indeed, legal positivism formed the theory used by jurists of the day to address the imposition of an essentially European body of international law on the peoples encountered through the annexation of Australia, the conquest of large parts of Asia, and the partitioning of Africa (Anaya 2004; Anghie 1999). With their growing statist focus, legal positivist theories of international law worked with colonialism to create both a statist and racialized order wherein international legal personality and legal subjectivity were associated with states that possessed a set of cultural characteristics "essential to the membership of the family of nations" and emanating from European states and European international society (Lawrence 1895, 58).[2]

In Australia, and elsewhere, legal doctrines of dispossession were developed to appropriate indigenous lands. According to the Roman law doctrine of *terra nullius,* which was incorporated into international law, vacant lands could be appropriated by states manifesting such intentions. As a result, a fictional representation was created that regarded the conquered lands as unoccupied, even though they were occupied by peoples, such as indigenous peoples. The underlying premise was that, as uncivilized peoples not forming a state, these people could not be recognized as exercising sovereign rights of occupation. Consequently, they did not possess the international legal personality required to constitute them as legal subjects capable of holding rights and enforcing international legal obligations.[3]

International law thus differentiated between civilized and uncivilized states and peoples, demanding different standards of law and diplomacy and recognizing different degrees of sovereignty and autonomy (Anghie 1999). Under nineteenth-century positivism, international law came to be regarded as "the body of rules framed between states" (Westlake 1894, 1).

Moreover, it was formulated epistemologically, not on natural, transcendent principles, as natural law would have had it, but as a science deriving from the actual practices of states (Lawrence 1895, 1). In creating a legal science based upon state action, positivists saw themselves as "creating order out of chaos" (ibid., 94; and see Kennedy 1988, 14; Cutler 2001) and rooting legal subjectivity in rational, scientific, and objective foundations. Increasingly, the authority of international law was traced to state practices since time immemorial, as a transhistorical authorization of the legal subjectivity of the state. This authorization was a move to the abstraction of law as part of the formalistic framing of the law as an independent, self-contained universe. It was a move outside of history, because it set up the analytical foundations of international law as a naturalized and transhistorical domain (see Cutler 2002a, 2003). These foundations permitted positivists to present statist international law as universal, eternal, rational, and natural. They also masked and neutralized the role of law in securing the political ambitions of European colonial powers and the economic ambitions of capitalist business enterprise.

Miéville (2005, 243) observes that a standard of civilization emerged in the middle of the 1800s "as a criterion without which a state could not engage in international legal relations." This standard was originally based upon "civilized, Christian nations" and later became one of "civilized nations." Increasingly, international law became that law created among sovereign European states. Legal positivists developed rules to regulate sovereign identity and created specialized legal arrangements to deal with non-European contacts. These rules disciplined the relations between states and non-state entities and between the civilized and uncivilized. Nineteenth-century legal positivists established the modalities of sovereignty in the legal requirements for establishing statehood. These requirements helped constitute a highly racialized order that differentiated between civilized, uncivilized, and semi-civilized nations, as well as between sovereign and quasi-sovereign (or not-full sovereign) states (Anghie 1999).

Thus legal doctrines regulating sovereignty that configured non-Europeans and indigenous peoples as outside the family of nations and European civilization helped enable the colonial expansion of European economic and political empires. Criteria of statehood were developed to facilitate the expansion of political control and capitalist accumulation and to regulate contact with the peoples of Asia, Africa, and the Pacific more generally. Today, we recognize the criteria governing statehood as including the existence of a permanent population, a defined territory, a government, and the capacity to enter into relations with other states. These are set out in the Montevideo Convention on the Rights and Duties of States of 1933. These criteria have their origins in state practice and the works of the nineteenth-century positivists. The requirement of a defined territory clearly ruled out sovereignty and property rights for nomadic and wandering tribes. As Lawrence (1895, 136) observes, "so entirely is its [international law's] conception of a state bound up with the notion of territorial possession that it would be impossible for a nomadic tribe, even if highly organized and civilized, to come under its provisions."

The requirement of a capacity to enter into diplomatic relations also ruled out tribal and nomadic peoples and resulted in differential and preferential treatment for states such as China, Persia, and Turkey, which had rich diplomatic traditions. Indeed, the treaties entered into between these states and European states, about which eighteenth-century jurists had written much, posed a real analytical problem for the positivists. How could non-sovereigns enter into treaties as subjects of the law? The only way of resolving these apparent instances of legal personality was to recognize a special category of not-full sovereign states. Such recognition began the practice of reconfiguring non-Europeans in the periphery of international law and international society.

While special legal arrangements were developed to regulate the relations between sovereign states and peoples of Asia, Africa, and the Pacific, different legal mechanisms were created to facilitate colonial expansion and to manage contact with indigenous peoples. They involved efforts to re-include these peoples in international society. The result, however, was a reconfiguration of indigenous identity, not as subject under international law, but as object, subservient to both the state and to the great trading corporations.[4] These special arrangements included colonialism through assimilation under treaty arrangements and rules regulating cession, discovery, annexation, conquest, occupation, recognition, and protectorate agreements. Legal doctrines were also developed to facilitate the activities of the trading companies. The latter were granted legal personality and state-like sovereign powers over non-European peoples, including the rights to trade, to war, to make peace with indigenous peoples, to impose customs duties, and to create money.

Another technique used by nineteenth-century jurists to manage colonialism that had a major bearing on property rights was the development of variations in the doctrine of sovereignty involving quasi-sovereigns.

Positivists reasoned that although non-European states were not proper sovereign members of international society, they were partial members. Although they had no legal personality, they were capable of entering into treaties insofar as they were recognized by European states. Rules governing recognition and the conditions under which quasi-sovereigns could enter into treaties were developed. Differentiations emerged between Asian and African states. The former were regarded as having the necessary capacity to understand the treaties to which they entered and, as a result, were recognized as quasi-sovereigns. African tribes, however, could not transfer their sovereignty because, according to nineteenth-century jurist John Westlake, they were incapable of understanding the concept of sovereignty. Accordingly, different rules developed on the basis of the private law of property to govern the acquisition of territory, including discovery, occupation, conquest, and cession.[5] Their application depended in part on how much sovereignty or autonomy a people or country was considered capable of holding. For example, the sovereignty of a European state could be affected only by conquest. In sharp contrast, if a territory was inhabited by a tribal people, who were not subject to international law, mere occupation was enough to establish property rights for the occupier on the grounds that the territory constituted terra nullius or unoccupied territory, as noted above (Anaya 2004, 29). If the tribal people were deemed politically organized, however, title, and thus rights over land, could only be established through something more than mere occupation, as in conquest or cession. Anghie (1999, 51) observes that each "of these doctrines relied upon different notions of native personality, as the particular means of asserting title depended upon the positivist assessment of the degree of civilization of the peoples occupying the land."

In this vein, the Asian empires were higher on the sovereignty pole, because they were regarded as capable of meeting European standards of civilization. In these instances, treaties of capitulation were imposed, giving Europeans special rights and jurisdiction over their own nationals while in these states. Protectorates were an additional legal category developed to partially incorporate non-European states into the family of nations towards the end of the nineteenth century. The European state would acquire complete control over the external relations of the protectorate, while in theory the protectorate was to retain domestic control, which is what differentiated it from a colony. Despite these rules, jurists were still prepared to recognize exceptions when so-called uncivilized nations required assistance in the maintenance of good government. Over time, the distinction between a colony and a protectorate disappeared as European states deepened their controls over non-European peoples.

In summary, different legal mechanisms resulted in differential inclusion of peoples in international law with variable sets of property rights and claims to autonomy through the extension of economic, political, and legal imperialism. The picture presented of nineteenth-century international law illustrates the development of legal subjectivity through the exclusion of non-Europeans from law's empire and their differential re-inclusion through racialized legal categories. Racialized legal categories are categories that confer identity, subjectivity, and autonomy, depending on differential assessments of the degree of civilization and humanity possessed by a "race." This assessment resulted in a fundamentally different form of sovereignty for Europeans and for non-Europeans and indigenous peoples as international law's reach extended beyond Europe. This differential treatment persists today, although the development of international human rights law has muted the influence of racial discrimination through law. However, differential legal capacities persist and in some cases are intensified and deepened through the globalization of capitalist legal forms under the new constitutionalism. The new constitutionalism extends special rights and protections to some non-state entities, such as transnational corporations, but continues to reproduce statist barriers to claims to legal subjectivity and autonomy coming from non-state entities, such as individuals and indigenous peoples.

Globalization of International Law, Imperialism, and the New Constitutionalism

As mentioned, the globalization of international law is an important element of the new imperialism that is knitting the world together and disciplining societies, a process Stephen Gill (2008) insightfully characterizes as the new constitutionalism. Both its neoliberal economic logic and its neoconservative politico-strategic logic are responding to a crisis of capital overaccumulation and the need to find what David Harvey (2003) refers to as spatio-temporal fixes to absorb capital and labour surpluses. Neoliberal logic solves the problem by facilitating capital accumulation through dispossession and the assignment of property rights as progressively more peoples, places, and spaces are opened up to capitalist exploitation.

Neoconservative logic lends coercive support by providing the political and military infrastructure to secure capital expansion and dispossession.

I have argued that non-state entities, such as individuals and indigenous peoples, existed historically, both analytically and materially, as dispossessed objects on the periphery of the international legal order. The movement to sovereignty discussed above — while putatively an embodiment of international law's universalizing, civilizing, and rationalizing impulses — may be seen more critically as a highly particularized and racialized movement. And it continues to haunt the articulation of indigenous claims to autonomy, identity, and subjectivity under international law. Indeed, a better approach is to view exclusion and re-inclusion as forming a continuing dialectical relationship under international law, a relationship powerfully characterized as one of continuing irresolution (Tully 2000, 40).[6] In contemporary times, international law continues to articulate a political economy and society premised upon the exclusion and re-inclusion of significant non-state entities under highly privatized and exclusive regimes of accumulation through dispossession. International law, in this way, continues to encode the cultural and material values and private property rights associated with international society, as framed by the European family of nations. But at the same time, the development of international human rights doctrines, the global emergence of a pan-indigenous movement, and the establishment of global institutions that recognize indigenous claims hold out the promise of enhanced indigenous autonomy and global citizenship (see Larson, Johnson, and Murphy 2008). Indeed, there is a continuing intersection, internationally, of conflict over identity and autonomy and conflict over property rights, which reflects the homology of the legal form and the economic or commodity form of global capitalism (Cutler 2003, 2005b; Balbus 1976-77; D'Errico 1996-97).[7] International legal forms both reflect and constitute the mode of production of global capitalism by regulating subjectivity through the empowerment or interpellation of specific entities as legal subjects and the identification of specific interests as actionable legal rights (Cutler 2009, 2010). International law reveals and isolates the tendency of state sovereignty and processes of capitalist accumulation and production to configure and reconfigure legal personality-identity as a type of sovereignty and as a form of property. In fact, sovereignty and property regimes are "complementary in the process of capital accumulation" in that "both work together in the commodification of life-forms" (Çoban 2004, 755).

Under international law, the state provides a site for the articulation and enforcement of rules about sovereignty, social identities, subjectivities, property rights, and the organization of labour. Although states undergo significant transformation relating to conditions associated with globalization, they continue to be privileged by legal regimes that accord them sovereign authority and control over social and economic development and commercial laws that privilege corporate property rights. In contrast, many non-state entities are marginalized by these sovereignty and property regimes, constituted as they are through the legal dialectic of exclusion and re-inclusion, in some cases as racialized and objectified entities. Moreover, significant elements of identity are framed by the commodity form of law, as commodified identities. The commodity form of law is the specific legal form that property rights take under the new constitutionalism, in that predominantly those interests that can be bought and sold in the market as commodities are recognized as protected property rights.[8] The operation of the commodity form of law as the juridical correlative to contemporary global capitalist structures of accumulation is visible in the framing of the right to self-determination of indigenous peoples under international law. Before examining the development of this right, further discussion of the new constitutionalism and the commodity form of law is in order.

As mentioned, *new constitutionalism* refers to the uneven emergence of a de facto constitutional structure for the global political economy. This development has largely coincided with the global expansion of capitalism since the 1980s and the pursuit over the past few decades by many states and associations of neoliberal policies and constitutional reforms, both domestically and globally. The new constitutionalism is further reflected in a proliferation of neoliberal trade and investment frameworks, such as the North American Free Trade Agreement (NAFTA) and the World Trade Organization (WTO), and in legal and institutional changes in macroeconomic policy, exemplified by politically independent central banks and currency boards. Changes in public service provision involving the privatization of education, health care, and many other aspects of life are linked to new liberal trade and investment frameworks and treaties, such as the General Agreement on Trade in Services (GATS) (Cutler 2008b, 2010) and the emerging intellectual property regime (Sell 2003), and are subordinated to the demands and regulatory power of transnational business corporations (Cutler 2009). The new constitutionalism increasingly informs bilateral and multilateral trade and investment agreements and other economic, social, and environmental policy frameworks (Schneiderman 2004).

It is redefining politics and governance globally and, in the terminology of the World Bank, involves "locking in" states to neoliberal frameworks of capital accumulation (World Bank 2002). The new constitutionalism is increasingly significant in shaping global public policy in ways that may have long-term effects on the ontological and epistemological bases of constitutionalism and, more broadly, on institutions of social reproduction associated with public service, care, and education (Bakker and Gill 2003). In this regard, it provides the template for contemporary economic, social, and political regulation; it is the legal rendering of economic constitutionalism.

Economic constitutionalism is the acceptance by society of the expansion of commodification through the legal protection of private property rights as natural, commonsensical, and rational modes of governance that serve the common interests of all, both the governors and the governed. Private appropriation becomes constitutionalized through law and state as a public good. Through economic constitutionalism, the communal protection of private property rights becomes a natural and organic accompaniment of global production and exchange (Cutler 2005b).

What is novel in the contemporary period is the globalization of new types of exclusion through the enclosure and privatization of more forms of common property and the hardening of global regimes of accumulation by dispossession. In these processes, the analytical and theoretical foundations of international law work with neoliberal constitutionalism and the commodity form of law to configure important dimensions of indigenous autonomy, not as inherent human rights to self-determination but as commodified property rights mediated by state sovereignty. Indeed, indigenous peoples have had difficulty inserting themselves into international law as a category because they are not states; they lack international legal personality as subjects and thus do not have legal standing to assert claims. Nor do they possess unmediated rights of access to and standing in international legal tribunals, and they are not regarded as legitimate participants in multilateral treaty negotiations (Koivurova 2008, 3).

The inability of non-state entities, such as individuals, to claim the protection of international human rights laws against states has been a major barrier to the development of international human rights and was the reason that the Optional Protocol to the International Covenant on Civil and Political Rights was developed. The Optional Protocol provides an individual situated within a state that is party to the covenant and the protocol to assert a human rights complaint against that state by petitioning the Human Rights Committee (HRC) established under the covenant

(Higgins 1985). However, the HRC has interpreted the right of access to be limited to individuals, not to collectivities. This interpretation has made it an awkward point of legal access for groups such as indigenous peoples and has conditioned the legal form in which indigenous autonomy claims have evolved under international law.

To illustrate, article 1 of the International Covenant on Civil and Political Rights provides that "all peoples have the right of self-determination" to "freely determine their political status and freely pursue their economic, social, and cultural development." In a number of cases brought by indigenous peoples, under this provision and through the Optional Protocol, the HRC stated that it could not hear a complaint brought by a collectivity. However, in the *Lubicon Lake Band* case and in a series of cases that followed, the HRC allowed the petition to proceed, recasting it as a submission of the chief of the band on behalf of the collective, not under article 1 of the covenant, but, significantly, under article 27, which provides for the protection of minorities' cultural, religious, and language rights (Koivurova 2008, 5).[9] This interpretation was crucial in recasting indigenous autonomy claims as cultural claims, a matter examined more closely below.

In addition, the statist ontology and racialized differentiations of international law do not extend the right of national self-determination to non-state entities or to indigenous peoples — they limit this right to nations emerging to statehood from former colonial settings. The saltwater thesis, articulated by the United Nations General Assembly, sets limits on decolonization by limiting the right of national self-determination to only those territories separated by water from the colonial power (Anghie 1999, 76; Koivurova 2008). Insofar as self-determination is recognized for indigenous peoples, it takes the form of self-governance arrangements within the existing territorial borders of the state. This position has been adopted by three of the most significant international processes addressing the right to self-determination of indigenous peoples: the United Nations Declaration on the Rights of Indigenous Peoples, the Nordic Saami Draft Convention, and the practices of the HRC in interpreting provisions relating to self-determination in the International Covenant on Civil and Political Rights. It is instructive that in adopting the United Nations Declaration on the Rights of Indigenous Peoples, four states (the United States, Australia, Canada, and New Zealand) opposed the final vote because they feared its terms would compromise their sovereignty and potentially lead to the political and territorial fragmentation of their states.[10] Byrd and Heyer (2008, 2) observe that the fact that "these four countries, whose origins are rooted in British colonialism and imperialism, continue to oppose indigenous peoples' recognition and rights within international forums demonstrates the degree to which issues of indigenous governance, sovereignty, and self-determination remain troubled and troubling sites of disruption to the nation-state." Indeed, Koivurova (2008, 18) similarly concludes that "it seems very difficult indeed to convince states that indigenous peoples should (re)gain their self-determination."[11]

As a consequence of the statist ontology of international law, the claims of indigenous peoples to autonomy and recognition under international law have not been able to proceed as claims to national self-determination that is both political and territorial or as holistic conceptions of a right to indigenous development. Rather, they have emerged as claims to protected cultures, traditional knowledge, and ways of life. As Byrd and Heyer (2008, 3) observe, "indigenous sovereignty is continually recast as cultural rather than political and territorial self-determination." Similarly, Larson, Johnson, and Murphy (2008, 56) note that the Japanese policy of defining Ainu issues as cultural matters "has kept Ainu claims to land rights, economic rights, and political rights off the national agenda." This separation of political from cultural autonomy is directly attributable to the statist analytical foundation of international law, which reserves legal subjectivity for states, and to the tendency flowing from the HRC's interpretation of the Optional Protocol to recast self-determination claims as cultural claims. As a consequence, indigenous peoples' claims to political and territorial self-determination have been reformulated as they are articulated through the prism of cultural rights. Accordingly, Holder (2008, 15) observes that indigenous peoples' "cultural rights can be fully understood only against the background of a fundamental and persistent denial of indigenous peoples' basic right to self-determination."

Moreover, Holder (2008, 8, 10) notes that, historically, international legal documents treated culture as a thing or an object or commodity to be owned, possessed, used, bought and sold, and conceived of "as rights of access and consumption." She adds, "there is a tendency to treat culture as a type of good — as an object or a state of affairs, valuable for its potential to be consumed, experienced or used," rather than as an activity to be enhanced and preserved.[12] Although Holder (ibid., 11-12) argues that this tendency has been valuable in protecting some indigenous rights of access to and control over ancestral lands and resources, it is also problematic because it tends to treat cultural rights as less fundamental than other human rights, such as freedom of speech or freedom from torture. Moreover, it "places important limits on the extent to which non-state groups can challenge state activities that threaten their continuing ability to live as a people" because it "sets a very high threshold for the impact that decision making must have on a group's way of life before it constitutes a human rights violation" (ibid., 13). Holder illustrates this tendency with examples of judicial failures to protect indigenous lands from logging and to protect Māori fishing rights.

In addition, by directing attention to the criteria of cultural impact and results, attention is diverted from the formation of deeper holistic conceptualizations of indigenous autonomy that recognize a right to indigenous, self-determined development (Gibbs 2005; Loomis 2000).[13] There is a tendency in adopting the discourse of rights to advance indigenous self-determination to overlook that this disclosure is limited by its Western epistemology and ontology. The legal forms proposed employ Lockean conceptions of property and commodity fetishism that privilege private rights and corporate capital.[14] This orientation neglects deeper ecological and philosophical issues of sustainable development, food security, and community renewal, and this neglect is due, in part, to the separation of "questions of homelands and natural resources from those of political/legal recognition of a limited indigenous autonomy within the existing framework of the host state(s)" (Corntassel 2008, 107). Corntassel (ibid., 109) identifies the significant limitations that these tendencies pose to indigenous autonomy and proposes an alternative conception of "sustainable self-determination" as "a credible benchmark for future indigenous political mobilization."

That rights discourse tends to frame indigenous autonomy in terms of enforceable (i.e., commodified) private property rights and not inherent, natural, or communal rights to self-determining development is also relevant to the emerging global intellectual property regime (May 2000).[15] This regime reveals "tensions between North and South in ownership and control of natural resources" and "between the growth of a market-based culture and a communitarian, gift-based culture" that have important implications for indigenous autonomy (Ghosh 2003-4, 497). The TRIPS agreement, the United Nations Convention on Biological Diversity, and the World Intellectual Property Organization's work on intellectual property, genetic resources, traditional knowledge, and folklore signal a transition from international to global regulation, albeit enforcement remains with the state. This new global intellectual property regime enables the creation and expansion of opportunities to commodify and market non-material sources of wealth (Cutler 2002b, 2005b), with the assistance of biotechnology and globalized knowledge and information technology. The commodification of genetic materials (Barsh 2003-4), germplasm (Aoki 2003-4), sacred traditional knowledge (Gervais 2003-4), and folklore (Austin 2003-4) exposes "a series of fault-lines dividing the technology-rich industrialized countries located primarily in the temperate zone of the Northern hemisphere, and the biodiversity-rich developing countries located primarily in the tropics and Southern Hemisphere" (McManis 2003-4; see also Coleman and Reed, this volume).

In this regard, the economic significance of the capacity to appropriate traditional or indigenous knowledge is profound. It is estimated that the annual market value of medicinal products derived by pharmaceutical companies under protected intellectual property rights (IPRs) from the traditional healing practices of indigenous peoples in the tropical rain forests is more than $32 billion, while 25 percent of US prescription drugs come from such plants (Oguamanam 2004, 140). The patenting of genetic resources and knowledge obtained from indigenous peoples in developing countries has occurred largely without their knowledge or consent, a process highly reminiscent of the dispossession of land in previous centuries (see Aoki 2003-4).

Just as the international law relating to title to land was incompatible with customary, communal holdings, many question the conceptual, theoretical, and functional propriety of addressing indigenous autonomy through the prism of intellectual property rights (Gervais 2003-4; Davis 2003-4; Graham and McJohn 2005).[16] For example, traditional knowledge is typically regarded by indigenous peoples as community property and, as such, is not subject to appropriation by any individual. The difficulty is that the community as claimant faces practical procedural problems of establishing the natural or corporate legal personality required to legitimately claim or hold an IPR. On a more conceptual and theoretical level, postcolonial theorists question the ability to advance notions of indigenous knowledge through a language of rights derived from Western concepts and institutions (Spivak 1988; hooks 1990; see also Coombe 1999). As Briggs and Sharp (2004, 667) note, dominant approaches to traditional knowledge adopted by the World Bank and other global development organizations provide "no sense of dealing with embedded knowledges which are part of the wider world-view of the people involved, such as understandings of social justice, gender relations, familial responsibility, and so on." They argue (ibid., 669) that some approaches to indigenous knowledge lead to a "freezing of traditional cultures and ways of knowing," as in protecting traditional knowledge by requiring indigenous peoples to maintain traditional fishing, resource use, or conservation methods.

There are also practical problems in enforcing rights over traditional knowledge, which is often passed on through oral traditions and, thus, not written down in a protectable material or publishable form and for which misappropriation is difficult to assess (Oguamanam 2004, 140). The idea that indigenous land is fungible as cash and that a claim to historical lands may be adequately settled through a monetary payment commodifies such claims and neglects losses suffered through the dispossession of a way of living and being (for an example of these processes, see Mackey, this volume). Finally, this process of commodification is being mediated by transnational corporations, suggesting that powerful corporate interests are at stake in the content to be given to indigenous culture (Macklem 2000-1). The value flowing from international legal recognition of a cultural right is not lost on peoples aspiring to autonomy. As Coombe (1999, 268) observes, those "who can make the strongest claims to possessing culture are more internationally empowered to protest local injustices. We should not be surprised, therefore, to witness the emergence of strategic rhetorical movements to 'indigenize' culture and to 'culturalize' knowledge in local articulations of sustainable development, because Indigenous peoples are those most accepted as having cultures worthy of respect and preservation." However, she also notes the doubtful political and functional capacity of achieving this through the existing intellectual property regime.

The creation of new technologies of appropriation through the globalization of IPRs is also giving rise to new forms of sovereignty and new claims to autonomy. To the extent that indigenous claims to identity are framed as claims to traditional knowledge and cultural property, they are constituted as commodifiable and appropriable property rights (Çoban 2004). The linkage of identity and property evokes images of primitive accumulation, a concept developed by Karl Marx to describe pre-capitalist patterns of wealth production (Harvey 2001b, 304-7; 2003, chap. 4).[17] Indigenous peoples and others on law's periphery are not being included as subjects at all but are instead excluded by intellectual property laws. These laws produce a commodification of important dimensions of indigenous identity, open it up to appropriation and dispossession by others, and then lock indigenous people out by making it increasingly difficult for them to compete with corporate rights holders or to constitute recognized legal claims of right (Anghie 1999; Boyle 1996). Indigenous peoples continue, then, to be dispossessed and configured as objects on law's periphery. Indeed, Harvey (2003, 147-48) is worth quoting at length:

> Wholly new mechanisms of accumulation by dispossession have also opened up. The emphasis upon intellectual property rights in the WTO negotiations (the so-called TRIPS agreement) points to ways in which the patenting and licensing of genetic material, seed plasma, and all manner of other products can now be used against whole populations whose practices had played a crucial role in the development of those materials. Biopiracy is rampant and the pillaging of the world's stockpile of genetic resources is now under way to the benefit of a few large pharmaceutical companies ... The commodification of cultural forms, histories, and intellectual creativity entails wholesale dispossessions (the music industry is notorious for the appropriation and exploitation of grassroots culture and creativity). The corporatization and privatization of hitherto public assets (such as universities), to say nothing of the wave of privatization (of water and public utilities of all kinds) that has swept the world, indicate a new wave of "enclosing the commons."

Although the rights to culture and to cultural property are being increasingly recognized in international legal documents as rights that reflect the special and intimate relationship between indigenous peoples and their lands and the traditional knowledge deriving from that special relationship, there are real limitations to achieving or preserving cultural identity through property rights (Holder 2008; Halewood 1998-99; Roht-Arriaza 1995-96; O'Keefe 1998). These limitations are particularly relevant when cultural recognition does not emerge as part of a protective regime oriented towards nurturing and preserving indigenous culture, but through a regime advancing commodified property rights whose functions and goals may be quite at odds with the achievement of indigenous autonomy: "A major goal of IP [intellectual property] is to alter, not preserve, its subject matter by encouraging innovation and thus modifications thought of as improvements, to existing inventive and expressive works" (Davis 2003-4, 817). As Coombe (1999, 263) observes, the "cultural logic of intellectual property law entrenches a European colonial worldview in which individuals (including corporations) lay claim to intellectual properties by means of deploying genius and innovation to transform resources, information and ideas into 'expressions' or 'inventions' which can be protected as 'works' of intellectual property. Nature is transformed into culture by such processes of human creativity, and such 'works' are encouraged as contributions to 'progress' in the arts and sciences."

Commodified identity formation thus becomes integral to common-sense understandings of indigenous peoples and to framing important dimensions of indigeneity under international law.[18] What appears on its face to be an exciting opportunity for emancipatory politics and the inclusion of indigenous peoples as subjects of international law in fact constitutes their further objectification. Their collective identity as peoples and their rights to culture are filtered through the lens of property rights that are difficult for them to acquire or enforce. International law facilitates the global expansion of capitalism and accumulation by dispossession through a globalized, exclusive, individualized, and privatized intellectual property regime that is most inhospitable to the recognition of indigenous collective identity.

Resistance in the Periphery

The globalization of international law gives rise to tensions between local and global politico-legal orders, tensions that raise questions about the potential for resistance at the local level, where hegemonic laws favour appropriation and dispossession and where common-sense understandings about power and authority may be challenged.[19] Resistance and contestation are thus linked to the dialectical operation of law as a mediator of local and global political economies and societies (Cutler 2003, 2005a). Gramscian political economy teaches that counter-hegemony involves wars of movement and wars of position (Gramsci 1971, 104-9, 229-32; see, generally, Amoore 2005). The former involve direct and open action against the dominant group or state, whereas the latter contemplate non-violent forms of resistance. The latter are also associated with passive revolution or revolution from above (Chin and Mittelman 1997) and the important concept of *trasformismo*. Trasformismo (Gramsci 1971, 58-59) is the process by which opposition and resistance to hegemony are absorbed into the dominant ideology, resulting in the decapitation and annihilation of the opposition. The adoption of non-binding declarations, such as the UN Declaration on the Rights of Indigenous Peoples, rather than the adoption of binding multilateral treaties, is an illustration of trasformismo, for non-binding declarations generate the appearance of legality and obscure the unchanging power relations that structure indigenous autonomy. The global promulgation of private, non-binding codes of corporate conduct and soft legal disciplines intended to foster corporate social, labour, environmental, or human rights responsibilities through voluntary self-regulation is likewise an example of trasformismo.[20] Soft law is promoted as the efficient and rational means for humanizing globalization, but this mythology conceals its nature as a safety valve for capital (Cutler 2005b). Similarly, hard legal disciplines that enforce private property rights in the trade, investment, financial, and intellectual property regimes purport to create an equal playing field for all. But the concealing and commodifying moves of such disciplines constitutionalize private regimes of accumulation.

The most acute example may be found in the interface of indigenous identity claims and the intellectual property regime in which trasformismo is reframing collective rights into commodified private property rights subject to dispossession through hard legal disciplines (see the chapters by Mollett and Mackey in this volume). Indeed, the acceptance of neoliberal market discipline in the idea that indigenous autonomy, cultural rights, biodiversity, and sustainable development are best achieved and protected through intellectual property rights informs "a new global bargain or transnational contract" in which the "'Northern We' now values 'Southern others' for maintaining cultural diversity because 'their' cultural difference ensures 'our' biodiversity" (Coombe 1999, 268). The idea that the intellectual property regime generates the sort of market-based incentive structures necessary and adequate for indigenous governance and is able to generate sustainability and preserve biodiversity, as promoted by liberal theories of economics and political economy, is an integral dimension of trasformismo. Governance through property plays directly into the hands of hegemonic corporate laws and institutions.[21] It is no accident that the movement to commodify and regulate germplasm through intellectual property rights occurred with the development of relevant technology by the seed industry and the concentration of the industrial sector dominated by transnational agrichemical and biotech corporations, such as Monsanto, Novartis, Ciba-Geigy, and DuPont (Aoki 2003-4, 303). It is also no accident that these and other transnational corporations control the content of the emerging global intellectual property regime (Sell 2003). As Graham and McJohn (2005, 316) note, "intellectual property law has been expanded for corporate interests in a number of sweeping ways ... Indigenous interests have hardly received the sort of attention that corporate interests have" (see, too, Cutler 2009).

Aoki (2003-4) describes the legal regime that governs patentable germplasm as the "apotheosis of germplasm as a commodity — the means of (re)production have now been separated from the commodity" because the farmer is now separated from legal ownership of the seed he farms.[22] The implications of this process for indigenous autonomy are great. Far from ensuring biodiversity, the intellectual property regime is producing genetic erosion in the developing world and genetic vulnerability in the developed world as genetic uniformity emerges because of the introduction of proprietary varieties and the increasing vulnerability of these varieties to new diseases and threats (Aoki 2003-4, 306-7). The situation is complicated further by distinctions between natural resources and artifacts that form part of the common heritage of mankind and are, therefore, not protectable by patents or copyright. These can be freely appropriated by all and sundry, including transnational corporations that profit from their collection and use. There is real asymmetry when supposedly primitive plant germplasm is legally constituted as the common heritage of (hu)mankind, enabling the free appropriation of genetic materials in the developing world by large corporations from the developed world who research, develop, patent, and sell the product at a premium. The possibility of indigenous dispossession through gene piracy was a very live issue in negotiations over biodiversity and traditional knowledge and has generated deep angst about the ability of intellectual property laws to function in a remedial way (McManis 2003-4, 548; Harding 2003-4).[23]

The relationship between indigenous peoples and transnational corporations is paradoxical. Today, neither indigenous peoples nor transnational corporations are recognized as subjects under international law. Both are objects, but with widely and wildly different powers. Without being formally recognized as subjects of international law, transnational corporations have configured themselves as objects and as subjects simultaneously, deftly managing the boundaries of international legality. Transnational corporations are actively involved in activities that bear directly on the autonomy and property of indigenous peoples but, by virtue of their invisibility under international law (Johns 1994; Cutler 2003), they remain unaccountable. As McLean (2003, 376) observes, "depending on the circumstances, the absence of legal personality can be a marker of both power and relative powerlessness. In fact, some collectivities, which exhibit enormous power, do not enjoy legal status. The WTO, for example, has no legal personality (as protestors found when they attempted to sue it). Lack of legal status can render a group above the law."

There is growing recognition that setting the rights of traditional knowledge holders up against those of transnational corporations tends to polarize positions and does not resolve the conflicting interests involved (Ghosh 2003-4, 501). More to the point, however, is the functional capacity and political legitimacy of addressing indigenous autonomy through the intellectual property regime (Davis 2003-4; Heald 2003-4). As Davis (2003-4, 829) cautions, "the solution is certainly not more IP [intellectual property], but to repeal TRIPS ... To suggest that the language of IP offers a remedy, when it is the language of IP that causes its poverty and misery is to trap indigenism into legitimizing the source of its tragic misery."

Transnational corporations and their laws continue to mediate indigenous autonomy (Macklem 2000-1). For example, in British Columbia, licences granted by the government to the transnational forest company Interfor, to log areas claimed as spiritual lands by the Kitkatla First Nation, pitted indigenous rights against the property rights of a powerful transnational company. In Nicaragua, the Awas Tingni claim forest granted under a timber concession by the government to the Korean corporation Solcarsa. In both cases, indigenous claims, rights, and property were mediated by corporate property rights granted by the state — the very same state that stands in the way of indigenous legal subjectivity. As a result, indigenous identity continues to be mediated by corporate and statist influences on particularized, partial, and racialized terms that work dispossessions of both culture and property. However, dispossession is no longer affected under doctrines of dispossession, such as *res nullius* and discovery, but by governments granting leases and concessions to forests, land, fisheries, mineral, and development rights to corporations. To the extent that such grants are made to transnational corporations, governments are participating in the delocalization and diminution of indigenous and local autonomy.[24]

The inadequacy of international legal protections for indigenous peoples has generated legal challenges to the operations of transnational corporations under domestic and regional systems of law. The Awas Tingni successfully challenged corporate conduct in the Inter-American Court of Human Rights, which found that Nicaragua had violated the indigenous community's right to property over their ancestral lands. In Canada and Australia, a number of high-profile cases have articulated principles that are building a body of jurisprudence that recognizes significant indigenous rights.[25] Extra-legal efforts include those of groups working to establish alternative localized regimes in the form of community-based intellectual property rights and resource rights regimes. Such groups are the Indian

NGO Gene Campaign; the Third World Network; GRAIN; the Research Foundation for Science, Technology and Ecology; and the International Cooperative Biodiversity Groups program (ICBG).[26]

Dissatisfaction among the world's indigenous peoples with the new constitutionalism and neoliberal economic discipline has generated an indigenous renaissance over the past decades. Examples of indigenous revitalization can be found in Bolivia, Ecuador, and elsewhere in Latin America (Fenelon and Murguía 2008). Māori resistance in New Zealand (Gibbs 2005; Austin 2003-4); Lakota, Navajo, and Wampanoag resistance in the United States; Zapotec and Zapatista-led Mayan resistance in Mexico; and Adivasi resistance in India are just a few examples of indigenous mobilization (Fenelon and Hall 2008). In these cases, as Fenelon and Hall (ibid., 1869) note, some of the "most significant forms of resistance are the various ways that resources are managed collectively for the communal good, and not solely as conventional 'public goods.'" Rather, the objective "goes deeper than collective ownership of goods," for there is a rejection of satisfying indigenous autonomy through commodification (ibid., 1870). The refusal of the Lakota to accept monetary compensation for land they claim as sacred in the Black Hills, which they insist must be returned, illustrates this form of refusal.

Organizations that deal with indigenous issues — such as Cultural Survival, the International Work Group on Indigenous Affairs, the Center for World Indigenous Studies, and the United Nations Working Group on Indigenous Populations — are assisting in providing sites to support collective approaches, resistance, and political participation (Fenelon and Hall 2008, 1871). Many indigenous peoples have benefitted significantly from these transnational networks. For example, the Ainu, who are not recognized as indigenous peoples by the Japanese state, have gained significant support and legitimacy for their claim to recognition through the transnational indigenous peoples' movement (Larson, Johnson, and Murphy 2008). Similarly, indigenous peoples in Indonesia have been able to "deploy indigenous identity as a strategy in their claim over land and natural resources," while indigenous identity is evoked in claims over cultural goods in China, where indigenous peoples are not recognized (Aikau and Spencer 2007, 6).

In fact, indigenous peoples have made some advances in gaining enhanced legal status in international society. Their legal personality as distinct societies with special collective rights and a distinct role in national and international decision making is gaining recognition. The International

Labour Organization (Convention 169) recognizes indigenous peoples' right to self-government. However, it is a right of internal self-government and not of secession in that it recognizes a collective right to participate in the state's internal decision making. This is also the situation with the UN Declaration on the Rights of Indigenous Peoples. The Earth Summit in Rio de Janeiro (1992) recognized indigenous peoples' right to environmental security — again, a right articulated within the context of the state, which contemplated, for instance, special land and development controls. The year 1992 was celebrated as the International Year of the World's Indigenous Peoples, while the UN General Assembly proclaimed a Decade of the World's Indigenous Peoples. To promote these developments, indigenous peoples are also demanding fuller representation in the UN system, in the World Bank, and in other assorted multilateral and regional forums. However, international legal doctrine is slow to recognize this enhanced profile (Barsh 1994). It continues to differentiate between the rights of indigenous peoples and the rights of "other peoples," such as colonized peoples. The international legal right to self-determination is being withheld from indigenous peoples in that it is regarded as appropriate only for peoples emerging from colonialism. To the extent that indigenous self-government is being recognized as a legal right, it must be exercised within the confines of an existing state. The explicit recognition of an unqualified right of indigenous peoples to self-determination therefore remains elusive. Recognition as "peoples" under the United Nations Charter would establish that indigenous peoples are members of international society possessing legal personality under international law; however, states have consistently resisted this recognition.

Other chapters in this volume show that there is increasing evidence of subordinate groups organizing and expressing their opposition to privatized legal regimes, which may construct an alternative counter-hegemony. Resistance to the intellectual property regime is mounting in India, Malaysia, Nepal, Indonesia, Thailand, Sri Lanka, Bangladesh, and the Philippines, as well as in Nigeria, where indigenous peoples are organizing and demanding compensation and remedies for rights dispossessed by transnational mining, logging, pharmaceutical, and oil corporations (see Obi 2000). Other examples of local resistance to the globalization of neoliberal market civilization include the mobilization of labour in Asia and Latin America (Schmidt 2000; Stevis and Boswell 2000) and in North America (Morton 2000; Pieterse 2000), challenges by citizen groups in Canada and the United States to corporate taxation laws and policies that shift tax burdens to individuals (Thomas 2000), Islamic social movements (Pasha 2000), opposition to structural adjustment policies in Bangladesh and Zimbabwe (MacLean, Quadir, and Shaw 2000), and civil society mobilization at anti-globalization protests during the WTO ministerial conference in Seattle in 1999. These are indications of fractures in the discipline of neoliberal economic law and the commodity form of capitalism.

Mark Rupert (2000, chap. 7) cautions that right-wing populist opposition to neoliberal discipline in the United States has been recognized and is generating trasformismo in the form of efforts by world leaders and international organizations to sustain globalization by giving it a human face. He also notes (ibid., 153), however, that "resistance to globalization has opened up possibilities for new forms of political practice which are not circumscribed by the territorial state or by the conventional separation of politics from the economy." Indeed, Oguamanam (2004, 166) argues that globalization has empowered indigenous peoples, because it "generates increased consciousness of cultural membership and identity. Indigenous renaissance and its impact on boosting various forms of cultural emancipation are incidences of globalization. In fostering homogenization, globalization also engenders resistance to domination and cultural appropriation, which the integration initiative symbolizes. Cultural preservation and expression are platforms for resisting domination." Oguamanam (ibid., 152-53) identifies proliferating conferences, workshops, resolutions, and declarations, such as the Mataatua Declaration on Cultural and Intellectual Property Rights of Indigenous Peoples as evidence of a growing solidarity among indigenous peoples.

Indigenous resistance is facilitated by the growing global network and strategic alliances of indigenous groups who are challenging the conventional intellectual property law regime (Coombe 2001, 278). There is a growing movement among indigenous peoples and international organizations, such as the World Intellectual Property Organization and operations pursuant to the Convention on Biological Diversity, to catalogue and develop localized *sui generis* intellectual property law regimes (see also Coleman and Reed, this volume). Some derive from customary laws and tribal rituals and provide protections for community-held property, collective rights and, in some cases, comprehensive local biodiversity legislation (Oguamanam 2004; McManis 2003-4).

However, there is also growing recognition that the rights-based approach to indigenous autonomy has profound limitations. Loomis (2000) argues that a new epistemology is required to create new governance structures that incorporate holistic, self-determined development for indigenous peoples. Awareness of the poverty of governance through property is echoed by Corntassel (2008) in his assessment of the Nisga'as' final agreement in the British Columbia treaty process. This treaty, in effect, extinguished indigenous rights for a cash payment and afforded little promise of cultural sustainability to the Nisga'a as a people. Johnson (2008, 31) speaks of indigenous self-determination in third spaces, spaces that lie "outside of the hegemonic control of the settler-state" and are created through bicultural and binational partnerships between indigenous peoples and states. Theses spaces are "holes in the fabric of the state that sit outside of this binary relationship [between the settler and the colonized]," and, Johnson (ibid., 31) argues, these spaces are transforming the meaning of citizenship in New Zealand.

Holder (2008) notes the emergence of a different approach to culture that is having a positive impact on state practices. This approach treats culture not as a noun or a good to be owned, bought, or sold but as an activity to be enhanced, nurtured, and preserved, and it is evident in recent international documents and interpretations addressing the cultural heritage of indigenous peoples. However, only time will tell whether local assertions of indigenous autonomy will succeed in disrupting the tendency of conventional IPRs and rights-discourse to embed globalized legal disciplines in localized practices and laws. Their existence, however, does suggest crucial openings at both the local and global levels for resisting the globalization of law.

Although Cox (1993, 65) instructs that "the task of changing world order begins with the long laborious effort to build new historic blocs within national boundaries," this examination of indigenous peoples and international law suggests a significant dialectic operating between local and global political economies and civil societies that provides openings for contestation and resistance.

chapter 3

Lifeworlds and Property: Epistemological Challenges to Cree Concepts of Land in the Twentieth Century

Susan M. Preston

To CONSIDER HOW WAYS of knowing — the epistemological bases for action in the world — are central to any discussion of property, we must begin with the recognition that the Western concept of landed property has a particular cultural and historical lineage and has been wielded against peoples of other cultures to justify the often violent imposition of new forms of governmentality. It has been used to assert and simultaneously deny rights and to assert or constrain autonomy between colonizers and colonized. And the application of this powerful concept has changed over time as people of influence adapt to changing social values and pressures.

Debate over property's applicability to North American indigenous peoples has been volatile and political for over a century. Much has been written *after* the assumption is accepted that landed property is a "natural" object. This chapter argues for the importance of reflecting on ways of knowing the world that do not presuppose the natural existence of landed property as a logical construct. Rather than arguing about whether indigenous peoples had an equivalent concept for landed property prior to colonization by Europeans, we may productively acknowledge that other ways of knowing the world have legitimacy and are deserving of historical and institutional recognition. They are, I argue, central to understanding and explaining cultural experience, change, and autonomy in light of globalization. In particular, it can be instructive to consider the communication challenges posed by culturally different ways of thinking about human relations with land and how these challenges actively drew the Eeyouch (as they self-identify) or Eastern James Bay Cree (as they have been known to non-Aboriginal people since 1853) into the dynamics of globalization.

Grounded in pre-twentieth-century Cree cosmology, this chapter considers the implication of colonial resource exploitation interests in the renegotiation of traditional meanings and the emergence of new ways of thinking about land. Interest in converting physical elements of the Cree lifeworld into extractable capital drove the colonial fur trade from the seventeenth century through to the early twentieth century. Far more intensive were twentieth-century mining and logging, especially hydroelectric developments since the 1970s. I propose that, during the postwar era and in response — at least partly — to these impositions and their associated policies, a concept of land as property has arisen alongside variations of traditional understandings within Cree culture.

Implicit in this interpretation is a view of globalization as the contemporary manifestation of a historical sequence of events characterized by imperialism and its expression through colonization and the global rise of capitalism *and* by forms of organized and everyday resistance to these expressions. Just as access to — and control over — natural resources was a key driver in premodern colonization and nation building, so too it remains in the era of globalization. The mechanisms, justifications, and language have changed, but the goals remain the same. Once presented as the vehicle for bringing Christianity and civilization to cultures deemed unfortunate enough to have not yet discovered them, new forms of colonization in the post–Second World War era are now framed rhetorically as developments that will bring human and economic development to impoverished regions. Following Toby Morantz (2002), current government-directed resource exploitation in the Cree landscape is thus understood as a continuation of colonialism.

Although the transition to the era of globalization — with its attendant characteristics linked to scale, time, communications, and power — is positioned historically by many (including this volume's editors) with Bretton Woods, the full dynamics of globalization are evidenced much later in the case of the Cree. The shape that these dynamics took on in the last quarter of the twentieth century was influenced by a period of struggle that had its origins much earlier in the century and that reflected earlier sets of relations. Using the concept of landed property as a lens to examine change, I reflect on how this struggle and the forces of globalization have both constrained and empowered the Cree and on how the nature of Cree autonomy has been transformed in the process.

Autonomy in this chapter is therefore, like concepts about human relations with land, not a static condition. Autonomy as it is explored here is relational, and it is considered at multiple scales relevant to changes across time, from the individual to the hunting group and extended family networks to the political entity "First Nation" and an entire culture. Of interest is the way in which autonomy has relevance and how that relevance can change as a result of changing relationships between actors regarding land. Its meaning at the cultural level over much of the past half century resonates with the combined views of Taylor and Appiah (cited by Prudham and Coleman, this volume) that autonomy is about the right to choose how to live, given a field of acceptable choices.

Most scholarly publications that describe the meanings Cree attach to land have by necessity focused on a particular period, event, or band with whom a researcher has developed a long-term relationship. As a result, most of these accounts depict so-called traditional meanings as somewhat static. I hope to add a depth of perspective by exploring the potential for changes in meanings over time. In this respect, I provide another side of the story of the entrenchment of common-sense understandings about property outlined by Eva Mackey in her chapter in this volume.

My inquiry centres on five initiatives by the Quebec and Canadian governments that, together, spanned the twentieth century. It is part of a larger research program to explore the connections between access, value formation, and environmental practice. My observations are intended to draw attention to the ways in which globalizing forces can be implicated in the dynamics of change in culturally based epistemologies. Because of the broad sweep of time represented, and the practical limits of space, I focus on the five initiatives as pivotal moments when the Cree were challenged to articulate their relationship with land in defence of their collective autonomy. The most critical of these moments took place in 1971, but the chapter illustrates that these moments occurred within a longer sequence of relations with outsiders focused on land and resources.

I begin by outlining the Cree concept of land prior to significant influence from other cultures and associated changes in Cree lifeways. I contrast this concept with the perspective of colonial interests in the same region. I then consider some of the ways that events in the interpretive framework are implicated in changing Cree autonomy and concepts of land. I am critical of the universalizing assumptions of Western Enlightenment thought relating especially to human-environment relations, and I am sympathetic to postcolonial (e.g., Nash 2004) and post-development (e.g., Escobar 2001) critiques. My relationship to the Cree began over forty years ago as a result of my father's commitment to learning from them. Family ties and friendships endure. I am sensitive to the disjuncture between the familial and the scholarly in my own endeavour, and my inquiry is intended to be one of compassion rather than objectification.

Historical Cree Concepts of Landscape

In the Western scientific view, land is generally thought of in abstract physical terms as a neutral entity that lacks personal agency. More recently, the cultural geographer's idea of landscape has been described as land plus the social and cultural values and perceptions based in experience that inform our understanding of it (Tuan 1979; Cosgrove 1984). Anthropologist shave expressed a similar understanding (e.g., Hirsch and O'Hanlon 1995). These definitions are more sympathetic to the historical Eastern Cree understanding of land than is the dominant scientific view, which informs Western notions of property.

Eeyou subsistence landscapes have comprised an area of approximately 345,000 square kilometres in the eastern Subarctic for as much as five thousand years. The environment and climate are varied, spanning a latitudinal distance of approximately 700 kilometres. Abutting the inland sea now known as James and Hudson bays, the land slopes upward to the east, and its myriad rivers and tributaries drain into the bays. Lakes and muskeg are common because of the underlying Precambrian Shield. The dominant vegetation regions are boreal forest in the south and tundra–open woodland in the north. In general, there is snow cover for at least half of the year.

Until the early twentieth century, Crees lived as seasonally mobile hunter-gatherers who had regional variations on a common subsistence pattern, language, and oral tradition. There are no ancient written texts explaining how the Cree lived and what they believed in the millennia prior to European colonization. Drawing on archaeological and archival evidence, Morantz (2002) argues that the typical hunting group of two to four families, or ten to twelve people, was likely a consistent size between the first and eighteenth centuries CE. She also cites evidence in support of a continuity of culture from the distant past to the late nineteenth century, and shows that participation in the fur trade had little influence on Cree culture and practices. Instead, she argues that the Crees mediated global economic interests through their own interests at least into the 1870s, thereby maintaining their autonomy and established system of social relations, including those with the land (Morantz 1983, 2002). It is therefore easier to speak of so-called traditional Cree concepts of land in general terms up to the late nineteenth century because of the consistency of subsistence practice throughout that period.

The region southeast of James Bay saw intrusion by whites on a sustained basis much earlier than did most of the Cree territory, and hunting and logging in particular caused problems by the 1880s. By the mid-twentieth century, Cree society overall had become more heterogeneous, largely because of colonial government impositions that began in the 1930s. These changes were amplified by dramatic increases in Cree population from about 2,200 in the mid-1930s to 6,000 in 1975 and 12,000 in 2000 (Morantz 1983, 2002).

Ethnographic sources, including recorded oral tradition and life histories from the early twentieth century, clearly express an Eastern Cree way of knowing and thinking about landscape that defines it in relational terms. For Crees, landscape consisted of what Westerners call geology, hydrology, soils, vegetation, animals, humans, weather, and spirit persons. It is an all-encompassing, holistic concept in which animals, humans, spirits, weather, and "some geophysical agents" (Scott 1996) have conscious autonomous agency and interact with one another on the basis of reciprocity and respect (Preston 1978, 1982; Feit 2001). Such a view is also borne out in my analysis of recorded oral tradition and life histories that reflect experience in the late nineteenth and early twentieth centuries among Crees associated with the Fort George (now Chisasibi), Eastmain, and Rupert's House (now Waskaganish) posts (Preston 1999, 2000). Recorded in the early 1960s, stories in the collection were not about places directly but rather the interactions of "the great community of persons," as Richard Preston (1997) describes it. Through these interactions, the experience and relational meanings of landscape were articulated in rich detail.

This world view should not be interpreted as animism, an understanding that is an unfortunate result of early anthropologists' inability to step outside of the limitations of Western epistemology (see also Bird-David 1999). Instead, it should be understood as a relational cosmology in which the lifeworld — the landscape — is a socially interconnected process of engagement. All participants are reflexive and adaptive in their actions. This understanding is, in fact, compatible with the view only recently articulated by Western specialists in environmental management: that the environment is in a constant state of dynamic change and has degrees of surprise and unpredictability that require an adaptive approach to engagement (read management). This thinking contrasts sharply with the long-standing positivist belief that the environment can be controlled in absolute terms if we simply develop the correct predictive models. Both scientific approaches are instrumentalist in their purpose and underlying assumptions. Although the Crees' adaptive practice was indeed practical, it was guided by ethical and moral values. When we speak of a hunting and gathering subsistence economy, the emphasis should be on the root origin of the English terms *economy* and *ecology*, which is the ancient Greek word for household: *oikos*. This emphasis shifts the concept from a monetary focus to one of familial environment.

Well into the early decades of the twentieth century, collective autonomy for the Eastern Cree existed at the scale of the individual and family hunting group. Individual autonomy within the group was recognized through the "ethic of non-interference" in the decisions of others (Preston 1986, 64). At the same time, it was "mediated by a strong sense of social practicality" (Preston 2002 [1975]), including the acknowledgment of one's own requirement for cooperation with others. Family hunting group autonomy was embodied in the need for, and ability of, the collective to be self-sustaining in often highly isolated settings.

Property: Conceptual Challenges

Both Colin Scott (1988) and Paul Nadasdy (2002) demonstrate that landed property — in the Western sense, as an inert object of individual ownership — was historically irrelevant to the Eastern Cree and many other First Nations cultures. Among the Cree, extended family groups were known, since earliest European contact, to have customary yet flexible hunting grounds; activities in each were overseen, typically, by a hereditary male hunting leader. Regions that comprised several such grounds and groups were mediated by an *Okimah* (Gorst [1675?], cited in Oldmixon 1969) or *Ouchimau*. The authority vested in these men by the collectives was based on demonstrable skill in negotiating complex social relationships among humans and other persons who collectively constitute the landscape. These relationships included the respectful hunting and killing of animals, who were understood to give themselves intentionally and lovingly (Preston 2002); the facilitation of others' subsistence needs through the social ethic of sharing, including access to land; and the management of food harvesting in a sustainable manner (Scott 1988). Scott (1988) identifies a set of complementary principles relating to property in traditional Cree culture, wherein the rights of the family unit are balanced with the rights of the collective so that no one is entitled to impede the ability of another for subsistence.

Beginning with Frank Speck's 1915 articles on "Indian" land ownership, anthropologists have debated whether Algonquian hunting territories were an artifact of the fur trade or a pre-historic form of social organization. Harvey Feit (2004) concludes that territories were one of a set of varied tenure arrangements adopted as needed, more likely in response to significant environmental change. Thus they plausibly existed in pre-contact times. Originally, the debate was spurred by recognition of the need to demonstrate persuasively to non-Aboriginal governments that indigenous peoples did indeed have landed property rights on the basis of Western criteria, including long-term, organized systems of residence and use. The challenge remaining is how to translate Aboriginal concepts and practices into something the dominant society can comprehend and its legal frameworks can accommodate (Scott 1988; Carlson 2004). By framing Aboriginal land tenure in these more Western terms, it would seem that adaptive systems were reconceived by some non-Aboriginal people as bounded objects. Herein lies a perhaps small, but I believe important, pair of errors. The first is the neglect of the cultural significance of an adaptive approach to the lifeworld, and the second is in the conflation of underlying conceptual categories with which to define land.

The importance of the adaptive, reflexive nature of the historical Cree lifeway cannot be overestimated. It informed most, if not all, facets of subsistence, including notions about land tenure. This adaptiveness was reflected in the flexible boundaries of customary family hunting grounds and in the mobility of individual hunters and families within and among such grounds, at least partly in response to variations in environmental conditions. In such a reflexive system, strict spatial boundaries would have been an impediment to equitable access to land to meet subsistence needs. By this reasoning, the European propensity for precisely articulating the boundaries of distinctly owned spaces could be seen as an unnecessary threat to the survival of at least some families.

Nadasdy (2002) points out that one of the failures of early anthropologists in their attempts to massage the concept of property to reconcile the Algonquian point of view was that they lacked reflexivity. They never questioned their underlying assumptions to consider the possibility of completely different ways of conceiving of human-land relations. He cites Strathern to suggest the need to step back from assumptions about what constitutes property to consider what constitutes personhood. These are completely divergent conceptual categories, even within the vocabulary of the Western mind.

As Eva Mackey and Sharlene Mollett demonstrate in their chapters, this challenge has taken varying forms right up to the present day. Negotiating the Crees' relational, flexible system vis-à-vis Western frameworks of property rights founded on notions of boundedness and individuality has, in some instances, meant the representation of Cree tenure in nearly Western terms by scholars, advocates, and governments. The extent to which this image has influenced Cree perspectives is discussed further below.

The Colonial Context

In 1610, Henry Hudson was the first Englishman to discover the waters since named for him: Hudson Bay. Whether other non-Aboriginal travellers preceded him is unknown. The Crown charter that established the Hudson's Bay Company (HBC) in 1670 granted the company control over all the lands draining into Hudson Bay, including the traditional subsistence landscapes of the Cree. The sole purpose of the company was to extract furs for European fashion markets. Following decades of competition with the French for control of natural resources in the Americas, Britain won out in 1763, and it was another century before the land was ceded from the HBC to the newly formed Dominion of Canada in 1869. As the country organized its territory administratively, the Cree homeland was assigned incrementally to the control of the Province of Quebec in 1898 and 1912.

The concept of landed property as it is understood in North American society, by its institutions and governance structures, is particular to seventeenth-century England and, later, western Europe. In the Introduction to this volume, Scott Prudham and William Coleman note the influence of Locke and Bentham and assertions that the act of improving land was the material means of legitimizing one's claim to it. By extension, unimproved land — that which was not brought under the plough or otherwise harnessed — was deemed unclaimed and empty of worthy human residents. The rhetorical supposition could thus be asserted that it was *terra nullius,* empty land available for exploitation by newcomers.

Although the British Crown had formally acknowledged Aboriginal rights to territory in North America well before the establishment of the Dominion of Canada, the assumption of terra nullius was sometimes (rhetorically) made by colonists and colonial governments. They justified this position by noting that the land in question had not been improved or settled according to European values and assumptions about legitimate land use and ownership (see Locke 1988 [1690]; Canada 1996).

This situation was compounded by the rhetoric of identity: Aboriginal peoples were portrayed by influential Euro-American authors such as Grinnell (1907, 3-6) as less evolved, more akin to the species of nature than to the civilized races. In this patronizing view, the civilized notion of property would simply not be relevant, and the best that could be hoped for the "natives" was total assimilation into the dominant society:

> The almost universal reverence of the Indians for the earth is interesting in connection with their feeling about the ownership of land. The earth is regarded as sacred, often it is called the "mother" and it appears to rank second among the gods ... That he has been expelled from the land which was too sacred to become even his own, is a bitter hardship ... Perhaps it is time and perhaps it is best that the Indians should fade away as we see them fading today ... We may regret the crushing out of the race before the march of civilization as we regret the extinction of other natural things, but we must recognize it as nothing more than the operation of the inexorable natural law that the weaker must perish while the fitter shall survive. Our notions of land ownership have developed through thousands of years. It seems to us now quite reasonable and expedient that one man should fence out others from his farm and that another should monopolize a lake and another a water power; but a primitive Indian can no more understand such private monopolies than the average American can understand how there could be a private monopoly of air or light. The Indian's notions of land tenure, so distinctly primitive, could not find acceptance in our day and our civilization. (Ibid., 4)

In the Eastern Cree context, in which land was constituted by social relations, the Western concept of property would have quite inappropriately involved claiming other persons as possessions.

In the James Bay region, fur-trading posts were constructed at strategic locations and repositioned periodically to try to access the Crees and others who hunted in the area. The earliest post in the Eastern Cree landscape was established in 1668, and many others followed, both along the coast and inland. With a few exceptions, Hudson's Bay Company managers were noted for rarely intervening in land management practices — at least partly because of the expectation that it would result in a lack of cooperation from Aboriginal people (Morantz 1983; Scott and Morrison 2005), upon whom their economy depended.

Resource interests expanded in the later nineteenth century as survey crews carried out intensive exploration and mapping for governments. Robert Bell (1881) reported to the Royal Geographical Society that his 1869-77 surveys had convinced him of the great commercial potential of the Hudson Bay area. He cited many kinds of natural resources as yet undeveloped, including minerals and timber for export. Bell's report illustrates the growing interest in the development of Canada's waterways for economic growth. When Bell reported on his 1895-96 season (1897), he was able to describe in greater detail much of the Cree landscape, and he reiterated his discovery of its natural resource potential. He commented that the Cree had no interest in (what he understood as) geography, and he interpreted their cultural difference from himself as naïveté — the implication being that the Cree's lack of interest somehow justified the imposition of colonial resource interests. Characteristic of terra nullius thinking about Aboriginal territories, Bell asserted that much of the southeastern James Bay area was suitable for settlement colonization and that the immigrants' property rights would be "as safe in this district as if it formed a part of England itself" (ibid., 17).

Plans for the use of the James Bay region's great rivers took a dramatic turn following the introduction of high-voltage transmission lines for hydroelectric energy production, first used in Canada at Trois-Rivières, Quebec, in 1897. A 1920 map, "Natural Resources, Transportation, and Trade Routes," published by the Department of the Interior, made note of furs throughout the northern part of the Cree landscape, fish in the lakes and bays, mica along the Eastmain River, timber and pulp wood in the far south, and waterpower along the Broadback and Eastmain rivers. By the time of the Second World Power Conference in 1930, government scientists had calculated and mapped in some detail the potential energy in horsepower of every major river in the eastern James Bay and Hudson Bay area. Studies were carried out between 1964 and 1967 that opposed hydroelectric development because of costs. Nonetheless, the decision to proceed with large-scale resource exploitation in the unceded Cree landscape was announced by Quebec's premier, Robert Bourassa, in 1971 as a grand economic development scheme. Bourassa wrote later that "Quebec is a vast hydroelectric plant in-the-bud, and every day millions of potential kilowatt hours flow downhill and out to sea. What a waste!" (Bourassa 1985).

While earlier activities reflect the interests of nation building by the Dominion, later developments reflect a similar form of nation building and efforts to secure economic autonomy by Quebec. In both cases, the act of quantification and plans for measured exploitation marked processes of inscription and legibility on the Cree landscape (Scott 1998) that extended into efforts to organize the Cree, both geographically and socially.

Non-Resource-Based Colonialist Influences

Before considering the influence of colonialist resource exploitation, the importance of two other colonialist influences on Cree concepts of land must be acknowledged: Christian missionizing and European-style schooling.

Jesuit missionary activity in the Eastern Cree landscape was limited, consisting of a few visits to southern posts in the seventeenth century. Methodist and then Anglican missionaries began working more earnestly towards conversion in the 1850s, building churches at posts and holding services, particularly in the summers when Crees arrived to trade furs for supplies. Missionaries tried to convince the Cree that their traditional beliefs were superstitious and to embrace the Christian cosmology instead. As has been documented for colonized peoples in other parts of the world, the eventual result was hybridization. Traditional values and practices were maintained, and a single Creator figure was gradually incorporated at the head of the spirit-person hierarchy (Preston 2010). In 1906, the Anglican missionary William Walton (Walton 1906) lamented: "Their lives are spent chiefly in the bush, away from all human help and counsel, so it cannot be wondered at that they are very superstitious in their habits, and go back to their old ways ... Nearly the whole of their heathen religion is connected with animals and departed spirits. It is practically stamped out among the 'coast hunters,' but the 'inlanders' still do all the old ceremonies. I ask the question, 'When do they give a thought to GOD?' 'Never,' was the reply."

Toby Morantz argues that it was only as a result of severe game depletions and epidemic diseases in the 1920s — both attributable to colonizers

— that the Cree engaged substantively with Christianity. She believes that these conditions made them "vulnerable to a religion that preached an afterlife and reunification with family" (2002, 89). The Christian message would have been understood from the Crees' frames of reference. John Long's analysis suggests that Crees saw in Christian practice the possibility of bolstering their personal power to affect outcomes of engagements with spirit persons in hunting relations (ibid., 90).

Non-Aboriginal education for Cree children was introduced in the late nineteenth century by missionaries, followed by day schools and then residential schools in the early twentieth century. Many children were removed from their families in the bush. Instead of receiving the traditional education in Cree life skills and beliefs, they learned according to the Western model, often through Christian institutions. There was for the first time a break in the transmission of traditional knowledge, practices, and beliefs. Many youth struggled with estrangement from the land. Schools were also built at trading posts, and the sites began to take on the identity of small villages in the late 1940s. Some adults remained for extended periods so that their children could attend day school.

By the 1970s, Western education and the effects of Christianity had made many Cree people feel that their traditional ways were antiquated and misguided (see Tanner 1979). Some carried on discretely in the bush, away from the critical eye of outsiders, and some abandoned many practices and beliefs (e.g., Etapp 2003). Rejection of traditional beliefs increased after evangelical Christianity and Pentecostalism became entrenched in the villages. Soon after, however, the rise of Pan-Indianism and the revaluation of cultural heritage led to attempts to reclaim or, at the very least, reinterpret that heritage for the later twentieth century.

Resource Exploitation and Cree Ties to Land

At this point, I step back in time to the first of what I argue are five pivotal events in Cree interactions with colonial governments over relationships with land, particularly regarding natural resource exploitation. Each of these events is complex, and most of them are subjects of detailed publications. I view them as a connected set and consider their incremental and cumulative influence on Cree concepts of land. Observations are based on an array of documentary sources, including Cree voices recorded between the mid-twentieth century and the present.

Creation of Beaver Preserves

Beaver meat was a staple of the Cree diet, both before and during the fur trade. Hudson's Bay Company records indicate that Crees resisted trapping more than they needed for food and for more than whatever small amount of trade goods they required (Morantz 1983). In other words, they were not motivated by an ideology of consumption and material wealth. Following a period of intense competition from white trappers spurred by high international fur prices, the beaver populations plummeted to near-extinction levels in the 1920s.

Out of concern for the Cree — and, no doubt, the fur trade economy — the HBC trader at Rupert's House, James Watt, and his wife, Maud, made arrangements with the Quebec government to create a beaver sanctuary of 18,500 square kilometres in 1932. They persuaded the HBC to adopt responsibility for it a year later (Morantz 2002). The sanctuary became the precedent from which a program of beaver reserves, each comprising numerous individual family hunting grounds, was gradually established throughout the Cree landscape over the next fifteen years. The initiatives engaged the provincial government's jurisdiction over land and resources, the dominion government's jurisdiction over Aboriginal peoples, the HBC's established presence by virtue of the fur trade, and Cree expertise and commitment to restoring a sustainable landscape (Feit 2005; Morantz 2002). Initially, there was a complete ban on beaver harvesting until populations recovered, at which time harvesting was re-opened — but with controls — the subject of the next section.

Harvey Feit (2005) presents a case for the Cree position in this event being one of an autonomous, self-governing people seeking the cooperation of governments for two specific purposes: honouring the Cree commitment to conservation and legitimating the exclusion of outsiders to help conservation succeed. Although some government and company representatives of the time are documented as acknowledging Cree rights in land and resources, James Watt, in notes made for his announcement of the sanctuary, made a comment that reveals the colonialist position vis-à-vis the Cree landscape. Watt planned to tell the Crees that once the animal populations were re-established, "all Beaver are going to be the property of the government" and that the government would dictate the timing, extent, and dollar value of the harvest (Morantz 2002; Feit 2005).

I have drawn attention to this initiative because it represents the first case of active government engagement in so-called resource management in the Cree landscape. It provided Quebec and Canada with an entry into the everyday negotiation of authority over the northern frontier. Feit's analysis suggests that Cree resistance to this imposition was implicit. For example, correspondence to the Department of Indian Affairs indicates that the scope of desired cooperation was explicitly limited to beaver conservation. Government involvement in other aspects of Cree lifeways or land relations was not being invited. The idea that beaver reserves influenced Cree ways of thinking about land and property is tied to the form of management implemented for them by the reserve managers, HBC employees. Feit (2009) elaborates on this point in a chapter in another book in this series.

Preserve Management, Mapping Traplines, and Tallymen

The logic of conservation for eventual harvesting called for a system of management, and the result was a program that Watt and other HBC beaver reserve managers believed was consistent with traditional Cree land tenure practices. One of the most symbolically important aspects of this program was the collective mapping of customary family hunting grounds by Cree hunting leaders, which created a documented system of traplines, each registered to its customary leader. Hunting leaders were given the role and title of tallyman and paid an honorarium, and at least some were given an official-looking document or badge (Feit 2005). Their tasks were primarily to monitor, record, and report the number of beaver and other fur-bearing animals present and harvested in the grounds each year. Based on these inventories, the reserve managers assigned the next year's quotas. Tallymen were also required to report the encroachment of any uninvited Aboriginal or white trappers to the managers (Scott 1988).

The system raises several issues of note. First, there is the potential conceptual impact, for a traditionally non-literate society, of men codifying the boundaries of individual hunting grounds in a semi-permanent form (on paper). In the process, an additional conceptual layer was created when it came to the possibility of thinking about landscape in clearly bounded portions rather than the flexible spaces of experience. Perceptions of that process, as recalled by Geordie Georgekish to Richard Preston in the 1970s, were that the HBC manager at Old Factory had "mapped out a strip ten miles wide along the coast, in sections about ten miles square." Georgekish noted that it was "just like a checkerboard" (Preston 1981, 198; 1990). The bureaucratic registration of bounded spaces to individual tallymen, and the status implied in the symbols of office, appear to have signalled the emergence of a sense of sanctioned proprietorship among at least some tallymen, institutionalizing their social authority over the area.

Second, this issue is complicated further by problems associated with the translation of meanings across cultures and languages. Third, and closely related to the issue of translation, there is a dearth of ethnographic documentation of Cree understandings prior to the early 1960s (Morantz 2002). Even then, few of the elder males, who would have been the tallymen, were bilingual. Therefore, when HBC records refer to tallymen using expressions such as *my land* or *my territory,* it is exceptionally difficult to ascertain whether the words reflect an emerging sense of proprietorship or were simply the easiest way to convey "the land that I am officially responsible for." The difference is subtle but potentially significant.

A final point that makes trapline registration historically pivotal is that the combination of mapping and imposing detailed management criteria provided the government with practical control over land for the first time. It also, for the first time, actively removed from the Cree *absolute* control over subsistence decisions.

Western environmental management has always taken the perspective that "man" is superior to nature and, as a result, entitled if not obligated to take the lead in dictating its path. There is no evidence to suggest that such an extreme view was adopted by the Cree as a result of reserve management strategies. But these underlying assumptions did, nevertheless, inform the strategy taken by the governments involved. We can say, then, that the initiative exposed the tallymen to a practical application of this alternative cosmology for the first time.

Contrary to Feit's (2005) empowering view of this system as a form of co-governance that included the colonizing government's acknowledgment of Cree land tenure, Morantz (2002) interprets beaver reserves and the trapline-tallyman system in the context of the immediate and overwhelming challenges of disease and starvation in the 1930s. "On the brink of physical and cultural annihilation," Morantz (ibid., 172) concludes, the Cree had no alternative but to accept the imposition of external management over their lands and hunting practices. It is conceivable that these experiences could have coexisted and that duress might have engendered flexibility without the abandonment of agency or long-standing spiritual understandings. In Feit's analysis, the Cree's autonomy was maintained if not extended by their collaboration with an external authority; in Morantz's view, Cree autonomy was severely diminished. My own view is that both individual and collective autonomy were beginning to be subtly undermined through the subordination of hunters to reserve managers and governments.

Hydroelectric Development in the 1970s

When the Quebec government announced in 1971 its intentions to harness the great rivers of the North for hydroelectric power generation, it was a major crisis for the Eastern Cree, who had not been consulted. In a reversal of the assimilationist precepts that had forced Western education on a generation, education now provided Crees with the means to fight against the government. A small group of southern-educated Cree men from the first generation to complete secondary school launched a legal challenge — a profound step forward in the struggle for collective autonomy. No longer focusing only on the individual or hunting group, autonomy became a broad cultural issue. The courts found in their favour, but the decision was immediately overturned. The Crees then entered into treaty negotiations with Quebec. The case brought the leaders of the Eastern Cree communities together for the first time, resulting in the construction of a clearly defined collective social and political identity represented by the Grand Council of the Crees (GCC).

Hydro development proceeded, but a modern treaty was negotiated: the James Bay and Northern Quebec Agreement (JBNQA). Extensive coverage of the case and its influence exists elsewhere (e.g., Carlson 2004; Moses 2002; Peters 1999; Richardson 1991; Rynard 2001). For present purposes, only a few issues are pertinent.

For purposes of administration, the JBNQA divided the Cree landscape into three classes. Category 1 (1.5 percent), where the Cree villages were situated, was designated as land for the exclusive use of the Cree. Category 2 (18 percent) encompassed adjacent lands, owned by the province but where the Cree have exclusive hunting rights. Category 3 (80.5 percent) refers to the remainder, which were conceived as public lands with controls on harvesting rights for Cree and non-Cree. Although the agreement states that Quebec and its agencies have development rights on Category 2 and 3 lands, Evelyn Peters (1999) claims that the province has expropriation rights for resource development in all three zones.

Once built, the Le Grande hydro reservoirs flooded 13,234 square kilometres of land, submerging twenty-six out of forty traplines that belonged to the Chisasibi Cree. In all, 41 of a total 286 lines (in 1989) were directly affected (Hayeur 2001). Access to subsistence landscapes was not only constrained; it was also permanently eliminated.

These categorizations of land and the explicit claims of the Province of Quebec as their primary owner constitute a bold challenge to the traditional Cree understanding of land. Beaver reserves and trapline registration had introduced bureaucratic management but with the implicit expectation that the landscape was still functioning essentially as a social ecosystem. Cree negotiators ensured that their right to access and to participation in decision making for the entire territory was entrenched in the treaty, but rampant disregard for state obligations by federal and provincial governments over subsequent years severely hampered the treaty's implementation.

The effects on autonomy in this case were two-sided. On the negative side, the Cree lost the potential for complete control over decisions on land use in the subsistence landscape, and the notion of village life as a permanent condition has become widely entrenched. Although evidence presented at the hearings demonstrated that nearly half of the Crees at that time still lived much of the year on their customary hunting grounds and that many others continued to hunt periodically, the government chose to view the Crees as living in settled, modern, assimilated communities. The collective autonomy to choose between long-standing ways of living and the ways of Quebecers was diminished significantly.

Mistissini tallymen interviewed in 1974 expressed concern for the survival of the animals, land, and future generations of Cree. They spoke of land — and its inheritance over generations, from the past and into the future — not as private property but as a place of living and a source of food. A frequently repeated concern was the hydro project's potential to destroy the land (Preston 2006b). The power of such a notion is profound, and it speaks to the survival not only of the Cree but also of the spiritual lifeworld. A few tallymen participating in these 1974 interviews expressed beliefs that may reflect the longer-term implications of trapline designation on the tallymen's conceptions of land and property:

> I believe the Indians own this land, for they have lived and hunted for as long as I remember ... I not only believe the Indians own this land, but I know it. (S. Mianscum, 1 April 1974)

> If my land should be flooded we won't have a place to trap. The workers that have been and are still working on that land have no manners why didn't they come to see us first about prospecting and

bulldozing their way into land which belongs to me? (I. Coon, 9 April 1974)

On the positive side, the treaty process has been enormously capacity building for the Crees in terms of knowledge, skills, and a sense of distinct identity, important tools for seeking collective autonomy within the political, economic, and cultural systems into which the Cree have been pulled. The Cree entered the global political arena by developing strategic positions vis-à-vis the United Nations, the International Labour Organization, and leaders of other nations, and they became leaders also in the development of the United Nations Declaration on the Rights of Indigenous Peoples. As Will Coleman rightly observes, they became active agents of globalization (personal communication with author, October 2005) in this process. One of the original Cree negotiators commented that although the Crees see the JBNQA as "a charter of Eeyou rights," the governments understand it as achieving the extinguishment of Cree rights, "taking of lands and resources, and the exclusive exercise of power" (Awashish 2002, 12).

By providing a one-way conceptual bridge, the process of negotiation also created opportunities for the Cree to think of land in ways more consistent with the Western world view. Hans Carlson (2004) demonstrates how the cultural bias of the Canadian legal system forced the Cree to find ways to represent their relationships with land in terms that were comprehensible to the courts. In the process, the discourse of Cree lifeways shifted into the language of resource management as an instrumental activity. The eventual establishment of a hierarchy of Cree governance and management under the agreement also followed the Western model and, with it, bureaucratic processes for land management.

The JBNQA originally included the payment of $135 million to the Cree over twenty years in compensation for their losses. This transaction introduced the idea that Cree land could be valued in terms of dollars — at that time what seemed like enormous sums. It should be understood that until the beginning of the 1970s, there were no popular sources of telecommunications in the northern Cree communities. People would occasionally go south to hospital or for other reasons, but from Waskaganish northward they were still isolated from the outside world. The exception is the northernmost community of Whapmagoostui, where a military base was built in the 1940s. Awareness of property in the Western sense would have been limited to what children learned in southern schools since the 1940s and to what a comparatively few men might have observed while doing wage work in the south. This economic valuation of Cree land may be the impetus behind several more recent cases of tallymen seeking personal compensation from the local band for overuse of their traplines by others (Richard Preston, personal communication with author, September 2005). It may be implicated further in cases of a few tallymen accepting money from lumber companies for extraction on their traplines, a practice that can be understood variously as payment for goods or as compensation for the use of viable hunting environments (Feit and Beaulieu 2001).

Hydro Development in the 1990s

While battles over the interpretation of the JBNQA waged on through the 1970s and 1980s, Hydro-Québec announced in 1989 that it would also launch hydro development on the Great Whale River. The plan was to flood another 9,000 square kilometres with reservoirs. With the devastating experience of La Grande still fresh and ongoing, and knowing the poor performance level of the government in meeting its agreed upon obligations, the Crees chose not to seek cooperative negotiation, as they had in the 1970s. Instead, they sought to prevent the development from occurring at all. Cree leaders took to the global media stage with their case, presenting to the world a view of Quebec's disregard for cultural and environmental protection in favour of wealth from development. The Cree engaged with local and international NGOs; they took their case to the International Water Tribunal. Sympathy for the Cree position was widespread and well publicized. American customers backed out, and Quebec shelved the project (on this case, see, for example, Jenson and Papillon 2000; McRae 2004).

I want to draw attention to just three of the different kinds of Cree voices that expressed feelings about the land in the public record about this case. First, environmental assessment interviews were conducted with Crees in 1994 by Colin Scott, Kreg Ettenger, Marie Roué, and Douglas Nakashima under contract to the Grand Council of Crees. Interviewees included people from Chisasibi, Eastmain, and Wemindji, who had experienced the La Grande Project, and from Whapmagoostui (formerly Great Whale), who would be most affected by the new project. They documented how people thought the proposed hydro project would influence the land. The frequency with which people expressed concern for catastrophic destruction within these transcripts is striking, and a profound sense of personal empathy with the animals, fish, and trees is also evident, especially among those who identify themselves as having lived on the land most of their lives. The following statement illustrates this position: "Some of the caribou are such a pitiful sight to see for they are so skinny, when they get here. This is what we know, so much is destroyed already, right through this land, where the caribou drowned. There is so much water on this side too, where the dam was built on the Chisasibi River and if ever the dam is built on the Whapmagoostui River, where will these caribou go, where will they find things to eat?" (Grand Council of the Crees 1994). I examine the theme of compassion in these and other statements made by Crees in the context of hydroelectric development in the 1970s in detail elsewhere (Preston 2006a).

Second, in public meetings about the Great Whale Project, a well-known socially and politically active man explained for the record that Crees' holistic understanding of land was the same in 1992 as it had been in the distant past:

> I would like to start by explaining that, to Crees, when you talk about the environment, many times they include themselves. They do not restrict their definition of environment to land, water, the air, but also include all living creatures including themselves. Crees see themselves as an integral part of nature. They are taught from when they are very young that they are part of the environment. They are one with nature. They are part of the land ... So the impact does not stay within that trapline. It affects the community members. It affects all those relatives that the trapper has in that community. (LePage and Blanchard 1992, 89)

One of the questions that arises is, to what extent has the enormously popular Western notion of indigenous wisdom begun to affect Aboriginal statements, especially public ones, about themselves? This third example is illustrative of how Cree political leaders regularly make public statements on issues of concern, just as other national leaders do. The challenge posed by translating concepts across cultures and languages is further compounded by the language of political rhetoric. For decades, Crees have explained that no one can own the land — the land owns the people. So, when Grand Chief Matthew Coon Come (1989) addressed the Grand Council with "we are the proper owner of this land," did he intend to refer to the land as property, or was he simply making a rhetorical statement about autonomy?

There is no question that the Cree definition of environment cited above is consistent with traditional Cree views. At the same time, changes in Cree lifeways, especially in the previous twenty years (including an astute awareness of politics and rhetoric), may result in strategic or rhetorical use of the traditional views by some people. The clear depth of meaning expressed in the interviews cited above, however, suggests that traditional values have endured, particularly among those who have continued to live on the land rather than shifting to permanent village life. Other interviews carried out in Chisasibi at the same time, but oriented to social services, revealed a widespread concern that "a generation has emerged that seems to have lost a close connection with the traditional lifestyle" and, thus, traditional values (Niezen 1993, 518-19). This disconnect may be reflected in the following comment from the Whapmagoostui Environmental Impact Assessment interviews:

> For the older people, their disagreement with the proposed project comes from a deeper level of their being. For them and I feel empathy for them, they know that it is not good to destroy the world as they know it, O.K., it's the only world they know. They see other "worlds" on TV but this is the world they know and they have known. Now they have not grasped that industrialization is almost destroying the whole planet anyway, but what they know of this part of the planet is a good functioning environment. Why change it? Why destroy it? Can we see other ways of using it so as not to upset the way it is functioning and not make massive changes to it? If you can satisfy my distress, maybe we will go somewhere with that. What about the children in the future? I mean, this is the basic Cree thinking about the future, what about the Cree children in the future? What can we, apart from destroying their history, their legacy, can we give them what will sustain them for all time in return for destroying the land their ancestors left behind for them? If the Cree people can be satisfied in that sense, I think they would agree to this project. (Grand Council of the Crees 1994)

Following the cancellation of this development by Hydro-Québec, many Crees must surely have felt that defending their traditions was in fact a powerful thing to do. Cree autonomy in terms of securing a way of living consistent with long-standing knowledge and ways of living within the Canadian socio-political context was gaining momentum.

A Negotiated Agreement: 2002

After the successful opposition to the Great Whale Project, it came as a surprise to many people when the Grand Council of the Crees announced in 2001 its agreement, in principle, for a new nation-to-nation relationship with Quebec regarding the development of natural resources. They had convinced the world of their commitment to the conservation of land and its necessity for their very survival so well that the new agreement seemed a betrayal. It was controversial within Cree communities as well. People were divided over traditional values, their relationship with the land, and the need for substantial economic stability to sustain a rapidly growing population in the twenty-first century. Half of the Cree population in 2000 was below the age of twenty-five. Statistics show that in 1999-2000 between 12 and 32 percent of adults were living on the land for one-third of the year or more, depending on their village of association (Quebec 2003).

In 2002, the grand chief and the premier of the Province of Quebec signed the Peace of the Braves. Among its many components, the deal allowed Quebec to proceed with more hydro development, a much-reduced version of the third major phase in its original plan to harness all of the great rivers of the Subarctic. In exchange, some of the failed promises of the JBNQA were revisited in new form in the expectation that the original objectives could be met. The Cree would receive $3.5 billion in compensation from Quebec over fifty years, and they would take on most of the responsibilities prescribed to government in the JBNQA. In principle, the deal gives the Cree much more involvement in decision making when it comes to resource exploitation by Quebec and its licensees. Several of the grievances expressed in the 1994 Environmental Impact Assessment interviews were addressed in the companion Nadoshtin Agreement, signed the same day, including mechanisms for the compensation of individual tallymen for the loss of land and resources resulting from hydroelectric development.

By that time, some of the Crees themselves had become involved in mining and logging initiatives and were benefitting directly from such activities. Others had gone into eco- and cultural tourism ventures as a form of economic development that relies on the landscape without destroying it. Environmental resource management practices now include many of the tools used by southern managers, such as digital mapping. For many Crees, the land has become an economic resource in contemporary Western terms; it has been abstracted from the spiritual world of their parents and grandparents. Yet the language of respect is still strong, and it has incorporated many popular Western — if not global — concepts such as ecosystem sustainability. Cree autonomy has been reconstituted within Canadian political structures, leading to the highest levels of self-determination since the 1940s.

Conclusion

In 2004, the former grand chief Matthew Coon Come (2004, 162) noted that $5 billion of natural resources are extracted from the Cree territory every year "by governments, crown corporations, and multinationals." There is no question that it will continue. But the Cree have developed the capacity to at least try to have a say in how it happens. "Our people and their way of life are still thriving; they are flourishing. We have learned to live with the animals. We have maintained some of our traditions and customs, but we have survived because we have adapted" (ibid., 153).

Although some adults have expressed chagrin that youth lack understanding of the old ways and values, there continue to be youth who opt for the bush life rather than that of the town or city. Still others straddle the two worlds, adapting their understanding of the old ways through the filter of experience; they struggle to define a distinctive and unified Cree identity and to nurture some form of spiritual relationship to the land.

The forces of globalization are significantly implicated in the history of the Eastern James Bay Cree, most particularly between the moment of rupture in 1971 and the present. In the face of extremely rapid changes to the conditions of daily life, Crees have both countered and employed these forces in defence of autonomy at both the hunting group and "First Nation" scales. As the nature of collective autonomy has been transformed, its integrity has been challenged and reclaimed. Colonialist natural resource exploitation has been a major impetus, and globalization has been an unexpected but well-engaged resource. The Cree have remained a substantial voice in global indigenism. They played a pivotal role in the UN Permanent Forum on Indigenous Issues, which led to the eventual adoption of the United Nations Declaration on the Rights of Indigenous Peoples in late 2007. (One of the last remaining UN parties not to ratify, Canada announced its intent to do so in late 2010.) Crees have shown continuing leadership in indigenous rights, for example, on the issue of climate change.

Concepts of land in relation to Western notions of property have been challenged as well. Although it would be incorrect to suggest that all

Eastern Cree share the same conceptions of land, notable changes can be observed among many whose voices have been documented in one form or another. In general terms, from a traditional position of land or landscape as social interaction in which the human person is but one participant with conscious agency, we can trace the emergence of other ways of thinking. These include notions of land as a working resource with internal functional boundaries, as cultural identity, as heritage, as property and, most recently, as an abstract economic resource. Traditional meanings have been retained and have been renegotiated to such a degree that complex layers of meanings now exist. With complex layers of meaning come new versions of autonomy, particularly a type of autonomy that involves "playing the game" within the Canadian and Quebec political systems, using Western legal means and understandings of land to build a new autonomous cultural space.

chapter 4

Making Forests "Normal": Sustained Yield, Improvement, and the Establishment of Globalist Forestry in British Columbia

Scott Prudham

IN BRITISH COLUMBIA, CANADA, globalization and industrial forestry have proceeded hand in hand. Indeed, as a resource hinterland serving a globalizing economy for much of the second half of the twentieth century, BC's environmental and social geographies have been actively produced in important ways by and through a globalist model of forest extraction, forest commodity production and exchange, and forest regulation. How was the province's model of globalist forestry established and consolidated and, in particular, how was this model enabled by the delineation of specific regimes of forest access and control?

In this chapter, in league with others in the volume, I seek to explore the significance of a singular globalist moment in which property relations were in significant measure fixed as a foundation for delineating relations of global integration. In BC, a dramatic post–Second World War takeoff of industrial, export-oriented forest commodity production and exchange was grounded in important ways by a regime of private forest tenures and forest regulation established in the wake of two provincial royal commissions on forestry during the 1940s and 1950s. Amid controversy and contestation regarding the province's nascent forest industry, these royal commissions (headed by BC Justice Gordon Sloan and hereafter referred to as the "Sloan Commissions") articulated new regimes of forest access that conferred lasting private rights to state-controlled forest lands in the province. At the same time, they also embraced a model of modernist and highly rationalized scientific forest management known as sustained yield forestry that was itself being globalized. Together, these positions would provide a foundation for propelling BC to global prominence as a forest commodity producer and exporter based on extracting the green gold of BC's accumulated inventory of old-growth timber and replacing it with scientifically managed cultivated forest regimes featuring younger trees, commercially oriented species, and ecologically simplified landscapes.

I briefly sketch the broad contours of the integrated and increasingly global model of industrial forest commodity production that has helped to shape BC forest policy since the mid-twentieth century, notwithstanding signs of serious decline in recent decades. My purpose is mainly to establish the Sloan Commissions as a globalist moment. I then provide some interconnected conceptual frameworks through which to view the establishment of modern forest tenures and scientific forest management regimes in BC, with an emphasis on the following: (1) the role of notions of social and ecological improvement resonant with Lockean discourses and pivotal in the political legitimation of property regimes as forms of enclosure; (2) interrelated notions of use value and exchange value that animate particular doctrines of improvement; (3) the ways in which contending logics of movement and fixity in commodity production and exchange were resolved or reconciled (if temporarily) through what I call a spatio-ecological fix predicated on the production of nature in the guise of scientifically managed forests rationalized for commodity production; and (4) the interplay of contending autonomies or claims to autonomy in the territorialization of BC as a postcolonial state achieved through forest administration and regulation. I emphasize all of these dynamics as facets of the postwar model of globalist forestry in BC, which was given significant shape by the extended globalist moment spanning the decade between the first and second Sloan Commission reports, issued in 1945 and 1957, respectively (Sloan 1945, 1957).

Postwar Industrial Forestry and the Sloan Commissions

For much of the period dating back to the Second World War, British Columbia has been known as timber country, and for good reason. The province contains more than 60 million hectares of productive forest lands (Council of Forest Industries 2000), 95 percent of it held (nominally) in public hands as Crown land. Home to a rich diversity of forest types, the province is particularly (though by no means only) well known in the public imagination for the temperate rainforests along its western edge, which are sustained by moist and mild air from the Pacific Ocean. These forests, among the most biologically rich and productive in the world, first attracted forestry capital to the province in the mid-nineteenth century and sustained a first wave of industrial expansion that extended well into the twentieth century. But it was only after the middle of the century that BC emerged as Canada's leading forest products producer and exporter, no mean feat for a nation-state that, in turn, is one of the world's forestry giants and a leading exporter of forest products.[1] Although beset in the last twenty to thirty years by a host of political, economic, and ecological challenges, the BC forest industry has shaped the province's postwar development, long serving as the largest single sector of manufacturing employment and income.[2]

The broad contours and controversies of BC's forest sector are well chronicled elsewhere. Geographers Trevor Barnes and Roger Hayter, for instance, have published extensively on the economic geography of the province's forest sector, dubbing it an example of permeable Fordism (Hayter 2000; Barnes, Hayter, and Hay 2001). Specifically, they highlight that, for most of the postwar period, BC was highly outward looking in terms of its dependence on foreign markets for the export of mass-produced wood commodities (90 percent going to the United States, the European Union, and Japan) and in terms of a pronounced reliance on multinational capital and foreign investment (Marchak 1983; Marchak, Aycock, and Herbert 1999; Hayter 2000).[3] As commodities flowed out, capital poured in, lured in no small measure by the existence of long-term, private, exclusive, renewable, and exchangeable access rights to Crown-owned forests, leases which accounted for over 80 percent of the provincial annual allowable cut by end of the twentieth century (Marchak, Aycock, and Herbert 1999).

Preference for big capital in conferring forest access rights has been a consistent feature of BC's forest policy framework, a feature based on the now highly questionable notion that larger companies are more stable and thus better partners in the economic development of hinterland communities (Bengston 1994; Tollefson 1998). Thus, by the late 1990s, approximately 85 percent of provincial cutting rights were controlled by fifteen large, integrated forest products companies (Marchak 1988; Widenor 1995; Marchak, Aycock, and Herbert 1999; Prudham and Reed 2001).[4]

At least for a time, globalist forestry in BC provided a basis of prosperity for forest-dependent communities (Hayter 2000, 2003). As Barnes, Hayter, and Hay (2001) note, for example, the community of Port Alberni, located in central Vancouver Island, boomed in 1976, boasting the third highest per capita income in all of Canada. And though exceptional, Port Alberni was hardly alone. The forest sector became the province's leading source of revenue, income, exports, and manufacturing employment.

In more recent years, coincident with high international log prices and decreasing terms of trade for more finished wood products, the province's forest industry has taken to closing mills and exporting more and more wood in the form of unprocessed or raw logs.[5] Fluctuating levels of performance and profitability have racked the industry since the 1970s (Marchak 1983; Hayter and Barnes 1997; Hayter 2000, 2003). In response, firms have consistently sought to shed costs through automation and employment rationalization. Consequently, there has been a dramatic reduction in levels of employment, including employment per unit volume of wood harvest (Marchak, Aycock, and Herbert 1999; Hayter 2000).[6] Many communities — including the aforementioned Port Alberni — have experienced the pain of layoffs and mill closures (Barnes and Hayter 1992; Hayter and Barnes 1997; Halseth 1999a, 1999b; Ostry 1999; Reed 1999; Barnes, Hayter, and Hay 2001; Hayter 2003; Prudham and Penfold 2005).

These dynamics have been complemented by sustained critique from multiple quarters of civil society. Environmentalist opposition to the liquidation of old-growth timber garnered headlines beginning in the 1980s and led to well-publicized standoffs and claims of a "war in the woods" (Wilson 1998; Braun 2002; McManus 2002; Satterfield 2002), fuelled by an increasingly conflicted scientific community (see, e.g., Franklin 1989a; Dietrich 1992; Swanson and Franklin 1992; Rayner 1996; Wilson 1998; Hayter 2000, 2003; Rayner et al. 2001; Braun 2002; Magnusson and Shaw 2003; Prudham 2005). At the same time, a resurgent First Nations movement has sought with some success to contest anew colonial displacements of Aboriginal peoples (see Cutler, this volume) by seeking stronger representation for BC First Nations in forest ownership and management, in the broader context of struggles over modern, comprehensive land claims (Blomley 1996, 2003; Rossiter and Wood 2005).

Despite seemingly clear signs that BC's globalist model of forestry is unravelling, it is worth considering the foundations of a way of doing forestry that, for several decades, propelled Canada's western-most province to prominence in the international forest sector and made it a singular example of a globally integrated, extractive economy. Strong property rights governing access to forests in BC is one of the lynchpins that has defined globalist forestry in BC, so much so that, despite the nominally public character of the province's forests, private lease rights to forests in

BC exhibit many of the characteristics of full-fledged, private, excludable, and exchangeable property rights. Banks, for instance, have for some time treated these rights as a form of private capital, loaning money to firms based on the expectation that the rights are renewable. Moreover, it is widely believed in forest policy circles that the threat of leaseholders suing the state for compensation has placed a chill on the provincial government's willingness to rescind access rights to enforce newer policy objectives (Haley and Luckert 1995; Clogg 1997). These lease rights, and the regime of forest regulation designed to prevail over them, were in substantial measure prescribed by the Sloan Commissions on forestry, marking a departure from prior, more laissez-faire modes of extraction and setting the stage for subsequent postwar expansion.

Improvement, Use and Exchange, Fixity and Movement

In his influential collection of essays *Property: Mainstream and Critical Positions,* C.B. Macpherson (1978) argues that property rights must always rely on a foundation of legitimacy. In his words (ibid., 11, emphasis in original), this is for two reasons: "First, that property is a right in the sense that it is an enforceable claim; second, that while its enforceability is what makes it a *legal* right, the enforceability itself depends on society's belief that it is a *moral* right." In essence, he seems to suggest that although force may well underpin any or even all exclusive property claims — and, as he notes, all property regimes (save extremely rare, truly open access regimes) involve some sort of exclusion — so too does the wider society's acceptance of those claims as legitimate rights. From an ideological standpoint, then, a key question emerges: what arguments (explicit or otherwise) circulate around particular property regimes as forms of exclusion that give them legitimacy? How are these exclusions made to make sense to a wider society?[7]

One pervasive discourse of legitimacy for enclosures of various kinds centres on the notion of improvement, the idea that somehow, in the enclosure of land, dispossessions are legitimate if the land enclosed has been in some sense improved for the benefit of all. As Macpherson discusses, the genealogy of this line of argument goes back at least to John Locke in his celebrated defence of the enclosure of private land in England as a natural right of those who mix their labour with the land. As Locke famously wrote, "As much land as a Man Tills, Plants, *Improves*, Cultivates, and can use the Product of, so much is his Property. He by his Labour does, as it were, enclose it from the Common" (John Locke "Of Property," reprinted in Macpherson 1978, 19, emphasis added). For Locke, this argument was underpinned by the idea that enclosed land would be made more agriculturally productive, and thus improved, ostensibly for the benefit of society more generally.

Locke's argument that the improvement of land makes private enclosure legitimate had an important influence in the natural rights paradigm and remains widely influential in the Western property right tradition. It was also an important intellectual and discursive underpinning of colonial enclosures (Weaver 2003) and the territorialization of colonial administrative rule (see, e.g., Vandergeest and Peluso 2001). Moreover, the Lockean notion of improvement, in so far as it links the efficient use of property with a socially just disposition of benefits from the use of property, underlies widely held contemporary arguments about the relationship between property rights and the distribution of social goods (e.g., income, resources) and social bads (e.g., pollution). This underpinning includes, for instance, the now widely influential idea that attributes excessive environmental damage stemming from economic activities to market failures or externalities. These failures impose, vis-à-vis production technologies, negative costs of production disproportionately on those outside the scope of decision making. The solution, according to this paradigm, is to get the prices right, a process that revolves to no small extent on assigning exclusive property rights and, thus, in theory, responsibilities. Perhaps the iconic statement along these lines remains Garret Hardin's (1968) essay "The Tragedy of the Commons." It is also a staple of contemporary, particularly neoliberal, prescriptions for redressing resource depletion and environmental pollution problems (see, e.g., Pearce and Turner 1990; Mansfield 2007).[8] In development circles, the continuing, albeit mutating, influence of the notion of improvement is widespread. Tanya Li (2007), for example, discusses improvement as a logic of governmentality whose aim is the right or correct ordering of things. In this respect, as she argues, the logic operates not only as a sham cover for dispossession but also as a kind of truth claim whose rationale, though never disinterested, works to enrol diverse subjects into a common project.

In what follows, I examine how a distinct logic of improvement, at once political and ecological, animated the proposed changes in forest access and forest administration envisaged by the Sloan Commissions in British Columbia. In this context, I argue that specific notions of use and exchange value are crucial to understanding how doctrines of improvement function as legitimating and enabling discourses. This was central for Locke, for instance, who maintained that enclosure for the sake of improvement was justified only if the land and the products of the land enclosed were actually used; it did not matter who used them. As Macpherson (1978) points out, despite arguing that enclosure could not be justified if it led to hoarding and waste, Locke makes the decisive (and, for Macpherson, highly problematic) argument that exchange is a form of use — that is, as long as the products of enclosed land are not wasted (whether directly used by their owner or not), then the enclosure is legitimate. Although one may quibble, as Macpherson did, with Locke's collapsing of exchange value into use value, the important issue for the current discussion is how specific notions of use and exchange value are understood as relational categories that are often highly intertwined in doctrines of improvement that underpin property regimes.[9]

Drawing on this framing, I focus on the particular valences of use value and exchange value embraced, sometimes implicitly, by Sloan in his reports and in the institutionalization of his recommendations. If, as Sloan argued, nominally public forests were to be (newly) enclosed, and if private forestry capital were to be granted enduring and exclusive rights of access to Crown lands, on what basis could state action to create these rights be considered legitimate as forms of enclosure and, specifically, as postcolonial dispossessions? For Justice Sloan, the normative or moral foundation for private, excludable rights to forested land lay in two fundamental logics of improvement. First, by being granted enduring rights to public forests, forestry capital would provide, *in exchange,* a stable basis for the economic and social development of BC's forest-based hinterland communities. Private rights to public forests would lead to the improvement of society more generally. Second, and drawing centrally on the Lockean tradition, capital and the state together would undertake the improvement of nature (land) via the exchange of BC's "untamed" forests for scientifically managed and rationalized forestry regimes prescribed along the lines of European ideals of the *Normalbaum* or normal forest (literally, from the German for *normal tree*). These ideals have since become known more familiarly as scientific sustained yield forestry.

Yet one of the particular registers through which I seek to examine notions of use and exchange value in the creation of modern forest tenures and forest management regimes in BC, particularly in thinking about globalization as territorial integration and articulation, is that of a dialectic of movement, on the one hand, and fixity or territorialization, on the other. That is, I see the particular logics of use and exchange value that animate the doctrine of improvement embraced by Sloan in terms that speak to resolution (even if temporary) of a fundamental geographical tension in capital accumulation and commodity circulation. On the one hand is a tendency towards movement (the ability of commodities, capital, information, and so on to move or circulate, more or less freely and quickly, between places). On the other is a somewhat countervailing tendency arising from the delineation of specific places and spatial arrangements to facilitate this movement. This dynamic tension between movement and fixity is surely at the heart of attempts to understand particular places and the evolution of their relationship to others via evolving spatial arrangements in a globalizing world.

David Harvey, drawing on Marx's analysis and critique of capitalism (primarily in Volume 2 of *Capital*), has written extensively on the notion of a spatial fix or a spatio-temporal fix (see Harvey 1982, 1989, 2001a; Schoenberger 2004; Jessop 2006). Although sometimes referring primarily to the spatial development of physical infrastructure, Harvey also hoped to theorize more general geographical dynamics and configurations of commodity circulation, including, for instance, specific property relations that govern access to territory and, thus, to nature. Bob Jessop (2006) provides a useful critical review of the scope of Harvey's thinking on the notion of spatio-temporal fixes. He notes two broad ways in which Harvey discusses the idea. One of these is in reference to the development of fixed capital in definite spatial arrangements typically coordinated by state action. The second, however, is a much more broad reference to the notion of a structured coherence very much in line with regulation theory, emphasizing not only the spatiality of physical infrastructure but also institutional, policy, and cultural norms that shape the trajectory of commodity production and circulation. As Jessop (ibid., 164) writes in his attempt to synthesize Harvey's writing on the topic, "Relevant spatial factors in these matrices include place-based social relations, the built environment, land markets, the rural-urban division of labour, urban hierarchies, locational policies, the territorialization of political power, and attempts to manage uneven geographical development." Enduring and exclusive property regimes are a prime example of the sort of institutional fixes that can both enable and impede circulation and exchange (see Introduction).

My interest is in drawing on and extending these ideas in ways applicable to a more rural context, one that corresponds to an extractive frontier. Such a place is one in which the nature-society relationship and the appropriation and transformation of non-human nature for commodity production in institutionally and culturally specific ways is seen as a central facet of the (formally) extra-economic context (using Jessop's language) that constitutes a regionally specific spatio-temporal fix. I find it useful in this respect to invoke Neil Smith's *Uneven Development* (2008 [1984]). Smith draws centrally on Harvey's conceptualization of the dynamics of uneven development but, in addition, he insists on interconnections between the production of space and the production of nature through logics of commodification and the progressive domination of exchange value. Along these lines, I argue that one of the achievements of the Sloan Commissions was that they helped establish the foundations of a spatio-ecological fix.[10]

And yet, also in keeping with one of the themes of this volume, the establishment of forest access and regulation subsequent to the Sloan Commissions must be seen as a form of territorialization that privileged some notions of and claims to autonomy over others. The Sloan Commissions clearly prescribed rights of forest access that effectively defined the terms of forest enclosure and thus the scope of autonomy for private capital. In addition, the Sloan Commission recommendations called for active state enforcement and administration of forest tenures and forest practices in ways that consolidated and extended the reach of state capacities, making nature and territory more legible while helping to make BC an administrative state.[11] But taking place as they did in the aftermath of the colonial dispossession of Aboriginal peoples, the commissions worked to confirm or entrench those dispossessions. Postcolonialism is a widely discussed and debated concept, one that I cannot delve into in any great length. However, I use the term to point broadly at ways in which developments in formerly colonial contexts renew or re-inscribe colonial dispossessions and forms of political domination (Braun 2002; Gregory 2004).

In this sense, a condition of postcolonialism is one in which colonialism cannot be relegated entirely to the past. If the Sloan Commissions did not directly prescribe the removal of First Nations people from forested landscapes, the embrace of scientific forestry was predicated on a notion that pervades the history of colonial dispossession in BC, namely, that the province's lands were essentially empty and available for administrative rationalization and commodification (Rossiter 2007). At the very least, the Sloan Commission recommendations and their institutionalization acted to further entrench dispossession of First Nations from their ancestral lands. And this was no mere negation, but rather an active postcolonial prescription for the extension, rolling out, and territorialization of the administrative state via its role in prescribing and regulating the transformation of BC's forested lands.

From Open Access to Sustained Yield

Prior to the establishment of the first two provincial royal commissions on forestry, private timber companies and sawmill operators in BC enjoyed relatively laissez-faire access to the province's extensive forests. With First Nations decimated by disease and largely (and forcibly) relocated to small reservations (Harris 2002; Blomley 2003), forests had become, in the eyes of Anglo-European settlers and their governments, Crown territory (despite the absence of formal treaties) and up for grabs (Rossiter 2007). The province's initial inclination towards these lands combined a predilection for outright transfer to private ownership (with no strings attached) in the form of railroad land grants and for grants of forest-harvesting rights (but not land per se) under extremely favourable, open access, and generally laissez-faire terms (Clogg 1997). This inclination played out during the administration of Premier Richard McBride, who, between 1905 and 1907, established a series of twenty-one-year transferable leases, which were slated to revert to Crown land once they were cut over but were otherwise accompanied by no conditions or restrictions (Rajala 1998; Hayter 2000), including requirements for reforestation.

Such laissez-faire disposal of land and quasi-permanent harvesting rights were halted in 1907 under pressure from conservationists. For the next two decades, the Crown reverted to one-time sales of cutting rights, again without transferring land title. By 1940, however, the forest tenure question had arisen again, owing to concerns about overharvesting and wild economic and geographical fluctuations as forestry operations cut and then moved on, leaving behind a growing inventory of cutover lands and abandoned milling sites for which no one in particular was responsible.[12] There was, at the time, nothing approaching what we would now call forestry or silviculture and little knowledge about the extent of the province's forest resources. In response to these concerns, in 1943, BC Justice Gordon Sloan was named to head the first of two royal commissions on forestry in an attempt to establish a system of property rights and forest regulations to guide the province into the postwar era. Sloan's first report became the basis of significant legislative changes to the regulation of forests, including forest tenure, in the form of An Act to Provide for Forest Management in 1947 (S.B.C. 1947, c. 38). A second report by Sloan, issued in 1957 and based on ten years' experience with the new regulatory provisions, helped to consolidate this system, the precursor of the modern system of forest tenure and forest regulation in BC (Sloan 1945, 1957).

Faced with what were considered socially and environmentally destructive cutting practices on the railroad grant lands (lands transferred outright to private hands in the hopes of financing the railroad), as well as in adjacent public forests, property rights became a key question for Sloan. Would the commission endorse privatization of public forests or turn to more public control and management of forest resources (Rajala 1998)? Opting for a decidedly liberal approach, Sloan (1945, 143, emphasis added) advocated "a form of tenure permitting the operator to retain possession *in perpetuity* of the land now held under temporary forms of alienation upon condition that he maintain these lands continuously productive and regulate the cut therefrom on a *sustained-yield* basis."

Although ostensibly maintaining forests in public ownership, the commission created new, exclusive rights to forests via forest management licences (FMLs). These tenures conferred exclusive rights of access to individual companies, which were, in turn, encouraged to retain and manage these areas according to the principles of sustained yield forestry. In addition, the Sloan Commission reports led to the establishment of public working circles in which shorter-term but renewable rights of access to specific volumes were created. Forest management licences became the basis of the tree farm licences (TFLs), most of which were firmly established by the late 1960s, that now constitute a prevalent form of private access rights to the valuable forest lands of Vancouver Island and parts of the Coast. Moreover, amendments to the BC Forest Act in 1978, consistent with the spirit of the Sloan Commissions' embrace of working circles, established forest licences as more secure, renewable, and transferable forms of volume-based tenures within prescribed timber supply areas (TSAs). Together, TFLs and forest licences accounted for about 80 percent of the annual allowable harvest in BC in the late 1990s (Clogg 1997; Marchak, Aycock, and Herbert 1999).

Sustained Yield and Social Improvement via Community Stability

A crucial element of Sloan's justification for the creation of enduring, exclusive property rights for private capital over public forests lay in his reasoning about the relationship between the forest industry and forest-based settlements in the hinterland. Linking private property rights to public forests, on the one hand, with the economic and social life of forestry communities, on the other, became a key normative argument offered by Sloan in defence of these rights. For Sloan, the strictly social justification for secure, private, excludable rights to public forests lay in stability, specifically in his vision of economic stability for forest-based settlements. Invoking a common trope articulated by advocates of private, individual, and exclusive forms of resource enclosure who link property rights to improvement, Sloan embraced the idea that owners of secure rights would be more likely to invest *in situ*, based on a long-term interest in exercising those rights. In the case of BC forestry, the particular argument was that secure access to sufficient and proximate fibre would help cure the industry's migratory boom-and-bust dynamics by encouraging long-term, larger-scale investments in processing facilities. In this respect, arguments in favour of fixing property rights and social relations were clearly tied to forest-based accumulation, but the use value reflected in Sloan's vision was refracted through the lens of a wider reformist agenda of taming the migratory character of the extractive frontier.

Employment was a key consideration. "Stability of employment," wrote Sloan (1945, 66), "is, of course, of manifest importance in fostering the establishment of permanent and prosperous communities." Referring to these very imperatives in relation to sustained yield regulation, Sloan (ibid., 127, emphasis added) wrote in his first commission report: "A sustained yield policy has, as one objective, the maintenance of forest cover and growth, thus ensuring a perpetual supply of raw material for forest industries *with consequent stability of industrial communities and assurance of permanent payrolls.*" Making the link to tenure reform, Sloan argued that "under our present system of temporary alienations of timber lands that revert to the Crown when logged, operators who cut these lands to secure raw material for their own conversion units are offered no encouragement to treat these lands as permanent tree-farms producing continuous crops. They are, therefore, of necessity forced to move from one area to another to maintain production" (ibid, 143). Sloan's solution was to foster exactly this type of encouragement. Thus, he argued, "The first step toward this objective would be a form of tenure permitting the operator to retain possession in perpetuity" (ibid.).

Emphasis on community economic stability as a rationale for sustained yield forest regulation was by no means unique to BC. Rather, it was also a feature of generally contemporaneous developments in the US Pacific Northwest (Robbins 1987; Schallau and Alston 1987; Robbins 1988; Prudham 1998), developments that clearly had an influence on the Sloan Commissions' deliberations. It bears noting that in BC, however, unlike the United States, the imagined link between tenure, sustained yield forestry, and community economic stability was formalized during the postwar period by the insertion of appurtenance clauses into TFL leases that required leaseholders to direct specified volumes of logs to mills in named settlements. Moreover, the province came to privilege large, increasingly corporate forest products companies because of a (questionable) expectation that these larger companies would prove more stable over time and, thus, better bets for providing an economic foundation for the province's remote, forest-dependent communities. As Justice Sloan wrote in his second report (1957, 94): "In award of management licences, first priority must be given ... to the pulp and paper industries and other large conversion units, especially the great integrated organizations, because of their relative stability, the enormous investment required for their establishment, their continuous prosecution of research and development of new and better uses for wood, their ability to offer continuous, profitable employment, the support of communities, and their direct and indirect contributions to the Provincial taxation structure."

Ecological Improvement and the Normalbaum

Also a rationale for creating secure tenure rights was the idea that they would help deliver sustained yield forestry, not only by encouraging firms to be less geographically mobile but also by encouraging them to reforest cutover lands. More generally, firms were expected to manage the lands to which they now had enduring rights in a more rational, predictable, and ostensibly renewable fashion. Linking community stability, forest regeneration, and property rights, Sloan (1945, 144, emphasis added) wrote, "The allocation or reserve of Crown timber for units of industry would serve two purposes: First, it would enable the operator to maintain production from the cut of mature Crown timber during the period necessary to restock his own land; secondly, the combined area of the private and Crown acreage should, on the second rotation, produce enough timber on a *sustained-yield basis* to maintain production of the unit in perpetuity, perhaps not at the peak of capacity, but sufficient to ensure a profitable operation with consequent benefit to those communities dependent upon the permanence of the industry." Institutionalization of sustained yield forestry was considered a key achievement of the first inquiry, one that echoed and reinforced parallel developments in US forest policy (Robbins 1982; Wilson 1988; Rajala 1998; Bridge and McManus 2000).

In seeking to transform BC's forests, the Sloan Commission reports embraced a second notion of improvement, one that was decidedly more ecological. Specifically, sustained yield forestry would entail replacement of nominally wild (i.e., not transformed by human labour) and unproductive forests with rationalized, productive forests. In this argument — although discursively echoing Locke's link between labour, private and exclusive property rights, and the improvement of land — the Sloan Commission reports also drew heavily on European and specifically Prussian traditions in scientific forest management and the ideal of the domesticated, ordered, and rational landscape of the Normalbaum.

The Normalbaum ideal emerged most directly from the Prussian and German traditions of scientific forestry, which in turn were a product of cameralism *(Kameralwissenschaft)* and its emphasis on scientific state administration of lands and populations. This paradigm of scientific forest rationalization conceptualized the forest in machine-like terms, abstracted from particular social and ecological contexts and subject to improvement and perfectibility via scientific forest management prescriptions (Scott 1998; Ciancio and Nocentini 2000). Cameralism became hugely influential in colonial forest administration, travelling the world via professional and colonial administrative networks during the late nineteenth and early twentieth centuries (Rajan 2006). Introduced in substantial measure by professional foresters trained in the German tradition, this paradigm also transformed North American forestry after the turn of the twentieth century (Clawson and Sedjo 1983; Demeritt 2001).

The central idea of orthodox sustained yield management is to convert natural forests into an ideal form of forest, one that has been defined as "an *ideally constituted forest* with such volumes of trees of various ages so distributed and growing in such a way that they produce equal annual volumes of *produce* which can be removed continually without detrimental impacts to future production" (Brasnett 1953, 16, emphasis added). Ostensibly both simple and elegant, the principle involves organizing a given forest into even-aged monoculture stands of commercially significant tree species. Each stand is harvested at a prescribed age — the rotation age — so that the total annual harvest from the whole forest remains constant over time (Fernow 1902; Society of American Foresters 1944). Reflecting the widespread influence of this idea in scientific forestry of the day, Sloan (Sloan 1945, 24, emphasis added) wrote in his first report that "the vast extent of our productive Coast acreage now occupied by mature and *overmature* timber illustrates the *unbalance of our forest resources*. These *virgin* forests are static and making no net growth and must be replaced by growing trees if we are to progress to within any reasonable distance of the *ideal* or normal forest cover."

It is notable that Sloan's language conveys negative connotations associated with old-growth forests, sentiments that are at odds with contemporary sensibilities, both environmentalist and scientific, that recognize such forests as aesthetically beautiful and biologically rich (Franklin 1989a, 1989b; Swanson and Franklin 1992; Marcot et al. 1994; Shannon and Johnson 1994; Marcot and Thomas 1997). In contrast, for Sloan, liquidating old growth and converting it to young growth would constitute a distinct improvement. An essentially static forest would be replaced with one always growing (i.e., adding commercially useful wood volumes) and supplying wood at the maximum sustainable volume over time.

The idea that a forest could be so converted draws on simple and elegant (though highly problematic) assumptions about the growth profile of forest stands under idealized (i.e., not actual) growing conditions. Generally speaking, the largely old-growth forests that typified BC at the time of the Sloan Commissions and that have since become a cause célèbre among environmentalists are characterized by stands with many trees at an advanced age adding little, if any, net wood volume and by many trees that are either dead or dying (Swanson and Franklin 1992; Marcot et al. 1994; Prudham 2005). By contrast, a *normal* forest is one converted so that all trees older than a prescribed age, which corresponds to their maximum annual growth rate, have been harvested. The scientific principle behind this prescription is that once the maximum annual growth rate or increment has been passed, the tree should be harvested and replaced with younger trees since the annualized average growth rate has been maximized and will subsequently decline. Managing forest stands in this manner on a perpetual basis will result in the maximum wood volume yield over time — a commercial (and ostensibly ecological) improvement.

Managing individual stands within a prescribed forest area or region so that an equal aggregate volume can be harvested each year also means that (in theory) a constant, non-declining, even flow of timber can be obtained from the forest more generally. While one stand is cut one year, another stand reaches culmination age the next year; harvesting pressure relocates within the forest while the previously harvested stand is allowed to regenerate, and so on. For any given volume of harvest required, a prescribed area of forest (given constant and known growth rates) can sustain this volume in perpetuity. This calculation is the basis of the idea of working circles that sustain mills or clusters of mills within a particular geographical setting on an ongoing basis. A normal forest, then, is actually a collection of forest stands at different ages, managed to yield a constant volume over time: the sustained yield (Demeritt 2001).

The Normalbaum prescription also equated ecological improvement with considerable ecological simplification. Old-growth stands, by contrast, are typically characterized by a diversity of tree species, not all of which are commercially valuable or desirable. Thus, for instance, in coastal BC, one can find mixes of commercially attractive species such as Douglas fir, western hemlock, western red cedar, Sitka spruce, and true fir but also less commercially desirable species of coniferous and deciduous trees. The Normalbaum prescribes the replacement of diverse, multi-species stands of trees with monocultures, a practice that very much (and by no accident) resembles an industrial agricultural setting rationalized for the production of a single crop (Scott 1998). Since all the trees in a stand would ideally be of the same age and species, they would be more likely to need the same management treatment (e.g., thinning, pruning, and herbicidal treatments), and this possibility would allow for not only more efficient but also more intensive forms of management.

In the Normalbaum model, the stands were not simply improved by being rationalized, however. Improvement was also defined by social and economic optimization that linked constant harvest volumes with predictability and stability in the forest sector. In BC, this type of optimization entailed the widespread conversion of largely old-growth or late-successional forests to those corresponding to the Normalbaum model. In this respect, embrace of sustained yield forestry endorsed by the Sloan Commissions (particularly the first) drew not only on the German and Prussian tradition of scientific forestry but also on innovations developed by the likes of forester E.J. Hanzlik in the 1920s (Hanzlik 1922; Perry, Vaux, and Dennis 1983) to convert massive areas and volumes of over-mature forests to the idealized model.

Producing Nature: Use and Exchange

The introduction of sustained yield forest regulation, combined with the establishment of new regimes of tenure that conferred exclusive and enduring rights of access to forests for private capital, entailed nothing less than a dramatic province-spanning exercise in the active production of nature in the image and service of the commodity. The province's forests would be remade in the image of the commodity by specifically tying the age profile and the types of trees regenerated to a market imperative. Forest management was transformed into a singular commitment to the goal of generating the maximum volume of merchantable wood. In short, the prescription was literally to liquidate old-growth forests and replace them with organic machines designed for commodity production.

Neil Smith's (2008) theory of the production of nature as a conjoined material and semiotic process of transformation is relevant in this context. For Smith, this combined process entails the literal production of biophysical nature in the sense of being physically transformed by and for commodity production and exchange, but it also entails the production of the idea or the ideology of nature seen in exchange value terms. Smith defines first nature as that nature that is physically transformed and produced as and for commodity exchange, and he defines second nature as that nature that is increasingly understood epistemologically in commodity terms. Both rely on the transformation and re-articulation of nature in use and exchange value terms, particularly the ascendance of exchange value as the prism through which nature takes on both form and meaning.

The Sloan Commissions constituted a globalist moment in that they crystallized reworked notions of use and exchange that would establish the discursive and institutional foundations of material transformations to come. These notions comprise highly interested, active, specific, selective, and postcolonial renderings of what a forest entails and what (and whom) a forest is for. This reworking includes, for instance, the re-articulation of forests through a process of ecological exchange and transformation that moves generally from complexity to simplicity and involves the discursive erasure of the interrelated physical and biological elements of the actually existing, uneven geographies of forests.

The displacement of a tangible, place-specific forest with a forest in the image of a generic idea of a forest is in itself a globalizing moment. The idea of the Normalbaum travelled over significant time and space —

through complex networks of transformations, institutions, and social relations — to arrive in BC as a template for forest management and transformation in the postwar period. And inasmuch as its arrival signified the exchange of a seemingly placeless and generic ecology for a place-bound and specific ecology, the institutionalization of the Normalbaum represented an erasure of place by space of the sort that, as has been argued, is quintessential to globalization. Put simply and in crude terms, land (and thus nature) must be known if and as it is owned.[13] Returning to Macpherson (1978), if property rights must have a moral basis in order to be seen as legitimate, and if nature's improvement is a key basis of this argument, then knowledge claims about the real and imagined natures to be improved are central elements of the moral economy of property.

I do not suggest, of course, that the movement and translation of generalized prescriptions for scientific forest management from Germany to British Columbia via colonial and postcolonial networks of scientific forestry and state administration were simple matters. Scholarship tracking such movements clearly indicates that local uptake of scientific forestry regimes involved active negotiation, not least to accommodate the local biophysical and social context (see, e.g., Rajan 2006; Vandergeest and Peluso 2006a, 2006b). As mentioned, the so-called old-growth problem alone, not to mention persistent challenges in achieving successful forest regeneration and rationalized growth in a new setting, required locally adapted strategies (see, e.g., Rajala 1998; Prudham 2003). Nevertheless, it seems to me quite important and profound that the embrace of the Normalbaum meant the embrace of an abstracted idea of a forest and its instantiation or "fixing" into a forested landscape that initially bore little resemblance to this idea. This is a critical facet of the dialectic of movement and fixity involved in the establishment of a spatio-ecological fix that made BC forests available for commodity production and exchange.

It is also important to emphasize that cutting old-growth stands diverse in both the age and species of trees and replacing them with even-aged monocultures represented a dramatic ecological conversion that had implications not only for the types of trees present but also for the entire ecosystems of which they were a part. Species that were dependent largely or uniquely on old-growth stands (e.g., the northern spotted owl) were actively managed out of existence when the prescriptions of the Normalbaum model were implemented. This logic of exchange as ecological simplification has since become one of the most controversial features of conventional sustained yield management in both the United States and Canada as forest types have been converted to younger and ecologically simplified communities. British Columbia's so-called war in the woods and similar conflicts in the western United States erupted in response to dwindling old-growth habitat and were fuelled by growing scientific documentation of some of the actual ecological implications (see, e.g., Wilson 1998; Bridge and McManus 2000; Braun 2002; Prudham 2005). Viewed increasing through the lens of less strictly commodity-driven environmental science and new environmental sensibilities, the use value of old growth has been redefined. This helps us to see in retrospect, however, that one of the dominant logics of the Normalbaum idea was precisely to define the use value of old growth as an exchange value, one that would see not only trees converted into commodities but also forest ecosystems converted into biological engines of commodity production. Thus the Sloan Commissions' vision for rational scientific management drew on an articulation of use and exchange that strongly echoed Locke's equation of exchange value with use value (via production for exchange) in his justification of enclosure.

In keeping with the parallel, it is important to understand that, in the context of the Sloan Commissions, this globalist moment was indeed an enclosure that involved not only the territorialization of some claims to the land but also the active displacement and denial (exclusion) of others. In particular, Sloan's articulation of a set of use values as ecological and economic exchanges effectively displaced more direct forms of use, including alternative values tied to the cultural and social reproduction of BC's First Nations.

Indeed, the idealist renderings of scientific sustained yield forestry, as Braun (2002) discusses, seldom mentioned (and by their silence helped to reproduce and consolidate) the removal of First Nations from their lands and the erasure of First Nations claims to land. Resurgent nationalism in recent decades among First Nations in BC, including the reassertion of land claims, has drawn attention to the ways in which the commissions were not only a key globalist moment but, in so being, also helped to secure the territorialization of postcolonial state authority by entrenching the marginalization of Aboriginal peoples. This perspective highlights what Vandergeest and Peluso (2001), in the context of Dutch and British colonial territories in Southeast Asia, call the political forest. They refer to the link between the emergence of modern regimes of professional, scientific forest management in colonial settings and the spatial deepening or internal territorialization of colonial authority. This process occurs not least via the conversion from customary and informal regimes of property rights and administration to more modern and formal regimes governing access to and control over forests (see also Vandergeest and Peluso [1995] and the Introduction to this volume).

From this perspective, the establishment of property and management regimes over forests in postwar BC must not be seen in terms of the familiar dichotomy of states or markets. Instead, state power and authority were territorialized through the creation and administration of private property rights and scientific forest management, processes that simultaneously made forests available for commodity production and solidified postcolonial territorial claims. In this complex set of transformations, autonomy as a set of claims to resources and territory was articulated, on the one hand, in terms of access rights for private capital and, on the other, in terms of an administrative logic of governmentality in which forested landscapes became the objects of an overarching scientific forestry elite embedded within and constitutive of the postcolonial administrative state.

Conclusion

British Columbia's Sloan Commissions on forestry represented an extended globalist moment in which the institutional foundations of contemporary forest access rights and regulatory regimes were "made." In part, this was accomplished through discursive "work" to define and establish the legitimacy of rights of access that were both enduring and exclusive. Sloan first reasoned that secure, exclusive, and ultimately transferable rights to forests, when conferred on forest capital, would help cement the economic and social future of BC's communities in the hinterland by providing them with stable income and employment from the manufacture of forest products. In this sense, the political and social logic of improvement served as a rationale for how the political economy of forest access and forest regulation would be organized. At the same time, the logic of ecological improvement was applied directly to the forests, a process that would see them rationalized, tamed, and modernized via the prescriptions of the Normalbaum ideal in the tradition of European scientific forest management. For Sloan, the constant timber harvests guaranteed by sustained yield regulation and private capital investment would secure the future of forestry communities. At the same time, sustained yield forestry would produce (or, more accurately, reproduce) forests in the image of highly rationalized, ordered, socio-ecological landscapes tailored to the needs of industrial forest management and commodity production. Nature would literally be retooled, engineered for commodity production and exchange through its material and semiotic transformation from wild, chaotic, and inefficient old-growth stands to tamed, rationalized, and efficient wood factories. Responsibility for prescribing and overseeing the sustained yield project would fall to the postcolonial state, whose territorialization was a spatio-temporal fix for commodity production that also consolidated exclusion of First Nations from their ancestral lands.

This broad architecture of postwar, globalist forestry has prevailed in British Columbia, more or less intact, since the mid-twentieth century and the days of the Sloan Commissions. It has proven extremely difficult for opponents to undo, despite entrenched opposition from environmental and community activists, deteriorating economic conditions in forest-dependent communities in the hinterland, and renewed claims to the land among First Nations, which have been bolstered by the Supreme Court of Canada's extension of Aboriginal title to the province in *Calder* (1973). Contemporary attempts to establish community forestry, for instance, have difficulty offering anything close to the livelihood promise contained in the deal proposed by Sloan for forest workers and forest-dependent communities (Prudham 2008). Moreover, the legacy of exclusive access rights to provincial and nominally public lands held largely by integrated and powerful forestry firms is a difficult obstacle for critics of globalist forestry to overcome. Perhaps more than any other facet of the Sloan Commission paradigm, it is the property claims that endure and continue to structure the dynamics of movement and fixity and, more generally, the conditions of possibility for BC's forested lands and political and cultural claims to them.

chapter 5

Contested Autonomy: Globalization and Miskito Customary Property Rights in the Río Plátano Biosphere Reserve

Sharlene Mollett

The globalization of the environment is reshaping indigenous space. In Honduras, state support for conservation and the adoption of global environmental norms and discourses are evident in the national landscape. Indeed, 20 percent of the nation's territory is enclosed in over one hundred protected areas (AFE-COHDEFOR 2000). Among these enclosures, 75 percent overlap with territories claimed by indigenous peoples (Martínez 2003). For many indigenous peoples living inside the Honduran Río Plátano Biosphere Reserve, protected-area policies and boundaries impinge on indigenous customary property rights and undermine the prospect for indigenous autonomy over ancestral domains.[1] In Honduras, the ways in which protected areas serve as obstacles to indigenous land rights illustrate how "global connections give grip to universal aspirations" (Tsing 2005, 1) and threaten to erode local indigenous land tenure securities. The goals of sustainable development and biological diversity also shape the prospect of autonomy by legitimating a long-standing set of ideas about indigenous and ladino identity and use of natural resources in Honduras.

The Río Plátano Biosphere Reserve encloses a significant portion of the Honduran Mosquitia, formally recognized as the Department of Gracias a Dios.[2] This region historically represents an important bastion of natural resource potential and racial and ethnic diversity. The reserve was established in 1980 under UNESCO's Man and the Biosphere Program; in 1982, as a result of international pressure, it was designated a United Nations

World Heritage Site (Herlihy 1997). An important resource to the state, the reserve is financed by the German government and is managed under the auspices of the State Forestry Administration (AFE-COHDEFOR).[3] As the largest protected area in Honduras, the reserve measures 815,000 hectares and is an essential component of the internationally recognized Mesoamerican Biological Corridor (Herlihy 1997), a transboundary conservation area that links the most biologically diverse regions in Central America into one large protected area. Because of the global importance of this corridor, the Honduran state also receives funds from many bilateral and multilateral donors such as the World Wildlife Fund, the Nature Conservancy, and the United States Department of the Interior to maintain conservation norms.

The reserve is also home to the Miskito, the region's most populous indigenous group. The Miskito share a mixed ancestry of Amerindian, European, and African heritages rooted in the mid-1600s. Although Britain dominated the colonial coastal trade in the Honduran Mosquitia until 1859, the Miskito, as their allies, controlled the region's natural resources in relation to other indigenous groups, relying upon de facto autonomy for almost four centuries (McSweeney 2004; Offen 1999). In recent years, however, in the context of increased state management of natural resources, Miskito territorial control and access to collective natural resources and property arrangements have been challenged by a steady influx of *ladino colonos* in search of land.[4] As a consequence, Miskito territories inside the reserve have become sites of struggle over natural resources.[5]

Miskito struggles in the reserve stem, in part, from state territoriality's reliance on a set of globalized norms and discourses — referred to as global environmental policy making (Sletto 2002) and environmental geopolitics (O'Tuathail 1998) — that have become the common-sense logic of mainstream conservation (Brockington, Duffy, and Igoe 2008). Critics of global environmentalism argue that its hegemonic norms have appropriated "Third World" natural resources into a global commons and that leaders in the Global North have both discursively and materially assumed leadership over this commons despite the needs of the people on the ground. Therefore multiple struggles are now occurring as indigenous and non-indigenous peoples face off over the environment. As West, Igoe, and Brockington (2006, 252) remind us, "protected areas matter because they are a way of seeing, understanding, and (re)producing the world." Given that the number of protected areas has increased around the world by 50 percent since 1996, indigenous dispossession — linked intimately with poverty, cultural change, and the intensification of struggles over livelihood — has also globalized (McKay and Caruso 2004).

In Honduras, the state draws upon the global ideology of conservation in a seemingly contradictory way. Despite demands from the United Nations to deter colono migration to the reserve — a development that has been blamed for deforestation and the endangerment of species (*La Prensa* 2003) — the state continues to facilitate colono incursions into Miskito space. Although state-sanctioned migration appears to contradict conservation norms, colono invasions are justified, in part, by the state's commitment to sustainable development, imbued with neoliberal paradigms that seek to expand the nation's export-oriented agriculture. These two entangled globalized processes, the globalization of the environment and the worldwide diffusion of neoliberal policies, I argue, grant legitimacy to a long-standing racialized project of nation building. This project, in the name of biodiversity protection and sustainable development, justifies the appropriation of indigenous territories and undermines the prospect for Miskito autonomy.

Miskito autonomy is contingent on the legal recognition of customary property rights and control over natural resources in ancestral domains. The Miskito seek collective territorial legislation accompanied by the right to use and control natural resources on their own terms and with the power to exclude others from appropriating resources inside Miskito space. The desire for autonomous spaces neither reflects aspirations of secession nor represents a challenge to state sovereignty; rather, the Miskito seek to legalize their de facto autonomy, a long-standing right that has only recently been eroded. Because they are rightful heirs to ancestral territories, the Miskito's autonomy to land and self-governance, particularly over natural resources, is intrinsic. Collective autonomy is critical to the Miskito's struggle to achieve human integrity, full equality as citizens, and a life unencumbered by racism and racial discrimination.

Miskito Customary Property Rights

Belen (pop. 859) is a small Miskito village located on the north coast of the reserve's cultural zone and nestled between the Caribbean Sea and Ibans Lagoon. As Miskito customs dictate, property rights are loosely arranged through familial social units. In Belen, Miskito family lands correspond to kin groups that share the same residential land unit. Most often, families are matrilocal; female children, once married, live in houses near their mother and father. When a couple unites, either through marriage or by shared residence, access to agricultural land and a house plot is provided by the family matriarch.[6] A system of *pana pana* (one another) also shapes access to both economic and natural resources. This local, cooperative work arrangement is based on reciprocity and involves family members assisting one another in livelihood activities such as clearing, planting, harvesting, and gathering (author's field notes, 2003).

The Miskito practice a variety of livelihood activities. Many villagers manage house or kitchen gardens on family land inside coastal villages. The majority of cultivation occurs on larger parcels situated across the lagoon in *kiamps,* secondary settlements upriver from the village. In Belen, most of the agricultural surplus is consumed by the household or shared and exchanged with other kin. Belen farmers also sell small surpluses to wealthier villagers. In addition, agriculture is supplemented by fishing, game hunting, gathering, and spiritual activities. Although most families typically plant from year to year (author's fieldnotes, 2003), purchasing power is achieved through a variety of wage labour: lobster diving, teaching, motorboat operating, and domestic service.

Free movement in the *monte* (forest) is inherent in Miskito land use practices. As swidden agriculturalists (Dodds 1994, 1998), farmers may have up to six *insla* (cultivated parcels of land) in production at one time (author interviews, Belen, April 2003). Swidden agriculture relies on unrestricted access to ancestral forest, for each insla is used for one to two years and then left fallow. Insla and fallow lands *(insla prata)* are typically not fenced but are delineated by the presence of fruit trees.[7] Since a farmer may have as many as six insla and insla prata in various stages and locations (author's field notes, 2003), customary property rights are sustained by a history of cohabitation and mutual knowledge of one another's field boundaries (Miskito farmer, personal communication, 2003).[8]

Customarily, land is not owned; rather, it is something to be held. The maintenance of standing forests around small agricultural plots reflects the Miskito's belief that trees are as important as land. Most Miskito publicly express the idea that forest products are free and belong to God. In the Mosquitia, the idea of possession is shaped by a labour theory of value. A Miskito who clears the land of primary forest has permanent usufruct rights to that land. Although many areas of the Mosquitia have been farmed for multiple generations and the original clearer has passed on, the notion that the first person to clear the forest (or his or her heirs) is the legitimate claimant remains rooted in local Belen discourse (author's field notes, 2003).

In contrast to land in Honduras' rural interior, land in the Mosquitia has traditionally held little money value (Helms 1971; Avila, personal communication with author, 2003). Similar to customary ownership, the value in land is derived from the work that is required to make a plot productive. For instance, elderly farmers question whether their children will tend to their work after their deaths (author's field notes, 2003). With an emphasis on work rather than ownership, Miskito notions of land possession allow villagers to loan land to fellow community members, often for a portion of the harvest. In areas of overlap between two different indigenous groups, farmers may knowingly plant in another's insla. But only certain crops — for example, annuals — may be planted on borrowed land. Perennial crops, such as coconut trees or plantain plants, suggest possession and are collectively understood as a direct claim to property (ibid., 2003).

Since the mid-1980s, Miskito leaders have sought to formalize their cosmologies into a system of land tenure that reflects the less visible aspects of Miskito customary property rights. Under the leadership of MASTA (Moskitia Asla Takanka/Unity of Mosquitia Peoples) and MOPAWI (Moskitia Pawisa Desarrollo de La Moskitia/Development of the Mosquitia), two Miskito-led grassroots and non-governmental organizations, the Miskito seek to formalize the Mosquitia region as a group of territorial blocs. These blocs would encompass open spaces that include not only agricultural parcels but also forests, water access, hunting lands, foraging lands, and sacred places commonly used by the Miskito, Pech, Tawakha, Garifuna, and native ladino residents (CACRC 2002).[9] Territorial blocs would also reflect intra-group cooperation in overlapping areas shared by indigenous populations in the cultural zone.

Miskito customary property claims have gained support in both national and global arenas. First, the International Labour Organization's (ILO) Convention 169, ratified by the Honduran Congress in 1994 (World Bank 2007), supports the legal recognition of customary property rights. The convention recognizes "the right of the [indigenous] peoples to use lands not exclusively occupied by them, but to which they have traditionally had access for their subsistence and traditional activities" (article 14.2; see also Cutler, this volume). Second, under the Rio Declaration on Environment and Development, indigenous people have "the right to a healthy and productive life in harmony with nature" (UN General Assembly

1992). In a similar vein, the United Nations Declaration on the Rights of Indigenous Peoples asserts that "indigenous peoples have the right to own, use, develop and control the lands, territories and resources that they possess by reason of traditional ownership or other traditional occupation or use, as well as those which they have otherwise acquired" (article 26, p. 2). States are also obliged to legally recognize and protect these "lands, territories and resources" (article 26.3). At the national level, the Honduran Constitution calls for the protection of the rights and interests of indigenous communities, "especially in the lands and forests where they are settled" (Honduras 1982, article 346, p. 131).

Most recently, international support for indigenous claims for autonomy and state recognition of customary property rights has gained legal precedent. In 2001, the Inter-American Commission on Human Rights ruled in support of the Mayangna (Sumo) community of Awas Tingni in a case concerning their ancestral lands located in the Nicaraguan Mosquitia. The community of Awas Tingni claimed that the Nicaraguan state had violated their customary rights to ancestral lands when the government granted concessions on Mayangna lands to Sol De Caribe, a Korean logging company. Although the state argued that Mosquitia lands were state property, the court ruled that maps, ethnographic studies, and community members' testimony served as evidence of indigenous customary territorial rights, despite the absence of land titles (Bryan 2007; Mylavarapu and Macdonald 2005). The Inter-American Commission for Human Rights in fact requires states to acknowledge and foster specific measures to protect indigenous rights to land and natural resources in line with their own customary use and tenure patterns (Anaya and Grossman 2002).

Globalizations: Conservation and Protected Area Management

This global movement of international and national legal instruments and norms governing indigenous people's rights to natural resources, however hopeful, has commonly been overlooked by nation-states in favour of two other intertwined globalized processes: the globalization of environmental norms and discourses (the globalization of the environment) and the global diffusion of neoliberal paradigms (see Coleman and Reed, this volume). First World architects, consisting of northern governments and their concomitant bilateral and multilateral institutions, circulate environmental norms through environmental discursive formations (O'Tuathail 1998; Sletto 2002). These so-called danger and crisis discourses, which predict widespread environmental decay, justify the creation of a global commons (Colchester 2003; Dalby 1998; Shiva 1998). Such rhetoric informs the transformation of Third World environments, such as tropical forests, into objects of natural resource management and control (Singh and Van Houtum 2002; Sletto 2002; Shiva 1998). This transnational network of epistemic communities (Brysk 2000) working against such global ailments as forest degradation and water contamination is embodied in institutions such as the World Conservation Union, the World Wildlife Fund, the Global Environmental Facility, the World Bank, and UNESCO's Man and the Biosphere Program. It is also represented at various conferences and in the creation of policy statements such as the Rio Declaration, Agenda 21, and the Convention on Biodiversity.

The ubiquity of these norms and discourses is evident in the preponderance of over 103,000 protected areas worldwide (Stevens 2005). Moreover, indigenous lands have overwhelmingly become enclosed through the conservation of protected areas. Indeed, in Latin America, almost 90 percent of protected areas overlap with indigenous territories (Colchester 2004; Negi and Nautiyal 2003). Although the number of inhabited protected areas in Asia and Africa is unknown (Colchester 2003; Oilwatch and World Rainforest Movement 2004), it is estimated that as many as six hundred thousand tribal people have been displaced by protected areas in India alone (Colchester 2004, 146). This expansion of environmental protection is supported by an ethic that encourages biodiversity protection as a global good, and the Brundtland Commission's *Our Common Future* (1987) has introduced sustainable development as part of the globalized ideal to "meet the needs and aspirations of the present without compromising the ability to meet those of the future" (Saha 2002, 21).

The globalization of the environment has also included the design of protected areas. Indeed, the move away from fortress conservation to community-based conservation (with similar labels) is well established. In this vein, long-standing "fences and fines" approaches, which keep people out of protected areas, and more coercive forms, often demonstrated by the use of state violence against local inhabitants of a particular area, have been well critiqued. Instead, community-based conservation, often undertaken through integrated conservation and development projects (ICDPs), is widely supported by global environmental organizations such as the International Union for Conservation, the World Wildlife Fund, and the United Nations Environmental Program. Integrated conservation and development projects were designed to permit human settlements inside parks, to raise the standard of living of communities residing inside or in close proximity to protected areas, and to include local communities (along with national park managers and NGO and government agents) as participants in protected area management (Wells, Brandon, and Hannah 1992). Although ICDPs are seen as a drastic improvement over coercive conservation (Peluso 1992) and fortress conservation models (Colchester 2003; Stevens 2005), they have not escaped critique. Despite praise, the notion that local participation will erase previous cleavages among the state and local communities over protected area policies and design has not been proven (Brockington, Duffy, and Igoe 2008; Chapin 2004; Sundberg 2006).

In particular, despite labels such as "community-based" and "participatory," state conservation practices have provoked specific conflicts for indigenous peoples inside protected areas. One such conflict has emerged from the continuing enclosure of indigenous territories inside protected area space. Brockington, Duffy, and Igoe (2008, 114) refer to this process as the "convergence of global indigenism and global environmentalism." Indeed, since the 1980s, indigenous movements and environmental movements have come together to challenge the state and multilateral interests inside forest regions populated by indigenous groups. According to Agrawal (2005), conservation discourses bolster notions of privation and recuperation, dispossession and struggle, all concepts that provoke the motivations that underpin indigenous territorial movements. But these alliances have frayed as NGO and state conservation agencies alike have moved towards market environmentalism, whereby private property rights determine the rights to use resources communally held and accessed (Liverman and Vilas 2006; Zimmerer 2006). Increasingly, protected areas serve as sites for the practice of biodiversity conservation *and* neoliberal market expansion. This unlikely alliance reveals a link between conservationist and capitalist agendas that is incongruent with how biodiversity conservation is understood and practised. The so-called alliance is based on powerful discursive claims that reflect how market expansion and economic growth are vital to biodiversity conservation (Igoe, Neves, and Brockington 2010). Thus, a heterogeneous movement that is "seemingly governed by a thin array of values, ideals and institutional goals" comes into play (ibid.). Brockington, Duffy, and Igoe (2008) describe this situation as mainstream conservation, by which dominant and elite ideas and values of nature and biodiversity are posited as widespread and global and operationalized in conservation NGOs and their practices.

Neoliberal policies that promote the privatization of natural resources are legitimated by the notion that the environment is best managed when natural resource rights are clear and defendable (Scott 1998; Liverman and Vilas 2006). Admittedly, in some cases, protected areas have been the means by which indigenous groups have been able to secure customary rights to lands and cultural resources, particularly when indigenous peoples perform identities and mobilize narratives that continue to preserve the conservationist ideal of pristine nature or where land use is limited to subsistence practices (Chapin 2004; Herlihy 1993). At the same time, there is overwhelming evidence that protected areas threaten to change or erase current customary tenure systems (Mollett 2010; Sundberg 2006; Vandergeest 2003; West, Igoe, and Brockington 2006). This situation occurs when indigenous groups are only casually involved and invited only after participatory and community-based conservation designs have been solidified (Lynch 2005; Tsing 2005). In such cases, the goals of sustainable development and biodiversity protection may threaten indigenous peoples' customary tenure arrangements. For indigenous groups who are commonly classified as "traditional" and "backward" and presumably operate outside the market, new regulations for protected area management tend to fix these identities in place. This fixing occurs in terms of their presence inside protected areas, to limit forest disturbance, and in terms of their imagined capabilities as productive citizens and contributors to national development. Protected areas serve as a means to acknowledge indigenous peoples' presence in forested areas, thereby territorializing their space through state regulatory control without recognizing indigenous people's rights to these same areas (Dove 2006; Li 2005). The interconnectedness of the globalization of the environment and the logic of neoliberalism empowers the territorial authority of the state to shape subject populations and Third World landscapes (Singh and van Houtum 2002; Ghate 2003).

Indigenous peoples and their customary territories are squarely implicated in this process. Embedded in the natural resource policies of the state, neoliberal rhetoric promises to erase and reduce inequities produced through former top-down protected area initiatives that silenced indigenous contributions in protected area design and management. In fact, proponents of this new common-sense conservation argue that "unfettered markets in choosing what to produce and consume, and patterns of natural resource use are best determined by market processes" (Hulme and Murphee 1999, 280). At the heart of conservation discourse and practice, neoliberal capitalism seeks to tie indigenous domains to global markets: "nature has become an emporium, a commercial warehouse awaiting its brokers" (Zerner 2000, 4). The exclusionary nature of conservation is condoned as an acceptable trade-off between national interest and indigenous claims. In Honduras, such interests have little to do with conservation and, as I argue in this chapter, warrant a postcolonial look at state imperialism (Stevens 2005) and state territorialization (Vandergeest 1996) in contemporary analyses of conservation. Because states frequently deny formal recognition of indigenous customary property rights and restrict access to natural resources under the auspices of conservation, protected areas have become a pronounced and geographically authoritative aspect of globalization (Stevens 2005). Since protected areas involve the enclosure of indigenous territories, boundary formation in the name of sustainable development, biological diversity, and the global commons (Dalby 1998) is imbued with strategic territorial meanings (Singh and van Houtum 2002). A number of recent studies seek to trace how protected areas are the sites of wealth accumulation for resource-poor nation-states (Goldman 2005; Brockington, Duffy, and Igoe 2008). Complementing these studies, this chapter demonstrates how, in Honduras, protected area boundary constructions, whether real or imagined, are buttressed by specific regional racial ideologies.

To illustrate this point, I examine Miskito colono land tensions in the Río Plátano Biosphere Reserve. In the Preamble of the reserve's management plan, *Plan de manejo* (2000), state objectives for the reserve include biodiversity protection and the economic promise of sustainable development as "enthusiastic injections" in conservation initiatives (AFE-COHDEFOR 2000, 11). Missing from the Preamble, however, is the recognition that contemporary state control over natural resource use falls in line with the state's long-standing preoccupation with the Mosquitia. In the past, the state was unable to incorporate the region's natural resources into the nation and, in part, blamed Miskito backwardness for failed attempts to nationalize the region (Barahona 1998; Thompson 2004). Today, however, state management of the reserve resembles previous attempts to integrate the Mosquitia's natural resources into the national economy, now legitimated in the name of conservation and neoliberal common sense.

The Miskito and Early State Representations

Contemporary interest in the Mosquitia's natural resources is rooted in a racialized past. Because "racial thinking was an organizing principle and a powerful rhetorical theme among colonial regimes" (Stoler and Cooper 1997, 10), state trials to incorporate the Mosquitia into national space reveal the persistent entanglement of racialization and natural resource control.[10] Like elsewhere in Latin America, nation-building projects have historically relied on the construction of the racialized Other to advance an image of racial and ethnic homogeneity within the nation (Medina 1997; Wade 2001). In Honduras, a nationalist ideology of *mestizaje* encouraged racial mixing between Europeans and Amerindians and the relinquishing of aspects of Indian cultural forms. Invoking this ideology, the state and ladino elite historically placed pressure on the Miskito to give up aspects of Miskito culture and assimilate to the ladino way of life (Alvarado Garcia 1958).

Notwithstanding Honduran independence in 1821, state control of the Mosquitia coast was not viable until the withdrawal of the British. In contrast to Nicaragua, where the Treaty of Managua (1860) compelled the state to recognize a self-governing Miskito district (Thompson 2004), in Honduras, the Wyke-Cruz Treaty of 1859 recognized juridical recognition of state claims to Mosquitia lands. In exchange, the postcolonial state was obliged to invest in "educating the Mosquito Indians to improve their social condition" (Honduras 1957, 2).

In 1868, the Mosquitia was incorporated administratively into the Honduran nation as the Department of the Mosquitia. As the state's attention to this new department increased, the Miskito became increasingly defined by the words and images of government officials and elite agents who, through the production of texts, endeavoured to incorporate an indigenous and black Mosquitia region into the newly formed ladino nation-state (Barahona 1998; Thompson 2004). In a collection of reports written in the late nineteenth century by departmental and central authorities, the inhabitants of the Mosquitia became known as *los indios selvaticos* (forest Indians) and *hordas* (nomads) and were assigned racialized labels such as *zambos, negros* (blacks), and *morenos* (brown-skinned).[11] Both race and custom came to define differences between the Miskito and the ladino majority of the interior (Alvarado García 1958). (Racialization is examined in a North American context in Mackey, this volume).

To explain such differences, Loreto Mazier, the Mosquitia's first governor, reasoned that the separation of the Miskito from the rest of the nation "deprived [the Miskito] of the great benefits of civilization, which the inhabitants of the rest of the *departamentos* are enjoying" (see also Thompson 2004, 25). State and elite representations of the Miskito assumed an innate primitiveness that compelled erasure and elevation through activities designed to "inspire in the savage Indians the pleasure for work" (Alvarado García 1958, 19-20). Implicit in Honduran postcolonial discourse was the notion that "natives" were amenable to being elevated to the likes of "civilized" humans, such as Europeans (McClintock 1995). This temporal narrative shaped state representation of the Mosquitia and its inhabitants (Barahona 2002; Barahona and Rivas 1998) and served as a means to determine the value of Miskito land use in the context of national development.

Civilizing the so-called savages of the Mosquitia was fundamental to the progress of the new nation-state. In 1882, Mosquitia integration was led by Governor Francisco Caceres, who led a special commission of men to conduct a so-called scientific study of the land and inhabitants of the Mosquitia (Barahona 1998; Thompson 2004). The commission produced a plethora of reports and articles loosely referred to as the Civilization Program (Barahona 1998; El Cronista 1930). Echoing an earlier reformist movement, the commission stated that commercial agriculture, industry, and exports, facilitated by foreign immigration, would come to represent "grand traits that will distinguish Honduras from other states. Nature appears destined to place Honduras among the richest and most powerful countries in all of the New World" (Barahona 2002, 253, translated by author). In the report and in reference to the Mosquitia, the commission noted that "it seems incredible that in a land where nature has concentrated so much mineral wealth, plants and animals have been left unattended for centuries without mankind offering to help; instead, this wealth of resources has been in the hands of wild people that seem to allow them to perish with calm and cold blood" (El Cronista 1930, 7, translation by author). This "finding" suggests that Native inhabitants lack the innate ingenuity required to use the region's natural resources adequately. Such findings justified non-Native or elite appropriation of indigenous resources. Arguments similar to these were made with reference to the Cayuga and Caldwell First Nations in the United States and Canada and in the forests of British Columbia (see chapters by Mackey and Prudham, this volume).

Unlike its inhabitants, however, the Mosquitia's natural resources represented potential wealth to the newly formed nation-state. Officials were amazed by the abundance of wild cattle, inexhaustible fish stocks, and miles of precious woods in which medicinal plants, "plantains and bananas grow spontaneously" (Thompson 2004, 26). State opposition to entrusting natural resources to the Miskito was underpinned by notions of *terra nullius,* a doctrine, as both Cutler and Mackey (this volume) argue, that justified the appropriation of indigenous lands through fictitious representations of their vacancy. Instead, the state offered foreign and national elites generous concessions to Mosquitia forest for timber (mahogany and pine) extraction and agricultural production (Rivas 1938; Revels 2003).

These favourable arrangements were not simply temporary installments of foreign enterprise, they also represented an ongoing initiative to civilize the region (Cruz 1926, 700). Concessionaries were permitted to import up to ten thousand colonists each to assist with extraction and agricultural production. Because concessionaries were from the so-called white nations of Europe and North America, colonists were also required to be of the white race. For their work, foreign concessionaries and their children were granted citizenship and property rights in *dominio pleno* (full ownership/fee simple ownership) (Rivas 1938).

After 1930, the state's presence in the region was intermittent as domestic and international issues diverted it away from its preoccupation with civilizing the Mosquitia (Barahona 1998). However, over the next seventy years, national representations of the Mosquitia and the Miskito peoples continued to problematize Miskito cultural landscapes, now classified as mysterious and impoverished (Frascara 1969; El Tiempo 1978). Following more than a century of postcolonial racial discourse, the state, through its goals for sustainable development and biodiversity conservation, renewed Miskito racial representations to justify contemporary interventions in indigenous space. Claire Cutler's chapter in this volume offers a general argument about racialization and international law.

Strategic Boundaries in the Mosquitia

In Honduras, neoliberal structural adjustment programs have linked agrarian reform to the market and pushed the state to move away from leading redistribution efforts. Neoliberal thinking in agrarian policy prescriptions has rendered the use of small parcels *(minifundios)* as inefficient land use. Under the law of modernization, small parcels are at risk of being redistributed to seemingly more productive farmers, namely, commercial producers. At the same time, the law of modernization legally sanctions farmer invasions of national lands as a method of making property claims (Honduras 1992). As a consequence, land displacement and growing landlessness among small-scale producers often occur in the settled agricultural regions of the southern and western departments and contribute to the increased migration of thousands of ladino colonos to the sparsely populated forests of the Mosquitia and to the Río Plátano Biosphere Reserve (AFE-COHDEFOR 2000; Herlihy 1997; Stonich 1993; Mollett 2006a).

Although it draws from international policies on protected area design, the practice of biodiversity conservation in Honduras is contingent on state practices and ideologies. For the Río Plátano Biosphere Reserve, state policy narratives explicitly recognize traditional societies and the need to protect indigenous peoples' "way of life, customs and traditions" (AFE-COHDEFOR, 2000, 78). This narrative, which is partial to the protection of indigenous peoples' traditional livelihoods, also problematizes ladino colono "migratory agriculture" and clear cutting (author's field notes, 2003). In this vein, the Río Plátano Biosphere was rezoned in 1997 as part of the Subzoning Project *(Proyecto de Subzonificacion)*. Although human activity in the nucleus zone is strictly prohibited, the project created two distinct areas on each side of the reserve's nucleus (AFE-COHDEFOR 2000).

The reserve's cultural zone (pop. 21,320) is inhabited primarily by indigenous peoples (Miskito, Pech, Tawahka, and Garifuna) and a small native ladino population. The Miskito were acknowledged officially for their historical stewardship of Mosquitia forests, which was made possible because of subsistence practices that maintained natural resource equilibrium and limited deforestation (AFE-COHDEFOR 2000). Unofficially, subsistence land use justified restrictions to commercialization because, it was presumed, indigenous people were situated outside the market (AFE-COHEDEFOR 2000; Mollett 2006b). Under the Plan de manejo, indigenous land was restricted to subsistence agriculture and only occasional and small-scale commercial production, woodcutting, gold panning, hunting, and fishing in certain areas. Despite these restrictions, livestock production is becoming increasingly important among the Belen Miskito.

In contrast, the buffer zone (pop. 19,111), located in the western and southwestern parts of the reserve, is overwhelmingly ladino. Ladino families, which have a myriad of tenure histories, hold de facto property rights to individualized farming parcels. As I argue elsewhere, reserve officials, most of whom are ladino or German, insist that "*ladinos* are more interested in producing for the market [than are indigenous people]" (Mollett 2006b, 7). Their market production is supported through the reserve's normative and legal framework outlined in the Plan de manejo. In addition to basic productive systems, the plan facilitates commercial activities in coffee production, timber exploitation, and cattle raising and beef production

(Vallejo Larios 1997; AFE-COHDEFOR 2000), three of the six most valued agricultural exports in Honduras.

These narratives and conservation designs, seemingly benign, highlight prevailing ideas among policy makers about the role of indigenous peoples, as subsistence producers, in protected area management. In practice, however, the state has actively renewed an earlier nationalist project to integrate the Mosquitia's natural resources into its national development agenda, condoning practices and ideologies that justify the dispossession of indigenous peoples. Indeed, in 1997, the National Agrarian Institute awarded AFE-COHDEFOR a land title of dominio pleno to reserve lands (Hablemos Claro 1997, 64; INA 1997). State officials maintained that the legal granting of land to AFE-COHDEFOR was necessary to protect biodiversity (AFE-COHDEFOR 2000). Yet, despite regional state reforms that have made multicultural citizenship possible and often marked with the legal recognition of indigenous lands and territories (Hale 2002; Hooker 2005), state ownership of reserve lands is a rejection of Miskito territorial claims. Honduran law prohibits more than one title of dominio pleno per parcel of land (Honduras 1992). Making matters worse, ladino migration inside indigenous territories enclosed within the cultural zone has legal support (AFE-COHDEFOR 2000). In 2000, the state declared that colonos who had settled inside the cultural zone by 1997 were legal residents (ibid.). Similar to the Civilization Program, state management of the reserve, conducted as a means for sustainable development and biodiversity protection, echoed early postcolonial narratives and manoeuvres. Today, however, the Mosquitia's integration and the transformation of the cultural landscape has been rendered less explicit by the seemingly unorganized ladino colonization of Miskito space.

In 2004, further heightening Miskito anxieties about land tenure, the state announced Catastro y Regularización, the Cadastral and Regularization Project. State rhetoric embodied in the framework of Catastro y Regularización mirrored mainstream property rights discourse and defined and institutionalized property rights as a critical criterion for social and economic development (Ferranti et al. 2004). According to the state, property rights were also needed to ensure conservation goals and sustainable natural resource use in the buffer and cultural zones (AFE-COHEDEFOR 2002). Indeed, "free markets ... cannot be expected to produce efficient and sustainable results when property rights are not clearly defined, complete, enforced and transferable" (Berry 2001, xxi). Thus, the state would award *contractos de usufructo* (usufruct contracts) to "augment the security of land tenure" in the reserve (AFE-COHDEFOR 2002, 3) and thereby "change the systems of production towards sustainable systems, the development of consumption markets, and to provide a base for an efficient and transparent taxation and territorial legislation" (ibid., 8).[12]

Since the state would own reserve lands, contractos would only recognize use rights *(dominio útil)* (Secretaría de Gobernación y Justicia and AFE-COHDEFOR n.d.). The project boasted a long list of assurances, including legal tenure security (individual or collective), an abatement of land conflicts, better access to credit, and incentives to invest. Additionally, reserve residents would have the right to bequeath contractos (and thus land) to their heirs. Although land would remain inalienable, in exceptional cases villagers would have the option to sell *mejoras* (improvements) either to other community members or to the *patronato* (village council). The project favoured a system of improvements congruent with ladino agrarian traditions.[13]

State plans to legalize Miskito territories have, however, left Miskito peoples skeptical of the project's design. Tasba and Rayaka (meaning "land" and "life," respectively), two local Miskito land organizations, have engaged in heated debate with the state and the municipality over the lack of consultation with Miskito communities and the overall conditions of the project that threaten to disrupt customary access to the forests (author's field notes, 2003). Although Catastro y Regularización promises collective arrangements, Miskito municipal officials, enticed by promises of additional economic resources from the state (ibid.), have been instructed by the state to encourage villagers to register their lands individually in preparation for cadastral surveying. These officials insist that land registration is crucial preparation "to protect the Miskito way of life against the *colono* invasion" (Belen village meeting, 13 August 2003).

Although the project allows villagers three years to register lands with the municipality, those villagers who fail to register lands as individual holdings may find their lands expropriated and declared state property. Subsequent clearing in these forests will be considered trespassing (Belen village meeting, 13 August 2003). In Belen, these measures are cast as foreign impositions. Prior to the mid-1980s, most villagers "didn't think about land titles [because] it is not in [Miskito] culture" (Rayaka, personal communication with author, 2003). Although a municipal land registry has existed since 1958, only a fraction of households have registered residential properties with the local municipality (author's field notes, 2003). Even fewer Miskito have registered agricultural lands.[14] Miskito leaders do not understand the need for individual registration as a prerequisite for contractos de usufructo to collective property (Ban, personal communication with author, 2003). They insist that "the existence of collective properties of land is threatened every day by the state and its hegemonic imposition towards an individualized property [system]" (TASBA 2003). So material is the imagined threat of individuation that official plans to individuate Miskito family lands quickly led to intra-Miskito struggles along gender and class lines (Mollett 2010).

A key source of Miskito land tenure insecurities concerns the distinction between dominio pleno and dominio útil (contractos de usufructo). Dominio pleno ensures that the state is legally bound to recognize the Miskito as owners and not just as users of their lands. This distinction is also conceptual. By definition, dominio pleno adds force to Miskito customary rights. Property rights in dominio útil, although they bear a close resemblance to current arrangements whereby indigenous peoples "hold" territories, demonstrate how the state imagines indigenous customary rights should be represented in national law. Yet this legal form leaves Miskito lands with little legal protection in a region envisaged by colonos as a "frontier."

In defence of their demands for legalization in dominio pleno, Miskito bolster their claims to ancestral lands with collective memories of "belonging" to the Mosquitia (Gordon, Guardian, and Hale 2003); for example, they assert, "We were here in 1502" (Avila, personal communication with author, 2003). The Miskito affirm that they deserve dominio pleno in Mosquitia territory by virtue of their rights as indigenous people, as *originarios* not "noble savages." Territorial rights are key to Miskito autonomy because, at present, Honduran law only offers communal titles to village boundaries, not territories (Honduras 1992). As originarios, the Miskito seek to exercise collective autonomy over ancestral territories, within which the forms of economic, social, and political norms can be arranged and advanced (Assies, van der Haar, and Hoekma 1998).

Colono Invasions in Miskito Space

The conflation of neoliberal paradigms and protected area conservation policy has undermined Miskito claims to customary property rights and autonomy. Officially, Miskito leaders blame the state for a lack of legal protection. Unofficially, colonos represent the greatest erosion to Miskito customary property rights and lack of autonomy over ancestral domains. In Belen, the arrival and subsequent land rights of colonos has penetrated the Miskito's everyday conversations (author's field notes, 2003). Villagers no longer accept colono claims of landlessness and need and instead insist that colonos are destroyers of the forest, speculators, and escaped convicts (Belen, author's interviews, 2003). As is revealed in the following excerpt from field notes, keeping colonos out of the cultural zone is as much about securing land rights as it is about protecting Miskito culture from foreign traditions.

> Nathanial Wilson, a highly respected Miskito farmer, was approached by a colono named Jesus Vargas from the Department of Olancho, located southwest of the Mosquitia. Jesus, a farmer, told Nathanial that he was poor and landless and asked if he could work for him on his chicken and cattle farm in Wawabila, south of Belen. Nathanial needed a *mozo* (labourer) and hired Jesus. In addition to a small monthly salary, Nathanial allowed Jesus to borrow a fallow parcel measuring about half a manzana to plant his own milpa.[15] In the first year, Jesus cleared the land and planted rice and corn, as per their agreement. But in the second year, in addition to replanting milpa, Jesus cleared an additional parcel of forest and planted grass. After a short time away in the "interior," Jesus returned with a young bull.[16] Suspicious of this "needy" hired hand, Nathanial fired him for violating their agreement and told Jesus to leave the land. However, Jesus refused to relinquish his parcel unless Nathanial compensated him for his house and the conversion of forest to pasture. Looking for a "just" price for his mejoras, Jesus threatened to kill Nathanial if he withheld payment. Disguising [his journey] as a trip to obtain money, Nathanial travelled to the department capital to seek legal support to evict Jesus. Back on the coast, however, Jesus found a buyer, a young Miskito. When Nathanial returned with an order of eviction, Jesus had already fled (see also Mollett 2011).

The Nathanial-Jesus story reveals how Jesus, through threats of violence, attempted to impose dominant ladino agrarian traditions in Miskito space. In Miskito culture, borrowed land is always returned, regardless of who ends the contract. But Jesus tried to force Nathanial to pay the mejoras he made to the land. This is a common form of exchange in settled ladino agricultural areas, where most small farmers are de facto property holders on national lands; thus, upon migration, they seek compensation for the improvements made on the land. A system of mejoras that benefits colonos makes capital mobile. But for the Miskito, the colonos' actions are disrupting indigenous customary rights to the *monte* (forest).

Colonos, nonetheless, have provided multiple justifications for their presence in the cultural zone. Just south of Belen, the colono village of San Arturo (pop. 60) emerged in the late 1990s. The hamlet's founders, Arturo and Duarte, defended their presence in the cultural zone as "an act of desperation" (San Arturo, author interviews, 6 November 2003), and women in San Arturo argued that they had "rights here because of [their] need" (ibid.). Furthermore, the founders insisted that they rightfully owned the land because they had purchased the mejoras for fifty manzanas from a ladino farmer in 1994 and worked part of the land for two years before moving their families from the neighbouring department of Colon.[17] In 2003, despite their need-based justifications, founders claimed at least five times the area: 250 manzanas and cleared forest.[18]

Colonos are very conscious of their so-called rights in the reserve. San Arturo farmers traded working on mountain sides with arid soil conditions and low yields in their areas of origin for de facto property rights and tenure uncertainties in the fertile lands of Mosquitia forests. When questioned about the possibility of having to relinquish lands in the reserve, all farmers in San Arturo stated that the opportunity to posses their own lands was worth the risk. If not, they claimed that the state "will have to pay us to leave" (San Arturo, author interviews, 6 November 2003), a reference to the widely advertised compensation made to ladino families displaced from the reserve's core. For Arturo, colono rights are supported by the Honduran Constitution, which allows Hondurans the right to live anywhere in the country (Honduras, 1982, c. 2., art. 81). Although he knows that his lands fall within the boundaries of a protected area, Arturo believes that efficient agricultural production, sanctioned by constitutional and agrarian legislation, supersedes conservation norms restricting forest clearance (San Arturo, author interviews, 6 November 2003).

Congruent with state conceptions, colonos envisage the Mosquitia as national lands (Duerte, personal communication with author, 2003), a notion reinforced by the transfer of reserve lands to the State Forestry Administration. Colonos reject the Miskito's claim as originarios and assert that "they do not have special rights to the land if they don't use it (San Arturo, author interviews, 6 November 2003). Considering themselves "far more dedicated to agriculture" (ibid., 17 August 2003), farmers in San

Arturo insist the Miskito "don't like to work" and barely farm enough for their families (ibid., 11 June 2003). Colonos are specifically critical of the small areas of cultivation typically found in Miskito subsistence-based agriculture. For instance, Miskito swidden plots range from less than one-quarter to six manzanas (Belen, author interviews, 2003). Echoing national agrarian legislation that supports the erosion of minifundios (Honduras 1992, 27, art. 34), colonos argue that "one *manzana* yields nothing" (personal communication with author, 2003). In contrast, colono cultivation in San Arturo ranges in area from two to fourteen manzanas (San Arturo, author interviews, 2003), bolstering colono assertions that they are real farmers.

Subsistence production, associated with Miskito agriculture, is represented as being synonymous with laziness because Miskito contributions to national development are considered insignificant and inferior to ladino production. Such representations reflect an "unequal quality of ethnically marked cultural elements and the presumed unequal innate intellectual and physical capabilities [plot size and subsistence production] of racially identified peoples" (Williams 1991, 171). This racialized form of land use — painted by colonos as an obstacle to national development and, more particularly, as an impediment to colono progress — symbolizes racial inferiority, despite Miskito narratives that they were here first.

Conclusion: Implications for Miskito Autonomy

The (re)fulfillment of Miskito autonomy depends on the legal recognition of Miskito customary property rights inside the Río Plátano Biosphere Reserve. Collective legal protections would allow the Miskito to "reconstitute themselves as closed societies" (Hiatt 1998, 209) in order to possess the means to control their lands and the degree of interaction with colonos in the Mosquitia (see Castree 2004). This aim, however, faces many obstacles, because the state remains a primary actor in shaping how policy making is conceptualized on the ground (Keeling 2004; Stevens 2005). Under the guise of biodiversity conservation, the Honduran government is quietly implementing a project of colonization, a twenty-first-century version of the failed Civilization Program. As before, narratives of race are being built upon a discursive history of representing Miskito as uncivilized, backward, and presumably incapable of development.

Although promises of collective property have been made, the history of state and Miskito relations offers no assurances that formalization will follow the registration process. Moreover, individualization in Miskito space is currently fragmenting Miskito territories (author's field notes, 2003), failing to acknowledge customary tenure arrangements, and disempowering customary structures of social organization, such as Miskito razas, through the drawing of boundaries (Sletto 2002). Furthermore, the stated goal of Catastro y Regularización — to improve tenure security — is unlikely. Individualization is disrupting Miskito collective arrangements, which are customarily amenable to a fluidity of needs and circumstances but neglected by neoliberal ideologies, and legitimated under the banner of sustainable development.

The mutual constitution of protected areas and racialized state development is contested by the Miskito. The Miskito challenge the proprietary claims of the state and colonos, and their collective territorial claims speak "a language that power understands" (Castree 2004, 160). Indeed, property rights are one of the most legally absolute and materially compelling rights that the Miskito can attain in their road to autonomous control over natural resources. Miskito claims as originarios threaten those with economic interests in the Mosquitia and compel justifications for intervention. Just as global, environmental policy makers argue that protected areas should be areas of public domain, the Honduran state's rejection of Miskito customary property rights in dominio pleno (a foundation for autonomy) is a historical reproduction of postcolonial state-centred efforts to subjugate the Miskito and appropriate control over their ancestral territories. In essence, Miskito territories exist as narrow spaces for autonomy (Assies, van der Haar, and Hoekema 1998) in the face of state ownership of reserve land and subsoil resources. Simultaneously, state ownership justifies a racialized preference for ladino market interests and system of *mejoras* over ascribed Miskito subsistence and customary property rights in the Mosquitia. Entwined in global processes with specific environmental perspectives and incentives that fix indigenous peoples and their identities in place, protected area policies and practices are buttressed by global conservation narratives that legitimate the rearrangement of indigenous customary systems in favour of state control of forests in the name of sustainable development. Whether intended, state actions deprive the Miskito of collective autonomy. In so doing, the state demonstrates its own continuing lack of autonomy in the global political system.

chapter 6

Globalization, Intellectual Property, and the Emergence of New Property Types

Daniel Gorman

A country without a patent office and good patent laws was just a crab and couldn't travel anyway but sideways or backways.
— Mark Twain, *A Connecticut Yankee at King Arthur's Court*

When the American scientist Ananda Chakrabarty applied to the United States Patent Office in 1972 for three separate patents, he was no doubt unaware that his application would touch off a global revolution in the regulation of intellectual property. Using new recombinant DNA techniques, Chakrabarty had invented a genetically engineered microorganism that could break down crude oil. This invention had many potential commercial applications, such as containing oil spills. He applied for a patent for the bacterium's production, another for the material carrying the bacterium and, finally, one for the bacterium itself. The patent officer granted patents for the first two applications but not the third. Chakrabarty appealed to the United States Court of Customs and Patent Appeals and won, thus achieving a patent for bacteria created through recombinant DNA technology, a global first. His patent was ultimately upheld by the US Supreme Court in *Diamond v. Chakrabarty* (1980).[1] The justices ruled in a five-to-four decision that non-naturally occurring genetic materials could be patented, but they stressed that naturally occurring organisms would not be patentable. This narrow interpretation of US patent law has subsequently led to a boom in patent applications for genetically produced material, including genetically engineered plants and animals, embryonic stem cells, and even human genes. As Karen Goodyear Krueger (1981, 165) observed in the *Columbia Law Review* shortly after the decision, "after *Chakrabarty* ... human-made microorganisms, by whatever technique they are made, should be considered 'manufactures' or 'compositions of matter.'"

Chakrabarty was thus a point of rupture in the history of intellectual property and genetic engineering because it established the world's first successful patent for an artificially created life form. The implications of this decision have been significant, propelling property debates into the realm of human autonomy. The significance of these debates was brought to the global public in late 2002, when Clonaid, the so-called scientific wing of the Raelians, a Quebec-based religious cult, announced that it had cloned a human being (*The Economist* 2003a). Although the claim was ultimately unsubstantiated, it highlighted profound questions regarding the status of the human body. Is it ethical to produce human beings in a laboratory? Who has jurisdiction over the human body? Are genetic substances property?

These fundamental questions of human autonomy have emerged as an unanticipated result of the global technological revolution that began in earnest in the 1970s and was itself a component of the integrative process of globalization outlined in this volume's Introduction. As *Chakrabarty* illustrates, however, we are still using pre-global concepts and institutions to meet this challenge. Although intellectual property has historically been the autonomous preserve of the nation-state, the growth of international bodies that seek to harmonize and thus globalize such regulations and concepts adds a key element to globalization's history. An examination of this system thus constitutes the first part of this chapter and is followed by an analysis of how the system has defined emerging genetic properties as a case study in the frictions created between competing ideas of globalization and autonomy.

Debates concerning property rights and globalization are not new. Negotiations over the relationship between individual ownership, the nation-state, and the broader world have been ongoing in the Western world since the Enlightenment. Two broadly construed positions have emerged. The first is that inventors have a natural property right in their invention or creation. This "proprietary rights" position took root especially in the English-speaking world, and its most important texts are John

Locke's *Second Treatise* (1690) and Edward Young's *Conjectures on Original Composition* (1759). Proponents of the theory see all creations of the mind as *sui generis* and conclude that the creator should therefore derive all subsequent benefits. In this respect, the position gives precedence to individual autonomy. The second position is that ideas, and thus the inventions or creations derived from them, are inherently social, the product of collective reasoning and endeavour (Hesse 2002, 33-37). Proprietary rights, the leading "collective rights" theorist the Marquis de Condorcet argued, hindered the process of enlightenment by impairing or enclosing the free exchange of ideas. This position stresses the importance of property rights for collective autonomy, the capacity of given communities to shape the conditions in which they live.

Property rights give their holder the exclusive right to determine how a particular resource is used; as a category, they encompass a bundle of use, usufruct, and transfer rights. Intellectual property rights are a specific subset of property rights that give people rights over the creations of their minds. Although property rights can be self-defined or derived from customary or traditional sources, they are usually licences of exclusive ownership granted by the state to an individual or group and thus require competent and stable central governments (Bently 2000, 1-10). The latter first emerged in western Europe and brought in their train the antecedents of modern property rights. In Britain, the Statute of Monopolies (1623) replaced exclusive royal monopolies with limited, fourteen-year letters patent (the first true patent in the modern sense). The ad hoc system, moulded over the next two centuries by case law, was well suited to the still limited pace of innovation. As the pace of industrialization increased, however, the statute grew to be obsolete. It was replaced in 1852 by the Patent Law Amendment Act, which created a Patent Office, licensed commissioners to regulate innovation, and reduced the cost of a patent from three hundred to twenty-five pounds. A subsequent Patents Act (1883) lowered the cost to four pounds. Applications increased twofold after the 1883 Act (MacLeod 1999, 18-21). Perhaps the most important historical shift in the nineteenth century, however, was the replacement of the amateur inventor by the specialized expert. Many of the modern era's most important discoveries — radio, the telephone, the airplane, assembly-line production, x-rays — were made or perfected early in the twentieth century. Western nations responded to this innovation revolution by developing intellectual property systems that, with minor amendments, are still used today.

The concept of intellectual property has been increasingly contested since the Second World War. Given the example of British patent law and the innovation revolution of the first age of globalization, however, it seems the apparent novelty of current debates about intellectual property may be a case of new wine for old bottles. The challenge of how to deal with new or emerging technologies and processes is being met in the global era in a manner remarkably similar to previous historical eras (see Feather 1994; Clark 1960). The manner in which global actors have administered intellectual property has remained largely consistent since the late nineteenth century. What is new, and thus part of the historical process of globalization, is a growing uncertainty as to what constitutes property. This uncertainly has created debates about how intellectual property should be used, and by whom.

Globalization has presented a challenge. Is an intellectual property system designed for the second Industrial Revolution, a revolution centred on industry and manufacturing and the nation-state system, suitable for a new, global economy built on information and design (see Drahos and Mayne 2003; Shiva 2002; Correa 2000)? Globalization "foster[s] a growing awareness of the deepening connections between the global and the local" (Steger 2003, 13) and has thus driven efforts to harmonize intellectual property systems at the regional and global level. This emerging world society is, however, in Ulrich Beck's terms, a "multiplicity without unity" (Beck 2000 [1997], 10-12) and, as yet, no truly global patent system has emerged. Such a system would entail either a world patent-granting body that would superseded or share the authority of national or regional bodies or a truly harmonized patent-granting system in which patents granted in one jurisdiction would be globally transferable. Neither yet exists. Instead, we have a highly internationalized patent system in which nation-states retain much autonomy. Globalization has created friction within this system, notably through the emergence of new property types such as those arising from genetic engineering, as addressed in *Diamond v. Chakrabarty*. A functionalist international property regime that has favoured wealthy nations' collective national autonomy and their citizens' individual creative rights has clashed with the desire for collective and individual self-determination in the rest of the world. At issue is whether the autonomy of individuals, usually employed by large corporations in the intellectual property areas, will be permitted to override the collective autonomy of societies and communities, which have fostered creativity over the centuries and made intellectual property part of a public commons.

The Global Regulation of Intellectual Property: A Historical Review

Overview of the System

The global intellectual property infrastructure has three public tiers of administrative bodies, as well as a growing number of private interests. The World Intellectual Property Organization (WIPO) is the only broad international institution. It does not grant patents per se, though it does administer the Patent Cooperation Treaty (PCT), an agreement that allows inventors to file simultaneous patent applications in multiple countries. The organization administers international treaties, encourages new developments in the field, and promotes the harmonization of intellectual property policy around the world (see WIPO website). Like many United Nations agencies, WIPO is slow moving, relies on consensus, and has limited jurisdictional authority. It is, however, an important public venue for debating intellectual property issues and is the body that has engaged most fully with the challenges of globalization.

Below WIPO there are several regional intellectual property agencies, including the European Patent Office (EPO), the African Intellectual Property Organization, and the Eurasian Patent Office. Finally, there are national offices, the most significant of which are the United States Patent and Trademark Office (USPTO), and the Japanese Patent Office (JPO) (see official websites). European Union nations also have separate patent offices, though the EPO has increasingly superseded their autonomy.[2] Intellectual property was first codified through national patent offices, and they remain the most important decision- and policy-making entities. Copyright and patent grants are sometimes handled by different national offices, sometimes together. National bodies are financed largely through renewal fees, money they use to stimulate activity in targeted industries. This power of the purse has historically preserved the national bodies' autonomy, for trans- and international patenting bodies rely on financial contributions from their member states (Doern 1999, 76-77). The large revenues generated by the PCT, however, have recently granted WIPO much autonomy of its own. Despite the growth of transnational patent-granting bodies and the PCT, there is as yet no global patent. Nonetheless, global, regional, and national intellectual property bodies share a belief that patents foster innovation and that the proprietary model of ownership is ideal.

Although the public players are most instrumental in dictating global intellectual property policy, private institutions and interests also have a role. These include corporations, international non-governmental organizations, and even individuals (such as powerful recording artists, film actors, or business leaders). Also important are private regulatory institutions such as the Internet Corporation for Assigned Names and Numbers.[3]

The continued importance of national patent bodies indicates that the developed nations, which dominate the policy-making field, have been best able to confront the challenges of globalization by retaining their regulatory autonomy. At century's end, the USPTO, the JPO, and the EPO accounted for an astounding 83 percent of all patents held worldwide.[4] This trend became particularly pronounced in the 1980s and 1990s, reflecting the interrelation between globality and patent protection. The number of patents granted in the United States between 1995 and 2000 jumped an astounding 64 percent, and the 56,076 new patents granted in this period were more than the USPTO had granted in its entire history to 1965. The increasingly global nature of patenting is evident in the fact that 29,542 of these new patents, or 53 percent, were granted to foreign residents.

The United States has the most comprehensive national intellectual property network. The USPTO, a branch of the Department of Commerce, administers the laws relating to patents and trademarks and advises the government on intellectual property and international trade. Closely related is the United States Copyright Office (USCO). Founded in 1790, the USCO upholds article 1, section 8 of the US Constitution: "The Congress shall have power ... to promote the Progress of Science and Useful Arts, by securing for limited Times to Authors and Inventors the exclusive Right to their respective Writings and Discoveries." The USCO also distributes licensing fees to copyright holders.[5] United States District Court clerks filed claims for copyright until 1870, when the USCO moved to the Library of Congress. In 1897, the Copyright Office became independent (United States Copyright Office website). In 1900, 95,573 copyright claims were filed. As with patents, the scale of copyright activity has increased substantially over the twentieth century; 601,659 patents were filed in 2001 (USCO annual report, 2000). There has been a decline in the 1990s, however, attesting to the more precarious nature of copyright protection in a global age. Unlike utility patents, copyrights are easily broken and difficult to monitor. Music file sharing, unlicensed photocopying, and unlawful digital reproduction challenge copyright. Although modern technology makes breaking copyright relatively simple, copyright piracy itself is not new. In the late nineteenth and early twentieth centuries, for instance, piracy of sheet music was curtailed by identifying the pirates as criminal conspirators and outlawing their network (Johns 2002, 75-77). Whether similar measures will work against global piracy rings remains to be seen.

The JPO, the world's second most important national patenting body, has also witnessed an increase in activity since 1980. According to its website, it plays a more firmly economic role than other national bodies: "The JPO contributes to Japan's industrial development through policy planning for the industrial property (IPR) system, which covers patents, utility models, designs, and trademarks." Like most national patent bodies, the JPO uses a first-to-file system. In contrast, the United States is one of the few countries to use a first-to-invent system, a main reason for the complexity and litigiousness of US commerce.

International Cooperation

The uneven distribution of the world's economy means that a truly global patenting system, such as that suggested earlier in this chapter, is unlikely. Fearing it would grant developing nations greater access to their markets, members of the Organisation for Economic Co-operation and Development (OECD) have opposed any truly global system. This opposition suggests that globalization is merely the naturalization of the West's interests (Steger 2003, 105-12), particularly the proprietary rights model dominant in the Anglo-American world. Some OECD nations, however, have supported greater harmonization in the form of regional bodies, following the pattern of the PCT. Regional patent bodies represent a halfway house between national interests and true globality. The largest such body, the EPO, is the European Union's centralized patent-granting system. Established in 1973 through the European Patent Convention, the EPO came into effect in 1977 and has headquarters in Munich. Applicants can secure a patent in all member states through a SINGLE grant (EPO annual report, 1996; European Patent Office 2001a). The EPO is self-financing through procedural and renewal fees. Its high costs, driven by translation requirements, and relative newness make its rise to prominence that much more impressive. Although such regional agreements may appear to be international rather than global (Scholte 2002, 8-10), this is a distinction without a difference, for such agreements have served to make the world both conceptually smaller and more closely integrated. This regionalization is consistent with the explosive growth of international agreements in the twentieth century, which Akira Iriye sees as a key formative element of globalization (Iriye 2004, 7-8).

Although nation-states have engaged with intellectual property rights since the early modern period, the concept of international intellectual property rights emerged only in the late nineteenth century, when industrial nations were keen to sell their wares beyond domestic borders. These entrepreneurial motives led to the first international agreements on intellectual property. When foreign exhibitors were leery of attending the International Exhibition of Inventions in Vienna in 1873 lest rivals steal their ideas, Europe's industrialized nations began negotiating what became, in 1883, the Paris Convention for the Protection of Industrial Property (Paris Union). Its key tenet is the national treatment provision — applicants from any contracting nation must be treated as nationals in any other contracting nation. The union also established the right-of-priority (the date of first filing applies to all contracting nations) and common-filing rules (Bodenhausen 1965, 5-15). These three principles still guide the global patent system, marking the Paris Union as a far-sighted document. It recognized the future importance of industrial property, and its modest legal skeleton — built on principles of right of priority and national treatment — has allowed it to adapt to future unanticipated challenges (Curchod 1999, 100).

A similar covenant for cultural products, the Berne Convention for the Protection of Literary and Artistic Works was reached in 1886. The Berne Convention protects copyrighted material, codifying the artist's right to her or his creation. These two conventions form the basis of the global intellectual property system, ensuring that signatory nations respect patents and copyrights filed in other signatory nations (Bogsch 1983, 133). The Paris and Berne unions are WIPO's core agreements and the source of all subsequent intellectual property agreements.

The two unions merged in 1893, forming the United International Bureaux for the Protection of Intellectual Property (known by its French acronym BIRPI). Working out of Berne, it coordinated the European cross-border trade in ideas well into the twentieth century. Beginning in 1960, BIRPI, under the guidance of its director G.G.C. Bodenhausen, collaborated with the United Nations and convened a conference in Stockholm in 1967 to create WIPO. Other figures instrumental in founding WIPO were the Swiss statesman, Jacques Secrétan, director of WIPO from 1953-63; the Hungarian-American delegate to BIRPI and later director of WIPO, Arpad Bogsch; and the French BIRPI chairman, Guillaume Finnis. The World

Intellectual Property Organization was inspired by the growing international interest in development in the 1960s, itself the product of increased decolonization. The UN General Assembly declared in 1961 "that it is in the interest of all countries that the international régime of patents should completely satisfy the special needs of the economic development of the less developed countries and also the legitimate claims of patentees" (Resolution 1713/XVI). Intellectual property officials were seen as "quasi-social technicians," and the United Nations Conference on Trade and Development declared in 1964 that "the developed countries should complete the efforts of the less developed countries by passing on to them modern methods of production and by giving them technical or other assistance" (Bystricky 1965, 91).

BIRPI/WIPO has therefore extended technical and administrative assistance to developing countries. Through the Libreville Agreement (1962), BIRPI negotiated a union of thirteen African states to standardize industrial property laws and establish a central patent office. The union became the African Intellectual Property Organization (OIPA) in the early 1970s, and it later expanded into copyright (WIPO 1976, 1-3). Since the early 1970s, WIPO has provided traineeships, run regional seminars, advised on new patent documentation centres, and drafted model laws and patent-licensing conventions for developing countries (WIPO 1972, 1-2; 1980; 1981, 4-10). Whether such aid reflects neo-imperialism or a growing sense of global interdependence remains open to debate.

Global cooperation and intellectual property as a tool of development constituted what the conference chair, Herman Kling of Sweden, called the Stockholm spirit (BIRPI 1967g, 798 50). The US delegate believed "the global character of the meeting clearly illustrated the importance most states attached to intellectual property"; the Soviet delegate praised "the prospect of worldwide cooperation" (BIRPI 1967h, 794 35.1; 1970a, 829 401). Key to the conference's success was its incorporation of both socialist countries, through the inclusion of inventors' certificates in the agreement, and the concerns of the developing world. Senegal's delegate represented a large African presence, while T.S. Krishnamurti, India's delegate, impressed upon the conference that "the developed countries ... had a responsibility to meet the demand for educational and scientific literature in the developing world. The world was shrinking so that it was no longer possible to have cases of prosperity in a desert of poverty, islands of knowledge in an ocean of ignorance" (BIRPI 1967f, 948 1993.12). This tension between trade and development was particularly apparent in discussions of the

Berne Convention. Mexico linked the extension of the Berne Convention to the extension of human rights (ibid., 949 1995.4; 1967a, 810 194.1), while Tunisia feared that colonial powers might withhold equal treatment for their remaining colonies. These concerns were addressed in the Protocol Regarding Developing Countries, which allowed for greater leeway in applying copyright. Most developed countries, believing the protocol was too permissive, refused to sign until it was scaled back in 1971.

The Berne Convention has historically been more contentious than the Paris Convention. The former was especially hindered by the absence of major content-creator nations such as the United States, the USSR, and China. In the interwar period, the United States pushed instead for a Universal Copyright Convention, with a shorter minimum duration of copyright protection and looser prohibitions on use (BIRPI 1929, 350, voeu 6). Article 6*bis* of the Berne Convention, the moral interests clause, has also been contentious: "For all its modest appearance, Article 6*bis* sets against the materialist currents which dominate present-day society that the right to respect for intellectual ideals in the name of which thousands of writers and artists, those artisans of civilization's real progress, work, suffer and struggle, indeed also fall, as men fall at their desks as well as on the battlefields, in the agonizing fatigue of the unattained ideal" (Caselli 1929, 292).

Revisions to Berne were not broached again until a 1963 BIRPI conference in Brazzaville, where developing countries sought to extend its terms to include folklore. India later put the issue clearly at Stockholm in 1967: folklore was one of the developing world's only unique resources, and it should be protected as a source of development income (BIRPI 1967b, 838 477.2). Cultural equity and recompense was a second motive — the Congolese delegate reminded the delegates "that African countries had been pillaged, that their treasures had been removed to foreign museums, and that people came to those countries to make recordings for which they subsequently reserved the exclusive rights of exploitation." Niger's delegate stated that, while in the developed world folklore was a matter of antiquity, in the developing world it was a contemporary phenomenon. Its appropriation was evident in such global developments as the genre of world music. A proposed solution, put forth by Bulgaria, was to extend article 6*bis* indefinitely and to recognize cultural groups as the authors of folklore (BIRPI 1967e, 913 1460.2, 914 1473; 1967d, 893 1156–1160.2).[6]

Despite professing sympathy, the developed nations rejected these proposals. Berne, they argued, was designed for individual authors. France argued that it would be difficult to distinguish folklore from the creations of a single author-creator, while Canada stated that its folklore had always been in the public domain and opposed any action likely to restrict such public use. In voicing these reservations, developed countries appealed to the interests of public utility, a position they rejected concerning other intellectual rights (BIRPI 1967c, 876 965.2, 966.1, 987). Developing nations were unable to use the principle of proprietary rights to their advantage, while several developed countries asserted their rights to autonomy when it suited their interests. The folklore question was not resolved at Stockholm, and WIPO has wrestled with it ever since. The WIPO Performances and Phonograms Treaty (1998) protects the rights of performers of folklore, and its committee on Traditional Knowledge, Genetic Resources and Folklore is moving forward with draft regulations for the protection of what WIPO calls traditional cultural expressions.

The Evolution of WIPO and the PCT

In 1974, WIPO officially became a specialized agency of the United Nations, and in 1996 it began coordinated work with the new World Trade Organization. Its philosophical foundation is the UN's Universal Declaration of Human Rights (1948), which states that "everyone has the right freely to participate in the cultural life of the community, to enjoy the arts and to share in scientific advancement and its benefits [and] ... everyone has the right to the protection of the moral and material interests resulting from any scientific, literary or artistic production of which he is the author." As a specialized UN agency, WIPO enjoys internal autonomy while remaining part of the international community (in 2004 it had 859 staff from 86 different countries). This special status is important, for it allows WIPO to act with comparative efficiency and to avoid the administrative stasis that bedevils formal UN agencies. The separate revenue stream accorded by the PCT underwrites WIPO's autonomy and gives its director general influence. WIPO shares, however, the UN family's voting structure — one country, one vote, regardless of size or financial contribution. As a result, WIPO works better as a global information hub for intellectual property than as a formal deliberative body.

Philosophically, WIPO has encouraged discussion of new developments in the field, professed a core desire to encourage global creativity and, especially under Arpad Bogsch, its director general from 1973 to 1997, tried to integrate the needs of developed and developing countries (Doern and Sharaput 2000, 76). Economically, "by providing a stable environment for the marketing of intellectual property products, it also oils the wheels of international trade" (WIPO 2004, 2). This work includes administrating international intellectual property treaties (divided into intellectual property protection treaties, global protection system treaties, and classification treaties), advocating for the harmonization of national and regional intellectual property rules, and providing a registration service for patents, copyrights, and trademarks (ibid., 5).

Harmonization is a recent historical development. BIRPI was unable to coordinate harmonization, and the Berne and Paris conventions served as a *modus vivendi* rather than binding international law. In this regard, intellectual property lagged behind other emerging global entities, such as radio communication, labour legislation, and railway and air conventions, all of which were harmonized internationally by the early twentieth century. The Council of Europe made progress in the 1950s on harmonizing patent legislation, and its efforts resulted in the Harmonization Convention (1963) and an European Economic Community draft patent law (1962) (Ljungman, 52-54).

These regional developments were overtaken by the formation of WIPO and the subsequent negotiation of the PCT (1971). The International Patent Institute, set up by a group of European countries in The Hague in 1947 as a common resource for patent searching and archiving, laid the groundwork for the PCT. Under Bogsch's leadership, the PCT was formally created in 1970, but it was not implemented until 1978. The delay was due to the European community's desire to first launch the EPO and to resistance from national patent bodies that feared the PCT would compromise their autonomy (European Patent Office 2001b, 21). The PCT facilitates the filing of multiple national applications for the same invention through standardized application formats and a centralized procedure. An applicant who files in a member state can choose to have the patent simultaneously filed in any other member nation. These records are then deposited in a central repository, making future novelty searches easier.

The PCT would have been unworkable without a little-observed but essential innovation, the International Patent Documentation Centre (INPADOC), founded jointly in 1972 by WIPO and the Austrian government. The centre records the bibliographic data (country, code, document number, filing date and, for some countries, name of inventor and invention) for patent documents filed by industrial property offices all over the world. It enables users to search for patents by family type, inventor, or International Patent Classification (IPC) symbol; publishes a weekly gazette of new patent applications; and provides an application copying service.[7] The centre initially relied on a Siemens 7-748 computer with a mere twelve disc drives and six tape drives but was an early convert to what would become the Internet. The centre allows the PCT to function smoothly. By 1979, the PCT's first year in full operation, INPADOC had processed over one million patents and contained 96 percent of the world's extant patents. The World Intellectual Property Organization helped bring developing nations from the African Intellectual Property Organization (OIPA) and Latin America into INPADOC in the 1970s and encouraged national patent offices to harmonize their systems with INPADOC in exchange for access to the growing global patent database (WIPO 1979, 5, 7, 12–14).

National patent bodies, however, retain their granting authority, a compromise between the globalizing imperative of the PCT and the desire among the nations of OECD to preserve their autonomy. Thus, the PCT has not created a global patent, but by making multiple jurisdictional filings easier, it circumvents some state power and increases individual inventors' autonomy. The PCT is a decisive global moment — "the biggest breakthrough in patents since 1883 [the birth of the Paris Agreement]" — because it is a working-level agreement, not simply a pledge of international harmony (BIRPI 1970b, 27).

Figure 1: PCT applications filed, 1978-2008

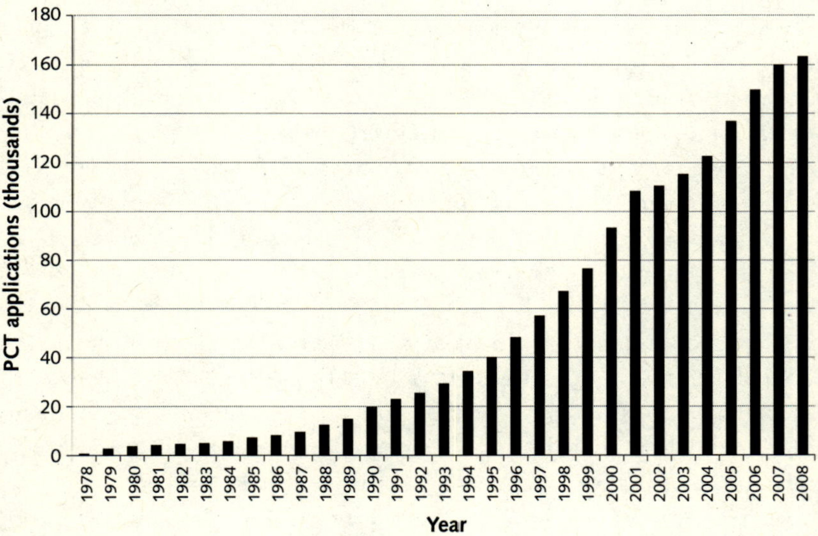

Source: World Intellectual Property Organization (2009).

Patent Cooperation Treaty applications increased from 2,586 in 1979, the treaty's first full year, to 67,007 in 1998, and 163,248 in 2008 (see Figure 1).[8] Revenues from PCT applications have made WIPO the UN family's most financially successful member. The organization retired its founding debt in 1993 (loans came from member states), and since 1982-83 it has shown a surplus that amounted to 47.7 million Swiss francs by 1991. The money is used to finance WIPO's activities, including a generous budget to help developing countries create and manage intellectual property mechanisms (Bogsch 1992, 32).

The PCT's genesis in the global political debates of the 1960s is evident in its attention to questions of development and modernization. The work of W.W. Rostow and other modernization theorists stressed the importance of technical and economic assistance, and the United Nations was entering its second Decade of Development (see Essid 2009). Although the United Nations Conference on Trade and Development (UNCTAD) advocated trade and foreign direct investment as the best tools for development, BIRPI gained support for the theretofore neglected issue of broader global intellectual property regulations as the necessary foundation of development. BIRPI's advocacy work in the 1960s established the international support for intellectual property without which WIPO might not have emerged. At the same time, the developing world was finding its voice on the global stage. The Bandung Conference in 1955 had pointed to a possible third way in international politics, and the Group of 77 had formed in 1964 to press for developing countries' interests at the United Nations, especially UNCTAD. Developing countries, led by Brazil, were also well represented at the PCT's founding conference. Brazil hoped that the PCT would facilitate technology transfer to the developing world: "No additional amount of financing or of foreign exchange earnings, however substantial, can be adequate substitutes for the full availability of modern technology; as few of the under-developed countries are able to devise through their own unhindered research the technological solutions that most adequately fill their specific needs, they will depend almost exclusively on an increasing volume of imported technology" (Bogsch 1992, 40). It appealed to fairness, arguing that developing countries should not have to bear the burden of costs "not applied to the countries in the vanguard of development" (ibid.).

Yet not all developing nations acted in concert during the 1960s and 1970s, the decades when the global patent system took shape. Although most developing countries were members of the Paris Union and joined the PCT by the early 1980s, hoping to gain from technology transfer and seeing no gain in staying out, there were exceptions. Many of the least developed countries were not members because they had no patent infrastructure at all and did not issue patents. India and Venezuela, which favoured autarkic economic principles, and OPEC countries, which sought to protect their revenues, also stayed out of the PCT in its formative period. Nonetheless, by 1981, 90 percent of patents were granted through Paris members, almost all through the PCT and most to OECD citizens, a sign that those countries with the most advanced legal and technical capacity have benefitted the most (Bogsch 1983, 16, 17, 23).[9] The PCT also reminds us that internationalism progressed alongside Cold War divisions. Indeed, the USSR attended the PCT founding conference, securing recognition of inventors' certificates (the socialist equivalent to the patent, it provides the inventor with remuneration but not sole proprietary rights) (BIRPI 1970b, 25; Iriye 2004, 96-125).

As a global information hub, WIPO has often relied on international non-governmental organizations (INGOs). The latter have both promoted the growth of intellectual property laws and education in developing and developed nations and mobilized civil society organizations that see such developments as a threat to their autonomy. Although INGOs are sometimes excluded from the global research-policy nexus because of their lack of size or technical sophistication (Appadurai 2000, 17), more than 170 enjoy observer status at WIPO. They include business interests, such as the Biotechnology Industry Organization, the International Federation of Pharmaceutical Manufacturers Associations, and the American Film Marketing Association; regional intellectual property interests, such as the Arab Society for the Protection of Industrial Property, the ASEAN Intellectual Property Association, and the Caribbean Broadcasting Union; and civil society interests, such as the Afro-Asian Book Council, the Ibero-Latin-American Federation of Performers, the International Association of Authors of Comics and Cartoons, and the International Federation of Reproduction Rights Organizations (Bardehle 1997, 194; WIPO 2003, 1-15). As this brief list indicates, INGO interests are wide and varied, and thus they perform an uneven advisory role in WIPO's deliberations. Nonetheless, they are able to influence intellectual property policy discussions at an early stage, avoiding the lobbyist role they must play in democratic politics. The World Intellectual Property Organization's development work and its active collaboration with INGOs define it as an epistemic community of disparate interests that share knowledge.

Although WIPO-BIRPI has historically sought to internationalize intellectual property relations, there have always been states that remained outside the organization. At present, approximately 10 percent of the world's countries are not members. With the exception of North Korea, nonmembers are mostly micro-states such as Vanuatu, where many Internet providers have set up shop to avoid international treaties. Such loopholes reveal a difference between the global nature of the recent past and older internationalism. The world governance structure established at Bretton Woods in 1944 was predicated on the primacy of the nation-state: the International Monetary Fund, the World Bank, and even the United Nations itself are extensions of the state system. These bodies are both not powerful enough, in that they are tied to national governments, and too powerful, in that they are accountable to no one in particular. They are too autonomous. Globalization has intensified this paradox. Global organizations must attain unanimity, or demonstrate an adaptability with which they were not bestowed, to be effective. Effective global institutions either rely on internal measures such as binding arbitration (the World Trade Organization) (Moore 2003, 64-65) or operate outside of the nation-state paradigm (Amnesty International, the Red Cross, or Médecins Sans Frontières). The latter groups' influence relies largely on moral persuasion, a tool not readily available to WIPO.

Instead, WIPO's legitimacy rests on its core belief that intellectual property is a necessary prerequisite for social and economic development. To achieve this goal, WIPO favours broad international harmonization, thus asking states to transfer to it some of their autonomy. In this sense, WIPO seeks to become, in Anne-Marie Slaughter's terms, an effective global network in which nation-states, groups, and individuals all relinquish some of their sovereignty or autonomy in pursuit of a larger goal (Slaughter 2004, 153, 160). Although a new international realm has thus been created for patent applications, one in which individual inventors enjoy the near-global principle of national treatment, the sovereignty of national law persists, meaning that a truly global patent system has not yet emerged. Time will tell if WIPO's proposed Substantive Patent Law Treaty, which its Standing Committee on the Law of Patents has been debating in various forms since the 1990s without resolution, will achieve this goal. Its proposed treaty suggests a true global patent in the form of standardized global filing processes, consistent with WIPO's goal of a Global Cooperation System (WIPO, Standing Committee on the Law of Patents, 2010). Thus, globalization and nationalism have so far formed overlapping concentric circles. In Scholte's (2002, 24-26) terminology, the supraterritoriality represented by WIPO's creation of a global social space is itself composed in part of the actions of territorially based, autonomous nation-states and INGOs.

The World Intellectual Property Organization emerged in the 1970s as part of a broader proliferation of global networks of interdependence, including the modern environmental and human rights movements, and the development of multilateral agreements between OECD states (Ferguson et al. 2010). Notable here is Tri-Lateral Cooperation, a loose cooperative agreement between the EPO, the USPTO, and the JPO. Founded in 1981, it facilitates the exchange of statistical data and promotes the harmonization of patent-granting processes between its members. Tri-Lateral Cooperation reflects its members' desire for open markets to create harmonized, global intellectual property standards. In 2007, its members processed 993,170 applications from both residents and non-residents, far outdistancing applications to other regional bodies such as the African Intellectual Property Organization and the Eurasian Patent Organization (Trilateral Cooperation Statistical Report, 37). Although the emergence of Japan is an important exception, the disparity in global patent activity and the interconnectivity of such activity supports Paul Hirst and Grahame Thompson's view that the modern global economy is not unprecedented but rather closely resembles the Western-dominated, highly internationalized economy of the first era of globalization, from roughly 1870-1914 (Hirst and Thompson 1999). Even new legal principles such as transjudicialism, whereby domestic courts employ foreign law in their jurisprudence, are nonetheless primarily confined to the developed world (Tawfik 2007, 573-74).

The decisive global moment in the history of intellectual property rights occurred in 1994, when the Agreement on Trade-Related Aspects of Intellectual Property Rights (TRIPS) was negotiated as an annex of the Marrakesh Agreement Establishing the World Trade Organization (WTO). The agreement incorporated into the WTO binding international regulations for private intellectual property rights, including patents, copyrights, and trademarks, as well as the collective intellectual property right of geographical indications. Unlike the intellectual property agreements administered by WIPO, the TRIPS agreement is backed by the WTO's binding dispute settlement system. Developed states, led by the United States, lobbied strenuously for the inclusion of TRIPS in the WTO, and the agreement reflects those countries' normative belief that the harmonization of intellectual property protection among member states facilitates innovation, trade, and development (Sell 2003; Drahos 2002). The TRIPS agreement has thus reinforced the OECD countries' dominance of the global patent system.

The TRIPS agreement, partly a response to developing countries' resistance to harmonization at WIPO, compels developing nations to strengthen their intellectual property legislation by outlawing, for instance, the mass production of generic pharmaceuticals upon which a patent is held elsewhere. As Susan Sell argues, "the global approach ensconced in the TRIPS agreement is a much less flexible regime for IP protection" than the Paris-Berne regime, which it has augmented (Sell 2003, 12). The agreement's importance, however, should not be overstated. It uses weak and sometimes vague language and in the last decade has been forced to become more flexible. Notable here is the Declaration on the TRIPS Agreement and Public Health (2001), which relaxed provisions for the purchase of generic drugs by developing countries and more broadly asserted that the TRIPS agreement "should not prevent members from taking measures to protect public health" (Amani 2009, 223-27; Drezner 2007, 176-78; Kapczynski 2002). The declaration was the result of a joint campaign by developing nations and global civil society actors such as Médecins Sans Frontières, Health Action International, and ACT UP (Drahos 2002). The declaration demonstrates that claims for autonomous decision making can be successful within the global framework of an international agreement such as TRIPS, in which a normative consensus can be built across global North-South lines.

The case of public health, however, is an aberration. Many developing states and INGOs have found the TRIPS agreement excessively restrictive and have consequently turned to other forums to press their various alternative positions on intellectual property. Such regime shifting has become increasingly common as global issues such as intellectual property have themselves become denser, both in their own complexity and in the number of interconnected policy areas in which they are relevant (Helfer 2004, 5-9). One such forum is WIPO, which, as discussed above, was a focus of Third World activity in the 1960s and 1970s and to which developing states have returned as a body that they feel better represents their development and human rights concerns. Although TRIPS remains significant because its regulations — unlike those of the Paris, Berne, and other unions administered by WIPO — are enforceable under threat of sanctions, WIPO's legalist infrastructure and organizational knowledge have established it as a global intellectual property information network.

The World Intellectual Property Organization is the leading Internet domain name dispute settlement body; has convened a working group on Intellectual Property and Genetic Resources, Traditional Knowledge and Folklore; and, in 2007, adopted a development agenda to foster technical assistance and capacity building in the developing world (de Beer 2009). The organization's funding structure, heavily dependent on industry and industrialized states, and its committees' advisory nature limit its ability to directly implement changes to "hard" international intellectual property law. These same limits, however, have paradoxically established WIPO as a global space where evolving intellectual property issues can be more freely debated and where innovative responses to intellectual property challenges — for instance, those pertaining to intangible property types such as certain biotechnologies or indigenous groups' folklore — can be generated free from immediate political and trade law pressures. Developing states, for instance, have embraced the WIPO Intergovernmental Committee on Intellectual Property and Genetic Resources, Traditional Knowledge and Folklore (the IGC) as a means to craft alternatives to the dominant private property model at the heart of the TRIPS agreement. The IGC gives them access to WIPO's technical expertise and allows them to work with like-minded INGOs, thanks to WIPO's relatively open observer status rules (as detailed above). Such arrangements can potentially create what Bita Amani calls a feedback loop, whereby WIPO's norm-setting endeavours create a framework for revisions to the TRIPS agreement similar to those inspired by the coalition of developing states and INGOs regarding public health provisions detailed above (Amani 2009, 285-86). Industrialized states have also endorsed the IGC, though for different reasons. The open-ended nature that attracts developing states to WIPO is also attractive to industrialized states because it can be used as a blocking mechanism to substantive change in hard international intellectual property law, as has been the case with WIPO's stalled Patent Law Treaty (Helfer 2004, 79-81).

The WIPO Development Agenda, meanwhile, has sought to bring its intellectual property work into closer accord with the UN's broader commitment to human rights and development (WIPO 2007b; May 2007; de Beer 2009). It asserts the public policy dynamics of intellectual property that are muted or absent within TRIPS. Even if the majority of its forty-five recommendations are not ultimately implemented, the development agenda's agreed upon principle that different levels of state development should be considered when WIPO establishes intellectual property norms (WIPO

2007a, Recommendation 15) explicitly acknowledges the importance of state autonomy in the international intellectual property policy-setting arena (Bannerman 2009, 25-28). This recognition of plurality rather than harmonization, as embodied in TRIPS, suggests that WIPO can exert moral suasion on member states through the development agenda's soft law status and potentially play a role in making the global intellectual property regime more flexible (de Beer 2009, 9; Gervais 2007). Like the IGC, the development agenda demonstrates how WIPO has functioned as a forum for counter-expressions of developing state autonomy in opposition to the WTO and its global TRIPS agreement.

The relative roles of TRIPS and WIPO in facilitating or restricting the autonomy of states to craft their own intellectual property policies over the past fifteen years have run parallel, and have been shaped by, the spread of intellectual property rights to new, intangible properties. The two most common technical fields for EPO applications in 2001, for instance, were computing and biochemistry/genetic engineering (European Patent Office 2001a, 19). The latter is especially relevant to considerations of globalization and autonomy, for it poses a challenge both to the prevailing paradigms of property ownership within TRIPS, national patent offices, and WIPO discussed so far in this chapter and to the nature of individual autonomy within the international intellectual property regime.

Competing Visions of Intellectual Property and Biotechnology

The history of global intellectual property rights in the twentieth century is largely one of growing institutional harmony, helping to create what Johan Galtung terms "the invisible continent of nonterritorial actors" (Iriye 2004, 133). In this case, internationalism has been the midwife of globalization, establishing parameters of cooperation and communication and an appreciation of shared goals or responsibilities. This growth was especially so in the 1960s and 1970s, when events such as the OPEC crisis, the creation of Greenpeace, and UNESCO's initiative to protect the world's heritage sites heightened awareness of the interconnection between economics, culture, and the natural world. The creation of WIPO and a global understanding of intellectual property was part of this history.

These developments have not been without critics. Some fear a rights creep, the trend towards absolute rights and the entrenchment of intellectual property holders as absentee landlords. Such absolutism would create excessive and socially detrimental rent seeking, potentially threatening capitalism itself and the world's poor (de Vuyst 2004, 130-33). Rent seeking disempowers those individuals still tied to the state or place of residence, pitting globalization directly against autonomy. Although strong intellectual property laws are supposed to encourage economic development, the abstract nature of intellectual property leaves it open to abuse (Hardt and Negri 2000, 302). Intellectual property also neglects the many intangible factors that aid economic development, such as social relationships, organizational knowledge, and non-monetary ideas of value.

These criticisms have encouraged alternative models of intellectual property rights, both new and old, including the idea of the commons, open or shared use ownership, and copyleft.[10] These models stress the moral weaknesses of the proprietary rights position, support greater autonomy for intellectual property users, and acknowledge intangible rights. They turn the neoliberal logic of intellectual property rights against itself. Intellectual property rights, they argue, should mimic the openness and permeability intrinsic to globalization itself, minimizing what Zygmunt Bauman calls the "new asymmetry ... between [the] exterritorial nature of power and the continuing territoriality of the 'whole life'" characteristic of globality (Bauman 2000, 8-9). Alternative models of intellectual property stress the idea of collective rights. The conflict between a global concept of intellectual property rights, based on the Anglo-American philosophy of proprietary rights, and weaker intellectual property rights — based on arguments of fair use, the commons, and autonomy — has been particularly evident in regard to new genetic property types.

Industry Canada defines biotechnology as "the applied use of living organisms or their components to make or modify products, to improve plants or animals or to develop microorganisms for specific uses" (Doern and Sharaput 2000, 68). The first patent for a microorganism, granted in the United States in 1873, was for a disease-free yeast created by Louis Pasteur. This patent established a precedent for the ownership of living organisms. Scientific progress was slow, however, and most inventors were narrowly concerned with industrial properties. New plant varieties were the earliest potential new genetic properties. Plants and other genetic resources, including new breeds created through animal husbandry, had historically been considered common property. The US Plant Patent Act (1930), an ad hoc response to lobbying by the ornamental garden breeders industry, thus broke new ground in allowing patents for asexually reproduced plants (also see Coleman and Reed, this volume).[11] It did not apply to bacteria,[12] which scientists classify as a plant but common usage does not, nor did it apply to products of nature.[13] This narrowly conceived Act established a precedent for later debates about the ownership of emerging genetic property types, with genetically modified foodstuffs and other agricultural products so far being defined as intellectual property because they are not expressly forbidden under the PPA. The question of what constitutes a product of nature, in particular, has informed whether new genetic discoveries, such as the well-known Harvard oncomouse, are deemed patentable.[14]

Support for broader intellectual property rights for genetically created plants increased from the late 1930s. European plant patent legislation appeared in the 1940s, and in the 1960s the European community allowed plant breeders to protect sexually reproduced varieties of plants if they were found to be stable and novel. The International Association of Plant Breeders for the Protection of Plant Varieties was founded in 1938, and the Union for Varieties of New Plants was formed in 1961, establishing a *sui generis* system for recognizing plant varieties. A further rupture occurred when the United States passed the Plant Variety Protection Act (1970), granting exclusive marketing rights for new types of sexually reproduced plants. The Act excluded basic organisms, seemingly drawing a legal line regarding biotechnology patenting. The development of recombinant DNA technology in the 1970s and 1980s, however, allowed genes to be transferred from one organism to another without the organisms interacting, thus creating the modern biotechnology industry (Coleman and Wayland 2005, 5-13). At this historical juncture, the property law model for plant types, and by extension for all genetic properties, broke down.

The legislative and philosophical breakthrough again happened in the United States. The discovery of the structure of DNA in 1953 first brought questions of intellectual property and genetic engineering to the public eye. The DNA code was deciphered in 1968; the first recombinant DNA experiments (in bacteria) occurred in 1973; and the first in vitro fertilization occurred in 1978. Until this point, the Plant Patent Act still prohibited life forms from being patented. *Diamond v. Chakrabarty* decisively changed the legal environment, opening the door to patents for artificially created life forms. Almost simultaneously, the Baye-Dohl Act (1980) decreed that non-profit organizations (primarily universities) could now apply for patents for publicly funded innovations.[15] The Act stimulated an increase in public sector research and development. The number of US university patents increased from three hundred in 1980 to two thousand in 1995. The Act's supporters believe it promotes the dissemination of knowledge, while critics argue that the exclusivity agreements, which public researchers must increasingly sign, harm accountability and allow private interests, rather than a commitment to the public good, to steer research (Brown 2000; Nelson 1998, 1460).

Chakrabarty opened the possibility of ownership over future genetically produced organisms up to and including human germline engineering. Moral arguments against the patenting of genetic properties quickly followed, especially from organized religion. In 1983, a coalition of US religious leaders presented Congress with a "Theological Letter Concerning the Moral Arguments," alleging that human germline engineering posed a threat similar to nuclear holocaust (Theological letter 1983). Moral arguments were outpaced, though, by scientific developments. The Human Genome Project, established in 1988 to map the human genetic code, was successfully completed in 2003. W. French Anderson began the first somatic gene transfer experiments in 1991 and obtained a US patent on all ex vivo gene manipulations in humans in 1995. Global attention to genetic engineering was galvanized by the cloning of Dolly the sheep in 1996, prompting the formation of international agencies to monitor such activity. The Council of Europe Convention on Human Rights and Biomedicine was adopted in 1997, prohibiting human germline interventions. It banned human cloning in 1998, and over 70 percent of European Union states had ratified it by 2000.[16] Like BIRPI-WIPO, the convention deliberately cited article 1 of the 1948 UN Universal Declaration of Human Rights, establishing genetic engineering as a global rather than a national human rights question. The UN itself, through UNESCO, adopted the Universal Declaration on the Human Genome and Human Rights in 1997, which banned germline interventions (Taylor 1999, 480; see also UNESCO's website). Fundamental moral differences as to what constitutes human life, however, have precluded a true international ban on cloning. Furthermore, biotechnology is largely the preserve of the world's wealthiest nations. Poor countries have little interest in creating regulation in this field and potentially leave their jurisdictions open to forum shopping by actors whose work might not be permitted in developed countries. Even among OECD countries, there is no moral or political consensus on the ethics of cloning (Caulfield 2003, 717). The United States has lagged behind European and international bodies in creating regulations covering human cloning, mainly because of strong lobbying by its biotechnology industry. The 1998 symposium "Engineering the Human Germline" at UCLA highlighted the industry's support for genetic research, stressing academic freedom and the prevention of disease. In 2000, the American Academy of Arts and Sciences publically supported such research. Despite tentative official movements in this direction, the United States has yet to completely ban human cloning.

Although arguments that stress moral autonomy have been most prominent, utility arguments have also been made. Some critics accept that biotechnologies should be patentable but are concerned about how they will be used and whether the genetic resources of indigenous or poor groups will be exploited. There are also parallels between the use of patented genetic resources and the history of slavery (Brewer and Staves 1995, 10-11). The state granted a monopoly to attract capital for a risky venture — slavery — which it believed was in the public interest. Debates about slavery, as with genetic properties, broke down on moral and utility lines. Some opposed the practice as morally offensive, while others merely wanted its excesses curbed, lobbying for better treatment or a ban on selling slaves as commodities. As with the slave trade, the search for new genetic properties, sometimes called biopiracy, has also brought the developed world into conflict with the world's poor (Shiva 1997, 5, 119-24).

Biopiracy or, less pejoratively, bioprospecting involves representatives of the industrialized world creating patented products from the genetic resources of developing countries (May 2000, 3). This practice has a long history that follows in the train of European overseas expansion. Colonial explorers, supported by bodies such as the London School for Tropical Medicine (founded in 1899), searched for cures for tropical diseases to which Europeans were vulnerable. Globalization has exacerbated bioprospecting. The US company W.R. Grace, for instance, has earned millions of dollars from its patent for BioNeem, an insecticide developed from the Indian neem berry. Indians, for whom the neem berry was a common resource, have earned nothing. Some efforts have been made to curb this exploitation of what Erica-Irene Daes calls indigenous heritage (Daes 1997, 3, para. 24), notably through partnerships between developing countries that assay or collect resources and biotechnology companies, who create the final product (Merson 2001, 285-86, 288-90, 295). Such partnerships are supported by the Convention on Biological Diversity (1992), an international agreement that includes provisions to allow signatory countries to control their genetic resources. Critics, however, fear these partnerships constitute a form of neocolonialism and especially harm indigenous groups, who are often at odds with their own governments.

Bioprospecting can also apply to the human body. The case of John Moore is notable. Moore unsuccessfully sued the doctors who removed his spleen and later developed a patented cell line from it. Following the same principle as the PPA, the human body itself is not patentable. Its formation and development are subject to discovery but not invention. However, isolated parts of the body, including gene sequences, can be patented. Controversy erupts over determining the line between discovery and invention. Although several international agreements have tentatively supported patents for partial genetic manipulations of both plants and human beings, such as the engineering of Moore's spleen, manipulations of the human genetic sequence (including cloning) — as discoveries, not inventions — have been deemed unpatentable.

The biotechnology industry's support for proprietary intellectual property rights and the threat of bioprospecting have created a potential genomics divide. Major pharmaceutical companies that lead the world in drug research are alleged to have a relative lack of interest in drugs for diseases prevalent in developing countries, favouring those in the developed world (Dowdeswell, Daar, and Singer 2003, 1-6; Glennerster, Kremer, and Williams 2005, 26-27). In response, public and private groups such as the Copenhagen Consensus have suggested direct international initiatives that target specific global problems. Such initiatives suggest an apparent end run around the patent system for those who believe it cannot be reformed. There are, however, internal systemic mechanisms that may help, such as differential drug pricing, voluntary licensing, generic drug production, benefit sharing, and public-private initiatives such as drug donation and delivery programs. Developing nations could also strengthen their intellectual property systems and technical infrastructure, as India has, to ensure they can retain their own innovators. The danger, however, as shown in Coleman and Reed's chapter, is that such a step may simply reinforce the existing asymmetry in genetic resource transfer between developed and developing nations. The WTO's Doha revisions have granted member states increased autonomy over public health, including the right to bypass patent protection for drugs needed to save lives and to allow compulsory licences for generic drugs (World Health Organization 2002, 132-34, 136, 141; Lomborg 2004). Although these reforms remain untested, member states seem to recognize the limitations of a one-size-fits-all global patent system and the weaknesses of TRIPS, which tries to make antiquated patent and copyright systems apply to properties for which they were not designed.

Conclusion

The challenge posed by new property types to the worlds' various intellectual property institutions is that of the prisoner's dilemma. Although it would arguably be in all parties' interests to adapt their policies to accommodate new potential property types, such adaptations are resisted for fear that competitors will reap greater economic rewards through inaction. After all, the framework of the world intellectual property system remains nineteenth-century national patent legislation. This resistance to change supports Susan Strange's contention that the Westphalian state model, which encourages national interest at the expense of cooperation, is ill-suited for globalization (Strange 2003, 127-29). Yet the emergence of new, global property types has forced nation-states in particular to confront their prisoner's dilemma. The risk of not acting globally has increased substantially since the early 1970s (Beck 2002, 40-41), whether it be developed nations seeking to protect their intellectual property rights through TRIPS, WIPO seeking to promote greater equity through development, developing nations seeking to protect their indigenous heritage through special arrangements such as compulsory licences, or all actors trying to come to terms with the implications of the biotechnology revolution.

The *Diamond v. Chakrabarty* case, with which this chapter began, has proved a decisive rupture in the historical evolution of global intellectual property regulation. Chakrabarty's legal victory meant that US patent law was no longer solely concerned with material creations (Krueger 1981). It now extended to life itself — a development fraught with uncertainty and troubling ethical decisions. The potential ownership of human beings is on the horizon. This development will bring the struggle over autonomy and the construction of common and personal property to individuals the world over. Whether the global intellectual property regime described in this chapter can address this prospect looks to be a central theme of globalization studies in the twenty-first century.

chapter 7

Competing or Relational Autonomies? Globalization, Property, and Friction over Land Rights

Eva Mackey

This chapter explores volatile, local conflicts over Aboriginal land rights in Canada and the United States as global moments in the evolution of property regimes. Although they are acted out, sometimes violently, at the local and national levels, such conflicts are deeply embedded in the global. Their material conditions of possibility, based as they are on earlier moments of global colonial power relations, were legitimated and are today enabled by global, supposedly universal, property ideologies. Furthermore, Aboriginal people often frame their contemporary struggles for autonomy and sovereignty by using a global vocabulary that defines their struggles as a continuation of earlier moments, moments when they, as sovereign nations, made international treaties with colonial powers. Indigenous land rights actions, including assertions about the relationship between land rights and global environmental issues, also mobilize international vocabularies and subject positions that have been forged by indigenous peoples over two decades, in part by taking on the global audience and framework of the United Nations.

At the same time, non-Aboriginal people often resist global assertions of land rights and autonomy or sovereignty, blaming governments and global governance organizations for betraying older yet essential common-sense ideals and social arrangements. Instead, these governments and organizations are viewed as promoting unequal, even race-based, rights that go against long-standing Western property ideologies. This chapter explores how discourses of rights, property, and justice are mobilized by divergent actors in such moments of friction. The focus is the Caldwell First Nation in Ontario and the Cayuga Indian Nation in New York State and their successful land claims of 1998 and 2002, respectively. An analysis of these claims demonstrates both the resurgence of oppressive universals based on Western property regimes and the possibility for alternative conceptualizations of property and personhood.

Globalization, Resistance, and Autonomy?

Studies of resistance to globalization tend to examine grassroots social movements that explicitly critique global capitalist processes such as the destruction of local and traditional cultures, the conditions in sweatshops and free trade zones, and environmental destruction. These movements may not define themselves as anti-globalist per se or even as anti-capitalist, but they often explicitly seek to promote human rights, social justice, and local autonomy (see Khasnabish 2008). Influential analyses of such movements suggest that they may be sites for the development of innovative forms of democracy and autonomy. Other analyses look to the structures of globalization and suggest that even in spaces of apparent resistance, global hegemony holds it grip. Surprisingly, however, little attention has been paid to right-wing and libertarian forms of resistance to globalization. These forms of resistance defend individual liberties such as the right to bear arms, they reject government (global, national, or local) intrusion into and control of private affairs, and they assert peoples' inalienable right to private property.

I suggest that neither globalization nor resistance to it emerges in clearly identifiable forms. Nor do they clearly signify freedom or oppression. Dichotomous views of anti-globalization as either resistance or accommodation do not shed light on the complexity of these processes. Following Tsing (2005), I contend that to comprehend how global processes work, we must examine how they are enabled and enacted through everyday encounters over the implementation of universals. The chapter therefore offers an ethnographic analysis of one site of friction in which we can see the production of such globalized complexity: struggles over Aboriginal rights and property in settler nations.

The conceptualization and negotiation of indigenous peoples' rights and citizenship within nation-states and on a global scale have shifted in recent decades, at least theoretically. Important legal decisions in British settler nations such as Canada, the United States, Australia, and New Zealand have recognized indigenous rights to autonomy and self-determination. Decisions such as the *Delgamuukw* decision in Canada and the *Wik* decision in Australia are often seen as part of the global development of frameworks for indigenous rights. Global governance documents such as the UN Declaration on the Rights of Indigenous Peoples explicitly recognize indigenous peoples' inherent right to collective autonomy, as well as the need for control over their own land to establish and maintain it.[1] Collective autonomy is generally understood as some form of self-regulation, self-governance, or self-direction. But what happens when Aboriginal collective autonomy conflicts with the individual autonomy of other members of nation-states?

Despite the assumed shared global moral community of the United Nations (Collier 2001), some members of local non-Aboriginal communities experience claims for Aboriginal autonomy — materialized in land and supported theoretically by global governance organizations such as the UN — as a threat to their individual autonomy and equal rights. They see collective autonomy for indigenous people as being in conflict with established notions of the sovereignty of nations and the autonomy of its citizens. They see indigenous land rights and sovereignty as an invasion of their lands; a violation of their rights as local, national, and global citizens; and a threat to their inherent right to control their own property and themselves. They also argue that nation-states cannot and must not have distinct forms of government for any of their citizens and that there should be one set of rules for all citizens. They see themselves as resisting a new global world order in which governments and global governance organizations now betray such long-established and common-sense ideals by promoting multiculturalism and Aboriginal rights. How do we interpret moments when it appears that local people are resisting the globalization of social justice?

Anna Tsing's book, *Friction: An Ethnography of Globalization* (2005), presents the argument that to avoid programmatic global predictions, it is important to emphasize the unexpected and unstable aspects of global interaction. Globalizing processes can best be understood through analysis of their moments of friction: moments in which the spread of supposedly universal categories and projects of the global are "charged and enacted" in the "sticky materiality of practical encounters" (ibid., 1). To me, practical encounters, such as the struggle over land rights, reveal complex and messy processes of conflict and misunderstanding in which people may be using the same key terms and ideas in different ways for different goals. There is a lot at stake for all participants. Furthermore, as Tsing suggests, the unstable and unpredictable nature of these encounters may offer productive conditions of possibility for developing new relationships grounded in both global and local realities.

A great deal of important research and analysis about legal decisions has been carried out regarding land rights, much of it focusing on legal issues.[2] Here, I explore friction over land rights by using an ethno-legal or vernacular-law approach. I do not, therefore, focus primarily on the law as enacted in legal decisions and documents; instead, I draw primarily on ethnographic data, collected during fieldwork since 1999, and on interviews with and observation of people in local communities experiencing conflict over land rights.

In ethnographies of globalization, focusing on local phenomena requires both the global and the universal to be in the lens. As Tsing (2005, 1) points out, it is "impossible to get very far in tracing global connections without running into claims about universals." Indeed, one of the characteristics of Western property ideologies, emerging from the Enlightenment as they did, is that they have been mobilized as if they were valid universal modes of characterizing human beings and their relationship to nature and to one another. They are models for how any society should "naturally" work. But the very specificity and complexity of local-global encounters is "an ever-present reminder that universal claims do not actually make everything everywhere the same. Global connections give grip to universal aspirations" (ibid., 1). People do not actually live the universal categories as imagined. Earlier global processes introduced Western property ideologies and practices around the globe, but they were taken up in exceedingly diverse ways.

Tsing (2005, 7) argues that it is necessary to "see generalizations to the universal as an aspiration, an always unfinished achievement, rather than the confirmation of a pre-formed law. Then it is possible to notice that universal aspirations must travel across distances and differences, and we can take this travel as an ethnographic object." Tsing argues that universalism is implicated in "both imperial schemes to control the world and in liberatory mobilizations for justice and empowerment. Universalism inspires expansion — for both the powerful and the powerless" (ibid., 9). Although it is important analytically to see universal frameworks as aspirations that travel and change, on the level of practice, during specific debates people often mobilize universal categories as if they reflect a natural truth. In the conflicts I discuss below, divergent actors mobilize discourses of rights, property, and justice in ways that show the resurgence of oppressive universal categories as well as alternative ways of imagining social relations.

Property and Universality

Property is one such apparently universal concept. It is powerful, persuasive, and ubiquitous. From early political thought onward, ideas about property have been central to conceptualizations of an entire nexus of themes: economics, civil society, government, gender relations, morality, individuality, autonomy, personhood, work, entitlement, and conquest. The concept of property has become what anthropologists Verdery and Humphrey (2004, 2-3) argue is a Western native category: its meanings appear self-evident and commonsensical in Western contexts. Furthermore, as a result of colonialism and globalization, property ideologies also "act powerfully" throughout the world. Although conceptions of property do transform in different contexts, property carries with it its own "implicit theories, which endow it with ideological effects" (ibid.)

Terra nullius, a Latin expression meaning "empty land" or "vacant land," is a framework for thinking about property that was influential in earlier global processes of colonization. The doctrine of terra nullius rationalized and authorized colonial processes that depended, to a great extent, upon the appropriation and redefinition of indigenous peoples' territories. It was important first in establishing so-called frontiers for exploration and then in transforming those indigenous lands into private or public property to be improved or exploited by newcomers. The theory that most epitomizes the terra nullius framework is elaborated by John Locke (1632-1704), especially in his *Second Treatise on Government* (1952 [1690]). Locke justifies the European conquest of the "New World" by arguing that Europeans were naturally entitled to the land because only they, not the original inhabitants, would develop private property and therefore improve the land (Verdery and Humphrey 2004, 4). Today, such frameworks are generally seen as colonialist, backward, and contrary to international law and global human rights regimes.

The underlying assumptions of older property ideologies, tied as they are to imperial and colonial moments, have a continuing and vibrant life today among people who oppose land rights. I found them very much alive during my fieldwork on local conflicts in Canada and the United States, despite national mythologies to the contrary.[3] My goal in this chapter is to explore how property ideologies behave in the moments of friction I describe. How do they legitimate and entitle some individuals' and communities' access to property while simultaneously denying or limiting the access of others? I suggest that Western property ideologies, and the body of assumptions that move with them, are persistent, embedded, and powerful in these conflicts. I argue that such bitter conflicts about property represent struggles of adjustment and deep-seated resistance to what anti–land rights activists perceive as a new global property regime. They are confronted by unexpected and unwelcome relations of power. In the process of resisting change, they mobilize common-sense property ideologies to discount Aboriginal peoples' world views, thereby refusing to recognize their historical interpretations and, most importantly, their claims to land. The implicit assumptions about personhood and relationships in Western property ideologies, and in modernist versions of nationhood and rights, allow for the dehumanization of Aboriginal Others. More tragically, they allow for a construction of a world in which collective (Aboriginal) and individual (non-Aboriginal) autonomies are constructed as competing and dichotomous.

As messy as these encounters are, they also offer possibilities for different forms of local engagement and mobilization and for creative ways of organizing around property, history, justice, and autonomy. Aboriginal groups and their non-Aboriginal supporters are finding their own ways to assert and establish autonomy that may offer alternatives to such an oppositional and dichotomous stance. They are developing, I suggest, forms of relational autonomy that avoid the dichotomies and limits of Western property ideologies. My ethnographic approach draws out the complexities of these encounters as they are played out in specific contexts.

The Caldwell First Nation and the Cayuga Indian Nation

Both the Caldwell First Nation in southern Ontario and the Cayuga Indian Nation in upper New York State have been landless for over two hundred years.[4] Extensive detail about the histories and present conditions of the First Nations and their relationship with the state is not possible in this chapter. What is significant is that both groups made land claims in the Great Lakes region of North America and that both succeeded at the federal court level. If implemented, neither claim will include defined pieces of land as settlement, as is usual in such cases. Instead, each nation will receive money to purchase land on the so-called open market. Finally, both nations have experienced a volatile backlash to their claims by local non-Aboriginal residents (Mackey 2005).[5]

In New York State, the Cayuga Indian Nation claims land and compensation for 64,000 acres of traditional territory on the northern edge of Lake Cayuga. In 2002, the Cayuga won $243 million in compensation. The backlash to the Cayuga land claim, by a group called Upstate Citizens for Equality (UCE), has been felt since the mid-to-late 1990s. It has included the posting of signs on lawns and fields that say "No Sovereign Nation — No Reservation," "One Nation," and "Equality Is Necessary for Justice." The UCE has organized demonstrations and a huge car rally; petitioned local, state, and federal governments; hired lawyers; launched court cases; attended local meetings and court hearings; and held money-making events such as bottle drives to have the claim rejected (Mackey 2005). In June 2005, the opponents of the Cayuga claim, including UCE, won an appeal of the Cayuga decision. The Cayuga have recently announced they will challenge that appeal decision.

The Caldwell First Nation in Ontario struggled for land rights for decades. In 1998, the federal government of Canada announced an agreement in principle with the band. If approved by band vote, the Caldwell would receive $23.4 million to purchase 4,500 acres of land over twenty-five years. Immediately after the announcement, over two thousand non-Aboriginal people from the area attended a meeting to express outrage at the government and to resist the claim. The Chatham-Kent Community Network (CKCN) was soon formed. The CKCN printed signs saying "Not for Sale," organized local meetings, sent submissions to the government and politicians, and hired lawyers to contest the claim. When I first visited Caldwell Nation members in 2000, they discussed the intense backlash they had experienced in the area, including graffiti on their buildings and nightly harassment. In 2000 and 2001, they organized Walks against Racism to make their plight public. Property, history, equality, and autonomy are hotly contested issues in both of these cases.

Furthermore, while members of the indigenous groups in the cases discussed in this chapter see themselves as local citizens who interact on a regional and national stage, they also position themselves as members of a global moral community and assert particular international forms of sovereignty, autonomy, and responsibility. The Haudenosaunee (which includes the Cayuga as one of the nations in their Confederation), for example, have never given up their sovereignty and see themselves as sovereign nations in the international sense. They define sovereignty as follows:

> Sovereignty is the state of existence as a self-governing entity, and it was in this capacity that ... members of the Haudenosaunee sat with delegates from England, France and the Netherlands in the years prior to American independence ... Early U.S. statesmen acknowledged the international status of Indian nations and the treaties made ... In 1871, the United States ceased treaty-making with native nations. It is the contention of the Onondaga Nation, then, that it maintains and has never relinquished either its national or collective sovereignty as a member of the Haudenosaunee. There has never been any provision for transferring that sovereignty to any other entity, nor have the traditional chiefs of the Haudenosaunee ever consented to such a transfer. (Onondaga Nation 2009b)

The Haudenosaunee have been negotiating such sovereignty for centuries. It is reflected in events such as the 1794 Jay Treaty (Onondaga Nation 2009a) and in the Haudenosaunee's refusal of the United States Citizen Act of 1924 (Onondaga Nation 2009b). In addition, from the 1920s to the present, Haudenosaunee leaders have appealed to and participated in international forums such as the League of Nations and the United Nations.[6]

In 1999, Caldwell Chief Larry Johnson also went to the United Nations. To publicize the backlash to their land rights and garner support for their struggle, he attended the UN Commission on Human Rights, Sub-Commission on Prevention of Discrimination and Protection of Minorities, Working Group on Indigenous Populations. The Caldwell and their supporters also use UN charters and frameworks as moral authorities in their discussions against the backlash. The Onondaga Nation, whose land rights case I discuss at the end of this chapter, asserts the importance of using land rights as a legal and moral force for the environment and the earth. These local and national struggles about land are therefore related to, and embedded in, global histories and property ideologies and, at the same time, address present-day manifestations and futures.

Property and People

Western property frameworks are connected to a range of related categories such as rights, equality, freedom, personhood, and autonomy. In current everyday usage, we normally think of property as a thing over which a person claims "more or less exclusive rights of ownership" (Hahn 1998, 4). For anthropologists and legal scholars, however, property is about human social relations rather than the inherent attributes of the object we call property. In other words, property is not a thing but rather "a network of social relations that governs the conduct of people with respect to the use and definition of things" (Hahn 1998, 4; see also Brace 2004; Rose 1994; Underkuffler 1990; Nedelsky 1991). Anthropologists have shown that there are, and have been, many possible ways to organize relationships between people with regard to things.

In contemporary global capitalist society, specific modern post-Enlightenment notions of property are dominant, although they are elaborated and contested in distinct ways within specific contexts. I find it useful, when thinking about conflict over land claims, to consider what Rose (1994) calls the broader property regime. For Rose, the term *property regime* denotes an entire historically developed institutionalized system of beliefs and practices about the correct way to deal with property.

The property regime that is now naturalized to the point that it appears to be common sense in many Western contexts nevertheless has a history. Within that history, even as aspects of the property regime change, there is a set of assumptions that move with it over time. Modern conceptions of property that constituted the rudiments of imperialism were based on a complex mix of ideas about individual ownership and control (Weaver 2003). British colonizers "primarily conceived of property as 'individual absolute domination' in which 'all the potential sticks in the bundle of property rights are gathered into a single owner'" (ibid., 49; see also McLaren, Buck, and Wright 2005) and in which private property signifies "autonomy and liberty," equality and freedom (Brace 2004, 101). Significantly, such ideologies also implied the superiority of those who shared them. They are integral to Western property regimes, even as they may appear to be changing.

The idea of land rights for Aboriginal peoples appears to disrupt unquestioned, long-standing assumptions about property. For example, activists against land rights whom I interviewed from CKCN and UCE often spoke as if their assumption of a safe and secure world was shifting profoundly before their eyes, and doing so in deeply unexpected and unjust ways. They felt that their unshakeable understandings about their own property, and their rights to control that property fully, were being betrayed by their government. The question of whether the legal recognition of Aboriginal land rights is in fact a shift in basic structures of the dominant property regime is not within the confines of this chapter. The important point is that these people believe and act as if it is. They construct their world as endangered and at risk.

Property in Practice

Within the context of Western property frameworks, as proposed by Locke and others, and in my fieldwork on conflicts about property rights, three interconnected frameworks emerge as persistently powerful organizing categories. First, colonizers in the past and non-Aboriginal people opposed to land claims in the present have assumed that they are superior and therefore possess unquestioned entitlements. These entitlements have permitted them to define others and to do so on supposedly God-given, rational, and universal terms. Second, individual and social personhood was, and still is, defined through such normative ideals as property, productive labour, and particular relationships to nature that can be traced to Locke and others. Finally, Lockean property ideology proposes specific normative notions about individuals and social groups. Similar concepts emerge in complex and interconnected ways in the property conflicts I examine below.

Universality and Labour

A sense of implicit superiority and a feeling of entitlement to define others — and to do so on the basis of supposedly rational principles — emerged in an interview I had with John, a supporter of UCE. He argued that land rights and sovereignty for Aboriginal people do not make sense: "I don't know of any other nation, empire, tribe, or whatever, that once it's conquered a people ... Those people [are] ... either ethnically cleansed, or they assimilate, or they're put into slavery. I mean there's some category. But I don't know of any historical example where those people reclaimed their sovereignty as a conquered people ... Look, this is not just a Western concept ... You have a war and the other guy loses; you don't have sovereignty, you've lost it" (John interview with author, 2002).[7] John asserted his authority by implying that his arguments were universally applicable. He claimed there was no evidence for contrary points of view and even pre-empted a possible critique that his argument was ethnocentric. He attempted to craft an authoritative discourse (Asad 1979, 621) that could not be countered.

Jim, a member of CKCN, combined "universal" assertions with the idea that the individual within a set of standard laws is the only rational approach to land rights.

> I know some Native people, and I respect them and think they're great people. I have nothing wrong with them maintaining their heritage, but the people living today ... What have we done to them that they should expect compensation and not have to contribute anything to society? Have all the benefits, plus ... You cannot build a nation where you have people with different rights. We've seen the results of that in recent times. You look at the Palestinian and Israeli people right today. Because you have two different peoples trying to live in the same place with different laws and different rights. You look at Yugoslavia: it doesn't work. Everybody has to abide by the same laws, and everybody has to contribute to society ... This isn't unique to Canada; this has happened all over the world. Canada's not the only one that's got problems: Australia's got problems, New Zealand's got problems, Africa's got problems. (Jim, interview with author, 2003)

Jim expounded on universal rules in an authoritative manner. Based on unquestioned yet widespread assumptions and presented as non-negotiable truth, his opinion sounded like law. His propositions that people must live in the present and not the past and that a nation must have a singular identity emerged as simple common-sense knowledge shared by all. Furthermore, his first few statements indicated how Aboriginal peoples' labour and their contribution to society were being assessed within this context. Jim asserted that indigenous people take but do not give. For him, equal productive labour is the basis of equal rights. Cultural difference is acceptable but separate rights are not. Only improving kinds of human labour are the basis of belonging.

Labouring for Rights

These activists' conceptions, which present labour as the basis of ownership and belonging, have a long history. Locke's labour theory of value, elaborated in his 1690 treatise, proposes that the right to property is derived from the labour of those who work and improve it. By implication, since property ownership is also the basis of citizenship, improving labour is necessary for full citizenship, belonging, and rights. Much Indian policy up to the late twentieth century was based upon this view: it was assumed that Aboriginal people needed to be educated to work hard and engage in agricultural labour in order to assimilate into modern society and to hold land. This idea is also not uncommon in more recent neoliberal discourse. In my interviews, normative judgments about labour and contributions to society were commonly used as a way to include and exclude Aboriginal people from belonging.

The Miller family, members of the UCE, discussed their move to New York and simultaneously defined normal and abnormal behaviour. According to James:

> We moved from Florida. We weren't natives of this part ... But everybody accepted us, [because] we do like everybody else does: we pay the taxes, and we live here and get along ... People accepted us because we *don't come here wanting anything for nothing*. We weren't freeloaders; we did what everybody does. When we got a tax bill, we paid the tax person. We never complained. We use the roads. We use the phones. We use the electrics. And, you know, everybody's supposed to do the same thing. If we had Indians ... they'd want to be able to hunt and fish in our lakes anytime of the year. They don't want to respect our months for hunting or fishing our laws. (James Miller, interview with author, 2005, emphasis added)

The repetition of *everybody* — juxtaposed with freeloading, non-tax-paying "Indians" — characterizes Aboriginal people as lazy members of a different class of citizenship, as people who are separate and different from everybody else. Non-tax-paying people (Indians), by implication, are freeloaders who want something for nothing and are, therefore, not part of *everybody.* They do not belong in *our* lakes.

One important aspect of assertions of proprietary interest and possession is that they also elaborate an ideal of normative personhood. Indeed, they characterize the kind of person and citizen who is and is not deserving of ownership of land. Furthermore, UCE and CKCN members feel entitled to make such normative judgments. These judgments occur in a number of ways that reflect complex and contradictory liberal ideals.

Aboriginal people (unless behaving like "the rest of us") are actively excluded from dominant ideas of "normal," which have multiple and shifting criteria.

Indeed, labour and its relationship to nature and normative society often plays a central role in how Aboriginal people are assessed by opponents of land claims. In Chatham-Kent, many defined the local community through characteristics related to intensive agricultural production. Such an approach to farming was even described by some as a culture or heritage that everyone shared and that the land claim threatened. They often described the Caldwell as outsiders because they did not share this culture based on interdependence and on hard agricultural labour and farming. In fact, in Chatham-Kent and New York, the Caldwell and the Cayuga developed plans for their land that were neither full-out capitalist farming nor wilderness conservation. It was assumed by many people, however, that if the Caldwell did finally get land, they would, of course, allow it to lie fallow and undeveloped. A local commercial farmer simply assumed they would want to "establish a swamp area," and his concern was that they would probably not take care of the land the way he did and clean the drainage ditches. Their idle behaviour would have an impact on upstream drainage, and he would, he said, "have trouble getting the water off" his land (interview with author, 2002).

The presumption that Aboriginal people would not engage in agriculture and would not care for their drainage areas was based on preconceived ideas. Indeed, when I asked people if they had heard anything specific and detailed about what the Caldwell planned to do with their land, none admitted to any knowledge. They assumed that the Caldwell would allow or establish a swamp. It is interesting that *swamp* is a derogatory term, unlike *wetlands.* Furthermore, most of the CKCN members assumed that the band would not respect provincial drainage regulations. Again and again, they brought up the issue that they did not know what the Caldwell intended to do with their land and that the Caldwell may not care for and repair the drainage system. They repeatedly argued that the Caldwell would follow their own rules and not work with the community or follow provincial regulations that they all share.

These arguments were made even though there is a clear and well-publicized federal requirement that the Caldwell must respect provincial drainage regulations. The regulations were communicated clearly by Indian and Northern Affairs Canada at a meeting with the municipality and

CKCN at least a year before my first interviews, and the rules also appear on the government's website.[8] Nevertheless, all CKCN members I spoke to consistently denied that they had any idea what the Caldwell planned to do and repeatedly discussed drainage. The stereotype of the lazy Indian was more powerful (and more useful perhaps) to their cause than more complex knowledge.

More importantly, the Caldwell clearly expressed their willingness to work with the local community on the issue of drainage. Caldwell Chief Larry Johnson said that he wrote a letter to the municipality in 1999 regarding drainage and also published it on the Caldwell website. In it, he assured locals that the Caldwell would respect drainage rules:

> We recognize that drainage is an important issue in low-lying agricultural country. We are prepared to enter into an agreement with the municipal government to provide for the identification and management of existing drainage works and the construction or alteration of future drainage works. Basically, we should agree that existing drainage will be maintained — and that where drainage works on our reserve, the responsibility for maintaining them is ours, financially as well as legislatively. Any proposed changes in drainage should be matters in which we would give each other notice ... as provided in the present provincial Drainage Act. We would like to see an effective, informal dispute resolution process, accessible to individuals as well as governments, as well as a clear environmental review of any proposed changes.
>
> We believe that, with the proper facts and a clear understanding of our intention, we can deal with these issues. We hope that this letter will clarify our views and will provide the basis for an understanding between our two governments. Our Council is a government, one that is recognized in Canadian federal legislation as well as in the Canadian constitution. We have the authority to make laws for our people and our land. We intend to do so — and we intend to do so in a way that also respects the rights of our neighbours. (Johnson 1999)

What is striking about the letter is the willingness of the Caldwell to work with the local community to resolve any drainage issues. Not a single CKCN member mentioned this readiness to negotiate and compromise. When I later asked CKCN members about the chief's letter and the federal rules, they replied that they did know about his supposed readiness to compromise, but even if he was ready, it would make no difference to their fears. Even if they made an agreement with this chief, they said, the agreement could change in the future with a different chief. They therefore refused to treat the Caldwell as a legitimate government with the authority, autonomy, and responsibility to make and fulfill agreements.

Perhaps one key to this response is also apparent in the letter. The end of the letter makes clear that the Caldwell, even as they compromise, assert collective autonomy as a separate government. They claim firmly that "our Council is a government, one that is recognized in Canadian federal legislation as well as in the Canadian constitution." The Caldwell assume the authority of a government, stating, "We have the authority to make laws for our people and our land. We intend to do so — and we intend to do so in a way that also respects the rights of our neighbours."

I would argue that the drainage is not the fundamental problem. Instead, it may be that although the letter expresses a willingness to compromise, it does not relinquish authority or collective autonomy. I wondered why most CKCN members repeatedly complained about their lack of control over the drainage issue when it seemed, according to official statements, the problem had been solved long ago. The Caldwell were required — and willing — to follow provincial guidelines. The argument about drainage is actually about who controls the law and who has autonomy and legitimacy. Members of CKCN refused to accept that there could be responsible interaction and compromise between the Caldwell and the government. By doing so, they made the collective autonomy of the Caldwell, on the one hand, and their individual autonomy, the autonomy of their community, and the autonomy of Canada, on the other hand, competitive rather than interactive and relational. By ignoring the possibility of making an agreement, and by constructing the Caldwell as an illegitimate government that would not fulfill its agreements, they ultimately devalued and disallowed any version of collective autonomy the Caldwell may claim. In turn, they continued to characterize the Caldwell as dangerous, undependable outsiders who would threaten their local community. By constructing the Caldwell as an illegitimate government, or simply as a group of individuals who could not be trusted, they dismissed the Caldwell's ability to be autonomous. They represented the Caldwell as asserting a version of collective autonomy inherently in opposition to, even a threat to, community norms and individual rights and autonomy. They perceive

Aboriginal collective autonomy as incompatible with the ideals of personhood in the community.

Personhood, Individualism, and Competing Autonomies

The normative model of personhood that excludes the Caldwell and Cayuga is surprisingly similar to Lockean and neoliberal ideals of the autonomous individual. Individuals are "expected to lead their own life, without being dependent on anyone else. They take responsibility for themselves, for their labour, their conscience, and their reason. They own themselves ... There is not much room for those who are characterized as irrational, vulnerable or uncivilized" (Brace 2004, 6). For Locke, how a person made use of his life, liberty, and possessions is the "outcome of a choice and connected to the process of development of an individual character" (ibid., 27-28). This means that individuals should choose to improve property and themselves, thus becoming "active proprietors" of their person and their property (ibid.). Individual autonomy is based on consent, morality, and self-development. Property is therefore tied to a notion of human beings, particularly men, "as masters of themselves" (ibid., 5). Through ideals of personal self-mastery and self-propriety, property is intrinsically connected to specific ideals of personhood (and masculinity).

This norm, as I discuss below, is based on a complex interpretation and assertion of many of the assumptions that now underlie liberal (neo-conservative) property and economic ideals. Most property theory takes this version of personhood for granted and assumes a universal normative subjectivity, which is, of course, not universally shared. Although this body of assumptions emerged from a long line of thinkers in the past, I suggest, based on my fieldwork, that this framework and others like it are actively mobilized today in judgments about the desirable and "natural" properties of personhood. For example, a member of CKCN in Chatham-Kent argued that when Aboriginal land was taken, it was somehow voluntary, based on his model of active, decision-making personhood. John argued, "If the Indians didn't think it was the right thing to do at the time, why did they participate? I completely believe that you are in charge of your own destiny. That's all there is to it. If you're being abused by society ... luckily I've never been in such a situation, but I'd like to think if it got to the point where I just couldn't deal with it anymore, then I'm going to move on. Not sit around and continue to be abused." I said to John, "some people would say that, in fact, Aboriginal people at that point didn't have a choice." He replied:

> No, I don't believe that. That's the victim mentality that a lot of people use, and that I think, in a country that's as social as Canada, is overused. The whole mentality of the victim is wrong. In this world, this day and age, the twenty-first century, you have choices ... In the past maybe it was true. I like to think if I get so unhappy with the way things are — if I don't like it — that I have control over my life, am not going to try to go to society and say, "I'm a victim. You owe me this, you owe me that." (John, interview with author, 2002)

John's discomfort with the so-called victim mentality is based on a normative model of personhood, within which individuals should be independent, self-interested, decision-making, and active. The victim mentality was also attacked by another member of CKCN. David suggested that

> there are people [who] come to this country with nothing in their pockets, nothing, and they've been very successful because they weren't always trying to blame somebody else for their problems. They said, "I got a problem, I got to fix it." The Natives continually try to blame us for their problems, and I don't think we're their problem; they're their own problem. Until they're willing to constructively try to make it in society, they're always going to have a problem. And it doesn't matter how much money we pour down the drain to them, it ain't going to fix it. (David, interview with author, 2003)

David's concern proposes a similarly normative model of hard-working, active, non-passive participants in society.

Underlying these ideals of personhood are specific notions of culture that define collective cultural differences as acceptable as long as only one culture and set of laws has priority. Mary, a member of the UCE, argued: "If they want to buy land here and farm it, or live there, or whatever they want to do with it, they should have to follow the same rules and regulations that we have to. It's the only fair way to do it" (Mary, interview with author, 2005). James agreed: "We have Amish and Mennonites. They follow their traditions. The Italians, they can follow their traditions. They have their food and their ceremonies and everything, and we're not going to keep the Indians from doing that" (James, interview with author, 2005).

In this model, collective traditions are acceptable, yet only up to a certain point (Mackey 2002). Collective traditions are still seen as a holdover from the past and are therefore potentially intolerable (even dangerous or savage) if they cross the line to archaic or uncivilized. Betty Miller argued:

> You know, everyone was indigenous to some place, and how far back do you go? The reality is, folks, that we're all here. This is 2002, and how far do you want to take your culture? Do you want to take it back to human sacrifices and cannibalism? [I once read] a first-hand account of a French missionary, and he talks about the Onondagas taking a Cayuga maiden as a sacrifice gift ... So, just how far back do you want to take your culture? What is that going to include? Do you get my drift? They say they want to practise their culture again. Well, it's fine to practise your beliefs, but just how far back? ... Do you want to do sacrifices again? What do you want to do? (Betty, interview with author, 2005)

Ultimately, the argument is for a single, unitary, modern, rational, civilized, national culture based on one's own culture. James interjected, "You can't have two cultures in one. You've got to be all one, with the same rules and regulations for everybody." Betty pitched in, "Like the pledge of the allegiance says, 'One nation under God, individuals'" (James and Betty, interview with author, 2005).

In this case, official US nationalist ideology and ritual legitimates the idea of rational cultural superiority and singularity. It is significant that James recites the Pledge of Allegiance incorrectly. Instead of saying, "One nation under God, indivisible," he mistakenly says, "One nation under God, individual." This slip makes sense within the modern neoliberal logic of property. Mark offered an example of this conception of the modern individual in his interview. As we were concluding, he summarized his views as a supporter of CKCN:

> I have two thoughts. The first one is, stop trying to solve problems in the year 2001 with solutions ... created in the 1700s. It's a different time; it's a different economy ... Stop trying to solve land claims with land ... It's an absolutely archaic system: the reserve system. Stop trying to solve land claims with land. The other point ... is, trust the individual. Again, not only has the economy changed dramatically over the last two hundred years, but so has people's sense of

> themselves: self-determination. We are much more aware of who we are and where we fit in society, and we're much more connected now to the rest of the world than we used to be. So start trusting the individual. If we have an outstanding claim, and 150 people are equally entitled to it, then treat them as equals: treat them as individuals. Show them that respect. So those would be my two thoughts. Stop trying to settle land claims with land, and trust the individual, empower the individual ... Pay off their mortgage. Put their kids through school. Be innovative; be creative; be supportive. Don't be archaic. (Mark, interview by author, 2002)

The autonomous, rights-bearing individual is proposed as the only rational and modern solution. There is only one permissible version of autonomy, and it is singular. In terms of property, Mark's definition of autonomy reflects an ideal of a despotic dominion in that each individual has his or her own defined property and rights with clearly defined boundaries and control. The problem is that Aboriginal people are inevitably required to assimilate to this normative ideal.

My point is that many present-day responses to land rights use older common-sense frameworks that likely make sense conceptually to people in liberal, individualist social contexts. However, these same frameworks also reproduce, in fundamental ways, the same problematic constructions of Aboriginal peoples and their cultures that we find in Locke's writings. Locke saw Aboriginal people as individuals who were entitled to equality as individuals but not entitled to collective political protection. Like the people I interviewed, Locke constructed Aboriginal societies as irrational, underdeveloped collectivities. They were not capable of collective autonomy in his view.

Although the individualist solutions voiced by Mark draw on older frameworks, they also reflect the changing and more globalized world in which neoliberal ideals of autonomous individualism are being constructed (Martin 1997; Wright and Shore 2001a, 2001b). Individualism, according to Mark, will empower; it will be innovative, creative, and supportive, not archaic. The fundamental assumption is, however, that to become equal and modern, one must become individual. Individualism is framed as a solution, and underlying it is a sense of entitlement to define others (on one's own terms) as less valuable and less progressive. Not coincidentally, in the process of defining indigenous autonomy as less modern, Mark also rejects indigenous people's collective claims for land and collective versions of autonomy. For Locke then, and for UCE and CKCN supporters now, it is not contrary to the ideals of equality to take or keep indigenous land in the name of individualism and progress.

In summary, global rights frameworks, when enacted in specific contexts concerning Aboriginal property rights claims, are seen by some non-Aboriginal people as disruptions to embedded racial and economic hierarchies that have long been viewed as eternal and commonsensical (Hage 2000; Mackey 2002). Bitter conflicts about property can be seen on one level as resistance and adjustment to what appears to be a new global property regime and, thus, a new, unexpected equation of power. People draw on older versions of autonomy to discount a supposedly new globalized version of human rights that includes self-determination for formerly colonized peoples. These rights are seen as unequal because they challenge or are seen to be in conflict with individualistic versions of autonomy non-Aboriginal people have had in the past. In the process, opponents of Aboriginal claims implicitly construct inferior and superior cultures and values.

Attitudes of cultural arrogance and superiority assumed by opponents of land rights assume the necessity of the subordination of Aboriginal world views and practices to so-called normal Western world views. Such attitudes, when enacted in this specific context of friction, create a situation in which the individual autonomy of non-Aboriginal people and the aspirations for collective autonomy articulated by their Aboriginal neighbours are placed in competition with each other. The individualist position appears to be anchored in making distinctions between those who are superior and those who are inferior.

Emergent Relational Autonomies

Are there other ways to imagine human-territorial relationships within nation-states and around the globe that do not reproduce problematic assumptions about personhood, property, and autonomy? Taiaiake Alfred (1999), Michael Asch (1984, 1992a, 1992b, 1994, 2002), Cole Harris (2002), Patricia Monture-Angus (1998), and innumerable other scholars and activists have argued for years that we need different ways of thinking about relationships between Aboriginal and non-Aboriginal peoples. They suggest that a first step is to recognize and value Aboriginal world views and not subsume Aboriginal life ways into Western and national frameworks of superiority.[9] Many Aboriginal people claim that control over their land is one essential aspect of asserting and developing autonomy and that land must therefore be more equitably shared or divided.

My examination of these encounters has so far focused mostly on anti-land-rights activists who propose a model of competing autonomies. During my fieldwork, however, alternative visions and practices of what I call relational autonomy emerged from the Onondaga Nation, near Syracuse, New York, just next door to the Cayuga.[10] In March 2005, the Onondaga Nation asserted its rights to a wide stretch of land in New York State. The difference between their claim and others is that the Onondaga did not frame it as a land claim but rather as a land rights action, through which they explicitly sought to work with other people in the community to improve human and environmental relations.

The Complaint for Declaratory Judgment begins with an inclusive and relational approach: "The Onondaga people wish to bring about a healing between themselves and all others who live in this region that has been the homeland of the Onondaga nation since the dawn of time" (Onondaga Nation 2005). According to the Onondaga, instead of opposing local residents and competing for land within a Western property paradigm, they hope to reach out and make links but retain autonomy: "We want justice. New York State took our land illegally and needs to acknowledge this injustice and our rights to the land. But we will not displace any of our neighbors — the Onondaga know all too well the pain of being forced to leave our homes and do not wish that on anyone" (ibid.).

From the outset of the action, the Onondaga refused Western legal concepts of property in which people own land as an object: "The Nation and its people have a unique spiritual, cultural, and historic relationship with the land, which is embodied in Gayanashagowa, the Great Law of Peace. This relationship goes far beyond federal and state legal concepts of ownership, possession, or other legal rights. The people are one with the land and consider themselves stewards of it" (Onondaga Nation 2005). The Onondaga believe that a broader collaborative project has emerged from this relationship to the land and that they have an important role: "It is the duty of the Nation's leaders to work for a healing of this land, to protect it, and to pass it on to future generations. The Onondaga Nation brings this action on behalf of its people in the hope that it may hasten the process of reconciliation and bring lasting justice, peace, and respect among all who inhabit this area" (ibid.).

The idea of labour proposed by the Onondaga is important because ideas about the relationship between property, personhood, and labour play a central role in the frameworks anti-land-rights activists use to delegitimize Aboriginal claims. In contrast to the Lockean notion that productive individual labour is about improving and developing property and land, labour here is both collective and protective. As a collective, the Onondaga are "one" with the land and are caretakers responsible for healing, protecting, and passing it on to future generations. Part of the productive labour of healing and caring is bringing about reconciliation "among all who inhabit this area" (Onondaga 2005). This is autonomy defined in more relational and responsible rather than rights-based terms.

The Onondaga certainly use Western frameworks of rights, but their claim is neither individualistic nor for humans alone. It is integral to their role as stewards and peacemakers. Sidney Hill, *Tadodaho* (spiritual leader) of the Onondaga Nation Council of Chiefs, states, "We intend to use our rights to this land as a legal and moral force for the environment and the Earth. We want to see polluted areas cleaned up and we want to protect those areas not yet defiled for generations to come" (NOON 2005). Again, the goal of legal and moral rights is not to separate and create boundaries but to be inclusive: "All people of Central New York can benefit from this action" (ibid.).

The Onondaga Nation has also distanced itself from other oppositional land rights cases in the area through its collaborative approach. Hill continues, "The Onondaga will not settle for methods used to resolve other Native American nations' land rights actions ... We do not want to open or operate casinos. Our values do not allow for the harm that casino gambling can cause. We want this action resolved in a way that preserves, not disrupts, the social fabric of our Nation as well as that of our neighbors" (NOON 2005). By refusing casino gambling on moral grounds, the Onondaga are, in some sense, more in line with their opponents, UCE.

The Onondaga also argued against government programs and policies. Hill stated, "The State has used [casinos] to attempt to divide us," and "our land and health have been disregarded by the Albany politicians for far too long" (NOON 2005). The members of UCE have consistently argued that the real problem is politicians. The Onondaga have therefore found a way to appeal to the deep anti-government sentiment that fuels UCE and other groups. They have created a situation in which the apparently oppositional interests and autonomies of Onondaga and UCE are parallel and related.

The Onondaga have also found a way to align themselves with the problems of other local people, such as unemployment and pollution. A major problem in Syracuse, New York, is the pollution left behind by large factories as business moves flexibly in the global economy to sites where labour and resources are cheaper. The polluted remains of industrial development are concentrated on Lake Onondaga, one of the most polluted lakes in the world and the most sacred site of the Onondaga. Perhaps one of the Onondaga's most unusual moves is that they include large corporations in their claim. The suit names as defendants the State of New York, the City of Syracuse, Onondaga County, and five corporations named for their environmental damage, including Honeywell International, Hansen Aggregates, Clark Concrete Company, and Valley Realty (Onondaga Nation 2005).

The Onondaga's commitment to the environment and to their neighbours goes further. As part of their stewardship, they have written environmental reports (see the official website) and are now collaborating with community and university sponsors to present an ambitious year-long and widely advertised educational series titled "Onondaga Land Rights and Our Common Future." Events explore topics such as "Environmental Stewardship: Finding Common Ground between Traditional Environmental Knowledge and 'Modern' Environmental Science" and "Why Native American Sovereignty Makes Sense for All of Us." Notions of individual autonomy and rights have been replaced by an idea of relational responsibility for the land and one another.

Whether this approach to resolving Aboriginal–non-Aboriginal relations concerning land will be fruitful is not yet known. In comparison to local reaction to other land claims in upper New York State, the response from local communities has been positive. There has been virtually no significant resistance from people who oppose land rights. Perhaps this lack of resistance has resulted in the Onondaga's tendency to frame their autonomy, territory, and relationships with neighbours in a non-oppositional manner. Their autonomy is relational, defined in a manner that goes beyond embedded ideas about territory and human relationships within Western property regimes.

Conclusion

This chapter explores how processes of globalization have been enabled and enacted through practical encounters that involve material resources (Tsing 2005, 1) and are informed by larger global ideologies and capitalist processes. I examine how universals, particularly concepts of property and personhood, played out in struggles over Aboriginal rights and property in two settler nations. These sites of encounter are productive because they allow us to see both the limits and the possibilities of global processes in specific contexts. Dichotomous views of anti-globalization — as either resistance or accommodation — do not help to explain the complexity of these processes. Universal categories, as we have seen, are re-hashed and reinforced in new contexts, but they are also transformed.

Tsing's metaphor of global encounters as sites of friction is apt here. She uses the concept of friction to avoid straightforward dichotomous understandings of globalization. The metaphor of friction suggests the effects of multiple forces interacting with one another, with sometimes unforeseen consequences. In the sites of friction I examine here, all sides drew on older universals and specific cultural traditions and then mobilized these frameworks creatively in new and changing environments to invent and defend their versions of autonomy. Neither the anti-land-rights activists nor the Cayuga, Caldwell, and Onondaga nations purely resisted or accommodated global capitalism and global ideologies. All sides rejected some aspects of globalization and used others to bolster and seek authority and autonomy in a complex context as they struggled to make their meanings stick in the messy day-to-day world of practical encounters.

chapter 8

Plant Genetic Resources, Farmers' Rights, and the Globalization of Intellectual Property Rights: Reinforcing Asymmetries in Autonomies

William D. Coleman and Austina J. Reed

In 2001, the international community of states reached agreement on a treaty that brought the concept of farmers' rights formally into international law, the International Treaty on Plant Genetic Rights in Food and Agriculture (ITPGRFA). These rights seek to protect collective intellectual property associated with traditional farming practices, that is, the planting and saving of seeds to improve yields, strengthen welcome characteristics of plants, and eliminate other characteristics deemed less useful, if not harmful, by farmers. Behind the concept of farmers' rights is an approach to conservation, knowledge sharing, and innovation that recognizes plant genetic resources as a common heritage of humankind and a global public good. Concerted promotion of farmers rights in the international domain began in 1983 and was led by some developing countries, the United Nations' Food and Agriculture Organization (FAO), and non-governmental organizations. They were concerned that a mounting interest in defining property rights for plant genetic resources because of the rapidly expanding agricultural biotechnology industry would overturn the idea of common heritage. Not only would the traditional farming practices of peasants and small farmers be threatened, but also biological diversity in agriculture would diminish over the medium to long term and have disturbing consequences on world agriculture.

As the chapters by Mollett and Gorman in this volume show, steps to enclose biological diversity, living organisms, and what might be termed traditional and indigenous knowledge of plants and their properties intensified significantly in the late 1970s. Research advances in biotechnology had significantly raised the importance and value of genetic structures themselves (Parry 2000, 2004). The push by biotechnology and pharmaceutical corporations to shift the site for international debate and decision making on these matters from the World Intellectual Property Organization (WIPO) to the trade regime was successful in the Uruguay Round. In particular, section 27(3) of the Agreement on Trade-Related Aspects of Intellectual Property Rights (TRIPS) confirmed steps already taken by the United States and western European countries to patent plant varieties or to set up *sui generis* systems of plant breeders' rights. Members of the WTO were now required to make provisions for one or both of these forms of intellectual property rights in domestic law in order to be in compliance with TRIPS. Over the same period, the notion of plant genetic resources (PGRs) as a common heritage of humankind was qualified significantly in the Convention on Biological Diversity (CBD) signed in 1993, thereby making PGRs subject to the sovereignty of nation-states.

For states in the Global South in particular, these changes in the trade, intellectual property, and biological diversity international regimes had mixed implications. On the one side, as the sites of the largest resources of biological diversity and thus plant genetic resources, the enclosure of these resources in the TRIPS agreement raised issues of biopiracy and appropriate compensation for appropriation of these resources. On the other side, the sovereignty provision of the CBD gave them some policy space to demand and shape processes for compensation. The ITPGRFA is a potential additional tool in that it could make the implementation of farmers' rights, however qualified, a responsibility of nation-states. Whether state sovereignty will be adequate to ensure ample diversity in plant genetic resources for future generations is unclear. Similarly, it is also unclear whether farmers' traditional knowledge in agriculture gained from small-farm agriculture will be protected and will remain available for humankind long into the future. The competing industrial model of agriculture is increasingly dominant not only in the wealthier states but also in large agriculture-exporting states outside the Organisation for Economic Co-operation and Development (OECD) such as Brazil, Argentina, and South Africa. This model has, in effect, been entrenched in global trade law in the WTO Agreement on Agriculture (Coleman 2009). In short, it is doubtful whether the collective autonomy over food and food security hoped for by states after the end of colonization and by farmers within those states will be realized.

Plant Genetic Resources: Towards Commodification

Until the middle half of the nineteenth century, plant genetic resources were developed and improved by farmers themselves. They would plant seeds, cultivate and harvest the plants, and collect seeds to be planted the following year. The collection of seeds was a careful process. Farmers observed that some plants were taller, more productive, more resistant to cold or heat, needed less water, or had other favourable traits. Those traits most valued by the farmers, given the particularities of their locality, guided the selection of seeds. Farmers would sometimes share or trade these seeds with one another. Fields were thus composed of landraces, an early cultivated form of a crop species that had evolved from a wild population and was composed generally of a heterogeneous mixture of genotypes. "Landraces form a major component of farmers' PGRs in gene bank collections, and this material provides the backbone of agriculture and plant breeding today. In addition, landraces are often rooted in local communities' culture and are often identified as part of cultural heritage" (Salazar, Louwaars, and Visser 2007, 1515). Over time, grasses that originally had a few tiny seeds were cross-bred with grasses producing bigger seeds or grains suitable for eating, grinding, and storing. Other commodities such as maize were developed from tiny plants that hardly resembled the large plants with ample ears found today. In short, the genetic resources in those plants are the product of constant innovation, sharing, and trading among farmers over millennia; their seeds concentrate the wisdom and hard work of millions of people over time.

In the 1920s, the Soviet botanist N.I. Vavilov identified a number of areas in the world particularly important for the development of plant genetic resources. For example, wheat — now a central crop in the United States, Canada, western Europe, Russia, Ukraine, India, Australia, and many other parts of the world — was first developed and domesticated in southwest Asia (Diamond 1999, 100). The coffee bean was nurtured in Ethiopia, corn or maize in Central America, the potato in the Andes region of South America, and rice in China. Relatively few plants originated in North America (blueberry, cranberry, Jerusalem artichoke, and sunflower) or northern Europe (currant, oats, raspberry, and rye) (Kloppenburg 2004, 48). By and large, the germplasm for the most important food crops in the world came principally from farmers' and indigenous peoples' continuous experimentation over time in the Global South or developing countries. (*Germplasm* refers to that part of the germ cell that bears the factors determining the transmission of characters from parent to offspring and is itself transmitted unchanged from generation to generation.)

As people moved from one part of the world to another, they took seeds with them and, as transportation technologies improved, the distances travelled by seeds increased. So the wheat developed in southwest Asia moved eastward to India with the Mughals and other invaders and northward and westward to Europe. When Columbus returned to the Americas on his second voyage, he carried wheat, olives, chickpeas, and sugar cane (Kloppenburg 2004, 155). (When he had returned to Europe from his first voyage, he had brought with him the seeds of the maize plant, long developed by indigenous peoples in the Americas.) As Europeans colonized what Crosby (1986, 3) calls the neo-Europes (Australia, New Zealand, parts of South America, Canada, and the United States), they brought with them their own plant varieties. Over time, the colonists, mainly farmers, took advantage of traditional knowledge accumulated by indigenous peoples and continued the processes of innovation and adaptation to ensure the new varieties would survive in new environments. These same areas now number among the world's dominant agricultural producers.

During these years, plant varieties, wherever they were developed in the world, were treated as if they were the common heritage of humankind (Brush 2004, 223). "Common heritage refers to the treatment of genetic resources as belonging to the public domain and not owned or otherwise monopolized by a single group or interest" (Brush 2007, 1499). Admittedly, the transfer of plant genetic resources was somewhat asymmetric; much of the wealth in plant genetic resources moved from resource-rich centres of diversity in the colonized world to resource-poor centres dominated by the major European imperial powers. They set up collection centres, often in the form of botanical gardens, which served to regulate the flow of collected materials as they were recirculated and redeployed on a global scale for imperial interests (Parry 2000, 380). The germplasm "contained in the resource has the public good characteristic of being 'nonrival' ... meaning that information itself is not diminished by its use. Maintaining crop and animal diversity therefore produces a public good ... with long-lasting effects over generations" (Eyzaguirre, De Grigorio, and Meinzen-Dick 2007, 1482). Seen as a free good, germplasm was appropriated at little cost. Although it amounted to billions of dollars in value over time, farmers and indigenous peoples in the source regions of the globe received no direct remuneration (Kloppenburg 2004, 15).

Within traditional farming practices, it was difficult for capitalists to commodify seeds, particularly in the absence of intellectual property regulation. Plant breeders could work to perfect a plant that could grow in a given climate and meet expectations for yield and quality. They could then sell the seeds to farmers, advertising the advantageous traits of the new plant. Farmers could buy the seeds once, gather the seeds at the time of harvest, and replant them the next year. Moreover, they could begin to experiment with the new seeds, mixing them with some of their own seeds, to see if they could do better still. Under such circumstances, the breeders' seeds could hardly support a profitable business.

As the neo-Europes were settled and grew in the nineteenth century, and as the possibility for trade in agricultural commodities became more promising, governments in these countries saw some advantage in sponsoring public research to improve their farmers' crops. Taking the lead in this kind of public research was the United States. When Congress created the United States Department of Agriculture (USDA) in 1862, it was mandated "to procure, propagate, and distribute among the people new and valuable seeds and plants" (Kloppenburg 2004, 59). In the same year, Congress authorized the founding of a number of land grant universities, which would grow to become important centres for research and development. Public laboratories working closely with the new universities sought to refine and improve seeds, while USDA employees, later to be called extension agents, lived and worked in the countryside and distributed them freely to farmers.

Improving seeds, however, required the continued procurement of landraces from other parts of the world with potentially useful characteristics for growth and survival in US conditions. To this end, the USDA set up the Section of Seed and Plant Introduction, whose staff of botanists was charged with identifying plant diseases and pests and then finding the germplasm needed to create new varieties to address such problems. Over the next quarter century, the section sponsored forty-eight expeditions all over the world to look for useful germplasm (Kloppenburg 2004, 67). These samples were available for the taking, with absolutely no compensation to the farmers whose work had produced the plants in the first place. Private breeders found it difficult to compete with the public breeding programs in the United States, neo-Europe, and western Europe. In 1934, for example, of the 128 wheat varieties in production in the United States, only 5 were from seed companies (ibid., 83).

This situation began to change with the development of hybrid corn plants. Shortly after the start of the twentieth century, drawing on Mendel's theories of genetics, botanists began to experiment with hybrids in an effort to grow new varieties in US laboratories. Over the first twenty years of the century, botanists and plant breeders worked to create and improve a hybrid version based on inbreeding among plants and then crossing the inbred plants. The results of these efforts culminated in seeds with two properties: the hybrid plants delivered significant increases in yields, and the seeds produced from these hybrids were ineffective in the following year. They could not be saved and reused for planting the next year's crops. Since the increased yields outweighed the added costs of buying seeds each year, however, farmers readily adopted the new technology. Furthermore, since seeds were no longer suitable for replanting, they were more easily commodified. Private seed firms moved quickly into the field.

With the arrival of hybrids in the United States, US private breeders succeeded in convincing legislators to provide limited patent protection. Congress passed the Plant Patent Act in 1930, making it possible to patent asexually propagated species such as most fruits and nuts and some flowers. Excluded from the Act were patents for sexually propagated species such as corn and wheat, as well as tuber species such as the potato. This exclusion was a concession to the demands of farmers, who could still follow traditional seed-saving practices for any of these new plants. Patents under the Plant Protection Act, however, differed from the industrial patent in one important way: plant breeders were not required to show that a new species was superior to an existing one.

Developments in Europe took a different path. Discussions at the United International Bureaux for the Protection of Intellectual Property noted the difficulty that new plant varieties might have in meeting the invention criteria required for industrial patents: as soon as conditions change — for example, in climate or soil properties — the plant itself changes from its original state. This instability contravenes a usual condition for a patent, the requirement that "any person skilled in the art should be able to carry out the invention, without having to do further inventive work" (Blakeney 2005, 370). So the Europeans moved towards a system of plant breeders' rights and plant variety protection (ibid. 2005, 370-77). The breeder of a new variety could apply for the right to be the sole seller under a "fancy name" (one that is unique to that new variety and thus links the new plant variety to a single breeder or group of breeders) (UPOV 1987, 68).

After the Second World War, and with considerable assistance from ASSINSEL (International Association of Plant Breeders for the Protection of Plant Varieties), five western European states — Belgium, France, the Federal Republic of Germany, Italy, and the Netherlands — agreed to the International Convention for the Protection of New Varieties of Plants (UPOV) in 1961. This agreement departed from the US legislation in three key respects: (1) it was not limited to asexually producing plants, (2) protection was to be gained either through a patent or a special title of protection developed by the country itself (later to be called a sui generis system), and (3) the new variety had to be "clearly distinguishable by one or more important characteristics from any other variety whose existence is a matter of common knowledge at the time when protection is applied for" (UPOV 1987, article 6). This latter requirement meant that a new variety had to improve on an existing variety, in some clear way, if it was to be recognized under the UPOV (Leskien and Flitner 1997, 52).

The European agreement, in turn, spurred activity among US plant breeders, who succeeded in pressuring Congress to pass a new Plant Variety Protection Act (PVPA) in 1970. The new law was more comprehensive than the 1930 legislation, covering asexual, sexual, and tuber propagation. It did not include, however, the idea of quality improvement found in the European legislation, leading Kloppenburg (2004, 140) to call it a marketing rather than a research Act. With the UPOV agreeing that the United States could keep its weaker patenting criteria, Congress revised the PVPA in 1981 to harmonize it with the UPOV, and the United States joined the international convention. This step triggered the global extension of developed countries' notions of intellectual property rights related to plant genetic resources.

Advancing Commodification: The Advent of Plant Biotechnology

Most agree that the crucial first step in the development of biotechnology was the description of the DNA structure published by James Watson and Francis Crick in 1953. In the subsequent quarter century, rapid progress occurred in the study of DNA and the enzymes present in cells that are linked to DNA. In the 1970s, scientists reported that they had constructed a DNA molecule by cutting viral and bacterial sequences with restriction enzymes and recombining them. They also discovered that the reconstructed molecule could be recombined with small self-replicating DNA molecules from bacteria called plasmids, which could then be reintroduced into bacterial cells, where they would replicate. Finally, scientists developed methods for determining the sequence of base pairs in a DNA molecule (Halford 2003, 18). With these discoveries, scientists now had the tools to cut DNA molecules at specific points and glue them back together in different combinations to make new molecules (i.e., recombinant DNA technology). The availability of these technologies led to a strong resurgence in the collection of biological materials as the agriculture, pharmaceutical, and cosmetics industries became increasingly biotechnology dependent (Parry 2000, 381).

The principal focus in agriculture was the development of plants engineered to resist pests or viruses and to tolerate some herbicides. These new varieties were tried and tested in the laboratory in the 1980s, field tested in the early 1990s, and released for commercial use in the mid-1990s. Four highly traded commodities now account for approximately 99 percent of commercially grown, genetically modified (GM) crops: soybeans, maize, canola, and cotton. Of these crops, soybeans lead in the number of hectares sown, accounting for 52 percent in 2009, followed by maize (31 percent), cotton (12 percent), and canola (5 percent). The United States was the leading country by far, accounting for 47.8 percent of the global total hectares, followed by Brazil (16.0), Argentina (15.0), India (6.3), Canada (6.1), China (2.8), Paraguay (1.6), and South Africa (1.5) (ISAAA 2010).

Two discourses have emerged regarding this technology and its contribution to agriculture. Those who favour the technology argue that it is a more precise method for plant development. Rather than the mixing of tens of thousands of genes found in conventional plant-breeding methods, single genes can be transferred using recombinant DNA technologies. They add that it is faster and more powerful compared to traditional techniques because it permits the movement of genetic information across species. They stress that the nature and safety of the protein produced by a gene can be studied before the gene is used in a GM program. Hence, they argue that the new commodities are safe (Paarlberg 2001, 1-2; Halford 2003, 37-38). One of the primary challenges facing these programs is more significant investments of time and money. Accordingly, proponents stress how innovative and research-and-development intensive the technology is and will continue to be and that developers need intellectual property protection to recoup their costs. Without this protection, they argue, the progress made thus far with the technology and through the GM program cannot be continued at its current pace.

Scientists who are concerned about the effects of this technology offer a counter discourse that takes issue with the notion of precision. They question the so-called central dogma in genetic science that came from Crick and Watson: "the premise that an organism's genome — its total complement of genes — should fully account for its characteristic assemblage of inherited traits" (Commoner 2003, 1). Behind this premise is the idea that genes "have unique, absolute, and universal control over the totality of inheritance in all forms of life" (ibid., 2). This proposition came into serious question when the Human Genome Project reported that humans only have about thirty thousand genes, close to the same amount as a mustard seed and far below the expected number based on the number of human proteins and inherited traits. The idea that one gene could give rise to multiple proteins has challenged the precision argument used by plant biotechnology corporations. It is becoming increasingly apparent that successful protein manufacture (the key to changing a trait) requires the involvement of more than one gene (Dutfield 2003, 163). If one gene can give rise to multiple variants of an intended protein, or even to proteins bearing little relationship to the original, one can no longer assume that a bacterial gene for an insecticidal protein in a given plant will produce precisely that protein and nothing else.

Moreover, some scientists argue that there is an important element of unpredictability to the technology: it is too soon to know the effects of gene splicing on the other genetic properties of the plant. Drawing on work by Robert Goodman, a plant pathologist, and Richard Lewontin, the eminent geneticist, Kloppenburg (2004, 311) notes that once a gene is inserted in a new species, it is no longer under normal control: "Lack of normal control could result in the production of new substances or in unexpected changes in the way the organism functions or interacts with other organisms and the environment." Evidence suggests that these effects could be harmful to human or animal health (Smith 2003, chaps. 1 and 2).

The development of recombinant DNA technologies for the genetic modification of plants has had three important consequences for the commodification of plant varieties and plant genetic resources. First, by altering its genetic structure, those developing a new plant variety may apply for patent protection for the discovery. The court ruling in the famous *Chakrabarty* case in 1980, discussed by Gorman in this volume, opened this path to scientists and corporations using these technologies in the United States.

The second consequence relates to how the information extracted from these resources is defined, handled, and catalogued. Biotechnologies have changed the commodity form of plant genetic resources from a corporeal one to a more informational one. Traditionally, collectors would search out cognate plants suitable for crossbreeding *within* a plant variety; the plants themselves or their seeds would then be collected and transported to another place. If the plants died or the seeds failed to grow in the new place, the information was lost. Parry (2000, 382; 2004, 32) notes that these parameters have now all but collapsed. With the advent of DNA technologies, potential collectors have the capability to extract materials from minute samples of plant, animal, or human tissue. Moreover, improvements in cryogenic storage technologies, cell preservation, and tissue biopsy techniques have transformed the archiving process by demanding less space, making long-term storage more sustainable.

Finally, DNA can now be extracted from minute samples of tissue and sequenced, and the sequences themselves can be stored in genomic databases. Bodies can also be dissected and scanned to create new electronic archives of 3D digitalized images. Parry (2004, 32) concludes, "These new artefacts, whether corporeal or informational in form, are set to play a central role in re-writing the dynamics of biological exploitation as they have the ability to act as 'proxies' that can effectively stand in or 'represent' whole living organisms in their absence."

When these biological materials are translated wholly into informational form, they can be stored in large digitalized databases, permitting them to be globalized in ways that were previously impossible. As a result, property relations have changed (Parry 2004, 38). In contrast to biological materials that have traditionally been bought and sold outright or taken by those with the resources to transport them and preserve them, information can be given away and still owned. As Gorman notes in this volume, the informational form makes it difficult to exercise complete dominion over information-based products such as books, films, and computer games. But an important new form of ownership has emerged as corporations develop, maintain, and then license or make information in databases temporarily accessible for a price. The implications for developing countries interested in receiving some compensation or benefits from their plant genetic resources are profound and disturbing.

In summary, the biotechnology revolution has globalized plant genetic resources in two ways. First, the availability of a technology that opens up the possibility of transmitting genetic information from one living organism to another, irrespective of place and species, has created a more profound global space in which plant varieties can be designed. Second, the possibility of changing plant genetic resources from a corporeal or material form to an informational one has increased the global extensity of the impact of those resources and the velocity of their transmission in ways not seen before in human history.

Globalizing Intellectual Property Rights for Life Forms

In a matter of a few short decades, changes in biotechnology — specifically those making possible the creation of new plant varieties — have had a ripple effect on agriculture, resulting in a massive-scale commodification of seeds. This rapid increase in commodification has prompted large transnational life sciences corporations to pursue the globalization of intellectual property rights in international law. Even with the changes in technologies, many of these corporations, which are based predominantly in the advanced capitalist countries, have remained highly dependent on the diverse plant genetic resources found in parts of the Global South. If anything, the new technologies mean that mining these resources is even more profitable than before (Parry 2000). For these reasons, transnational life sciences corporations took the lead early in the Uruguay Round of international trade negotiations, arguing the case for including intellectual property protection of new life forms as part of an overall treaty on the regulation of trade.

They succeeded, perhaps beyond their wildest dreams. The World Trade Organization's TRIPs agreement required all WTO members to abide by a comprehensive set of intellectual property protection standards (Helfer 2004, 23), including providing patent protection for new life forms or for a system of plant variety protection that would have the same net effect as patent protection. Remarkably quickly, the intellectual property regime for plant genetic resources first instituted in leading developed countries has now become mandatory for developing countries, the home of the largest and most diverse plant genetic resources.

Section 27 of the agreement, which defines patentable subject matter, is the most crucial. Subsection 3(b) defines what can be excluded from patentability when it comes to living matter: "plants and animals other than micro-organisms, and essentially biological processes for the production of plants or animals other than non-biological and microbiological processes. However, members shall provide for the protection of plant varieties either by patents or by an effective *sui generis* system or by any combination thereof."

Although existing plants and animals cannot be patented, new plant varieties are eligible. If countries choose not to permit the patenting of plants, they must have an *effective* sui generis plant variety system in place. Furthermore, by making microorganisms and non-biological and microbiological processes patentable, the agreement extends intellectual property protection to the key tools of the biotechnology industry. If non-biological and microbiological processes have been used to create the new variety, these living products are likely patentable (Çoban 2004, 748; Plahe and Nyland 2003, 32). Clearly, section 27 marked a stronger and more expansive intellectual property regime for PGRs (Oguamanam 2006, 441). Yet the section does not specify any particular sui generis system and makes no reference to the UPOV system. Accordingly, there is some leeway in domestic law for the formulation of sui generis systems (Blakeney 2005, 382), a point to which we return below.

At the time the TRIPS agreement was being negotiated, developed countries were agreeing on changes to the UPOV. In particular, the corporations were not happy with article 5(3) of the convention because it left the door open for farmers to reuse and breed protected seeds from their fields and to exchange seeds informally "over the fence" as long as they did not do so commercially (Borowiak 2004, 518). They lobbied intensively against this article, and a new version of the UPOV was agreed upon in 1991. Through article 14(2), the new agreement closes the exemption for farmers found in the 1978 agreement (Blakeney 2005, 376). In addition, article 3(2) of the 1991 version requires all new signatories to the convention to abide by the revised version. Earlier adherents, mostly developed countries, had the option to keep the 1978 version or change to the 1991 one. As we note below, India subsequently overlooked this requirement.

Prior to the signing of the TRIPS agreement, virtually no developing country had permitted the patenting of life forms or had enacted plant variety protection legislation because the UPOV was confined largely to developed countries. Most developing countries are, however, members of the WTO. Intellectual property protection for life forms has therefore been globalized because all countries belonging to the WTO must enact legislation consistent with section 27 of the TRIPS agreement. They must protect their plant varieties either through patents or a sui generis system such as the UPOV or of their own design (Cullet 2004, 269; Leskien and Flitner 1997, chap. 5).

The TRIPS agreement therefore strengthens the hand of the rather narrow set of large OECD-based corporations that dominate the field of plant biotechnology. This group is "now dictating what kinds of research are permissible and which technologies and products should be available in the marketplace" (Kloppenburg 2004, 314). The Indian ecologist and human rights activist Vandana Shiva (2004, 665) summarizes the reaction of many in developing countries when she writes: "It is the ultimate enclosure of the commons and the public domain, both as domains of cultural and social creativity and productivity, and as domains where the public interest and human rights to basic needs such as health and nutrition are protected." In contrast, the transnational plant-breeding companies were clearly satisfied with the legislation. As their association, ASSINSEL, writes: "Without appropriate intellectual property protection, as soon as a promising new variety appears on the market, it will be bought up and multiplied by seed traders to sell on, or by farmers for their own use ... Breeding, in those circumstances, cannot be carried on as a profitable commercial activity" (Borowiak 2004, 520).

In the eyes of some, the TRIPS and UPOV agreements have only exacerbated the power imbalance between developing and developed countries and the life sciences corporations that the latter harbour. The millennia-long contributions of farmers and indigenous peoples to innovation and conservation of plant genetic resources go unrecognized in these agreements. "Rather than being subjects of agricultural innovation, farmers are made into discursive and regulatory objects" (Borowiak 2004, 520). Thomas (2002, 187) adds, "The fundamental concern of developing countries lies in built-in biases that accrue from the fact that patent protection must be extended to high-technology fields like biotechnology but that there are really at this time no practical answers for the protection of their traditional intellectual property rights." The appropriation and uncompensated taking of the traditional knowledge inherent in plant genetic resources have gone unaddressed (Anuradha 2001, 35).

The Struggle for Autonomy: Farmers' Rights

There are conflicting sites of authority in play when it comes to the control and regulation of plant genetic resources. First, the scope of state autonomy is changing. As we have demonstrated, the OECD countries succeeded in writing intellectual property rights into international economic law that they themselves had formed in the preceding century through legislation to protect patents and plant varieties. Many developing countries have responded by seeking to protect or expand their autonomy when it comes to the regulation of plant genetic resources by shifting the struggle to other sites of international authority. Helfer describes their strategy as regime shifting, that is, they are trying to pursue the struggle in other international legal regimes, specifically the Convention on Biological Diversity (CBD), negotiations for an international agreement based on the International Undertaking on Plant Genetic Resources (IU) of 1983, and WIPO (Helfer 2004). A campaign for global recognition of farmers' rights is emerging among poorer states and farmers' and peasants' movements as a means to engage alternative sites of authority.

Farmers' rights are, as we shall see, loosely defined and seek to acknowledge the contributions that traditional farmers make to the preservation and improvement of PGRs (Helfer 2004, 37). As such, they are also global in that they incorporate practices common to farmers all over the world (Oguamanam 2006, 443-44). We examine how the concept of farmers' rights has been incorporated into other international treaties: the IU, the CBD, and the International Treaty on Plant Genetic Resources for Food and Agriculture (ITPGRFA). We then conclude by examining how one state in particular, India, has struggled to find a balance between the conflicting ideas and policy goals found in these treaties. For developing countries such as India, the difficulty for their governments lies in fulfilling their responsibilities as members of the WTO and responding to the demands made by private sector companies for better intellectual property protection, while at the same time attempting to secure their own autonomy and the autonomy of their farmers and indigenous communities.

Farmers' Rights and International Law

The concept of farmers' rights emerged out of discussions at the United Nations Food and Agriculture Organization (FAO) in the late 1970s and early 1980s. These debates focused on asymmetries in a system that gave corporate breeders in the developed countries free access to germplasm created and nurtured by farmers in the developing world (Girsberger 1999, 186; Brush 2004, 247). At its twenty-second session in 1983, in response to an initiative by developing countries, the FAO adopted an International

Undertaking on Plant Genetic Resources (IU). Article 1 of the undertaking referred to the "universally accepted principle that plant genetic resources are a heritage of mankind and consequently should be available without restriction." Based on this principle, PGRs were to be globally conserved and shared when it came to plant breeding and other scientific purposes. It was eventually adhered to by 113 countries. Notable for their absence were the United States, Canada, Japan, China, Brazil, and Malaysia.

One of the first attempts to define farmers' rights emerged later in the decade when the FAO passed two resolutions to assist with interpreting the IU. Resolution 4/89 stipulated that plant breeders' rights as contained in an agreement such as the UPOV were not inconsistent with the undertaking, and it recognized the "enormous contribution that farmers of all regions have made to the conservation and development of plant genetic resources, which constitute the basis of plant production throughout the world, and which form the basis for the concept of Farmers' Rights." Resolution 5/89 then went on to define the term *farmers' rights:* "Farmers' Rights mean rights arising from the past, present and future contributions of farmers in conserving, improving, and making available plant genetic resources, particularly those in the centres of origin/diversity. These rights are vested in the International Community, as trustee for present and future generations of farmers, for the purpose of ensuring full benefits to farmers, and supporting the continuation of their contributions."

Farmers' rights differed from intellectual property rights in not being assigned to individuals but rather to the international community. This conceptual foundation challenged the individualist basis of intellectual property rights. By passing resolutions 4/89 and 5/89, the FAO was seeking to define a space where farmers would be considered on equal footing to plant breeders (Borowiak 2004, 523). In effect, the farmers' rights concept was an attempt to weaken, if not overturn, plant breeders' rights. Not surprisingly, the concept was resisted by developed countries, prolonging attempts to build an international treaty on PGRs based on the IU (Brush 2004, 248). At the same time, by not specifying what genetic materials were covered and who could claim ownership, the FAO definition was problematic from the start (Brush 2007, 1508).

Two years later, in 1991, the FAO sought to give developing countries more control by making common access subject to state sovereignty. Resolution 3/91 states: "The concept of mankind's heritage, as applied in the International Undertaking on Plant Genetic Resources, is subject to the sovereignty of the states over their plant genetic resources." With this resolution, states agreed that their sovereignty should take precedence when it came to controlling those plant genetic resources found within their borders. The gradual encroachment of intellectual property rights claims in their territories and the expanding use of genetic engineering, both of which signalled a potential windfall in benefits and royalties for the state, made the sovereignty principle crucial for securing more control over the use of plant genetic resources (Çoban 2004, 749). Signed in 1993, the CBD enshrined this sovereignty principle, while conceding that biological resources were a "common concern of humankind." This latter notion implied that states have a concomitant duty to foster the sustainable conservation and use of these resources (Cullet 2004, 268).

The introduction of the sovereignty principle provided an opening for developing countries to increase their autonomy when it came to intellectual property by devising their own means to manage the use of plant genetic resources and to demand benefits from their use. The common heritage principle had functioned first under imperialism in support of a major transfer of germplasm from the developing world to the developed countries. In turn, article 15 of the CBD required the "sharing in a fair and equitable way [of] the results of research and development and the benefits arising from the commercial and other utilization of genetic resources." It also called for developing countries to have "priority access on a fair and equitable basis" to biotechnologies "based upon" their genetic resources (G. Rose 2004, 75). These vague provisions, however, required further discussions and negotiations among states who had signed the CBD, which have continued without final resolution to the present day.

By not challenging the developing international law on intellectual property, the CBD sanctioned an emerging market-oriented regime for plant genetic resources (Kloppenburg 2004, 337-38; Brush 2004, 238-43). The shift to the sovereignty principle and the CBD's recognition of the validity of intellectual property rights in the area of genetic resources also led member countries of the CBD to call upon the FAO to resolve outstanding issues related to plant genetic resources. In 1994, the FAO initiated negotiations on a revision of the IU to bring it more in line with the CBD (Thomas 2002, 190; G. Rose 2004, 57-58). The negotiation of a revised undertaking was protracted and featured sharp debates between developed and developing countries over a series of issues. The negotiating parties finally agreed on a new treaty, the International Treaty on Plant Genetic Resources for Food and Agriculture (ITPGRFA), in November 2001. It finally came into force in 2003, after a sufficient number of countries ratified it.

The ITPGRFA is complex and provides for a multilateral access system for benefit sharing, among other things. Helfer (2005, 220) sees this aspect as significant: the treaty is "thus the first binding international agreement to expressly recognize the public domain status of certain genetic materials and to create a concrete, mandatory funding mechanism to preserve the global genetic commons." Like its predecessor, the IU, it invokes farmers' rights both in its Preamble and in article 9. Similar to the IU, the ITPGRFA begins in section 9.1 by recognizing the enormous contribution made by farmers and indigenous communities to the conservation and development of plant genetic resources. Section 9.2 clearly delegates responsibility to the state to ensure the protection and realization of farmers' rights. Furthermore, it enjoins states to consider protection of traditional knowledge, benefit sharing, and participation in decision making when designing policies. It also asserts the existence of what some call farmers' privilege, notably the right to save, reuse, exchange, and sell farm-saved seed.

Nonetheless, for many of those interested in promoting farmers' rights as a framework for challenging the advance of capitalist intellectual property rights into all aspects of the use of plant genetic resources, the ITPGRFA was a disappointment. Gregory Rose comments that the articulation of farmers' rights in the agreement is "merely a symbolic expression of gratitude" (G. Rose 2004, 86). He notes (ibid., 87) that the four so-called rights in article 9 of the ITPGRFA are written in non-mandatory language and that three of those in section 9.2 are subject to national legislation. He does commend the treaty makers for attempting to graft together complex regimes for agricultural development and biodiversity conservation. As the only global sustainable agriculture treaty, it is "a new direction in international law" (ibid., 90). Brush (2007, 1511) concurs: "Farmers' Rights are a moral but largely rhetorical recognition of the contribution of farmers to the world's stock of genetic resources, and they provide only a limited mechanism to share benefits from using crop genetic resources or to promote their conservation." Cullet and Raja (2004, 100) reach similar conclusions but are more optimistic, seeing the agreement as a legal framework upon which states, particularly from developing countries, can build. Rose (2004, 90) writes: "From this small, fragile hybrid, many branches will grow." Finally, Oguamanam (200, 445-53) describes farmers' rights as being stymied by the ITPGRFA and concludes that the fight for such rights should be shifted to the CBD, whose article 8j seeks to protect traditional knowledge.

Farmers' Rights in India

Given that international law has evolved to acknowledge state sovereignty when it comes to the realization of farmers' rights, it is useful to review how one developing country, India, has moved on farmers' rights to date. We chose India because it has moved quickly to incorporate the concept of farmers' rights into national law and, in this respect, might have provided leadership to other less wealthy countries. The country's territory is one of the richest sources of biological diversity on the planet. As the TRIPS negotiations gathered momentum during the Uruguay Round, it was the site of highly contested politics that included large street demonstrations, civil disobedience, and occasional acts of violence. These demonstrations often drew attention to the dangers of strengthening global law on intellectual property rights. Leading public intellectuals such as Vandana Shiva, M.S. Swaminathan, and Arundhati Roy, as well as a wide range of farmers' organizations, participated in these events. At a rally of two hundred thousand people in New Delhi on 3 March 1993, Dr. Shashidhar Nanjundaswamy, a farmers' leader, summarized the thoughts of many, to loud cheers, when he said, "We are going to launch a one-point programme — to drive out the multinationals. *Our genetic resources are our national property*" (Gupta 1998, 202, emphasis in original). Although ultimately unsuccessful on the international stage, these actions did help create a policy environment in India that supported serious thinking about how farmers' rights might be protected and advanced. India's efforts also became a model for the thinking of other countries.

Agriculture is an important part of India's economy and society. It still counts for 23 percent of the country's gross national product. Over 70 percent of its 1.1 billion citizens live in rural areas, and 54 percent of its territory is arable land (compared to 15 percent in China) (Louwaars et al. 2005, 50). Small farmers dominate the agricultural economy: those with fewer than two hectares constitute 80.3 percent of all holdings and occupy 36 percent of agricultural land. Major advances in productivity and yields came with the introduction of hybrid plants and chemical farming in the 1970s and 1980s as part of the Green Revolution (ibid., 48). Since that time, productivity growth has slowed. The extent of traditional farming practices — saving, sorting, exchanging seeds — varies by commodity and region. For example, only 11 percent of rice seed, 25 percent of maize seed, and 65 percent of cotton seed (where hybrids and, more recently, genetically modified seeds have become very common) is purchased from formal sources (ibid., 62).

When it comes to intellectual property protection, India passed its first Patents Act in 1970, after many years of debate. The legislation sought to balance the patent regime inherited from the colonial period by subordinating it to food security and access to affordable drugs. The Patents Act also explicitly banned the patenting of living organisms (Cullet and Raja 2004, 102). After considerable protests and much debate, the Act was finally amended in 2002 to bring it into line with the TRIPS agreement. The government, however, made full use of the ambiguities and exceptions available. It specifically ruled out the patentability of living things or non-living substances occurring in nature and also the patentability of plants and animals (ibid., 106). The Act also excludes the patentability of biochemical, biotechnological, and microbiological processes. Finally, the Act requires the disclosure of the source and geographical origin of biological material used in an invention. Failure to do so constitutes grounds for opposing or revoking a patent. Further amendments in 2005 continued this pattern of ensuring minimal compliance with TRIPS but opened the door a little bit towards permitting product patents on biotechnological inventions.

Prior to the 1980s, India was reluctant to introduce plant breeders' rights, relying instead on the common heritage principle and support for public research laboratories to improve seeds. Public policy focused on the idea of ensuring that local farmers would be able to benefit from any new plant varieties created in public laboratories. Accordingly, similar to farmers in the United States prior to its Plant Protection Act, farmers in India had ready access to improved varieties of seeds, which were seen as part of the public domain (Dhar 2002; Seshia 2001).

This situation changed with the formation of the Seed Association of India in 1985, which began to promote the need for plant variety protection. The New Seed Policy of 1988 allowed private firms entry to the sector, thereby creating the basis for a strong lobby in favour of plant variety protection (Ramanna and Smale 2004, 427). Following the conclusion of the WTO treaty and the CBD, India introduced draft plant-variety protection legislation in 1994. Significant mobilization of farmers and others concerned about the entry of multinational corporations into India's agricultural sector followed. Farmers' leaders compared multinational seed and agricultural chemical firms to the East India Company, which had "stolen"

India's wealth under British rule. Referring to the US transnational agribusiness firm Cargill, one farm leader said: "We call Cargill the West India Company. We don't want a West India Company to once again dominate our economy, our freedom, our politics. We are prepared to die for this" (Gupta 1998, 323). In such circumstances, the legislation followed a long journey of debates, amendments, and drafts before the Protection of the Plant Varieties and Farmers' Rights Act was approved by Parliament in 2001.

The Act featured a creative balance between international legal constraints and concerns for national and farmers' autonomy by defining four types of plant varieties eligible for intellectual property rights (Ramanna and Smale 2004, 428-30). By protecting new varieties, India protected the right of plant breeders and borrowed largely from the UPOV. The protection of essentially derived varieties provided plant breeders further protection by extending the scope of the initial right to varieties whose genetic content and pedigree were not much different from the original variety. The Act broke entirely new ground, however, in its definitions of the remaining two varieties. A farmers' variety is one that has been traditionally cultivated and evolved by farmers in their fields or is a wild relative or landrace of a variety of which farmers possess common knowledge. An extant variety is one that has been registered under the Seed Act, is a farmers' variety or a variety about which there is common knowledge, or any other variety that is in the public domain. The definitions of these latter varieties seek to reward past innovation and to recognize farmers' rights, as defined in the IU. Although the first two varieties are of finite duration so as to promote innovation, the latter two are of infinite duration in order to promote conservation (Srinivasan 2003, 424).

In his review of the legislation, however, Srinivasan (2003) sees considerable obstacles to realizing the promise of the farmers' variety and extant variety provisions of the law. Although these varieties are economically viable, they do not meet the strict criteria of uniformity and stability. Conferring property rights on these varieties involves "fairly heroic assumptions about identifying specific communities ... to whom the development of individual varieties can be attributed. Traditional varieties may be in use over large and dispersed areas" (ibid., 426). Srinivasan goes on to examine the benefit-sharing components of the legislation (ibid., 429-42). After a complex statistical analysis based on an examination of plant pedigrees, he concludes convincingly that there will only be limited appropriation of returns based on the provisions in the law.

Srinivasan also turns his attention to a proposal to set up a centralized fund to support conservation activities related to extant and farmers' varieties. This approach was originally broached on an international level in the IU and is also the thinking behind the Multilateral Access Agreement of the ITPGRFA. The Indian law conceives of a National Community Gene Fund that will reward farming communities for their role in conserving traditional varieties. The logic behind the ITPGRFA's Multilateral Access Agreement was one that envisaged a fund created and financed by the levies collected from the benefits or royalties stemming from the commercialization of a new plant variety. But obstacles to implementing an effective and equitable benefit-sharing plan like the Indian Community Gene Fund are as equally daunting as those associated with the other two approaches. For example, Falcon and Fowler (2002) worry that the assessment of these kinds of royalties will be determined on a narrow financial basis and that the administration costs for maintaining a centralized community fund will be too great

India's plant variety legislation, in effect, tries to accomplish two contradictory goals. It seeks to advance the commodification of plant varieties by defining provisions for plant breeders' rights. In the same law, however, it also attempts to find a legal platform or procedure to recognize the innovations and traditional knowledge of farmers. India's approach to innovation in plant variety development has long relied on the sharing of knowledge between scientists working in public laboratories and farmers' own plant-breeding experiments. These innovations in new plant varieties first originated from the interbreeding of what we now know to be farmers' varieties and extant varieties with public varieties. As we have discussed in previous sections, we also know that private breeders follow a similar process, using traditional germplasm from extant and farmers' varieties to improve commercial varieties. Putting into practice the recognition of extant and farmers' varieties will involve publicly employed scientists and private seed firms seeking informed consent from farmers and indigenous communities prior to experimentation and negotiating with them to determine a benefit-sharing arrangement. Both Srinivasan (2003) and Ramanna and Smale (2004) worry that these negotiations will slow down innovations and increase the cost of plant development in both the public and private sectors. Consequently, private breeders may feel compelled to switch to patents or to rely on technological solutions such as hybrids. Public breeders may find themselves in increasingly adversarial relationships with farmers, thus undermining a long-standing alliance in Indian agriculture. For his part, however, Brush (2007, 1512) is more impressed by the Indian law because of its emphasis on multi-community solutions and its move away from individual contracts to access crop resources and share benefits from their use.

Conclusion

Even before the most recent steps to globalize intellectual property rights, the distribution of power in the control, use, and realization of benefits from plant genetic resources was asymmetrical. The European empires and the softer imperialism of the United States created considerable autonomy for individuals and corporations interested in transferring germplasm from the so-called developing world to metropolitan centres. Drawing on extensive experimentation and expertise in the growing field of microbiology, researchers in public laboratories and in corporations "improved" this germplasm, and corporations then gradually secured intellectual property protection for these works. No benefits from the use of this germplasm were paid back; in fact, the germplasm returned to these countries was in the form of commodities to be purchased.

The development of intellectual property rights for life forms in the OECD countries has effectively removed plant genetic resources from the public commons; they are now private goods destined for commodification. In the process, the role of state-sponsored public research has declined, as has the partnership developed in the nineteenth century between public researchers and the farmers who have long held traditional knowledge and practices. In the wake of this change, a rather small group of life sciences corporations has come to increasingly dominate the use and development of plant genetic resources.

The globalization of the approach to intellectual property rights developed by OECD countries, which came as a result of the TRIPS agreement, has reinforced this asymmetry. By requiring the adoption of patents or plant variety protection, the agreement has reduced the options available for developing countries to regulate plant genetic resources in their territories. They have lost collective autonomy in the form of self-determination — that is, the capacity to decide their own laws and to put them into effect as they see fit. The principal recourse left to developing countries is to pressure OECD countries into some form of benefit sharing, with funds going to the conservation of plant genetic resources. This avenue is outlined in both the CBD and the ITPGRFA.

Farmers' rights originated as a defensive manoeuvre to protect the knowledge and innovations of farmers and indigenous peoples. As collective rights based upon the idea of a global public commons, they contradicted both the commodification of life forms and those modes of intellectual property protection favoured by corporations and governments in the OECD. Building on loopholes in international law and its own autonomy as a sovereign state, India has sought legislative means to put these contradictory principles into simultaneous practice. The Organization of African Unity has also developed model legislation for the implementation of farmers' rights (Brush 2004, 253). Like the Indian legislation, it would guarantee that farmers would be exempt from restrictions to protect plant breeders' rights when it comes to collective saving, using, multiplying, and processing the seeds of protected varieties. Although these endeavours are heroic ones, it remains unclear whether such strategies and policies will work (ibid., 254).

Meanwhile, as an indigenous biotechnology sector grows in importance, the constellation of domestic forces in India is being pulled more and more in the direction of the OECD approach. The realization of farmers' rights will depend, in part, on whether India is able to develop its own sui generis system for plant variety protection that meets the requirements of TRIPS but avoids the wholesale commodification of genetic resources already built into the UPOV. Leskien and Flitner (1997) show that there is considerable space for building a sui generis system that meets TRIPS requirements, without reinforcing private plant breeders' rights as much as is found in the UPOV. Moreover, these systems could be adapted to the particular strengths and weaknesses of a given country's agriculture. Securing farmers' autonomy would require India's strong public research system to remain an alternative source of innovation to the private sector. Consequently, farmers and indigenous peoples do not find themselves in any better position to build autonomy than they were under imperialism. Boxed in by international economic law, they may fare worse.

chapter 9

Globalization without World Order: Intellectual Property and Its Discontents

Anna Greenspan

Social machines make a habit of feeding on the contradictions they give rise to, on the crises they provoke, on the anxieties they engender, and on the infernal operations they regenerate. Capitalism has learned this and has ceased doubting itself, while even socialists have abandoned belief in capitalism's natural death by attrition. No one has ever died from contradictions.

— Giles Deleuze and Felix Guattari, *Anti-Oedipus*

FOR A COSMOPOLITAN METROPOLIS, Shanghai — at least on the surface — is pretty disappointing for film buffs. The government places strict restrictions on the number of foreign films allowed in, and those that are imported are heavily censored.[1] The way out of this protectionist bubble is to purchase a DVD player. Popular in Shanghai long before they were common in the West, the machines are cheap, and prices continue to plummet as international brands such as Sony and Philips, which are sold in the plush boutiques of fancy malls, are forced to compete with Chinese-made knock-offs stocked in local supermarkets.

Buying a DVD player banishes isolationism by opening up the world of pirated DVDs. Contrary to some reports in Western media (Blodget 2005), no local knowledge is required to access this thriving underground economy. DVD stands — ranging from legitimate-looking stores to semi-permanent stalls to a guy with an open suitcase — can be found in almost every corner of the city. At the time of writing, there were at least four DVD stands in a one-block radius from my apartment in the Xuhui District of Shanghai. Films are sold for an average of eight yuan each (about US$1) — a pretty good deal even for those living on a local salary. Piracy thus allows the residents of Shanghai not only to enjoy Hollywood blockbusters and high-rated TV serials — which arrive with a shocking speed and efficiency — but also to appreciate Japanese manga cartoons, Hong Kong kung fu flicks, Taiwanese music videos, and the works of Antonioni, Fellini, Kurosawa, Zhang Yimou, Wajda, Fassbinder, and other classics of world cinema.

The prevalence of piracy in China is, of course, well known. *The Economist* calls the country "the international capital of counterfeiting." In an article in the *New York Times Magazine*, Ted Fishman (2005) writes that "counterfeiting and pirating are at the heart of the Chinese economic boom." The figures are indeed astounding. According to *The Economist* (2003b), "the International Intellectual Property Alliance claims that 90% of musical recordings sold in the country are pirated." The same is true for software, while more than 95 percent of the video games used in China are thought to be pirated copies (Blodget 2005). "According to one conservative estimate," writes *The Economist* (2003b), at least US$16 billion worth of goods sold each year inside the country are counterfeit. Henry Blodget (2005), writing for *Slate,* estimates that "as much as a third of China's GDP comes from piracy and counterfeiting."

Although staggering, these statistics seem increasingly plausible the more familiar one becomes with the tech-savvy youth culture of cities such as Shanghai. In these circles, the big issue with regard to getting hold of global media is not whether to pirate but which form of piracy to use. Is it better to buy copied disks, download free from the Internet, or get hooked up to a pirated satellite TV?

Although software and entertainment are at the forefront of counterfeit culture, piracy in China is in no way limited to digital technology. As Blodget writes (2005), "it's not just DVDs that are being ripped off, of course. It's everything." On consumer day, workers with megaphones stage mass events in public parks to warn people about everything from fake bags and watches to medicine and food. On one occasion, people gathered nearby discussed one of the more remarkable recent scares — fake eggs. Although it seems unbelievable — surely it is harder and more expensive to counterfeit an egg than to procure a real one — research on the Internet confirmed that Xinhua (China's official news agency) has indeed reported a case of pirated eggs ("Beware of Fake Eggs," *Danwei,* 28 December 2004).

Although there are, no doubt, factors specific to China that contribute to its particular affinity for piracy (Stevenson-Yang and De Woskin 2005), it is no accident that in Asia in general, and in China in particular, the problems surrounding intellectual property are so acute. Systems often tend to be most intense at the edges, and today it is Asia that marks the frontier of a global economy that is becoming evermore reliant on the global trade in intellectual property.

Intellectual Property and the New World Order

In the second edition of his book *Globalization: A Critical Introduction,* Jan Aart Scholte (2005, 59) defines globalization as "the spread of trans-planetary — and in recent times also more particularly supraterritorial — connections among people." Understood in this way, the process of globalization has been occurring for centuries. Nevertheless, events in the past few decades — especially the collapse of the Soviet Union, the subsequent rise in influence of China and India, and the planet's intense interconnectedness because of the spread of information technology — make it possible to speak of a contemporary phase of globalization that is unlike anything that came before it.

In 1991, President George H.W. Bush spoke dramatically of the emergence of this current phase. In a speech to the US Congress at the end of the Persian Gulf War (Bush 1991), he declared that, with the end of a "world divided — a world of barbed wire and concrete block, conflict and cold war," a new world order was coming. This contemporary stage of globalization would be characterized by the renewal of international regulatory bodies, which would unite the planet into a single consistent regime. Bush himself referred directly to the United Nations, which, "freed from the cold war stalemate," was now "poised to fulfill the historic vision of its founders" (Bush 1991). Four years later, at the end of the Uruguay Round trade negotiations of the General Agreement on Tariffs and Trade (GATT), this vision was reinforced by the establishment of the World Trade Organization (WTO), an organization dedicated to facilitating global trade by implementing a consistent set of global rules. The war in Iraq, crises at the UN, and protests aimed at the WTO have strained, if not destroyed, the 1990s vision of a new world order. In one of the key structural elements of contemporary globalization, however, the protection of intellectual property rights, there is now an unprecedented degree of international harmonization.

The new global regime in intellectual property protection, however, has not gone unchallenged (see Gorman, this volume). Critics claim that intellectual property laws privilege the high-technology industries of the rich while ignoring the needs of poorer countries such as China. The new world order has thus been pitted against the collective autonomy of the national governments and economies of the developing world. The institutions of global law, including the Agreement on Trade-Related Aspects of Intellectual Property Rights (TRIPS), tend to favour developed countries. Less wealthy countries, therefore, wonder what degree of autonomy will be made accessible to them. The TRIPS agreement, in particular, was pushed for ardently by transnational corporations from the pharmaceutical and biotechnology sectors, entrenching in the process immense privileges for these corporations and the states supporting them (Sell 2003).

Piracy and Global Disorder

Although it is easy to be snared by the binary logic of this debate, the activity of pirates fundamentally challenges the idea of a homogenous globalization that is structurally opposed to the autonomy of developing states. The technologies of the information age require an immense amount of research and development and creative investment, which depends on a uniform worldwide set of laws to protect intellectual property. These very same technologies, however, and the global conditions in which they are produced increasingly facilitate piracy. The result is a fractured global economy — split between the legitimate world of corporations and international law, with their formalized system of contracts in which intellectual property protection is rigorously and uniformly enforced, and the informal, shadowy world of pirates and fakes, which functions according to its own set of rules. Autonomy from below can flourish even, or perhaps especially, when autonomy from above is hobbled by global legal regimes.

In an article in *Wired* magazine, cyberpunk author and theorist Bruce Sterling (2005) argues that trade in fake goods constitutes a sham economy that "subverts conventional multi-national commerce" by creating a dark parallel process, which he calls black globalization. "Bogus products," he writes, "are part and parcel of the worldwide marketplace — more so than dated symbols of globalization like Coca-Cola." "Black globalism," he goes on to warn, "extends well beyond easy, offhand intellectual property thefts like videotaping first-run films and burning them onto DVD. It commandeers the manufacturing, distribution, and business infrastructure in a parasitic rejection of the global order."

The Janus-faced nature of the global economy and its implications for autonomy have engendered a highly polarized debate. While one side argues for increased enforcement to stamp out the criminal underground, the other seeks to roll back existing laws so that the legal structure can keep pace with the reality on the ground. Both of these positions, however, rest on highly fantastical visions aimed at formalizing the entire world economy and eliminating its informal twin. They both therefore seek to produce a type of globalization that operates as a single, unifying, integrated whole and that has only one path for building collective and individual autonomy.

In contrast, I argue that globalization is best understood as a system of intrinsic hybridity. What Sterling calls black globalization does not subvert multinational commerce but rather works alongside it. Although the market in fake goods and intellectual property protection are conceptual opposites, in the real world they work together to create a functioning machine. As philosophers Deleuze and Guattari (1977) note, machines work by breaking down. Rather than being a single unified regime, world trade, whether in goods or ideas, is built on differences, areas of fragmentation, and border zones of varying degrees of autonomy. Shanghai's pirated DVD market, for example, depends on the intersection of a zone of production in which intellectual property is protected, a state that closes its borders to all but a handful of foreign films, and the producers, traders, and consumers of pirated goods that operate relatively independently of the state. These differences create the breeding ground of a globalization that continuously escapes world order and creates unforeseen spaces for autonomy making in the process.

Intellectual Property against Autonomy

Intellectual property is the means through which people obtain legal rights over things they create or invent.[2] The main argument for the protection of intellectual property is that it is a vital incentive for innovation. Creators, in both the arts and sciences, need a temporary monopoly in order to provide an adequate return on investments. Simply put, without intellectual property protection, there is no mechanism for society's innovators to get paid for their work. This problem has become increasingly intense in the contemporary global economy, in which technological advancements require a steady increase in research and development expenditures and in which creative content can be duplicated perfectly and almost instantaneously spread throughout the globe. "Most of the value of new medicines and other high technology products lies in the amount of invention, innovation, research, design and testing involved. Films, music recordings, books, computer software and on-line services are bought and sold because of the information and creativity they contain, not usually because of the plastic, metal or paper used to make them" (WTO n.d., para. 1). In short, intellectual property is the means through which value in the information economy is leveraged for commercial use.

It has long been recognized that in an era of transnational trade, intellectual property protection requires a global regime. The Paris Convention of 1883 and the Berne Convention of 1886 were early attempts to harmonize global intellectual property laws (see Gorman, this volume). It is only in the past few decades, however, that a set of global norms really began to take hold. Today, the internationalization of intellectual property is primarily upheld by the World International Property Organization (WIPO), a specialized agency of the UN that came into force in 1970 and is devoted to administering treaties signed at these earlier conventions.[3] The organization promotes international laws in intellectual property protection and aims to create a world order in which a single system of intellectual property protection will encompass the globe.

That WIPO lacked any real means of enforcement, however, led many producers of intellectual property, particularly in the United States, to believe that it was too weak an organization upon which to rely.[4] These producers brought their concerns to the WTO and, by the end of the Uruguay Round in April 1994, succeeded, through intense lobbying, in establishing TRIPS as one of three integral parts of the WTO (for elaboration, see Gorman, this volume).[5] "The extent of protection and enforcement of [intellectual property] rights varied widely around the world; and as intellectual property became more important in trade, these differences became a source of tension in international economic relations," explains the WTO on its website. "New internationally agreed trade rules for intellectual property rights were seen as a way to introduce more order and predictability and for disputes to be settled more systematically." The aim, then, was to "narrow the gaps in the way these rights are protected around the world, and to bring them under common international rules." The

TRIPS agreement accomplished this task by establishing minimum levels of protection to which any country wishing to join the WTO must adhere. Current intellectual property laws have thus helped create a comprehensive world order that puts limits on the freedom of manoeuvre for states seeking more autonomy from OECD-based transnational corporations and, with it, the autonomy of individual innovators within their own boundaries.

Autonomy against Intellectual Property

All members of the WTO have necessarily agreed to implement TRIPS, and all members, including China, have had to adjust their legal system to agree with the accord. Nevertheless, strong objections to TRIPS continue to be raised. Critics of the agreement maintain that current intellectual property laws are an unfair imposition and have no regard for the autonomous interests of the indigenous economies of the developing world. Because it grants monopolies to large corporations, the current regime of intellectual property protection is seen to operate as a form of First World protectionism. Its main effect, in the short term at least, "will be a large transfer of resources from net users of ideas (often in poor countries) to net developers of ideas (e.g., America)" (*The Economist* 2001b). Thus, as *The Economist* (2001b) states, "governments of poor countries are being asked to co-operate in a redistribution of global income that will cost them hundreds of millions of dollars." Poor countries, it concludes, "have every reason to question the terms of this particular trade-policy bargain."

The economic case against intellectual property protection has a parallel in the cultural field, where it is argued that the global spread of intellectual property laws is a vital part of the Westernization of the world.[6] "Copyright as a legal and ideological concept," contends theorist Alan Story, echoing a commonly held belief, "is the product of Western societal development at a particular historical moment and remains a foreign concept in many other societies" (2002, 129). In Asian culture, for example, artists and scientists are not traditionally judged by the originality of their work but rather on the skill and technical competence of their reproductions. "So far as Korean culture was concerned," write Drahos and Braithwaite (2003, 21), authors of the book *Information Feudalism: Who Owns the Knowledge Economy?* "copyright was the most foreign of foreign transplants. Copying was regarded as a sincere form of flattery, something that should gladden authors rather than anger them."

In his book *Copyright in China,* Sanqiang Qu writes that the idea that there is something morally wrong with copying contradicts the basic principles of Confucian philosophy. Confucianism commends those who build on the work of others. Confucius famously said of his own teachings, "I transmit rather than create" (Qu 2002, 8). Moreover, claims Qu, the legal basis of copyright is alien to the Confucian ideal of *li,* "a concept which has been translated as ceremonies, rituals or rules of social conduct" (ibid., 6). In the Confucian tradition, li replaces law when dealing with social relations: "In the conception of li, there is no place for law in the Latin sense of the term. Strictly speaking, there are not even individual rights sanctioned and guaranteed by the law. There are only duties, mutual permeations, governed by notions of order, responsibility, hierarchy, harmony ... The Confucianist saying *cun tanli, mie renyu* (observing the belief in li and destroying individual desire) leaves little room for the Western concept of copyright that is vested in the individual" (ibid., 7).

Chinese culture is opposed to intellectual property rights not only on religious and philosophical grounds but also for political and economic reasons. The idea of the right to private property, which can be enforced or maintained against anyone, even the state, has no place in either ancient or modern China. "Throughout the imperial Chinese history the government's interest in publication remained focused on the control of ideas and the maintenance of order ... rather than on the protection of private property" (Qu 2002, 24).

This lack of attention to the personal rights of an individual creator, and thus to personal autonomy, was further reinforced by the modern adoption of communism. During the Cultural Revolution in particular, writes Qu, "all fledging attempts at copyright protection the PRC had made were destroyed." As evidence, he cites a popular saying at the time: "Is it necessary for a steelworker to put his name on a steel ingot that he produces in the course of his duty? If not, why should a member of the intelligentsia enjoy the privilege of putting his name on what he produces?" (Qu 2002, 38). It is not only the devaluing of ideas that is at work here but also the widespread propensity to put a greater emphasis on society over the rights of individuals. This tendency is doubly compounded in China in that it is both inherent in communism and also viewed as one of the key features of so-called Asian values.

Those who seek to challenge the current global regime of intellectual property protection — whether on economic or cultural grounds or both — aim their critiques at the legitimacy of both TRIPS and WIPO. From the beginning, the "developing nations were hostile to the very idea of TRIPS. They believed that IP protection fell outside the basic purview of GATT and that WIPO, not GATT, was the forum for such discussions" (Nair and Kumar 1997, 9; see also Gorman, this volume). Having succeeded in getting the WTO to take up the issue of intellectual property, many feel that these countries were bullied into complying. As Carlos Correa (2000, 3) writes, though they did "finally acquiesce in making important concessions in terms of reforms of their intellectual property legislation, they did not obtain any compensating concessions from industrialized countries." Many argue, therefore, that the TRIPS agreement embeds an intrinsic injustice into the very fabric of the WTO. And to the extent that the collective autonomy of societies is enhanced by fostering innovation and inventions within their own borders, the agreement puts additional obstacles in front of less wealthy states.

Among those who contend that TRIPS is an unfair agreement are some of the most well-known proponents of free trade. The editors of *The Economist* (2000), for example, question TRIPS' inclusion in the WTO. "Raising intellectual-property standards," they argue, "is fundamentally different from lowering trade barriers." Jagdish Bhagwati, author of the book *In Defense of Globalization* (2004), makes the same point even more forcefully. Intellectual property protection is not a trade issue, he writes, "the WTO ought to be about lowering trade barriers and tackling market access problems. The inclusion of IPP [intellectual property protection] has turned the organization into a royalty collection agency" (2002). Bhagwati's concern is that the inclusion of intellectual property protection in the WTO has set a precedent for labor unions, environmentalists, and other lobby groups who demand that their concerns also be incorporated into the WTO rules. If these demands are met, the end result will be a drastic curbing of global trade. Because of TRIPS, he maintains, "it is hardly surprising that poor countries see the WTO increasingly as the target of western lobby groups determined to exploit the WTO to their own advantage, using the specious argument that their causes have to do with trade in some intrinsic way" (ibid.).

Although the attacks on TRIPS are — so far at least — only theoretical, the challenges to WIPO have recently taken a far more tangible form. In the fall of 2004, WIPO adopted a proposal put forth by Brazil and Argentina that calls for the establishment of a development agenda. Although the plan encompasses a variety of complaints and ideas, the crux of the issue is that the globalization of intellectual property does not allow for a self-reliant, autonomy-reinforcing development strategy. The development agenda, writes Chee Yoke Heong in the *Asia Times* (2004), "is against the harmonization of intellectual property laws that leads to higher protection standards in all countries, irrespective of their levels of development, and instead calls for the integration of the 'development dimension' into policymaking on intellectual property protection, saying assessment should be done on a case-by-case basis." This demand that intellectual property laws cease to be internationally harmonious and take into account the autonomy of developing nations' power to legislate was supported by hundreds of non-profit organizations, scientists, academics, and other individuals who signed the "Geneva Declaration on the Future of WIPO." This document urged the organization "to abandon its 'one-size-fits-all approach'" and "adopt a more balanced view of the relative benefits of harmonization and diversity, and seek to impose global conformity only when it truly benefits all of humanity."

What the attack on intellectual property protection comes down to, then, is a challenge to the globalization of intellectual property. Whether it is extracting intellectual property protection from the WTO, rolling back intellectual property laws or requiring greater flexibility in their implementation, placing greater demands on intellectual property producers, or asking for exemptions of various kinds in order to allow for the preservation, if not enhancement, of the autonomy of states in the developing world, the desired results are the same: less integration, the rolling back of harmonization, and the dismantling of a global regime.

Piratical Disturbances

Those who seek to adjust WIPO and TRIPS, however, are still on the side of a single world order; their aim is to formalize the entire global economy by adjusting the laws in such a way that nothing can, or need, escape. They thereby stand in opposition to the actual hybrid system, which comprises both formal and informal economies and various zones in between. Although intellectual property laws demand international harmony, the treaties and conventions on which these laws are based are simply impossible to enforce. The flexibility, ingenuity, and skill of pirates coupled with the fact that actually implementing these laws requires manpower and resources that many governments, particularly in the developing world, see as better used elsewhere has led to a giant underground economy. Despite WIPO, TRIPS, and all its powerful allies, "the Counterfeiting Intelligence

Bureau (CIB), part of the International Chamber of Commerce, estimates that 7-9% of all world trade is in counterfeits" (*The Economist* 2003a).

Although DVDs, like all pirated goods, are illegal in China, and although newspapers report constant raids and seizures, the slackness of enforcement is everywhere apparent. This was abundantly clear one day in Shanghai when, upon approaching our local DVD stand, I noticed with some alarm that there were a couple of police talking to the seller. I tried to catch his eye because I believed that, despite my pidgin Chinese, we had developed a certain rapport and that he would warn me to stay clear if the situation required it. I was therefore somewhat puzzled when he seemed to ignore me entirely. Curious but wary, I cautiously approached. Noticing a foreigner, the cops immediately took the opportunity to practise their English. Standing close by as I flicked through the films, they enthusiastically recommended the latest thriller and were eager to discuss the merits of the various actors who play James Bond.

For many of those who support the free use of intellectual property (see, for instance, the online publication *Electronic Freedom Frontier*), this unenforceability makes abundantly clear the absurdity of the laws governing intellectual property protection; their distance from on-the-ground reality is yet more proof that they must be reformed. Yet, even in China, focusing solely on the laws' lack of implementation does not account for the complexity of the situation. Although many DVD sellers operate openly, for example, it is also not uncommon to see small traders frantically packing up their suitcases and fleeing from the police. Like all countries in both the developed and developing world, China is torn between pressure and a desire to comply with intellectual property laws and the practical difficulties and various disadvantages in executing them.

The result is that the so-called global intellectual property regime is made up of continuously shifting fractured zones of relative autonomy in which the producers, traders, and consumers of intellectual property operate within different jurisdictions and with varying degrees of enforcement. This fracturing has produced a gradient between formal and informal economies that is based on differences in price, marketing, and distribution. It is these differences and the disordered system that they create that feed today's hybrid globalization.

The underground or sham economy does not subvert the above-the-board world of commerce and trade but rather operates at its edges. The utopian ideal of fully implementing intellectual property laws, either by increasing levels of enforcement or by rolling back the laws, amounts to a desire to swallow these edges, bringing the periphery into the core. Both globalization and development depend on these margins since they are where real innovation occurs. Enterprise itself is never fully formal but instead operates in between the formal economy and the informal zones of invention and trade. Accordingly, global capitalism began with piracy, and piracy will always be with it.

Piracy and Economic Development

Piracy, in fact, is so common a feature in the process of development that it appears to be one of the key features of economic progress. During the initial period of industrialization in the United States, artists and scientists borrowed heavily from Europe. "American companies," writes Ted Fishman in his article "Manufaketure," "paid industrial spies to steal the designs of British machines. American theatrical producers routinely staged foreign operas and plays without permission; publishers sold dubious editions of English novels" (2005, 43). Moreover, *The Economist* (2002) reports that the United States, in a move that echoes the arguments of developing countries today, "provided no copyright protection for foreign authors, arguing that it needed the freedom to copy in order to educate the new nation." Similarly, it is no accident that Europe's own process of modernization occurred at precisely the same time that traders and explorers were encountering other cultures whose inventions and discoveries could be copied and used. More recently, the Asian tigers — countries such as South Korea and Taiwan — have used a similar strategy. As Ted Fishman (2005, 44) points out, emerging economies in "Southeast Asia, Latin America, Africa and the former Soviet Union still operate well outside the developed world's norm for intellectual property protection."

Piracy's vital role in the process of development is tied intimately to the practice of reverse engineering. Common throughout the developing world, reverse engineering involves taking foreign technology apart and then building it back up again with cheaper components and labour. It thus effectuates a remarkably efficient mode of technology transfer from the rich to the poor.

Reverse engineering is a vital component of China's dizzying boom. A particular high-tech example is the Shanghai Maglev Train, said to be the fastest in the world, which now runs a short line from Pudong airport to the start of the subway line. The maglev was built by German companies who invested massively in what they viewed as an opportunity to showcase a technology that the Chinese government expressed interest in spreading throughout the country (there is talk, for example, of constructing a maglev line to connect Shanghai and Beijing, and a line linking Shanghai to the nearby town of Hangzhou has recently been announced). Yet, as Fishman (2005, 43) writes, the intellectual property involved in this cutting-edge technology was not well protected:

> Workers for the German operation videotaped Chinese engineers poking around the maglev train's maintenance building in Shanghai at 3 a.m. one Saturday, apparently in search of confidential information. The manager of the Chinese operation that was a partner of the Germans clumsily excused the prowlers by saying they were merely taking part in a "research and development" exercise. Later that month, the government said that to save money it would eschew foreign designs for Chinese trains and, instead, employ newly developed indigenous maglev technology. Soon China could be exporting maglev trains for half the price Germany or Japan demand.

China's automobiles and pharmaceuticals, to name just the two most notorious industries, are based almost entirely on this type of "borrowing." Foreign companies swept up by "China hype" enter the market with great excitement and enthusiastically introduce their latest brands. The enthusiasm quickly fades, however, when they are faced with heavy competition from cheaper fakes, which are sometimes indistinguishable from the real products they imitate. This same blatant abuse of intellectual property occurs throughout the Chinese economy, from handbags to buildings. China's great construction boom, for example, has been a fabulous opportunity for foreign architects. But the mode of granting contracts leaves the field wide open to piracy. It is not uncommon to hear stories of architecture competitions in which foreign firms are invited to bid on huge projects. Once they submit their blueprints, and sometimes even after they win competitions, the projects are officially postponed or cancelled. Favourite design ideas are then used by local workers who complete the cancelled projects at a fraction of the cost.

Although it preys on research and development fostered elsewhere, reverse engineering is not without its own unique creativity. The attempt to make copies bigger, better, faster, and cheaper, along with the practice of shifting already-existing technology to fit particular geoclimactic and market conditions, sometimes allows for important innovation. This innovation, however, falls outside the spectrum of protected intellectual property since it is based on incremental improvements of existing production rather than on sudden and dramatic technological breakthroughs (Correa 2000, 38). Nevertheless, these incremental innovations often occur at the cutting edge of high technology, introducing the pirated goods of the developing world back into the core.[7]

Besides operating as a means of technology transfer, piracy allows the entrepreneurial poor to create successful small enterprises. Although the West tends to portray the poor as destitute beggars and starving children who lie helpless on the streets waiting for charitable donations, the truth, as development economist Hernando de Soto points out, is much more inspiring: "The grimmest picture of the Third World is not the most accurate. Worse, it draws attention away from the arduous achievements of those small entrepreneurs who have triumphed over every imaginable obstacle to create the greater part of the wealth of their society. A truer image would depict a man and a woman who have painstakingly saved to construct a house for themselves and their children and who are creating enterprises where nobody imagined they could be built" (de Soto 2000, 35-37).

One example of this heroic entrepreneurship is taking place on a folding table located on the corner outside my apartment in the former French concession of Shanghai. In the morning, the table is used to sell breakfast pastries and snacks; at noon, it holds a buffet lunch; and in the late afternoon, two years ago when I first arrived in Shanghai, it was used as a DVD stand. The young family that had this evening slot would stand outside year round, playing with their young daughter and eating their dinner on sidewalk stools. When I returned from a recent trip to Canada, however, I noticed with some alarm that, after lunch, the table was no longer being used. Upon further inspection, I was relieved to realize that one of my favourite DVD stalls had not, in fact, disappeared. Rather, it had instead graduated to a small store nearby, where the family that ran it could now enjoy the luxuries of an air conditioner, indoor heating, and a colour TV.

The most important role of pirates, however, is, of course, to bring down the price of existing technology. It is in this effort that they fulfill their most crucial entrepreneurial function. The very use of the term *pirates* for copyright infringers comes from precisely this type of activity. In the 1800s, when advances in the technology of the printing press made duplications easier and more accurate, entrepreneurs exploited the difference between the developed and developing worlds. At the time, publishing in Britain was tightly controlled by a core group known as the London book cartel. Publishers in Scotland defied this early monopoly by taking advantage of the new technology to print texts at much lower prices than their London competitors. Using the exact same strategies as today's entertainment industry, the London cartel attacked the Scottish booksellers as villains and pirates and used their actions to justify new copyright law (Halbert 1999, 6-7).

According to economist Joseph Schumpeter (1947, 83), "the fundamental impulse that sets and keeps the capitalist engine in motion depends not only on the new consumer goods, but also the new methods of production or transportation, the new markets, the new forms of industrial organization that capitalist enterprise creates." Even when pirates sell perfect reproductions of existing goods, they innovate massively at the level of distribution by continuously opening new markets at the edges of the capitalist world. Here on the periphery, where costs or other prohibitive factors make legitimate trade in core technologies impossible, it is often a choice between the sham economy or none at all.

It is therefore highly misleading to accuse pirates of stealing customers.[8] They are more often engaged in creating markets where none existed previously. Jagdish Bhagwati (2004, 184) makes this point with regard to the pharmaceutical industry. Although "poor countries have need for newly invented drugs," he writes, prohibitive costs mean that they have "no effective demand." DVDs are another obvious example. China's pirates are making available products of global culture that are not only unaffordable but also unavailable on the legitimate market. Price is one factor, censorship another. It is not uncommon to find films marked "Banned in China" on sale at the local DVD stand.

This situation explains why multinational companies, when they are honest, must admit to a complex connection to the distribution of their (faked) brands. One of the most famous tourist attractions in Shanghai is Xiangyang Market, where you can take advantage of China's role as factory to the world and buy fake Prada bags, Nike shoes, and Rolex watches, which, though often shoddy, are sometimes indistinguishable from their genuine counterparts.[9] Those that wear these goods are not — at least for the most part — the company's regular customers but rather people who are being introduced to the brand through their more affordable imitations. It was perhaps for this reason that Giorgio Armani, who recently opened a store in a luxury complex on the Bund, was said to be delighted at the copies of his goods and boasted to local reporters that he had bought himself a fake Armani watch. Although Armani is undoubtedly concerned about stolen intellectual property devaluing his brand, he nevertheless recognizes that fake Gucci shoes, Prada bags, and Armani watches work as free advertising for the brand-conscious upwardly mobile urbanites of Asia.

Nowhere is this insight more apparent than in the realm of intellectual property. Microsoft surely knows that copies of the latest Windows are being sold at five yuan apiece. At least part of the lack of enforcement, however, has to do with the fact that the company is keen to lock in a market that would never be able to afford its product at legitimate prices. Similarly, a company such as Philips, which owns patents on the technology needed for DVD players, is eager to enforce its own patent while surely recognizing that it is benefitting from the thriving market in pirated DVDs.

Just as piracy is vital to the development process, so too is the protection of intellectual property. As soon as countries shift from being consumers to producers of intellectual property, they start to demand that the laws securing their own ideas and inventions are enforced. Governments then become more focused on securing the economic rights and autonomy of producers of intellectual property and less on the autonomy of consumers and those pirating information. States become more interested in securing respect for global norms that can protect their intellectual property. One of the best contemporary examples is India. Although once heavily reliant on copying ideas and reverse engineering technology, the innovations of the indigenous software and film industry, along with its new role as outsourcing capital of the world, have resulted in increasing attention to intellectual property laws. India, as the *Wall Street Journal* (2005) writes, has become an "IP powerhouse," and as the "economy opens up, its best companies are innovating to stay competitive." "The winner used to be the guy who could copy faster," says Shrikumar Suryanarayan, president for research and development at Bangalore biotechnology concern Biocon. "Now that has completely changed so that companies that don't innovate will die."

This type of indigenous pressure is much more effective than complaints by foreigners in convincing countries to become stricter enforcers of intellectual property protection. Places such as Japan and Hong Kong that once subscribed to the view that piracy had both an economic and cultural justification are now — having climbed sufficiently high on the value chain — some of the strongest backers of the stringent protection of intellectual property. "Growth and home-grown invention are the most effective remedies to counterfeiting," writes *The Economist* (2003b): "In the 1960s, Japan was a hotspot for copying; in the 1970s, that dubious distinction passed to Hong Kong; in the 1980s, it was Taiwan's and South Korea's turn in the spotlight; and today it is China's. As each of the pioneer countries has developed its own industry, it has introduced laws and penalties to clamp down on counterfeiting. China will, at some point, follow the same route."

Chinese companies are already beginning to see the value in securing their own ideas and, as Mithras Consulting firm states on its website, there is an "increasing reliance among Chinese firms on the court system to protect their own IP, with the vast majority of cases in China involving only Chinese firms." In China, as elsewhere, it is this home-grown demand, which arises as soon as enough local businesses shift from copying to innovation, that will eventually force a genuine clampdown on the counterfeit economy. "Foreign lawyers have long despaired at the apparent failure of outside pressure to get the Chinese to combat piracy of all sorts," writes *The Economist* (2001a),

> but they are becoming increasingly optimistic that a new breed of Chinese firms may succeed where international law has failed ... High-tech stars such as Kexing ... Haier in white goods, Legend in computers and Konka in television sets are all examples of Chinese firms with strategies based on their own brands or other intellectual property. "Their biggest worry is not foreign rivals but local rip-offs," says Zili Shao, who runs the Chinese operations of Linklaters, a British law firm. And once they, rather than foreigners, start lobbying Communist Party chiefs to enforce the rules, the cadres might just do it.

As China becomes increasingly legitimate, producing its own technological breakthroughs that it is anxious to protect, it will eventually lose its status as part of the periphery, and the edges of global capitalism will inevitably shift elsewhere. It is there, in the zone of the most rapid development (Africa, perhaps, or a reformed Middle East), where the so-called sham economy will boom. Piracy has and will always work through these frontiers.

Counterfeit culture thus offers an alternative scale of development in which countries are measured not by their GDP or other conventional indicators but rather on the scale and intensity of their indigenous economy in pirated goods. The difference between the copiers and the copied, however, divides not only the developed from the developing world. Piracy also fractures the developed world from within. First, fractures occur because copied goods from the periphery flow into the core, thereby affecting the legitimate economy from outside. More importantly, however, if piracy is how one judges development, no country can be seen as a homogenous unit. Since developed countries, eager to profit from their higher position on the value chain, tend to become stricter enforcers of intellectual property, there are always zones of piracy that persist in their midst. This situation is true of a country such as India, which, despite the boom in its local information technology industry, has a piracy rate of over 70 percent when it comes to business software. It is also true of the United States, where the rise of one of the hottest new "legitimate" technologies — Apple's iPod — fed directly off of the amazing popularity of Napster and the free downloading of MP3 files.

These phenomena point to a crucial flaw in plans such as WIPO's Development Agenda, which presumes that a country as a whole is an autonomous unit locked at a particular stage of development. The idea of a flexible law that can be adjusted according to the stage of development a given country is thought to have reached is unfair to both the developed and developing worlds. It ignores the peripheral zones that exist within the core and blocks the most advanced industries of the developing world — India's software industry, for example — from freely competing on the global stage.

Conclusion

Despite intensifying cries over the ever-growing problem of intellectual property protection (see Livanos Cattaui 2005), contemporary global capitalism, as philosophers Deleuze and Guattari (1977) point out, works best through the crises, anxieties, and contradictions it produces. The fake software that is sold to run on legitimate brand name machines; the pirated DVD market, which creates an ever-increasing demand for brand name, patented DVD players; and the boom in MP3 players brought about by the ability to freely download MP3s are proof that the underground economy does not function as a "parasitic rejection of the global order." Effective parasites, after all, embrace rather than reject their hosts.

The hybrid mixture of formal and informal economy defies the idea that the globalization of intellectual property consists of a single world order pitted against the autonomy of government and indigenous economies of developing states. Instead, a hybrid globalization consists of a network of actors — the producers, protectors, and pirates of intellectual property — each of which operates with varying degrees of autonomy. The intersection of these autonomies from below with those from above is a sign of a disordered and decentred globalization, one that innovates at its edges no less than in its core.

Coda

chapter 10

Property Rites: Cultural Narrations of the Palestinian Catastrophe

Jasmin Habib

The State of Palestine is the state of Palestinians wherever they may be.
— Palestinian Declaration of Independence, 1988

I built with words a homeland for my nation and for myself.
— Mahmud Darwish, interview in *Ha'aretz*, 14 July 2007

ON 15 JULY 2007, AFTER receiving clearance by Israel's Ministry of Defence, Palestinian's most revered and celebrated poet, Mahmud Darwish, returned to Haifa, Israel, to participate in a poetry reading at a Mount Carmel Auditorium. Why would a Palestinian poet with Israeli citizenship need permission to return? What threat could he have posed that a state would feel it necessary to involve its Ministry of Defence?

Dangerous poets? Poets who express the will of the people? What is the place of poetry or the meaningfulness of its expression in this community? Why was I directed to this literature by my interlocutors? Why these texts and not others, such as history books, UN resolutions, or biographies? What does this advice tell us about transnational Palestinian identities or the experiences of exile?

In this chapter, I deal with a long-standing crisis — the displacement of Palestinians from their land. Concurrently, I perform a series of experimental gestures. I examine the appeal to the right to autonomy through property in its collective — that is, cultural or communitarian — form and orient this appeal through an exploration of the poetry written by Palestine's dispossessed. In these attempts and appeals, I remark upon the degree to which theories of globalization processes hastily embrace the logic of modernization focused on economic processes and thus fail to account for land-based resistance that is neither productivist nor anti-capitalist.

Relying on historical geographers and commentators on international law, I provide some background details of the process of dispossession. In particular, I show how Israeli law denied Palestinians their property rights in the period following the Nakba (Catastrophe) after the war (known in Israel as the War of Independence) in 1948. Lockean justifications for the appropriation of Palestinian land, which are now familiar to readers of this book, emphasized its alleged unproductive nature and its inhabitants' backwardness. The potent Zionist myth of "a land without a people for a people without land" has taken decades to dissipate.

I gained an unexpected insight while conducting research among Palestinians living in Canada in the period following the signing of the Declaration of Principles (also known as the Oslo Peace Accords) between the government of Israel and a new entity, which had emerged from within the leadership of the Palestine Liberation Organization, the Palestine Authority. In my attempts to understand exiled and diasporic relationships to Palestine, I learned something about the meaning of property — a cherished trope in the West that embodies the ideal and the route to autonomy, individuality, and wealth. Members of the '48 generation had vivid memories of their villages in what was once Palestine, but they spoke of their losses in cultural terms and sensory ways. No one ever referred to dunams lost, the economic potential of the land, or its current market value; not even once was the issue of compensation raised.

In her work "1948: Law, History, Memory," Samera Esmeir (2003, 25, emphasis added) writes:

> One of the difficulties in discussing violence against Palestinians during the 1948 war is that *"Palestine,"* the site of the violence, *both persists and has ceased to exist.* Its simultaneous presence and erasure occurs in part through the survival of Palestinians from the 1948 war in what has ceased to be Palestine. Their scattered yet persistent presence constitutes a threat with which one can return to that moment when Palestine was ruined. They embody the survival of Palestine,

yet they also stand for its death. This death continues both to impede their memory of what happened in 1948 and to structure it.

During fieldwork on transnational Palestinian identity conducted between 2000 and 2002, my interlocutors urged me to read poetic reflections narrating Palestinian history, memory and identity: "Haven't you read Darwish? He tells our story"; "We lost Fadwa Tuqan just recently. She was our voice."[1] After several such admonitions, I set out somewhat sheepishly to discover more about "our national treasures," "our spokespeople," and "our visionaries." I quickly discovered that poets and writers in exile reflect on the land in much the same way as my ethnographic informants, not as a property right — alienated and sovereign — but rather as a lived and embodied relation: a rite of property. Palestine's story of loss was not simply of the loss of property and its attendant rights but of property rites and the meanings associated with their loss.

Although this chapter is neither entirely an ethnographic nor a literary analysis, it does examine the role of Palestinian poetry in articulating the depth of these losses. This chapter emerges from the breach between an analysis that would take as its point of intervention the politics of poetic expression by poets and the ritual or rites of poetic expression in the community from which the poets' expressions emerge (Clifford 1997; Lavie and Swedenburg 1996; Slyomovics 1998; Swedenburg 1995). That is, the chapter is part literary criticism, part ethnography. It places poetry within community members' sense of identity and autonomy — not so much to understand this practice as a means of resistance (see, for example, Barbara Harlow's [1987, 1998] work) but as one of resilience. I pursue an understanding of how poetry has played a vital role in the everyday expressions of attachment to Palestine and dreams of its autonomy among Palestinians in exile.

The chapters in this volume show how globalizing processes have favoured the implantation of individual property rights around the world. Drawing on discourses such as the doctrine of improvement, the need for innovation and productivity and, more recently, neoliberalism and the conservation of biological diversity, cultural communities have been violently dispossessed of their lands, their knowledges, and their art. This analysis usually focuses on the economic and political aspects of these struggles, paying less attention to the emotional and cultural pain and sense of loss involved. In this respect, the analysis can tend to anaesthetize the effects of these globalizing processes. I propose to counter this tendency by drawing on nationalistic poetry that circulates through and among communities in exile.

The choice of poetry for this task is by no means accidental. Although it is true that many of my interlocutors were of the '48 generation — personally experiencing the displacement from their home and village — it is they who repeatedly chose to direct me to the poets and their poetry. As an example, and notwithstanding critiques by literary scholars of the propagandistic nature of such work, the book *A Lover from Palestine and Other Poems: An Anthology of Palestinian Poetry* (1970) — edited by Abdelwahab M. Elmessiri, illustrated by Kamal Boulata, and published by the Palestine Information Office in Washington, DC — seemed to have circulated throughout the community even in photocopied form.[2] Copies were twice handed to me. In effect, Palestinian poets have taken to the world stage, globalized their works, regardless of whether Israel (or the world) offers them permission to narrate (Said 1984). Their works circulate across the very boundaries meant to deny them a voice, constituting a form of transnational resistance that parallels those discussed in chapters by Cutler, Preston, and Coleman and Reed in this volume.

Moreover, I note that such a form of transnational resistance is not new by any means. I take as my cue for this research work on the survival of the Jewish diaspora — dispersed over centuries — as the "people of the book." It was poetic expression of loss and desire for return that sustained them as a collectivity. The irony of this position is self-evident, but it explains the force of property rites as a response by Palestinians to their encounter with settler colonialism — at the turn of the last century and ever since 1947. Although they are unable to reclaim their lands by military force or political means, Palestinians continue to resist military occupation and the confiscation of their lands and to defend their right to return. They have also been moved to write and to recite poetic expressions of their experiences, sharing the depth of their losses among themselves and others.

Global Contexts

There is a range of globalizing processes that need to be understood to appreciate the complexity of the Palestinian catastrophe and its continuing effects. One could begin with the Second World War and the devastating effects that it had on Europe's Jews. Such a choice, however, would assume that the catastrophe that befell the Palestinians in the postwar period was based on a world responding to the horrors of the Holocaust. In doing so, we would ignore other globalizing processes such as the European refugee crisis, a complex interplay of forces described as Zionism, the decline and end of the British Empire, the ascendancy of the US and USSR empires, and the spread of Arab nationalism.

As Israeli historian Tom Segev (1993) and US historian Peter Novick (1999), among others, point out, political and global consciousness about the Holocaust did not begin to emerge in either the United States or Israel until the mid- to late 1960s, and it was not fully formed and politically framed until the 1970s. Although the events and aftermath of the Holocaust have since been mobilized to affirm the right of Jews to a place of refuge — that is, to a Jewish state — it was not the reason that the international community represented by the United Nations would come to propose the partition of Palestine in 1947.

Tragically, the "solution" for one refugee community (European Jewry) meant the displacement of another (Palestinians) from their homeland. Linked to these proposals, in ways that are too complex to elaborate on here, the Zionist movement, which had emerged in the late 1800s in parts of Europe but which had all but collapsed prior to the war, also gained political currency at the international level at a later point. Before the war, few Jews chose to go to Palestine, preferring instead to migrate to other parts of Europe, the United Kingdom, and North America. In ways associated with, but also autonomous from, the globalizing process of Holocaust consciousness, Zionism's impact would not be felt within the Jewish community in the North American context until the late 1960s and 1970s. Until that period, although there was the idea of the Temple and of a historical connection with the region rooted in Judaism, there was little support for Zionism among North American Jews. Just as the Holocaust has become a global cultural phenomenon — with monuments, films, and museums — so too has the Jewish experience of loss been framed and globalized in the form of Zionism. Tragically, the experiences of Palestinian refugees have perhaps been diminished as a consequence.

The Palestinian experience of dispossession and nation building occurred in a period of decolonization throughout most of Africa and Asia. In the immediate postwar period, Palestinians primarily engaged with the United Nations, the only international institution or regime available to them. Especially important as a means of support was the United Nations Works and Relief Agency, which continues to provide social services to the refugee camps in the region. Politically, Palestinian concerns were raised in the Security Council as well as the General Assembly. A host of UN conventions on genocide, refugees, and other instruments were mobilized and adopted through the efforts of Palestinian and Arab representatives trying to engender support for the Palestinian cause. In the end, however, these legal efforts have offered less protection than their architects might have intended or hoped.

With the founding of the Palestine Liberation Organization in the 1960s came alliances with other resistance movements caught in the same backward spiral of neocolonization in a period of global decolonization. These included the Irish Republican Army, the African National Congress, and the American Indian Movement. The salient characteristics of Palestinian resistance in these periods (and to this day) were identification with a global struggle against colonial domination and suspicion of cultures or communities that supported Western versions of the good (in particular, individualism) and its attendant values, including Western-style property rights. By engaging with these globalizing processes and resistance movements, the Palestinians sought to create the basis for collective autonomy and national sovereignty.

On Palestine

Following the adoption of the UN's 1947 Partition Plan, the subsequent war, and the Declaration of the State of Israel on 15 May 1948, Palestine disappeared from the map and, for many, from history. More than sixty years have passed since the Palestinians' initial displacement, and although international legal instruments have been debated, few have been applied or implemented. The designation "refugee" is ascribed only to those whose homes or properties were taken and who have been prevented from returning to their property since 1948. In subsequent periods of violence and upheaval, however, including 1967, the disappearance of Palestine has meant the dispossession, for all, of their homeland. Accordingly, although not all Palestinians are by definition refugees, it can be argued that all Palestinians identify with the refugee experience of displacement, dislocation, and exile.

According to the *Supplement to the Survey of Palestine,* prepared for the United Nations Special Committee on Palestine in 1947 by the British, Palestinian Arabs outnumbered Jews in the mandate territory. Of an estimated 1.8 million people, approximately 1.3 million were Arabs and 600,000 were Jews. Jewish ownership of the land was estimated to be about 10 percent. The Palestinians were more generally engaged in a non-industrial, peasant economy, while the Jewish population was more prominent in industry (UN Special Committee on Palestine 1947).

Opinions about the amount of property lost and its value vary widely for a number of reasons, including record-keeping practices that did not always accurately reflect ownership and, of course, the effects of war. In their examination of Ottoman, British, Israeli, and United Nations land registration surveys and other related records, historical geographers Geremy Forman and Alexandre Kedar report on, for example, a 1951 United Nations Conciliation Commission for Palestine (UNCCP) study that establishes that 16.3 million dunams, including privately and communally held land, were lost, while a 1964 UNCCP document estimates that 7 million dunams were lost. Palestinian and Arab researchers have given estimates of between 5.7 million and 6.6 million dunams, whereas Israeli officials and researchers have consistently estimated between 4.2 million and 6.5 million dunams (Forman and Kedar 2004). Frank Lewis, who relies on the UNCCP's report in "Agricultural Property and the 1948 Palestinian Refugees: Assessing the Loss," notes that it was not simply that land was lost: "As important as the loss in the area was the *quality* of the abandoned land," which produced vegetables, fruit (especially olives, citrus fruits, melons, and bananas), tobacco, and cereals (Lewis 1996, 179, emphasis added).[3]

The state of Israel consistently rejects any right of Palestinian refugees to return to their homes inside the 1948 armistice lines. Resettlement outside Israel's Green Line (or Armistice Line) has remained the only option allowed by the Israeli government. As Palestinians argue, international law is on its side, with UN Resolutions 181, 194, and 242 forming the legal basis for their claims. However, Israel's interpretation of these same resolutions differs, and it is able — both politically and militarily — to enforce and maintain its position.

Israel's interpretation of UN Resolution 194 has had the greatest impact on Palestinian life. The Resolution's Paragraph 11 reads as follows:

> Resolves that the refugees wishing to return to their homes and live at peace with their neighbours should be permitted to do so at the earliest practicable date, and that compensation should be paid for the property of those choosing not to return and for loss of or damage to property which, under principles of international law or in equity, should be made good by the Governments or authorities responsible.

> Instructs the Conciliation Commission to facilitate the repatriation, resettlement and economic and social rehabilitation of the refugees and the payment of compensation, and to maintain close relations with the Director of the United Nations Relief for Palestine Refugees and, through him, with the appropriate organs and agencies of the United Nations.

It is this resolution that Palestinians interpret as establishing their right of return to their homes but that Israel refuses to acknowledge as such, let alone implement. According to Terry Rempel (1999), Israel interprets the text of the resolution, and especially Paragraph 11, in a narrow and technical sense, focusing on the word *should* as in "should be permitted to return." Israel argues that if the UN had intended a stronger meaning, the authors of the resolution would have used the word *must* as in "must be permitted to return." Moreover, Israel interprets later UN covenants, including the International Covenant on Civil and Political Rights, in such a way as to reject the notion that the covenant applies to Palestinians, for they return not to their country, Palestine, but to Israel, which did not exist at the time of their displacement. Israel's position is based on the state's 1952 Nationality Law, which prescribes the criteria for Israeli citizenship. Whereas Jews claim that their residency rights are several thousand years old and that they may acquire citizenship under the Law of Return, "the concept of residency for Palestinians is limited" (ibid., 212-14).

Lastly, at the core of Israel's opposition to the right of return is the interpretation of that right as one that is individual and not collective, a position consistent with Mollett's analysis of the Miskitos in Honduras and with Mackey's study of Aboriginal peoples in contemporary southern Ontario and upper New York State (see their chapters, this volume). Rempel (1999, 214) notes the irony of this position: "By the same logic, massive Jewish immigration to Palestine of displaced Jews under the British Mandate, based on the Zionist assumption that the refugees were returning to their country, although they were never citizens of Palestine, was illegal."

Nonetheless, in losing their rights to their land, Palestinians also lost a crucial base for the constitution of their collective autonomy as a community (see especially Khalidi 1997), a process also reflected in chapters by Mollett and Mackey.

Land, Law, and Loss

The price that has been paid for the compulsive power of the absolute dominion trope has been a heavy one, a maddeningly persistent tendency to suppress and to deny the collective and collaborative elements, the necessity of mutual dependence, inherent in social endeavour, and a consequently enormous distortion in our common capacities to understand and regulate our social life.

— Robert Gordon, *Paradoxical Property*

Although few deny that Palestine experienced changes in land tenure and administration that had tremendous socio-economic effects, it must also be remembered that, for more than forty years, the Palestinian narrative of violent dispossession was denied by the Zionist movement and the Israeli establishment. In a recent book titled *State Lands and Rural Development in Mandatory Palestine, 1920-1948,* P.N. Tyler Warwick (2001) provides a much-needed analysis of British policy on state land. Unfortunately, he adopts an Orientalist perspective, for example, writing: "Palestine was in a sorry state when the British assumed control. This ... 'the most beautiful of all lands,' promised by God to the ancient Israelites, had suffered over the centuries from misrule, misuse, neglect and the depredations of man, beast, and war" (ibid., 152). His analysis is informed by the Lockean premise that Palestinian culture was backward and that only a Zionist, Euro-colonialist presence could redeem the waste of the land that resulted in the exodus of the Israelites. Furthermore, and in keeping with arguments put forward by other authors in this book, Robert Home (2003, 305), citing de Soto (2000, 55), notes that what Palestinians owned was dead capital and that Israel's confiscatory processes, which had been "prepared by the British Mandate," had denied Palestinians their property rights.

Much of the ideological underpinnings of the Zionist project have since been debated or debunked, and Israel's New Historians have asserted that the Palestinians were violently displaced. Some argue that this displacement was a matter of war (e.g., Morris 1987, 1999), while others argue that it was a matter of policy (e.g., Pappe 2004). Whatever the interpretation, there can be no denying that Israel's mobilizations did not simply expropriate the land or appropriate land through the war: it invented laws to secure the process of dispossession, a common step, as the Introduction to this book and Cutler's chapter reveal. Israeli historical geographers, among others, have contributed to the critical legal scholarship on the violence of settler colonialism and the resulting regime of property rights. As Forman and Kedar (2004, 810) write: "One relatively constant element of dispossession has been the use of law in effecting and/or normalizing the outcome. The central role of legislation in such situations derives from the fact that the provision, or, alternatively, the transformation or negation of property rights, is invariably institutionalized by some type of law."

In the Israeli case, militarization separated the people from the land, while the law provided the ideological and political investment to legitimize and perpetuate the situation (see Blomley 2003, 2007).[4] Michael Fischbach's *Records of Dispossession* (2003) reveals the importance of this ideological dimension. His starting point is that refugee property losses are a matter of humanitarian concern. Drawing extensively from UN records, specifically the reports of the UNCCP, Fischbach argues that Israel entered all discussions of Palestinian compensation with the goals of permanently resettling Palestinians in other Arab countries and precluding their right to return.[5]

The question of how Israel furthered its land dominance has been taken up in a number of fields. Robert Home (2003, 293) discusses how the conquest of Palestinian land was facilitated by "applying, modifying, and selectively using Ottoman and British colonial law and regulations." In addition, Israeli historical geographer Geremy Forman (2006, 801) establishes that "in contrast to the primarily development-oriented aims of Mandate land settlement, the main aim of Israeli land settlement during [the postwar] period was securing state title to land in order to 'Judaize' the central Galilee through Jewish settlement."

Forman and Kedar (2004, 811) establish that beyond the "wartime seizure of millions of [Palestinian] dunums ... by Jewish (turned Israeli) forces," Israel embarked on a four-stage process over a twelve-year period that resulted in an integrated system of expropriation, appropriation, reclassification, and reallocation. By the fourth phase, Israel had transformed "appropriated Arab land into 'Israel Lands,' a new system of Jewish-Israeli 'national land.'"

In "Law and the Historical Geography of the Galilee: Israel's Litigatory Advantages during the Special Operation of Land Settlement," Geremy Forman (2006, 799) writes: "Israel's special operation of land settlement reflects this interdependence of law and space: not only did authorities apply this legal process in the Arab Galilee to achieve spatial goals, and not only was the process itself transformed by geographical realities in the region, but the product of the process — settled title to land — was as legal as it was spatial." In all of these ways, then, Israel has ensured that Palestinians are outside the state. This is literally true for those cast as refugees and practically true for those who are members of the state, for example, "non-Jewish" citizens of Israel. As a landless and stateless people, Palestinians also remain outside the law (in a Derridean sense) in a global system that privileges institutions of the nation-state (Ashcroft 2004).[6] As Robert Home (2003, 303-4) writes:

> Not only were Palestinians discouraged from living on their agricultural land, but that land could be transferred to Jewish-controlled local authorities or to the state for forestry or green space. Once transferred, such land could be fenced off, with army patrols to prevent trespass, and local Palestinians wanting to cultivate the land that was once theirs under miri rights were often forcibly excluded. Olive plantations (99 percent of which were owned by Palestinian Arabs, and which took decades to grow to full yield) were not allowed to be tended if belonging to "absentees," and the trees could be dug up for various official reasons (defence, reforestation, Jewish settlement). Often the appearance of a bulldozer and Israeli soldiers was the first indication that land had been confiscated. Thus the Palestinian agricultural base has been eroded, and farmland next to Palestinian communities transferred to the ILA [Israel Land Authority], which can then only be used by Jews ... Thus the planning system operates along two separate tracks worthy of the British dual mandate ideology, expanding Jewish settlements but restraining Palestinian.

Interestingly, and despite all the work that has been completed to date on property losses, the emphasis in works compiled by Palestinians is not on individual property owners but on the villages themselves. *Before Their Diaspora* (Khalidi 1984) and *All That Remains: The Palestinian Villages Occupied and Depopulated by Israel in 1948* (Khalidi 1992) are two widely referenced texts produced by the Institute for Palestine Studies. I refer to them here not because I think they are more reliable or historically accurate, but because they are produced by Palestinians and thus can be said to reflect how Palestinian nationals may officially represent their loss.

In *All That Remains,* editor Walid Khalidi (1992, xvii) draws on the work of Palestinian and Israeli historians, demographers, and geographers to "breathe life into a name, to give body to a statistic, to render to these [418] vanished villages a sense of their distinctiveness. It is meant to be a memorial." In these texts, property is never assigned to individual owners. In fact, no individual owners are named. Rather, every village is located by its proximity to a major centre, its elevation, its population in 1931 and in 1944-45, and its number of houses. Its communal use — Jewish, Arab or public — is also presented. The village, as it is found today, is described in some detail, as are the number and location of Israeli settlements. Land use statistics based on documents from the 1940s give a count of the dunams, and we learn that rarely did a village have less than 50 percent cultivable land; many had 90 percent or more. Khalidi (1992, xxxiv) writes: "The dispossession of the Palestinian village population of 1948 did not involve transient or migratory populations, but an ancient indigenous farmer community as settled as any in the Mediterranean basin or indeed anywhere else ... They were no less rooted in their patrimony and communal associations than any other people anywhere. It should not therefore be difficult to imagine the depth and longevity of the trauma that afflicted the generations that were uprooted in 1948 or to understand why their state of mind has been transmitted to their descendents in their Diaspora." The photographs of some 230 of the 418 villages visited are the most haunting aspect of the book. Khalidi (ibid., xxiv) writes of these photographs: "It should also be borne in mind that the photographs have been selected to 'show' something — the remains of houses, public structures, current uses of what remains. In this sense, they are not representative, as the vast bulk of the photographs show largely empty sites."

The above observations regarding law's spatializing power constitute the framework for considering Palestinians' relationships with their land. Following Roger Heacock's work (2004), but taking it in a slightly new direction, I argue that Palestinian poetry — its circulation across the boundaries of exile — is also evidence of autonomy. Heacock outlines how the relationship between land-related discourse and tenure has proven to be an inverse one and that political observers have not only misunderstood but also underestimated the Palestinians' bond to the land and their ongoing resistance to its loss. He notes, "The calculation is that by depriving the Palestinians of access to what is left of their land, they will be forced to give up their counterproductive resistance, and only then resume discussions on the disposition of (part of) the occupied territories" (ibid., 156). He argues that there is a rational basis for Palestinian behaviour. As their material or physical relationship to the land has declined, their attachment to it has intensified. This apparent paradox "can only be resolved if one gives due appreciation to the 'de-connection' and decentralization of Palestinian resistance" (ibid.).

In part because there has been no organic ruling elite — whether in the refugee camps, in Israel, or in the occupied territories — Palestinians have resorted to a form of localism. This tendency has allowed them to survive in times of crisis, but it has also contributed to their collective sense of identity — and perhaps also a sense of duty, regardless of their geographic location. I recognize that I am extending Heacock's work beyond what he might have intended. He does note, however, that destroyed villages and towns have reconstituted themselves in exile (see especially Peteet on the refugee camps in Lebanon, 2000, 2005). And Heacock (2004, 158) notes that "there was a tendency, however, to treat the phenomenon as an interesting ethnological vestige ... [rather than] that localism is the operative principle in the political realm as well."

Over the years, displacement forced Palestinians to survive in conditions in which official channels of support — whether local or international — were often unreliable. Heacock (2004, 160) concludes, then, that "the very primacy of their attachment to the land in the most specific sense, that is to say, their historic[al] rootedness in locale, has made it virtually impossible to defeat their movement, short of a new mass transfer of populations." I would differ with Heacock on this last point because even the transference of the population — which happened in 1948 and since — has not defeated the bond to the land or the politics and representations of the desire to return.

Those who continue to deny the very existence of Palestinians as a national collective cannot so easily dismiss the cultural saliency of the poetic tradition that their catastrophe has engendered. These poets write the life of Palestine into the memory and history of a world that seeks to make them invisible. Lines drawn on a map are constructs of a geopolitical reality, to be sure. Poets capture the lived realities.

Julie Peteet, an anthropologist who has spent decades working in the Palestinian refugee camps in Lebanon, comments on the problem of essentializing Palestinian identities. She writes:

> Palestinian in-group essentialism is hardly a surprise ... It has been produced in a context of violent displacement and exile and a continuing project to deny return ... Evoking Palestinian national identity in definitions of self and community is central to resisting a

> project in which nonrecognition is pivotal — the myth of the empty landscape or, in other variations, of people who could be moved at will to make way for those possessed of both more rights and technologies to render them possible ... Indeed, at some historical points, the very identity "Palestinian" — being and voice — constituted a form of resistance. (Peteet 2000, 186)

It is to these sites of being and voice — of the interaction and rearticulations of identity — that I want to now turn.

Property Rites

The poetry selections I present here — and which I was introduced to by community members — trace how social and historical memories constitute radically autonomous identities; autonomy in the absence of a state.[7] Much of the scholarly attention to Palestinian poetry provides us with critical analyses. Ashrawi (1978) is one example among many here (e.g., Amireh 2006 [2004]; Broderick 2003; Boullatta 1980; Boullatta and De Young 1997; Furani 2004; Hassan 2003; Somekh 1999; Tibawi 1963). While useful, it is not my intention to read the poetry as a literary scholar. That is not how my interlocutors read it; why should I? While scholarship on these works as forms of resistance (Antoon 2002; Harlow 1987, 1998; Palatella 2007) certainly informs my own analysis, this focus, too, is not my own. Rather, I stress how we might come to understand and appreciate poetry as an ethnography of identity. The poems are the maps that locate the scene, but these sites are culturally constituted sites of belonging and fix the location of the rites that have been narrated for me by those in exile.

> "On the Trunk of an Olive Tree," by Tawfiq Zayad[8]
>
> I shall carve my story and all the seasons of my tragedy,
> My sighs,
> My grove and the tombs of my dead.
> I shall carve the number of every usurped plot
> Of our land,
> The location of our village and its boundaries,
> In people's houses that have been razed,
> My uprooted trees,
> And every wildflower that has been crushed ...

I shall carve 'Kafr Qasim, I will not forget,'
I shall carve 'Dayr Yasin, It has taken root in my memory' ...
I shall carve all that the sun tells me,
What the moon whispers to me,
And what the lark relates
At the well forsaken by its lovers.
In order to remember
I shall remain here carving ...
On the olive tree in the courtyard of the house!
...

The most tragic verse in this poem by Zayad is the expression of the wish to die in a land one might not otherwise have access to. Zayad cannot write (because of censorship), so he carves. Zayad's turn to write the nation's history of dispossession and violence on the olive tree is not surprising, for the olive tree is symbolic of the Palestinians' rootedness to the land, their care for the land, and its bounty. The juxtaposition of death and destruction with the persistence and insistence of carving is also striking.

"Enough for me," by Fadwa Tuqan

Enough for me to die on her earth
be buried in her
to melt and vanish into her soil
then sprout forth as a flower
Played with by a child from my country.
Enough for me to remain
in my country's embrace
to be in her close as a handful of dust
    a sprig of grass
        a flower. (Selection from Jayussi 1992, 314, published in English)

Tuqan here projects an organic and embodied relation to the land and landscape. She expresses the tragic wish to die in a land to which she has no access. Tuqan's reference to a child raises the theme of regeneration and timelessness, for it is to a child that she refers but not to a child of any specific generation. In the following poem, note how Jabra expresses a love not only for the beauty of the land but also for its most bountiful harvest.

"In the Deserts of Exile," by Jabra Ibrahim Jabra

...

Our Palestine, green land of ours;
Its flowers as if embroidered on women's gowns;
March adorns its hills
With the jewel-like peony and narcissus;
April bursts open in its plains
With flowers and bride-like blossoms;
May is our rustic song
Which we sing at noon,
In the blue shadows,
Among the olive-trees of our valleys,
And in the ripeness of the fields
We wait for the promise of July
And the joyous dance amidst the harvest.

O land of ours where our childhood passed
Like dreams in the shade of the orange grove
Among the almond-trees in the valleys –
Remember us now wandering
Among the thorns of the desert,
Wandering in the rocky mountains;
...
Remember us
With our eyes full of dust
That never clears in our ceaseless wandering.
...
Our land is an emerald,
But in the deserts of exile,
Spring after spring,
Only the dust hisses in our face.
What then, what are we doing with our love?
When our eyes and mouths are full of frost and dust?
(Selection from Elmessiri 1982, 69-71, published in English)

Again, the olive tree is noted as part of a larger theme about a bountiful harvest. But Jabra goes on to contrast the "shade of the orange grove" and "the almond trees in the valleys" with the "desert of exile," the barrenness of the parched earth, and "eyes full of frost and dust" in the "desert of exile."

"To A Cloud," by Rashid Husayn[9]

I am the land ... do not deny me rain
I am all that remains of it.
Plant my brow with trees
And turn my poetry into vineyards
And wheat
And roses
That you may know me,
And let the rain pour down.
...
Waiting for you, my poetry turned to earth,
Became the fields,
Turned into wheat
and trees.
I am all that remains of our earth,
I am all that remains of what you love,
So pour ... pour with bounty
Pour down the rain. (Selection from Elmessiri 1982, 103, published in English)

Like Tuqan and Jabra, Husayn stresses the bountifulness of the land but then adds that the poetry itself becomes the earth, and the poems themselves are all that remain of the earth. In this context, the rain — all that feeds the land — is life giving. As with the previous poem and its mention of spring time, the rain and the appeal for rain connote regeneration. But the rain may also symbolize tears shed by the poet and the people: a sadness that also sustains the collective, for to mourn one's losses, one must remember their passing.

"We Go To A Country," by Mahmud Darwish

We go to a country not of our flesh. The chestnut trees are not of our bones.
Its stones are not the goats in the mountain song, and the eyes of pebbles are not lilies.
We go to a country that does not hand a special sun over us.
...
You have your glory, we have our glory. Ah, the country where
We see only what is not seen: our secret.

The glory is ours. A throne on legs chapped by the roads that
Take us to every house except our house.
The soul should find its soul in its own soul or die here.
(Darwish and al-Qasim 1984, 33, published in English)

"I Belong There" by Mahmud Darwish

I belong there. I have many memories.
... I have a wave snatched by seagulls, a panorama of my own.
I have a saturated meadow. In the deep horizon of my word,
I have a moon,
A bird's sustenance, and an immortal olive tree.
I have lived on the land long before swords turned man into prey.
I belong there. ...
I have learned and dismantled all the words in order to draw
from them a
Single word: Home. (Selection from Darwish 2003, 7, published
in English)

Darwish echoes earlier themes: the attachment to the land and the way a foreign place cannot sustain the same attachment because it is "not of our flesh" and it has no "special sun over us." Again, the olive tree appears as a central symbol of the land. And he finishes with a phrase that summarizes the feelings in all of the poems: "Single word: Home." All of the poems resist the disappearance of a culture; they memorialize and memorize its presence. It is in these senses that we can speak of property rights as property rites.

Poetry's Presence

Are the poetic narratives solely about loss, or are these lyrical expressions of the catastrophe a form of resistance? Could they be part of another performance of identity? Could it be that by memorializing place these narratives also produce or create and enhance new time (utopian) and (re) order history and thus the future? Could it be that in narrating these poems for me — in asking me to read them in(to) the present, these poems that reflect on the past, highlight the fragrance, the light, the sensual moments of Palestine — that Palestinians are remaking Palestine in the everyday? Could it be that these poems seek through me and other readers a reclamation that is not simply a longing for the material loss — in the sense of the property itself — but one that is also sensory? And could it be that through these readings we are bearing witness to an act of autonomy? By fostering these property "rites," are we not confronted with communal property shared among the dispossessed and disenfranchised? If, as Simon Schama (1995, 61) writes in *Landscape and Memory*, "landscapes are culture before they are nature," then reclaiming the land through poetry may be one more step to revisiting and revisioning Palestine.

What, too, of the poetic renditions of history, of the memories reflected in the poetry of the displaced? Could it be said that Palestinian poetry is a form of testimony caught between the written and the oral, for while it is published as the written word, it is meant to be heard, read aloud, and shared and experienced in communion? Is it meant, then, to hold open the connection between past and present, to make the connection between those who experienced the dispossession first-hand and those who are left only to ponder "all that remains"? Are those who introduced me to the importance of Palestinian poetry also asking me (and other readers or listeners) to act, to take responsibility for what they have been exposed to through these texts?

In short, why do I focus on rites and not rights? My references are both to the everyday and the ritualized — as poems are spoken and read in communal settings. In this way, Palestinian expressions of belonging to the land appeal less to the law than to the human current. In a recent interview, Darwish stressed: "In the end ... poetry has one meaning, it creates a reality, a linguistic reality which human beings need in order to survive their own reality and dilemmas." He also noted: "The role of the poet as witness ... has declined [with CNN], because the camera is more accurate than the writer. I believe the poet must write the unseen" (Darwish 2002, 77). Is autonomy not one of the unseen things?

In large measure, then, the profiles of the Palestinian that one encounters in this poetry are documentary, often autobiographical in nature. They seek to give voice to history and to community. In many fundamental respects, the landless refugee holds the key to comprehending the Palestinian condition, and Palestinian poetry offers valuable insights into the complex experience of the dispossessed. As we have seen in this volume, this dispossession remains a global phenomenon, and one wonders whether the insights from these poems speak to shared feelings of loss. Although the lines drawn to designate Israel-Palestine or Aboriginal–non-Aboriginal in North America and Miskito Indian biosphere preserve in Honduras are geopolitical constructs of the law, poetry captures the living experiences of those in exile. Rights in the form of resolutions have diminished Palestine. The poetry makes it real, serving to fictionalize the maps. Although no poetic effort can restore what Israel's devastating practices have destroyed, the poets have recorded the tragic accounts and their consequences.

In "Trajectories of Memory: Documentary Film and the Transmission of Testimony," Roxana Waterson (2007, 52) notes that although Maurice Halbwachs' important book *On Collective Memory* (1992) is routinely acknowledged, "remarkably little is said about the processes of transmission." Although her focus is on the role of the documentary, I think it applies to poetry as well. For while Halbwachs did write about "the manner in which individual memory is caught up in the 'social frameworks' provided by groupings such as families, religions," Waterson (2007, 52) rightly notes that he never analyzed or extended his analysis to appreciate the "potential of mass produced visual media" and, I would argue in the case of the Palestinians, poetry to change or constitute community members' "perceptions of history and value."

Conclusion

Almost nothing has been written in the social sciences about the role of poetry and nationalism; this promising area of study has been left to literary critics, whose analyses are limited to the poet and the text and not necessarily its audiences — Palestinians and others.[10] This chapter addresses this limitation by specifically considering Palestinians; however, the implications extend beyond the relationship between autonomy and property rights in Palestine.

My last argument is that autonomy — read here as *freedom* — necessarily involves a performative aspect, and this aspect requires us to ask what effect these kinds of nationalistic poetic expressions have on their audiences. Following Roxana Waterson's (2007) work on testimony and the documentary film, Rosemary E. Shinko's (2004) work on the discourses of denial, and Linda Zerilli's (2005a, 2005b) work on the imagination, I argue that the need for an audience or reader implies a dialogical relationship. This implication is vital both for how one interprets these poems, particularly if they are read as testimony or history, and for our understanding of the processes by which exiled identities are transmitted and thus become social (Waterson 2007, 53). Communal autonomy is built upon such collective identities. And the need for such building and reconstruction is a central aspect of the information age and globalization, as Castells (2003) argues at length. Poetry is performative — not simply in the sense that it may be read to an audience but also as a performance or act of autonomy in the face of the Zionist logic of disappearance and denial. As Linda M.G. Zerilli notes (2005b, 166): "Politics involves the exchange of argument in the sense of opening up the world that has been disclosed to us through language, our criteria or concepts ... Opening up creates the context in which a change in perspective may happen and things we may have known all along get counted differently." The force of the poetry that speaks of and to the land is that it insists on a presence. It is a rite of property in the absence of and in the struggle for property rights.

The force of the poetry is precisely that it requires others to confront a certain reality: we, as Palestinians, exist, and this is where we live! As Rosemary E. Shinko (2004, 48) writes: "Discursive and representational practices not only serve to define situations and events, but, more significantly, they are the means through which some actors are legitimized while others are marginalized. Frames of reference define who is a legitimate actor and who is not ... Speech and action create a political space, which enable[s] identities to emerge ... Identity requires the presence of 'others' who acknowledge and witness an individual's speech and acts. In essence, recognition confers identity."

Part of the urgency of the poetic project (and tradition) is to ensure that Palestine's history is acknowledged. It is — along with wedding songs, oral histories, and other everyday acts — a part of the struggle against forgetting. Giving voice to the Palestinians' loss, the narratives also present sensory accounts of the attachments to place.

Beginning with Heacock's (2004) article on Palestinians' self-organizing practices in the West Bank and Gaza, I would also like to argue a more forceful point in this regard: without a state, there may be a state of anarchy — with all the insecurity it entails. There may also be the self-governing and self-organizing principles and precepts we witness in these communities. Palestinian identity is articulated throughout communities, regardless of geographical location. We may need to learn more about how this kind of articulation can be facilitated through communication avenues opened up in this current era of globalization (see Habib 2008).

Critchley (2004, 183) writes, "politics consists in the manifestation of dissensus, a dissensus that disturbs the order by which government [or the state] wishes to depoliticize society. If politics can be understand as the manifestation of the anarchic demo, then politics and democracy are two names for the same thing. Thus, democracy is not a fixed political form of society, but rather the deformation of society from itself through the act of political manifestation." In the same way, a refugee people — landless, stateless — destabilizes the myths of property and autonomy, identity and territory, nationality and state. It disassembles the constituent elements: a people with a poetic tradition that emplaces their history, memory, and identity against Zionist, European, and global politics invented to exclude them. To simply dismiss these works as nationalistic or, worse yet, as anachronistic because they are so nationalistic is to fatally undermine their resonance in communities linked not so much (or any longer) by geography (a misreading of the issue) but rather by history and culture. To paraphrase Jacqueline Rose from *The Question of Zion* (2005, 13), this chapter asks its audience to do what may be impossible for some: to suspend both belief and disbelief. One is asked to enter the imagination of Palestinian nationals in order to understand why they command such passionate allegiance. More generally, as the coda to this book, these poems direct us to think more deeply about the violence of dispossession that has accompanied the globalization of property rights over the past three centuries.

Notes and Acknowledgments

Chapter 1: Introduction

1 To be clear, there is widespread recognition in the sprawling literature on property that property rights and regimes come in many guises. But we follow the likes of Macpherson, and more recently Gordon and Blomley, in noting with discomfort the tendency to "forget" this diversity. Gordon's point, for instance, is not that property really does (almost always) mean individual absolute dominion, but rather that the way we talk about property, particularly in the era of neoliberalism, often suggests the opposite, so much so that the common-sense notion of property is of individual freehold rights (see Blomley 2005).

2 *Species rights* means, as may be inferred, rights to specific species. But it also refers more generally to rights that are defined in relation to specific elements in the landscape as opposed to territorial rights to more or less monopoly control over discrete parcels of land (or water).

3 To be clear, Hardin does not use the phrase *selfish genes* per se. But in the almost entirely overlooked section titled "Conscience Is Self-Eliminating" of the original 1968 paper, Hardin (in a direct echo of Malthus) makes an explicitly Darwinian argument that natural selection would eliminate conscience as a check on anti-social behaviour. In his words (1968, 162), this would apply to "any instance in which society appeals to an individual exploiting a commons to restrain himself for the general good — by means of his conscience. To make such an appeal is to set up a selective system that works toward the elimination of conscience from the race."

4 As Polanyi (1944) notes, Bentham argues that prosperity in agriculture was facilitated by freedom in the disposition of land, and this form of freedom constituted, in significant measure, Bentham's conception of individual liberty. We do not, however, want to suggest that Bentham belongs in the natural rights tradition from which he clearly distanced himself.

5 For discussion of the character and significance of the Bretton Woods institutions, see Eichengreen and Kenen (1994).

6 For strongly parallel discussions of the continuous character of primitive accumulation throughout the history of capitalism, see De Angelis (2001) and Perelman (2000, 2007). See also Glassman (2006) for a discussion of the lineage of debates about primitive accumulation and accumulation by dispossession.

7 We also acknowledge the deeper and in some ways continuous history of enclosures and dispossessions that runs through colonialism and capitalism alike.

8 For an excellent empirical discussion of the role of classification in the dynamics of commodity exchange, see the chapter on wheat titled "A Sack's Journey" in Cronon (1991).

9 Some of this literature is aimed at sorting out the tendency to confuse communal with open access regimes. This confusion has been sewn in part by the widespread influence of Garrett Hardin's (1968) essay. Hardin clearly recognized that both individuation and strong state intervention could provide a check on the tendency among individuals to exploit socially important but unowned resources. But in doing so, he conflated open access regimes (available to anyone) with communal regimes, which are exclusive but at the level of a specific collective or community (Feeny et al. 1990; Swaney 1990). This misunderstanding, sadly, persists (for discussion, see, e.g., Mansfield 2004a, 2004b).

10 And as Macpherson himself notes, truly open access regimes are remarkably rare in historical and anthropological records, a finding that has generally been upheld by empirical scholarship differentiating between common property (i.e., communally held property) and truly open access regimes. See Berkes and IUCNNR (1989) and Mansfield (2007).

Chapter 2: The Globalization of International Law, Indigenous Identity, and the New Constitutionalism

1 See Cutler (2003, chaps. 2 and 3) for different theorizations of the role of law in the global political economy, and see Hunt (1993) for discussion of constitutive theories of law.

2 See Anghie (1999) for a full exposition of the racialized and colonial foundations of the conceptual absence of indigenous peoples in the field of modern international law as it took shape in the nineteenth century. For a parallel account of the colonial nature of the field of international relations, see Beier (2005).

3 This is not to say that indigenous peoples have not been accorded rights under national legal systems of law — see Wilson (2002), Aikau and Spencer (2007), and Byrd and Heyer (2008) for examinations of indigenous rights under various national jurisdictions — but rather that international law historically recognized their lands as terra nullius or as vacant lands open to acquisition. The doctrine of terra nullius was widely applied in South Africa and Australia, although it was abandoned by the Australian Supreme Court in *Mabo and Others v. Queensland* (No. 2) [1992] HCA 23; (1992) 175 CLR 1 F.C. 92/014 (see Russell 2005).

4 See Higgins (1985, 478) for what continues to be a very useful discussion of the subject-object distinction in international law.

5 Anghie (1999, 50n173) emphasizes the significance of understandings of private property law deriving from Roman law to the development of international legal conceptions governing the acquisition of property.

6 Tully (2000, 40) uses the term *irresolution* to refer to the colonial relationship between indigenous peoples and the state, which he characterizes as internal colonialism to capture its temporary, "as in unresolved," nature: "It is irresolution, so to speak, of the relation: a matrix of power put in place and continuously provoked by and adapted in response to the arts of resistance of indigenous peoples."

7 Ikeda (2004) presents this intersection as three cycles in citizenship participation/exclusion that correspond to three different structures of capitalist accumulation. The imperial subject corresponds to sixteenth-century imperialism and colonialism, the national subject corresponds to state-building projects of the eighteenth century, and the corporate subject coincides with the current conjuncture of neoliberal globalization.

8 Marx (1976) regards capitalism as developing initially through a process of primitive accumulation, by which producers were dispossessed of the means of production and alienated from the products of their labour, commodities, through the wage contract. Thus, workers or farmers, once dispossessed of the fruits of their labour or their land, were deprived of accumulating surplus value from exchange, which accrued to the owner through the commodity system. This dispossession, Marx argues, produced alienation and resulted in the fetishism of commodities: the commodities appeared to take on a life of their own, divorced as they were through market exchange from their human creators. For further theorization of the commodity form of law and its application to international law, see Cutler (2005b, 2008b, and 2009) and Miéville (2008).

9 See Anaya (2004, 254-55) for a discussion of these cases and the HRC's interpretations.

10 The Declaration on the Rights of Indigenous Peoples was adopted only after a guarantee was secured providing that self-determination meant self-governance within the existing territorial boundaries of the state (Koivurova 2008, 19).

11 After the Rudd government took power in Australia in 2008, that country changed its position and agreed to the declaration.

12 Holder (2008, 10-11) identifies this commodification of culture in a number of central international legal texts, including the UNESCO Declaration of the Principles of International Cultural Cooperation, the UNIDROIT Convention on Stolen or Illegally Exported Cultural Objects, and the European Charter for Regional or Minority Languages.

13 The concept of the right to development in international law can be traced back to the Universal Declaration on Human Rights, the Charter of the United Nations, multiple United Nations General Assembly resolutions and, finally, the non-binding Declaration on the Right to Development adopted by the United Nations General Assembly in 1986. It is interesting that international recognition of the right to development under international law has paid such little attention to indigenous peoples, although, as Gibbs (2005) notes, the application and development of the right to the Māori peoples in domestic practices in New Zealand may well have far-reaching implications. Increasingly, the right to development is being folded into the notion of sustainable development. See Loomis (2000) for analysis of the limitations of deriving a holistic conceptualization of self-determined development from dominant conceptualizations of sustainable development and for the need for a new epistemology of development.

14 See Cutler (2002a, 2000b, 2008) for analysis of the epistemological and ontological foundations of different conceptions of property and their relation to the mode of production of capitalism.

15 D'Errico (1996-97, 109) develops a similar analysis of the economistic and commodified definitions of freedom and civil rights that emerged as the commerce clause was used as the constitutional legal form to realize the human rights of blacks in the United States: "The essence of commodification is the transformation of unique individuality into generic form. In this case, the uniqueness of black people's historical relation to the Constitution was transformed into the generic form of the consumer in a market economy ... The market-based civil rights in the promised land of the 'Great Society' translated human values into an abstract context. It rested on and reinforced a system of

human relations in which people are subordinated to property and have 'rights' and 'freedoms' only on the basis of marketability." Moreover, as White (1986-87, 191) notes, the dominant tendency to root the total culture in capitalist market economics results in "the greatest difficulty in reflecting the reality of human community and the value of communal institutions. Its necessary tendency seems to be to destroy the idea of public action, indeed of community itself."

16 Increasing reliance on private bioprospector contracts (Roht-Arriaza 1995-96) raises still another issue of dispossession through the imperialism of contract law, which is a vehicle for universalizing the commodity form of law.

17 Marx (1976, 875) defines "primitive accumulation" as "nothing else than the historical process of divorcing the producer from the means of production. It appears as 'primitive' because it forms the pre-history of capital, and the mode of production corresponding to capital." He continues, "the expropriation of the agricultural producer, of the peasant, from the soil is the basis of the whole process" (ibid., 876).

18 Davis (2003-4) argues that indigenism or indigeneity involves at least five different goals that illustrate the extent to which indigenous autonomy is today infused by market culture: the ownership and control of cultural information, the ability to exploit and profit from the use by others of that information, the promotion and encouragement of cultural information, the protection and preservation of biocultural information and biodiversity, and the protection and preservation of cultural artifacts.

19 See Amoore (2005) for a collection that provides an inspirational introduction to analyzing and theorizing resistance.

20 See Cutler (2008a) for a critical analysis of corporate social responsibility initiatives as examples of neoliberal market discipline that function to obscure corporate power and influence by neutralizing opposition.

21 The ideological foundation of belief in governance through property is beyond the scope of this chapter, but it lies at least in part in the law and economics movement, which has had a profound influence on modern law (see White 1986-87). For champions of the governance capacities of private property law, see Graham and McJohn (2005) and Ghosh (2003-4) and see Coombe (1998, 1999) for more nuanced support. For a classic statement of the liberal economic view concerning the efficiency of property rights regimes in supplying common goods, see Ostrom (2002); for a review of liberal political economy theories advancing the governance capacities of economic markets and corporate actors in governing through the supply of common goods, see Keohane (1984), Rittberger and Nettesheim (2008), and Cutler, Haufler, and Porter (1999). For a critique of the logic of the private provision of common goods, see Cutler (2008a), and see Heald (2003-4) for an insightful analysis of the inability of neoliberal economic theory to ground indigenous autonomy claims through intellectual property rights.

22 *Monsanto Canada, Inc., v. Schmeiser,* T-1593-98, 2001 FTC 256 is the celebrated case in commodification of germplasm.

23 Note that the International Treaty on Plant and Genetic Resources for Food and Agriculture negotiated in the Food and Agriculture Organization abandons the designation "common heritage" and makes states responsible for the exploration, conservation, and sustainable development of plant resources. See Coleman and Reed, this volume.

24 The deterritorializing and delocalizing nature of global international economic law and practice is growing even more acute through the proliferation of bilateral investment treaties that are knitting global production, investment, and trade into a seamless, delocalized web of legal transactions and dispute settlement mechanisms.

25 See Keal (2003, 124-25) for summaries of the Australian *Mabo* case referred to above and the key Canadian cases — *Calder, Sparrow,* and *Delgamuukw* — that involve indigenous rights.

26 The ICBG program operates as a public-private partnership that involves scientists, government agencies, corporations, and others engaged in agricultural research and production in projects concerning terrestrial plants of medicinal significance. One project, the ICBG-Peru project, is a partnership with the Aguarna peoples of Peru that is exploring the patenting of indigenous medicines (McManis 2003-4).

Chapter 3: Lifeworlds and Property

This research was supported by a Postdoctoral Fellowship from the Social Sciences and Humanities Research Council of Canada. I would like to thank Harvey Feit and Richard Preston for access to research collections and for their thoughtful advice and feedback. The statements by Mianscum and Coon came from the field notes of Harvey Feit and are printed with permission.

Chapter 4: Making Forests "Normal"

1 For example, the province accounted for about one-third of Canada's annual timber harvest, averaging over 72 million cubic metres between 1993 and 1997.

2 For an excellent overview of the provincial forest industry, see Hayter (2000).

3 BC's forest industry paralleled the global articulation and integration of Canadian resource extraction and processing more generally. See Drache (1982), Hayter and Barnes (1990, 2001), and Innis (1956).

4 Some argued that control was even more concentrated given the various financial and administrative interconnections among forest industry giants. See Wagner (1988).

5 Between 1994 and 2001, raw or unprocessed log exports from BC increased almost six times from just over 0.5 million cubic metres to about 3.0 million cubic metres and from about 1 percent of the provincial harvest to 6 percent (Marshall 2002). This trend has been, if anything, encouraged by changes in provincial regulations that make it easier for firms to export logs without clearly demonstrating the absence of a domestic buyer.

6 Total employment in BC's forest sector peaked in 1979 at over eighty thousand workers. By 1995, total employment in the sector had dropped to under sixty-four thousand workers. Controlling for changes in the annual allowable cut, this change represents a decrease in employment per 1,000 cubic metres of harvest from 1.06 workers to 0.85 (Marchak, Aycock, Herbert 1999).

7 I draw here as well on E.P. Thompson (1975) and his seminal arguments about ideology and the rule of law in the context of Whig-era enclosures in England. For Thompson, the rule of law, even if it enables mass dispossession, must somewhat paradoxically be seen even by the relatively marginalized as a potential weapon to be used in their own defence. See also the Introduction.

8 A similar line of reasoning also underpins classic work undertaken on the fisheries by Gordon and Scott (Gordon 1954; Scott 1955; see also Mansfield 2004b).

9 My use of the terminology of use and exchange value is meant to correspond loosely to the classical tradition in political economy, wherein *use value* refers, as the term suggests, to the value of a thing unto itself, encapsulating both its physical attributes and the cultural context that defines its use. *Exchange value,* again as the term suggests, refers to the

value of some entity in exchange or for exchange. Neither of these terms, however, is meant to simply convey value as expressed in monetary terms, nor even in narrowly economic terms. That is a reified form of exchange value. I do draw specifically on Marx (1976) in insisting that the categories make little sense unless understood in dynamic relation to one another, particularly, though perhaps not only, in a capitalist political economy and on Graeber's (2001) more recent development (also influenced heavily by Marx) of the categories of value as categories of meaning.

10 Others have also attempted to extend the broad notion of the spatio-ecological fix to consider modes of environmental transformation and regulation (see, e.g., While, Jonas, and Gibbs 2004; Castree 2008).

11 My terminology and conceptualization here draw on Scott (1998).

12 It was estimated at the time of the first Sloan Commission that in excess of 20 million acres (8 million hectares) of forest land in BC had been cut over and not reforested (Sloan 1945).

13 I see this also as a strong theme in William Cronon's *Changes in the Land* (1983). However, more generally, I have in mind the idea of framing space and the ways in which representations of space become constitutive of the production of space (including ecological space), an idea that draws variously on Said (1979), Mitchell (1991), and Gregory (1994). For a close parallel argument, see Demeritt (2001).

Chapter 5: Contested Autonomy

I would like to thank the Miskito village of Belen and neighbouring communities inside the reserve for their participation in this research project. I also thank the Social Sciences and Humanities Research Council of Canada, the International Development Resource Center, and the Department of Geography, University of Toronto, for supporting the broader research from which this chapter draws. I am also indebted to the anonymous reviewers and the editors at UBC Press for their constructive comments. All errors in interpretation are my own.

1 This chapter draws primarily from my ethnographic fieldwork conducted over fourteen months from January to December 2003 and from January to March 2005. During this period, I conducted village-based interviews with Belen villagers. These interviews were conducted throughout March and April 2003, and follow-up questions were conducted during the rest of the research period. In this text, these interviews are organized and labelled as author's interviews. In-text citations to field notes refer to notes produced during ethnographic research in 2003. Ethnographic observations, interviews, and personal communications were obtained with informed consent both at the level of the individual (interviews and ad hoc conversations) and at the level of the village. I sought permission to conduct research from Miskito village authorities in 2002 and again in 2003. To maintain confidentiality, all names and some place names that appear in this chapter are pseudonyms.

2 *Departamentos* are administrative territories.

3 AFE-COHDEFOR was renamed the National Institute for Conservation, Forest Development, Protected Areas and Wildlife Refuges (ICF) in 2008.

4 *Ladino* refers to a person of mixed European and indigenous ancestry and is used synonymously in Honduras with *mestizo,* a term that celebrated mixed heritage throughout the era of Latin American independence. In Honduras, *ladino* can also refer to an

indigenous person who speaks Spanish and self-identifies as ladino. *Colono* is the Spanish word for colonist. In this chapter, all colonos are ladinos.

5 *Struggle* not only refers to acts of physical violence but also to threats, intimidation, theft, sabotage, deception, and bribery.

6 Although inheritance rules normally follow the maternal line, these rules are quickly changing as some new couples either clear their own agricultural lands or buy a village plot away from the family lands unit (author interviews, Belen, 2003).

7 Fruit trees and perennials crops such as guineo (a form of plantain) located on insla prata also communicate possession.

8 This is not romantic reproduction. Indeed, respect for existing land claims is fostered through various informal controls (Rudel 1995) found not only in indigenous domains but also throughout rural Latin America.

9 *Native ladino* refers to ladinos born inside the Mosquitia. This arbitrary category, however, also includes ladinos that have lived in the region for more than fifty years and participate in Miskito community practices, particularly reciprocity (author's field notes, 2003).

10 When social groups are differentiated and vulnerable to discriminatory and unequal treatment based on constructed biological, phenotypical, and cultural characteristics, racialization is unveiled (Dei 1996).

11 *Zambo* is a derogatory (colonial) term to describe the offspring of an Amerindian and black union and is most often used in reference to the Miskito.

12 Usufruct allows only use rights. The state retains ownership of the land; therefore, the sale and transfer of land is limited.

13 Mejoras are improvements made on the land such as crops, pasture, animals, or shelter.

14 Registering lands simply means having parcels measured and recorded in the municipal log (a tattered notebook with missing pages located in the village of Brus Laguna).

15 A manzana is a common measurement in Miskito and ladino land discussions. One manzana is equivalent to 0.67 hectares. *Milpa* refers to maize crops.

16 Acquiring a bull is another strategy by colonos to legitimate their presence and show "improvements."

17 This is contested by the Miskito, who insist that the founders arrived in 1997 and the rest of the settlement in 2000, which would make them illegal, according to the Plan de manejo (AFE-COHDEFOR 2000).

18 On each occasion that I and two Miskito research assistants took the two-hour (each way) walk to San Arturo and around the village, we passed through smoldering embers; in some cases, trunks were still burning.

Chapter 6: Globalization, Intellectual Property, and the Emergence of New Property Types

1 *Diamond, Commissioner of Patents and Trademarks v. Chakrabarty,* 447 U.S. 303, 100 S. Ct. 2204, 65 L. Ed. 2d 144 (1980).

2 National European offices both collaborate and compete with the EPO. National bodies had the initial advantage of an extant patent list upon which to collect renewal fees, while the EPO had to charge higher licensing fees. This comparative advantage diminishes each year, while the transnational applicability of an EPO patent has made it more attractive.

3 For an extensive discussion of ICANN, see Pal (2009).

4 Thirty-four percent (1,594,000) were in force in European Patent Convention states, 27 percent (1,295,000) in the United States, and 22 percent (1,041,000) in Japan. Seventeen percent (794,000) were held in other jurisdictions. See Japan Patent Office (2001).

5 It dispensed $187 million in compulsory licence fees in 2001.

6 In common law countries, moral rights are covered both under copyright and other legislation, such as defamation. In civil law countries, where copyright is perceived as a common good, there was less resistance to an indefinite extension of attendant moral rights.

7 The CAPRI system (Agreement Concerning the Computerized Administration of Patent Documents Reclassified according to the IPC) harmonizes pre-1970 patents with the IPC system.

8 The 67,007 applications in 1998 led to 3,463,147 applications at the national level.

9 In 1983, patents were not yet available in Afghanistan, Angola, Bhutan, Burma, China, Ethiopia, Laos, Mozambique, Oman, Papua New Guinea, Saudi Arabia, the United Arab Emirates, and Yemen. In 1981, India granted 1,289 patents, Venezuela 813. The heaviest users of the PCT in 1981 were the United States (65,770), Japan (50,904), the United Kingdom (22,994), Canada (22,696), France (21,447), the Federal Republic of Germany (13,429), Brazil (10,292), Switzerland (8,289), Spain (7,255), and Italy (6,500).

10 Copyleft is a form of licensing that allows others to use and or modify a product without being required to pay for it and that requires them to adhere to the same agreement if they choose to pass the product to a third party.

11 *US Plant Patent Act,* 46 Stat. 376 (1930), 35 U.S.C. ss. 161-164.

12 See *re Arzberger,* 112 F.2d 834 (C.C.P.A. 1940).

13 *Funk Brothers Seed Co. v. Kalo Inoculant Co.,* 333 U.S. 127, 68 S. Ct. 440, 92 L.Ed. 588 (1948).

14 Although Harvard obtained a US patent for the oncomouse in 1988 (US Patent No. 4,736,866), some Western countries have rejected the application. Drawing on patent legislation dating to 1869 (and last substantially altered in 1923), Canada's Supreme Court ruled in 2002 that the oncomouse is not a composition of matter but a naturally occurring entity and, thus, not patentable. *Harvard College v. Canada (Commissioner of Patents),* 2002 SCC 76, [2002] 4 S.C.R. 45.

15 *Patent and Trademark Amendment Act of 1980,* Pub. L. No. 96-517, 94 Stat. 3015-3027, 1984 amendment, Pub. L. No. 98-620, 98 Stat. 3362-3364.

16 Council of Europe, *Convention for the Protection of Human Rights and Dignity of the Human Being with regard to the Application of Biology and Medicine: Convention on Human Rights and Biomedicine,* Oviedo, 4.IV.1997. Article 1 of the *Universal Declaration of Human Rights* states that "all human beings are born free and equal in dignity and rights."

Chapter 7: Competing or Relational Autonomies?

I am grateful to the Social Sciences and Humanities Research Council and the McMaster University Arts Research Board for funding the research discussed in this chapter.

1 The UN Declaration on the Rights of Indigenous Peoples states that "Indigenous peoples, as a specific form of exercising their right to self-determination, have the right to autonomy or self-government in matters relating to their internal and local affairs, including culture, religion, education, information, media, health, housing, employment, social welfare, economic activities, land and resource management, environment

and entry by non-members, as well as ways and means for financing these autonomous functions" (article 31).

2 See, for example, Feit (1989, 1995, 1998), Wilmsen (1989), Asch (1984, 2004), Biolsi (1991, 1992), Culhane (1998), Dyck and Waldram (1993), Dyck (1985), Mohawk (2000), Monet (1992), and Waldram (1988). A few notable examples of analysis of Aboriginal-white relations and conflict are Landsman (1985, 1987), Landsman and Ciborski (1992), Feit (1995, 2004), Hodgins and Cannon (1995), Menzies (1994), Pertusati (1997), Purich (1991), Frideres (1988, 1996), Furniss (1999), Nadasdy (2002), and Harris (2002).

3 The correct terminology for these conflicts is complex. There is a problem with using the term *claims* instead of *rights* because it does not account for the broader political discourse of indigenous rights, a framework that is much more inclusive than *land claims* suggests and may include ideas about title to culture (see Coombe 1993; Mackey 1995, 1998). Furthermore, to claim something may imply that a request is being made, not that one is inherently entitled. On the relationship between property and rights, see also Asad (2003), Coombe (1993), Mackey (2005), Merry (2003), Rose (1994, 1998, 2004), Sarat and Kearns (2001), Speed and Collier (2000), Verdery and Humphrey (2004), and Wilson (1997).

4 The Cayuga are one of the Haudenosaunee Six Nations, who have been studied extensively for over 150 years, from Lewis Henry Morgan onward. For bibliographies, see Johansen and Mann (2000).

5 These particular case studies are not intended to represent all land claims in North America. This study is a qualitative examination of land rights conflict; therefore, the cases were selected precisely because they offer data for an in-depth analysis of the public backlash that emerged from First Nation claims.

6 In the 1920s, Desgaheh was the *Tadodaho* (or speaker) for the Iroquois Grand Council at Grand River, the traditional longhouse government that asserted independence for the government system. He presided when Canada closed down the traditional governments and imposed a band system that would answer to the Indian Affairs bureaucracy. With the "Canadian police about to arrest him, Desgaheh travelled to the headquarters of the League of Nations in Geneva, Switzerland, carrying a Haudenosaunee passport, with an appeal for support from the international community" (Johansen and Mann 2000, 73-74).

7 All interviews were conducted by the author between 2001 and 2008. Names are withheld by mutual agreement. All names used are pseudonyms.

8 According to the Indian and Northern Affairs website, "Caldwell First Nation lands are held in fee simple and are subject to all provincial laws ... The Caldwell First Nation will be required to address reasonable concerns with the municipality on the drainage issue and will be required to come to a formal agreement on how the drainage issue will be dealt with."

9 This is a developing literature. See, for example, Asch (2002), Muehlebach (2003), Monture-Angus (1998), Alfred (1999), and Feit (2004).

10 Relational autonomy is a framework being developed by feminist thinkers such as Mackenzie and Stoljar (2000), Nedelsky (1991), and Young (2001). Also see Feit (2005). The idea is that autonomy is a liberal philosophical framework that has historically valorized problematic ideals of boundedness and independence from others. These authors instead re-theorize autonomy to make it philosophically compatible with lived realities of social interdependence and render it capable of recognizing and supporting deep commitments to others and to collectivities.

Chapter 9: Globalization without World Order

1 Since joining the World Trade Organization, China has doubled (from ten to twenty) the number of foreign films it allows to be imported each year. Among the most absurd examples of Chinese censorship are cutting the so-called nudity scenes in *Schindler's List* and postponing the third part of the *Lord of the Rings* for fear that it would promote feudal superstition.

2 Intellectual property encompasses trademarks, patents, and copyright. Although each of these has its own unique traits, in this chapter *intellectual property* is used as a general term to designate them all.

3 The WIPO Convention was signed at Stockholm on 14 July 1967. It entered into force in 1970, and WIPO has operated as a specialized agency of the United Nations since 1974. See Gorman, this volume.

4 According to Alan Story (2002, 129), "core US copyright industries had contributed an estimated US$457.2 billion to the US economy ... the value of such industries to the gross US domestic product had increased by an astounding 360 percent between 1977 and 1999."

5 The other two are GATT (for trade in goods) and GATS (General Agreement on Trade in Services).

6 In addition to the perceived injustice of encouraging vast sums of money to flow from developing countries to the developed world, there is a general suspicion about attempts by intellectual property producers to equate copying with stealing. After all, unlike in theft — the producer of intellectual property does not lose the information. Instead, piracy damages intellectual property producers by introducing competition.

7 As Carlos Correa (2000, 128) points out, reverse engineering is a "crucial element in the competitiveness of the software industry" since "software products are generally developed using previously existing programs and algorithms."

8 Figures for dollars lost to pirates are highly misleading because the calculations make the absurd assumption that purchasers of fake goods would, if these markets didn't exist, buy the real thing.

9 Sometimes pirated goods are sloppy imitations. Other times, however, factories producing brand name products sell some of their extra stock out the back door. In these cases, the pirated goods are the exact same product.

Chapter 10: Property Rites

This chapter is dedicated to my father, Na'aman Habib. Among his many books, one will also find a well-worn photocopy of "A Lover of Palestine." This essay developed over the course of several years, beginning in 2002 with William Coleman's invitation to participate in the Globalization and Autonomy research project at McMaster University. I would like to thank Maria di Cenzo for reading and commenting on an early draft. Thanks to Iris Bruce, Len Friesen, Derek Hall, Audra Simpson, and Jackie Solway for their invitations to share my research with their colleagues and students at the "Art of Development Conference" sponsored by the World University Services of Canada, Trent University, McMaster University, and Cornell University, respectively; Dominick Boyer, Jane Fajans, Eva Mackey, Samah Sabra, Terence Turner, and John Weaver for their comments; my students in Global Studies and Cultural Analysis and Social Theory courses at Wilfrid Laurier University, including Brittan Coghlin and Joseph Farag, who focused their attention on the poetic tradition and the Israel-Palestine conflict; and the anonymous reviewers who made helpful suggestions that were incorporated into this work. Special thanks to Amit Habib and Jim Novak who listened to, read, and commented on the many iterations of this piece. This research was sponsored by Social Sciences and Humanities Research Council of Canada research grants.

1 Anthropologist Julianne Hammer (2005, 178), who studied Palestinians born in exile, writes: "Poetry, fiction, and music were important to me because a review of the repertoires of Palestinian poetry, short stories, novels, and nationalist songs shows that they can help young exiled Palestinians learn about their national culture. In many cases, they directly reflect on political issues; in others they simply reflect that the preservation of the Palestinian heritage is an important part of preserving national and cultural identity."

2 Salah Hassan's (2003) critique is that the focus on occupation literature distorts and limits perspectives on Palestine. See also Hanan Ashrawi (1978) on this issue.

3 Lewis (1996, 184) addresses the unreliability of Granott's statistics as follows: "The only other estimate we have is from Granott (1956, 254), who reports Israeli 'official sources' as putting the total area of abandoned land at 4.8 million dunams of which 3 million were cultivable. Without a description of the Israeli procedure, which was never made available, one wonders what to make of these numbers. Certainly, they are inconsistent with Village Statistics and with the Agriculture Department's estimates of the actual Arab area under cultivation before and after the 1948 war ... The CCP produced area estimates that approximate mine, but it seriously understated the value of this land." Furthermore, "Where this paper deviates from previous work is in the valuation of the land ... The United Nations has often been viewed, certainly by Israelis, as favouring the Arab side; yet, the UN estimate of lost Arab agricultural property is less than half the value derived here" (ibid., 187). Lewis understands the political implications of the numbers and their uses, noting value underestimations on the Israeli and United Nation sides, as well as, for example, the degree to which "the productivity of the land the Palestinians gave up was significantly lower than the productivity of their holdings outside of Israel, located on what is now the West Bank and Gaza" (ibid.).

4 Blomley (2003, 130) in "Law, Property, and the Geography of Violence: The Frontier, the Survey, and the Grid" writes: "Violence is not only a product of power, but also its vector ... Yet the violence that is done in the name of law appears uncoupled from the legal enterprise ... The effect is to make the words of law — for example, judicial decisions — appear uncoupled from their deeds ... At its core, property entails the legitimate act of expulsion, devolved to the state."

5 Forman and Kedar (2004, 822) write: "Dispossessed Arab citizens and Israeli officials alike regarded compensation as legal and moral recognition of expropriation. This was one of a number of reasons why many owners refused to apply, and it also explains why Israeli authorities regarded compensation as critical."

6 See also Long (2006, 115-16), who notes, following Agamben, "that the concept of humanitarianism, and the doctrine of inalienable and indefeasible human rights which goes along with it, is enormously problematic with respect to bare and sacred life since it is deeply implicated within the system of biopolitical sovereignty which it is out to challenge ... With the rise of the nation-state, however, birth has become intimately and inextricably linked with nation ... Problems therefore arise with respect to the refugee ... As such, refugees fracture the supposed continuity of nativity (man) and nation (citizen), making them very hard to define politically and also very hard to deal with."

7 I do not present the poems in their entirety, only extractions. Some of the poets that I was directed to are represented here. Although I did not select two of the most famous poems — Mahmoud Darwish's "We travel like other people" and "Identity Card" — I believe the ones that I have selected are reflective of popular sentiment about the Palestinian relationship to Palestine among those living in North America. When I found more than one version of a poem translated to English, I discussed it with at least one community member, and I chose the one that we thought most closely represented its original meaning in Arabic.

8 I came across several versions of this poem. An older version titled "The Olive Tree" appears in *A Lover from Palestine and Other Poems,* edited by Abdelwahab M. Elmessiri (1970). I used what appears to be a newer translation here, but I cannot locate its source. It was given to me as a photocopy.

9 This poem has also been cited with the title "I Am the Land." See Sakkal Design, http://www.sakkal.com/Guest_Gallery/hasan/hasan04.html.

10 On the poetry of occupation, see Hanan Ashrawi (1978); see also Darwish on the poet's prerogative to be non-nationalist (in Palattella 2007) and some of the ethnography collected by Furani (2004) on the role of the poet in community.

Works Cited

AFE-COHDEFOR (State Forestry Administration). 2000. *Plan de manejo: Reserva del hombre y la biosfera del Río Plátano*. Tegucigalpa: Proyecto Manejo y Protección de la Biosfera Río Plátano.

—. 2002. *Informe estudio de factibilidad: Proyecto reserva del hombre y la biosfera del Río Plátano, componente catastro y titilación*. Tegucigalpa: Proyecto Manejo y Protección de la Biosfera Río Plátano.

Agrawal, Arun. 2001. Common property institutions and sustainable governance of resources. *World Development* 29 (10): 1649-72.

—. 2005. *Environmentality: Technologies of government and the making of subjects*. Durham, NC: Duke University Press.

Aikau, Hokulani, and James Spencer. 2007. Introduction: Local reaction to global integration: The political economy of development in indigenous communities. *Alternatives* 32 (1): 1-7.

Alfred, Taiaiake. 1999. *Peace, power and righteousness: An indigenous manifesto*. Don Mills, ON: Oxford University Press.

Alvarado García, Ernesto. 1958. *Legislación indigenista de Honduras: Recopilación e introducción de Ernesto Alvarado García*. Ediciones Especiales, Número 35. Mexico: Instituto Indigenista Interamericano.

Amani, Bita. 2009. *State agency and the patenting of life in international law: Merchants and missionaries in a global society*. Burlington, VT: Ashgate.

Amireh, Amal. 2006 [2004]. Between complicity and subversion: Body politics in Palestinian national narrative. In *Diversifying the discourse: The Florence Howe Award for Outstanding Feminist Scholarship, 1990-2004*, ed. Mihoko Suzuki and Roseanna Dufault, 288-308. New York: Modern Languages Association.

Amoore, Louise, ed. 2005. *The global resistance reader*. London: Routledge.

Anaya, S. James. 2004. *Indigenous peoples in international law*. 2nd ed. Oxford: Oxford University Press.

Anaya, S. James, and C. Grossman. 2002. The case of *Awas Tingni v. Nicaragua:* A new step in the international law of indigenous peoples. *Arizona Journal of International and Comparative Law* 19 (1): 1-15.

Andreasson, Stefan. 2006. Stand and deliver: Private property rights and the politics of global dispossession. *Political Studies* 54 (1): 3-22.

Anghie, Antony. 1999. Finding the peripheries: Sovereignty and colonialism in nineteenth-century international law. *Harvard International Law Journal* 40 (1): 1-80.

Antoon, Sinan. 2002. Mahmoud Darwish's allegorical critique of Oslo. *Journal of Palestine Studies* 31 (2): 66-77.

Anuradha, R.V. 2001. IPRs: Implications for biodiversity and local and indigenous communities. *Review of European Community and International Environmental Law* 10 (1): 27-36.

Aoki, Keith. 2003-4. Weeds, seeds and deeds: Recent skirmishes in the seed wars. *Cardozo Journal of International and Comparative Law* 11 (2): 247-331.

Appadurai, Arjun. 2000. Grassroots globalization and the research imagination. *Public Culture* 12 (1): 1-21.

Appiah, Anthony Kwame. 2005. *The ethics of identity.* Princeton, NJ: Princeton University Press.

Arrighi, Giovani. 1994. *The long twentieth century: Money, power, and the origins of our times.* London: Verso.

Asad, Talal. 1979. Anthropology and the analysis of ideology. *Man* 14: 607-27.

—. 2003. *Formations of the secular: Christianity, Islam, modernity.* Palo Alto, CA: Stanford University Press.

Asch, Michael. 1984. *Home and Native land: Aboriginal rights and the Canadian Constitution.* Toronto: Methuen of Canada/Assembly of First Nations.

—. 1992a. Aboriginal self-government and the construction of Canadian constitutional identity. *Alberta Law Review (Constitution Series)* 30 (2): 465-49.

—. 1992b. Errors in *Delgamuukw:* An anthropological perspective. In *Aboriginal title in British Columbia: Delgamuukw v. The Queen,* ed. Frank Cassidy, 221–244. Vancouver/Montreal: Oolichan Books/Institute for Research on Public Policy.

—. 1994. To negotiate into Confederation: Canadian Aboriginal views on their political rights. In *Readings in Canadian history: Post-Confederation,* 4th ed., ed. R. Douglas Francis and Donald R. Smith, 561-78. Toronto: Harcourt Brace and Company.

—. 2002. From terra nullius to affirmation: Reconciling Aboriginal rights with the Canadian Constitution. *Canadian Journal of Law and Society* 17 (2): 23-37.

—. 2004. Reflections on relations between indigenous peoples and the Canadian state. *American Anthropologist* 106 (1): 165-68.

Ashcroft, Bill. 2004. Representation and its discontents: Orientalism, Islam and the Palestinian crisis. *Religion* 34 (1): 113-21.

Ashrawi, Hanan Mikhail. 1978. The contemporary Palestinian poetry of occupation. *Journal of Palestine Studies* 7 (3): 77-101.

Assies, Willem, Gemma van der Haar, and André J. Hoekema, eds. 1998. *The challenge of diversity: Indigenous peoples and reform of the state in Latin America.* Amsterdam: Thela Thesis.

Austin, Graeme W. 2003-4. Re-treating intellectual property? The WAI 262 Proceeding and the heuristics of intellectual property law. *Cardozo Journal of International and Comparative Law* 11 (2): 333-63.

Awashish, Philip. 2002. *From board to nation governance: Eeeyou Tapay-tah-jeh-souwin (Eeyou governance) and economic development in Eeyou Istchee.* Paper presented at the "Conference on

Reconfiguring Aboriginal-State Relations," Queen's University, Kingston, Ontario, November 2002.

Bakker, Karen. 2005. Neoliberalizing nature? Market environmentalism in water supply in England and Wales. *Annals of the Association of American Geographers* 95 (3): 542-65.

Bakker, Isabelle, and Stephen Gill. 2003. *Power, production and social reproduction: Human In/security in the global political economy.* Houndmills: Palgrave Macmillan.

Balbus, Isaac D. 1976-77. Commodity form and legal form: An essay on the "relative autonomy" of the law. *Law and Society Review* 11 (3): 571-88.

Bannerman, Sara. 2009. The WIPO Development Agenda Forum and its prospects for taking into account different levels of development. In *Implementing the World Intellectual Property Organization's development agenda,* ed. Jeremy de Beer, 24-33. Waterloo: Wilfrid Laurier Press.

Barahona, Marvin. 1998. Introducción, imagen y percepción de los pueblos indígenas en Honduras. In *Rompiendo el espejo: Visiones sobre los pueblos indígenas y negros en Honduras,* ed. Marvin Barahona and Ramon Rivas, 17-41. Tegucigalpa: Servicio Holandés de Cooperación al Desarrollo/Editorial Guaymuras.

—. 2002. *Evolución histórica de la identidad nacional.* Tegucigalpa: Editorial Guaymuras.

Bardehle, Heinz. 1997. AIPPI and the Patent Cooperation Treaty (PCT). In *AIPPI and the development of industrial property protection, 1897-1997.* Basle: AIPPI Foundation.

Barnes, Trevor J., and Roger Hayter. 1992. The little town that did: Flexible accumulation and community response in Chemainus, British Columbia. *Regional Studies* 26 (4): 647-63.

Barnes, Trevor J., Roger Hayter, and Elizabeth Hay. 2001. Stormy weather: Cyclones, Harold Innis, and Port Alberni, BC. *Environment and Planning* 33 (12): 2127-47.

Barsh, Russell Lawrence. 1994. Indigenous peoples in the 1990s: From object to subject of international law? *Harvard Human Rights Journal* 7 (1): 33-86.

—. 2003-4. Pharmacogenomics and indigenous peoples: Real issues and actors. *Cardozo Journal of International and Comparative Law* 11 (2): 365-92.

Bauman, Zygmunt. 2000. *Globalization: The human consequences.* New York: Columbia University Press.

Baxi, Upendra. 2005. Market fundamentalisms: Business ethics at the altar of human rights. *Human Rights Law Review* 5 (1): 1-26.

Beck, Robert J., Anthony Clark Arend, and Robert D. Vander Lugt. 1996. *International rules: Approaches from international law and international relations.* New York: Oxford University Press.

Beck, Ulrich. 2000 [1997]. *What is globalization?* Cambridge: Polity Press.

—. 2002. The terrorist threat: World risk society revisited. *Theory, Culture, and Society* 19 (4): 39-55.

Beier, J. Marshall. 2005. *International relations in uncommon places: Indigeneity, cosmology, and the limits of international theory.* New York: Palgrave Macmillan.

Bell, Robert. 1881. On the commercial importance of Hudson's Bay, with remarks on recent surveys and investigations. *Proceedings of the Royal Geographical Society and Monthly Record of Geography,* n.s., 3 (10): 577-86.

—. 1897. Recent explorations to the south of Hudson Bay. *Geographical Journal* 10 (1): 1-17.

Bengston, David. 1994. Changing forest values and ecosystem management. *Society and Natural Resources* 7 (6): 515-33.

Bently, Lionel. 2000. *Intellectual property law.* Oxford: Oxford University Press.

Benton, Lauren. 2002. *Law and colonial cultures: Legal regimes in world history, 1400-1900.* Cambridge: Cambridge University Press.

Berkes, Fikret, D. Feeny, B.J. McCay, and J.M. Acheson. 1989. The benefits of the commons. *Nature* 340 (6229): 91-93.

Berkes, Fikret, and IUCNNR (International Union for Conservation of Nature and Natural Resources). 1989. *Common property resources: Ecology and community-based sustainable development*. London: Belhaven Press.

Bernstein, Steven, and William D. Coleman, eds. 2009. *Unsettled legitimacy: Political community, power, and authority in a global era*. Vancouver: UBC Press.

Berry, Sara. 2001. *Chiefs know their boundaries: Essays on property, power, and the past in Asante, 1896-1996*. Portsmouth, NH: Heinemann.

Bhagwati, Jagdish. 2002. Patents and the poor: Including intellectual property protection in WTO rules has harmed the developing world. *Financial Times*, 17 September. http://www.cfr.org/publication/4847/patents_and_the_poor.html.

—. 2004. *In defense of globalization*. New York: Oxford University Press.

Biolsi, Thomas. 1991. Indian self-government as technique of domination. *Indian Quarterly* 15 (Winter): 23-28.

—. 1992. *Organizing the Lakota: The political economy of the New Deal on the Pine Ridge and Rosebud reservations*. Tucson: University of Arizona Press.

—. 1995. Bringing the law back in: Legal rights and the regulation of Indian-white relations on Rosebud Reservation. *Current Anthropology* 36 (4): 543-71.

Bird-David, Nurit. 1999. "Animism" revisited: Personhood, environment, and relational epistemology. *Current Anthropology* 40: S67-S91.

BIRPI (Bureaux Internationaux Reunis pour la Protection de la Propiete Intellectuelle). 1929. *Acts of the Rome Conference, 1928*. Berne: BIRPI.

—. 1967a. Plenary of the Berne Union, summary minutes. WIPO Archives KMCEL WIPO S/1.

—. 1967b. Stockholm Conference, Main Committee I, summary minutes, 1st meeting, 13 June 1967. WIPO Archives KMCEL WIPO S/1.

—. 1967c. Stockholm Conference, Main Committee I, summary minutes, 11th meeting, 20 June 1967. WIPO Archives KMCEL WIPO S/1.

—. 1967d. Stockholm Conference, Main Committee I, summary minutes, 15th meeting 27 June 1967. WIPO Archives KMCEL WIPO S/1.

—. 1967e. Stockholm Conference, Main Committee I, summary minutes, 20th meeting, 29 June 1967. WIPO Archives KMCEL WIPO S/1.

—. 1967f. Stockholm Conference, Main Committee II, 1st meeting, 21 June 1967. WIPO Archives KMCEL WIPO S/1.

—. 1967g. Stockholm Conference, Plenary of the Conference, summary minutes, 14 July 1967. WIPO Archives KMCEL WIPO S/1.

—. 1967h. Stockholm Conference, Plenary of the Conference, summary minutes, 1st meeting, 12 June 1967. WIPO Archives KMCEL WIPO S/1.

—. 1970a. Plenary of the World Intellectual Property Organization, summary minutes, 2nd Meeting, 12 July 1970. WIPO Archives KMCEL WIPO S/1.

—. 1970b. Transcripts of the Proceedings of the Washington Conference on the Patent Cooperation Treaty, Plenary Session, 2nd Plenary Sessions, 25 May 1970. WIPO Archives KMCEL WIPO E 2316g173112 BIRPI.T.

Blakeney, Michael. 2005. Stimulating agricultural innovation. In *International public goods and transfer of technology under a globalized intellectual property regime*, ed. Keith E. Maskus and Jerome H. Reichman, 366-90. Cambridge: Cambridge University Press.

Blaser, Mario, Ravi de Costa, Deborah McGregor, and William D. Coleman, eds. 2010. *Indigenous peoples and autonomy: Insights for a global age*. Vancouver: UBC Press.

Blodget, Henry. 2005. How to solve China's piracy problem: A dozen ideas — Maybe one will work. *Slate,* 12 April. http://www.slate.com/id/2116629/.

Blomley, Nicholas. 1996. Shut the province down: First Nations blockades in British Columbia. *BC Studies* 111 (August): 5-35.

—. 2003. Law, property, and the geography of violence: The frontier, the survey, and the grid. *Annals of the Association of American Geographers* 93 (1): 121-41.

—. 2004. Un-real estate: Proprietary space and public gardening. *Antipode* 36 (4): 614-41.

—. 2005. Remember property? *Progress in Human Geography* 29 (2): 125-27.

—. 2007. Critical geography: Anger and hope. *Progress in Human Geography* 31 (1): 53-65.

Bodenhausen, G.H.C. 1965. Paris Convention — General questions. BIRPI lecture course on industrial property, Geneva, 1965.

Bogsch, Arpad, ed. 1983. *The Paris Convention for the Protection of Industrial Property from 1883-1983.* Geneva: World Intellectual Property Organization.

—. 1992. *Brief history of the first twenty-five years of the World Intellectual Property Organization.* Geneva: World Intellectual Property Organization.

Bonefeld, Werner. 2001. The permanence of primitive accumulation: Commodity fetishism and social constitution. *The Commoner* 2 (September): 1-15.

Borowiak, Craig. 2004. Farmers' rights: Intellectual property regimes and the struggle over seeds. *Politics and Society* 32 (2): 511-43.

Boullatta, Issa, ed. 1980. *Critical perspectives on modern Arabic literature.* Washington, DC: Three Continents Press.

Boullata, Issa, and Terri De Young, eds. 1997. *Tradition and modernity in Arabic literature.* Fayetteville: University of Arkansas Press.

Bourassa, Robert. 1985. *Power from the North.* Scarborough, ON: Prentice Hall.

Bowden, Brett, and Leonard Seabrooke, eds. 2006. *Global standards of market civilization.* New York: Routledge.

Boyle, James. 1996. *Shamans, software, and spleens: Law and the construction of an information society.* Cambridge, MA: Harvard University Press.

Brace, Laura. 2004. *The politics of property: Labour, freedom and belonging.* New York: Palgrave MacMillan.

Brasnett, N.V. 1953. *Planned management of forests.* London: George Allen and Unwin.

Braudel, Fernand. 1980. *On history.* Chicago: University of Chicago Press.

Braun, B. 2000. Producing vertical territory: Geology and governmentality in late Victorian Canada. *Ecumene* 7 (1): 7-46.

—. 2002. *The intemperate rainforest: Nature, culture, and power on Canada's West Coast.* Minneapolis: University of Minnesota Press.

Brewer, John, and Susan Staves. 1995. *Early modern conceptions of property.* London: Routledge.

Bridge, Gavin, and Phil McManus. 2000. Sticks and stones: Environmental narratives and discursive regulation in the forestry and mining sectors. *Antipode* 32 (1): 10-47.

Briggs, John, and Joanne Sharp. 2004. Indigenous knowledges and development: A postcolonial caution. *Third World Quarterly* 25 (4): 661-76.

Brockington, Dan, Rosaleen Duffy, and Jim Igoe. 2008. *Nature unbound: Conservation, capitalism and the future of protected areas.* London: Earthscan.

Broderick, Richard. 2003. Ours is the earth of drowned gods. Review of Darwish and Youssef. *Ruminator Review* 1 (Fall): 54-56.

Brown, James Robert. 2000. Privatizing the university — The new tragedy of the commons. *Science* 290 (5497): 1701-02.

Brown, Wendy. 2006. American nightmare: Neoliberalism, neoconservatism, and de-democratization. *Political Theory* 34 (6): 690-714.

Brownlie, Ian. 2008. *Principles of public international law.* 7th ed. Oxford: Oxford University Press.

Brush, Stephen B. 2004. *Farmers' bounty: Locating crop diversity in the contemporary world.* New Haven, CT: Yale University Press.

—. 2007. Farmers' rights and protection of traditional agricultural knowledge. *World Development* 35 (9): 1499-1514.

Bryan, Joseph. 2007. Map or be mapped: Land, race and property in eastern Nicaragua. PhD diss., University of California, Berkeley.

Brydon, Diana, and William D. Coleman, eds. 2008. *Renegotiating community: Interdisciplinary perspectives, global contexts.* Vancouver: UBC Press.

Brysk, Alison. 2000. *From tribal village to global village: Indian rights and international relations in Latin America.* Palo Alto, CA: Stanford University Press.

Bush, George. 1991. President Bush's speech to Congress. *Arab Gateway,* 6 March. http://www.al-bab.com/arab/docs/pal/pal10.htm.

Byrd, Jodi A., and Katharina C. Heyer. 2008. Introduction: International discourses of indigenous rights and responsibilities. *Alternatives* 33 (1): 1-5.

Bystricky, Rudolf. 1965. The protection of industrial property in socialist countries." BIRPI lecture course on industrial property, Geneva. BIRPI No. 633(E).

CACRC (Central American and Caribbean Research Council). 2002. *La comunidad de Ibans: Diagnóstico del uso y tenencia de la tierra en comunidades Garifunas y Miskitas de Honduras.* Austin: CACRC.

Canada. Royal Commission on Aboriginal Peoples. 1996. *Report of the Royal Commission on Aboriginal Peoples.* Ottawa: The Commission.

Canclini, Nestor Garcia. 2005. Hybrid cultures in globalized times. In *Hybrid cultures: Strategies for entering and leaving modernity,* ed. N.G. Canclini, xxiii-xlvi. Minneapolis: University of Minnesota Press.

Carlson, Hans M. 2004. A watershed of words: Litigating and negotiating nature in eastern James Bay, 1971-1975. *Canadian Historical Review* 85 (1): 63-84.

Carolan, Michael S. 2009. The problems with patents: A less than optimistic reading of the future. *Development and Change* 40 (2): 361-88.

Caselli, Eduardo Piola. 1929. *Acts of the Rome Conference, 1928 — General report.* Berne: BIRPI.

Castells, Manuel. 1999. The *rise of the network society.* 2nd ed. Oxford: Blackwell.

—. 2003. *The power of identity.* 2nd ed. Oxford: Blackwell.

Castree, Noel. 2003. Commodifying what nature? *Progress in Human Geography* 27 (3): 273-97.

—. 2004. Differential geographies: Place, indigenous rights and "local" resources. *Political Geography* 23 (2): 133-67.

—. 2008. Neoliberalising nature: The logics of deregulation and reregulation. *Environment and Planning A* 40 (1): 131-52.

Caulfield, Timothy. 2003. Human cloning laws, human dignity and the poverty of the policy-making dialogue. *BMC Medical Ethics* 4 (3): 3-10.

Chapin, Mac. 2004. A challenge to conservationists. *World Watch* 17 (6): 17-31.

Chin, Christine, and James Mittelman. 1997. Conceptualizing resistance to globalization. *New Political Economy* 2 (1): 25-37.

Ciancio, A., and S. Nocentini. 2000. Forest management from positivism to the culture of complexity. In *Methods and approaches in forest history,* ed. Mauro Agnoletti and Steven Anderson, 47-58. New York: CAB International Publishing.

Ciriacy-Wantrup, S.V., and R. Bishop. 1975. "Common property" as a concept in natural resource policy. *Natural Resource Journal* 15 (October): 713-27.

Clark, Aubert J. 1960. *The movement for international copyright in nineteenth-century America.* Washington, DC: Catholic University of America Press.

Clawson, M., and R. Sedjo. 1983. History of sustained yield concept and its application to developing countries. In *History of sustained yield forestry: A symposium,* ed. Harold K. Steen, 3-15. Portland, OR: Forestry History Society.

Clifford, James. 1997. *Routes: Travel and translation in the late twentieth century.* Cambridge, MA: Harvard University Press.

Clogg, J. 1997. Tenure reform for ecologically and socially responsible forest use in British Columbia. Master's thesis, York University.

Çoban, Aykut. 2004. Caught between state-sovereign rights and property rights: Regulating biodiversity. *Review of International Political Economy* 11 (4): 736-62.

Code, Lorraine. 2000. The perversion of autonomy and the subjection of women: Discourses of social advocacy at century's end. In *Relational autonomy: Feminist perspectives on autonomy, agency and the social self,* ed. Catriona Mackenzie and Natalie Stoljar, 181-209. New York: Oxford University Press.

Colchester, Marcus. 2003. *Salvaging nature: Indigenous peoples, protected areas and biodiversity conservation.* Montevideo: World Rainforest Movement.

—. 2004. Conservation policy and indigenous peoples. *Environmental Science and Policy* 7 (2): 145-53.

Coleman, William D. 2009. Universals, global trade law and agriculture: Toward a cultural study. *Journal of International Trade and Diplomacy* 3 (1): 1-32.

Coleman, William D., and Sarah Wayland. 2005. The origins of global civil society and non-territorial governance: Some empirical reflections. Working Paper 05/1, Institute on Globalization and the Human Condition, McMaster University, Hamilton, Ontario.

Collier, Jane F. 2001. Durkheim revisited: Human rights as moral discourse for the postcolonial, post–Cold War world. In *Human rights: Concepts, contests, contingencies,* ed. Austin Sarat and Thomas R. Kearns, 63-88. Ann Arbor: University of Michigan Press.

Commoner, Barry. 2003. Unravelling the DNA myth. *Seedling* (July): 1-8. http://www.grain.org/seedling/?id=240.

Coombe, Rosemary J. 1993. The properties of culture and the politics of possessing identity: Native claims in the cultural appropriation controversy. *Canadian Journal of Law and Jurisprudence* 6 (2): 249-85.

—. 1998. Intellectual property, human rights and sovereignty: New dilemmas in international law posed by the recognition of indigenous knowledge and the conservation of biodiversity. *Indiana Journal of Global Legal Studies* 6 (1): 59-116.

—. 1999. Culture: Anthropology's old vice or international law's new virtue? *American Society of International Law — Proceedings of the Annual Meeting* 93: 261-70.

—. 2001. The recognition of indigenous peoples' and community traditional knowledge in international law. *St. Thomas Law Review* 14: 275-85.

Coon Come, Matthew. 1989. A word from the grand chief: Remarks to the General Assembly of the Grand Council of the Crees, 19 March. *Politics and Society* 28 (2): 245-64.

—. 2004. Survival in the context of mega-resource development: Experiences of the James Bay Crees and the First Nations of Canada. In *In the way of development: Indigenous peoples, life projects and globalization,* ed. Mario Blaser, Harvey Feit, and Glenn McRae, 153-64. London: ZED Books/IDRC.

Corntassel, Jeff. 2008. Toward sustainable self-determination: Rethinking the contemporary indigenous-rights discourse. *Alternatives* 33 (1): 105-32.

Correa, Carlos M. 2000. *Intellectual property rights, the WTO and developing countries: The TRIPS agreement and policy options*. London: Zed Books.

Cosgrove, Denis E. 1984. *Social formation and symbolic landscape*. Kent: Croom Helm.

Council of Forest Industries. 2000. *British Columbia forest industry fact book 2000*. Vancouver: Council of Forest Industries.

Cox, Robert. 1993. Gramsci, hegemony and international relations: An essay in method. In *Gramsci, historical materialism and international relations*, ed. Stephen Gill, 49-66. Cambridge: Cambridge University Press.

Cox, Susan Jane B. 1985. No tragedy on the commons. *Environmental Ethics* 7: 49-61.

Critchley, Simon. 2004. Five problems in Levinas's view of politics and the sketch of a solution to them. *Political Theory* 32 (2): 172-85.

Cronon, William. 1983. *Changes in the land: Indians, colonists, and the ecology of New England*. New York: Hill and Wang.

—. 1991. *Nature's metropolis: Chicago and the Great West*. New York: W.W. Norton.

Crosby, Alfred W. 1986. *Ecological imperialism: The biological expansion of Europe, 900-1900*. Cambridge: Cambridge University Press.

Cruz, R. 1926. La ley de inmigración y el problema de la raza negra en la costa norte. *Revista Ariel* (October): 700.

Cullet, Philippe. 2004. Intellectual property rights and food security in the South. *Journal of World Intellectual Property* 7 (3): 261-86.

Cullet, Philippe, and Jawahar Raja. 2004. Intellectual property rights and biodiversity management. *Global Environmental Politics* 4 (1): 97-114.

Curchod, François. 1999. Is the Paris Convention for the Protection of Industrial Property still relevant today? In *Global perspectives of contemporary intellectual property issues*, ed. Gert Egon Dannemann and Maria Thereza Wolff, 93-101. Rio de Janeiro: PVDI Design.

Cutler, A. Claire. 2001. Critical reflections on the Westphalian assumptions of international law and organization: A crisis of legitimacy. *Review of International Studies* 27 (2): 133-50.

—. 2002a. Critical historical materialism and international law: Imagining international law as praxis. In *Historical sociology of international relations*, ed. Stephen Hobden and John Hobson, 181-99. Cambridge: Cambridge University Press.

—. 2002b. Historical materialism, globalization and law: Competing conceptions of property. In *Historical materialism and globalization*, ed. Mark Rupert and Hazel Smith, 230-56. New York: Routledge.

—. 2003. *Private power and global authority: Transnational merchant law in the global political economy*. Cambridge: Cambridge University Press.

—. 2005a. Critical globalization studies and international law under conditions of postmodernity and late capitalism. In *Critical globalization studies*, ed. Richard P. Appelbaum and William I. Robinson, 197-205. New York: Routledge.

—. 2005b. Gramsci, law, and the culture of global capitalism. *Critical Review of International Social and Political Philosophy* 8 (4): 527-42.

—. 2008a. Problematizing corporate social responsibility under conditions of late capitalism and postmodernity. In *Authority in the global political economy*, ed. Volker Rittberger and Martin Nettesheim, 189-216. Houndmills: Palgrave Macmillan.

—. 2008b. Toward a radical political economy critique of transnational economic law. In *International law on the Left: Re-examining Marxist legacies*, ed. Susan Marks, 199-219. New York: Cambridge University Press.

—. 2009. Constituting capitalism: Corporations, law, and private transnational governance. *St. Antony's International Review* 5 (1): 99-115.

—. 2010. Unthinking the GATS: A radical political economy critique of private transnational governance. In *Business and global governance,* ed. Morten Ougaard and Anna Leander, 78-96. New York: Routledge.

Cutler, A. Claire, Virginia Haufler, and Tony Porter. 1999. *Private authority and international affairs.* Albany: State University of New York Press.

Daes, Erica-Irene. 1997. *Protection of the heritage of indigenous people.* New York: United Nations.

Dalby, Simon. 1998. Introduction: Environmental geopolitics. In *The geopolitics reader,* ed. Gearóid O'Tuathail, Simon Dalby, and Paul Routledge, 179-89. London: Routledge.

Darwish, Mahmud. 2002. A love story between an Arab poet and his land: An interview with Mahmud Darwish. *Journal of Palestine Studies* 31 (3): 67-78.

—. 2003. *Unfortunately, it was paradise.* Ed. and trans. Munir Akash and Carolyn Forché, with Sinan Antoon and Amira El-Zein. Berkeley: University of California Press.

Darwish, Mahmud, and Adonis Samih al-Qasim. 1984. *Victims of a map.* Trans. Abdullah al-Udhari. London: Al Saqi Books.

Davis, Michael H. 2003-4. Some realism about indigenism. *Cardozo Journal of International and Comparative Law* 11 (2): 815-30.

de Beer, Jeremy. 2009. Defining WIPO's development agenda. In *Implementing the World Intellectual Property Organization's development agenda,* ed. Jeremy de Beer, 1-23. Waterloo: Wilfrid Laurier Press.

de Soto, Hernando. 2000. *The mystery of capital: Why capitalism triumphs in the West and fails everywhere else.* New York: Basic Books.

de Vuyst, Bruno. 2004. The uneasy case for intellectual property rights. In *About globalization,* ed. Bart de Schutter, 113-35. Brussels: Brussels University Press.

Dei, George J. Sefa. 1996. *Theory and practice: Anti-racism education.* Halifax: Fernwood

Deleuze, Gilles, and Felix Guattari. 1977. *Anti-Oedipus: Capitalism and schizophrenia.* Ed. and trans. Robert Hurley, Mark Seem, and Helen R. Lane. New York: Viking Press.

Demeritt, David. 2001. Scientific forest conservation and the statistical picturing of nature's limits in the progressive-era United States. *Environment and Planning* 19 (5): 431-59.

D'Errico, Peter. 1996-97. Corporate personality and human commodification. *Rethinking Marxism* 9 (2): 99-113.

Dhar, Biswajit. 2002. Sui generis systems for plant variety protection: Options under TRIPS. Discussion Paper, Quaker United Nations Office, Geneva. http://www.geneva.quno.info/pdf/sgmono1.pdf.

Diamond, Jared. 1999. *Guns, germs, and steel: The fates of human societies.* New York: W.W. Norton and Company.

Dietrich, W. 1992. *The final forest: The battle for the last great trees of the Pacific Northwest.* New York: Simon and Schuster.

Dirlik, Arif. 2007. *Global modernity: Modernity in the age of global capitalism.* Boulder, CO: Paradigm Publishers.

Dodds, David. 1994. The ecological and social sustainability of Miskito subsistence in the Rio Plátano Biosphere Reserve. PhD diss., University of California.

—. 1998. Lobster in the rain forest: The political ecology of Miskito wage labor and agricultural deforestation. *Journal of Political Ecology* 5 (1): 83-108.

Doern, Bruce C. 1999. *Global change and intellectual property.* London: Pinter.

Doern, Bruce C., and Markus Sharaput. 2000. *Canadian intellectual property: The politics of innovating institutions and interests.* Toronto: University of Toronto Press.

Dove, Michael. 2006. Indigenous people and environmental politics. *Annual Review of Anthropology* 35: 191-208.

Dowdeswell, Elizabeth, Abdallah Daar, and Peter Singer. 2003. Bridging the genomics divide. *Global Governance* 9 (1): 1-6.

Drache, Daniel. 1982. Harold Innis and Canadian capitalist development. *Canadian Journal of Political and Social Theory* 6 (1-2): 35-60.

Drahos, Peter. 2002. Developing countries and international intellectual property standard-setting. *Journal of World Intellectual Property* 5 (May): 765-89.

Drahos, Peter, and John Braithwaite. 2003. *Information feudalism: Who owns the knowledge economy?* New York: New Press.

Drahos, Peter, and Ruth Mayne, eds. 2003. *Global intellectual property rights: Knowledge, access and development.* New York: Palgrave Macmillan.

Drezner, Daniel W. 2007. *All politics is global: Explaining international regulatory regimes.* Princeton, NJ: Princeton University Press.

Dutfield, Graham. 2003. *Intellectual property rights and the life science industries: A twentieth-century history.* Aldershot: Ashgate Publishing.

Dyck, Noel, and James B. Waldram, eds. 1993. *Anthropology, public policy and Native peoples in Canada.* Montreal and Kingston: McGill-Queen's University Press.

The Economist. 2000. The standard question. 13 January.

—. 2001a. Have patent, will travel. 28 June. http://www.economist.com/displaystory.cfm?story_id=677617.

—.2001b. Markets for ideas. 12 April. http://www.economist.com/displaystory.cfm?story_id=574263.

—. 2002. Patently problematic. 12 September. http://www.economist.com/displaystory.cfm?story_id=1325219.

—. 2003a. Copy or counterfeit? 4 January.

—. 2003b. Imitating property is theft. 15 May. http://www.economist.com/displaystory.cfm?story_id=1780818.

Eichengreen, Barry, and P.B. Kenen. 1994. Managing the world economy under the Bretton Woods Agreement: An overview. In *Managing the world economy: Fifty years after Bretton Woods,* ed. P.B. Kenen, 1-23. Washington, DC: Institute for International Economics.

Eisenberg, Robert S. 1992. Genes, patents, and product development. *Science* 257 (5072): 903-8.

El Cronista. 1930. *La importancia siempre creciente y siempre de actualidad de extenso y fértil territorio de la Mosquitia Hondureña.* 15, 19, 21, 22 April. Pp. 7, 15, 19, 21, 22.

El Tiempo. 1978. *Contacto directo con la miseria.* 13 March. Pp. 28-29.

Elmessiri, Abdelwahab M. 1970. *A Lover from Palestine, and other poems: An anthology of Palestinian poetry.* Washington, DC: Palestine Information Office.

—. 1982. *The Palestinian wedding.* Washington, DC: Three Continents Press.

Escobar, Arturo. 2001. Culture sits in places: Reflections on globalism and subaltern strategies of localization. *Political Geography* 20: 139-74.

—. 2008. *Territories of difference: Place, movements, life, redes.* Durham, NC: Duke University Press.

Esmeir, Samarah. 2003. 1948: Law, history, memory. *Social Text – 75* 21 (2): 25-48.

Essid, Yassine. 2009. A globalizing moment: The "UNO Decades for Development" and the North African countries. In *Empires and autonomy: Moments in the history of globalization,* ed. Stephen Streeter, John Weaver, and William D. Coleman, 212-31. Vancouver: UBC Press.

Etapp, Charlie. 2003. Narrative biographical account of conversion. In *Dab Iyiyuuu: Absolutely Cree.* Directors Neil Diamond, Philip Lewis, and Ernest Webb. Winnipeg: Aboriginal People's Television Network.

European Patent Office (EPO). 2001a. *Facts and figures.* Munich: EPO.

—. 2001b. *Serving industry and the public.* Munich: EPO.

Eyzaguirre, Pablo, Monica De Grigorio, and Ruth Meinzen-Dick. 2007. Introduction to special issue, "Property rights, collective action, and local conservation of genetic resources," *World Development* 35 (9): 1481-88.

Falcon, W.P., and C. Fowler. 2002. Carving up the commons: Emergence of a new international regime for germplasm development and transfer. *Food Policy* 27 (2): 197-222.

Feather, John. 1994. *Publishing, piracy and politics: An historical study of copyright in Britain.* London: Mansell.

Feeny, David, Fikret Berkes, Bonnie J. McCay, and James M. Acheson. 1990. The tragedy of the commons: Twenty-two years later. *Human Ecology* 18 (1): 1-19.

Feit, Harvey. 1989. James Bay Cree self-governance and land management. In *We are here: Politics of Aboriginal land tenure,* ed. Edwin N. Wilmsen, 68-98. Berkeley: University of California Press.

—. 1995. Hunting and the quest for power: The James Bay Cree and white men in the twentieth century. In *Native peoples: The Canadian experience,* 2nd ed., ed. R. Bruce Morrison and C. Roderick Wilson, 181-223. Toronto: Oxford University Press.

—. 1998. Reflections on local knowledge and institutionalized resource management: Differences, dominance, decentralization. In *Aboriginal environmental knowledge in the North,* ed. Louis-Jacques Dorais, M. Nagy, and L. Müller-White, 123-48. Quebec City: Laval University.

—. 2001. Hunting, nature, and metaphor: Political and discursive strategies in James Bay Cree resistance and autonomy. *In Indigenous traditions and ecology: The interbeing of cosmology and community,* ed. John A. Grim, 411-52. Cambridge, MA: Harvard University Press.

—. 2004. Les territoires de chasse algonquiens avant leur "découverte"? Études et histoires sur la tenure, les incendies de forêts et la sociabilité de la chasse. *Recherches Amérindiennes au Québec* 34 (3): 5-21.

—. 2005. Recognizing co-management as co-governance: Visions and histories of conservation at James Bay. *Anthropologica* 47 (2): 267-88.

—. 2009. Government rationalities and indigenous co-governance: James Bay Cree coexistence, from mercantilist partnerships to neoliberal mechanisms. In *Unsettled legitimacy: Political community, power, and authority in a global era,* ed. Steven Bernstein and William D. Coleman, 97-128. Vancouver: UBC Press.

Feit, Harvey, and Robert Beaulieu, 2001. Voices from a disappearing forest: Government, corporate, and Cree participatory forestry management practices. In *Aboriginal autonomy and development in northern Quebec and Labrador,* ed. Colin H. Scott, 119-48. Vancouver: UBC Press.

Fenelon, James V., and Thomas D. Hall. 2008. Revitalization and indigenous resistance to globalization and neoliberalism. *American Behavioral Scientist* 51 (12): 1867-1901.

Fenelon, James V., and Salvador J. Murguía. 2008. Indigenous peoples: Globalization, resistance, and revitalization. *American Behavioral Scientist* 51 (12): 1656-71.

Ferguson, Niall, Charles S. Maier, Erez Manela, and Daniel J. Sargent. 2010. *The Shock of the global: The 1970s in perspective.* Cambridge, MA: Harvard University Press.

Fernow, Bernhard. 1902. *Economics of forestry.* New York: Thomas Y. Crawell.

Ferranti, David, Guillermo Perry, Francisco H.G. Ferreira, and Michael Walton. 2004. *Inequality in Latin America and the Caribbean: Breaking with history?* Washington, DC: World Bank Group.

Fischbach, Michael. 2003. *Records of dispossession: Palestinian refugee property and the Arab-Israeli conflict.* New York: Columbia University Press.

Fishman, Ted C. 2005. Manufaketure. *New York Times Magazine,* 9 January. http://www.engin.brown.edu/courses/en100/IP/manuFAKEture.html.

Forman, Geremy. 2006. Law and the historical geography of the Galilee: Israel's litigatory advantages during the special operation of land settlement. *Journal of Historical Geography* 32 (4): 796-917.

Forman, Geremy, and Alexandre (Sandy) Kedar. 2004. From Arab land to Israel lands: The legal dispossession of the Palestinians displaced by Israel in the wake of 1948. *Environment and Planning D: Society and Space* 22: 809-30.

Foucault, Michel. 1991. Governmentality. In *The Foucault effect: Studies in governmentality,* ed. Graham Burchall, Colin Gordon, and P. Miller, 87-104. Chicago: University of Chicago Press.

Franklin, J.F. 1989a. The new forestry. *Journal of Soil and Water Conservation* 44 (6): 549-61.

—. 1989b. Toward a new forestry. *American Forests* 95 (11, 12): 37-44.

Frascara, A.M. 1969. Yo, pobre Zambo: La vida del hombre en apartadas regiones. *Revista Ariel* (May): 7-11

Frideres, James S. 1988. *Native peoples in Canada: Contemporary conflicts.* 3rd ed. Scarborough, ON: Prentice Hall Canada.

—. 1996. The Royal Commission on Aboriginal Peoples: The route to self-government? *Canadian Journal of Native Studies* 16 (2): 247-66.

Friedman, Marilyn. 2003. *Autonomy, gender, politics.* Oxford: Oxford University Press.

Furani, Khaled. 2004. When poets go to sleep: An anthropological inquiry into modernizing Arabic poetic forms. PhD diss., City University of New York.

Gervais, Daniel J. 2003-4. Spiritual but not intellectual? The protection of sacred intangible traditional knowledge. *Cardozo Journal of International and Comparative Law* 11 (2): 467-95.

—. 2007. TRIPS and development. In *Intellectual property, trade and development,* ed. Daniel Gervais, 3-60. Oxford: Oxford University Press.

Ghate, Rucha. 2003. Global gains at local costs: Imposing protected areas — Evidence from central India. *International Journal of Sustainable Development and World Ecology* 1: 377-89.

Ghosh, Shubha. 2003-4. Reflections on the traditional knowledge debate. *Cardozo Journal of International and Comparative Law* 11 (2): 497-510.

Gibbs, Meredith. 2005. The right to development and indigenous peoples: Lessons from New Zealand. *World Development* 33 (8): 1365-78.

Giddens, Anthony. 1990. *The consequences of modernity.* Palo Alto, CA: Stanford University Press.

Gilbert, Richard J., and David M.G. Newberry. 1982. Preemptive patenting and the persistence of monopoly. *American Economic Review* 72 (3): 514-26.

Gill, Stephen. 2008. *Power and resistance in the new world order.* 2nd ed. Houndmills: Palgrave Macmillan.

Girsberger, Martin A. 1999. *Biodiversity and the concept of farmers' rights in international law: Factual background and legal analysis.* Bern: Lang.

Glassman, J. 2005. The "new" imperialism? On continuity and change in US foreign policy. *Environment and Planning A* 37: 1527-44.

—. 2006. Primitive accumulation, accumulation by dispossession, accumulation by "extra-economic" means. *Progress in Human Geography* 30 (5): 608-25.

Glennerster, Rachel, Michael Kremer, and Heidi Williams. 2005. The price of life. *Foreign Policy* (May-June): 26-27.

Goldman, Michael. 2005. *Imperial nature: The World Bank and struggles for social justice in the age of globalization.* New Haven, CT: Yale University Press.

Gong, Gerrit W. 1984. *The standard of "civilization" in international society*. Oxford: Clarendon Press.

Gordon, Edmond, Galio C. Guardian, and Charles Hale. 2003. Rights, resources and the social memory of struggle: Reflections on a study of indigenous and black community land rights on Nicaragua's Atlantic Coast. *Human Organization* 2 (4): 369-81.

Gordon, H. Scott. 1954. The economic theory of a common property resource: The fishery. *Journal of Political Economy* 62: 124-42.

Gordon, Robert W. 1996. Paradoxical property. In *Early modern conceptions of property*, ed. John Brewer and Susan Staves, 95-110. New York: Routledge.

Graeber, David. 2001. *Toward an anthropological theory of value: The false coin of our own dreams*. New York, Palgrave.

Graham, Lorie, and Stephen McJohn. 2005. Indigenous peoples and intellectual property. *Washington University Journal of Law and Policy* 19: 313-37.

Gramsci, Antonio. 1971. *Selections from the prison notebooks of Antonio Gramsci*. Ed. and trans. Quintin Hoare and G.N. Smith. New York: International Publishers.

Grand Council of the Crees. 1994. *Great Whale environmental assessment*. Vol. 1, *Community consultation: Final report for Whapmagoostui*. Grand Council of the Crees Archives. http://www.gcc.ca/archive/article.php?id=47.

Gregory, Derek. 2004. *The colonial present: Afghanistan, Palestine, Iraq*. Malden, MA: Blackwell.

Grinnell, George B. 1907. Tenure of land among the Indians. *American Anthropologist* 9 (1): 1-11

Gupta, Akhil. 1998. *Postcolonial developments: Agriculture in the making of modern India*. Durham, NC: Duke University Press.

Habermas, Jürgen. 1996. *Between facts and norms: Contributions to a discourse theory of law and democracy*. Trans. William Rehg. Cambridge, MA: MIT Press.

Habib, Jasmin. 2008. Transnational transformation: Cyberactivism and the Palestinian right of return. In *Renegotiating community: Interdisciplinary perspectives, global contexts*, ed. Diana Brydon and William D. Coleman, 183-202. Vancouver: UBC Press.

Hablemos Claro. 1997. INA entrega a la AFE-COHDEFOR: Presidente Reina participa en traspaso de tierras nacionales. *Revista Hablemos Claro* (August): 64.

Hage, Ghassan. 2000. *White nation: Fantasies of white supremacy in a multicultural society*. New York: Routledge.

Hahn, C.M. 1998. Introduction: The embeddedness of property. In *Property relations: Renewing the anthropological tradition*, ed. C.M. Hahn, 1-47. Cambridge: Cambridge University Press.

Halbert, Debora J. 1999. *Intellectual property in the information age: The politics of expanding ownership rights*. London: Quorum Books.

Halbwachs, Maurice. 1992. *On collective memory*. Ed. and trans. Lewis A. Coser. Chicago: University of Chicago Press.

Hale, Charles. 2002. Does multiculturalism menace? Governance, cultural rights and the politics of identity in Guatemala. *Journal of Latin American Studies* 34 (3): 485-525.

Halewood, Michael. 1998-99. Indigenous and local knowledge in international law: A preface to *sui generis* intellectual property protection. *McGill Law Journal* 44: 953-96.

Haley, David, and Martin Luckert. 1995. Policy instruments for sustainable development in the British Columbia forestry sector. In *Managing natural resources in British Columbia: Market, regulations and sustainable development*, ed. Anthony Scott, John Robinson, and David Cohen, 54-79. Vancouver: UBC Press.

Halford, Nigel G. 2003. *Genetically modified crops*. London: Imperial College Press.

Hall, Stuart. 1988. The toad in the garden: Thatcherism among the theorists. In *Marxism and the interpretation of culture*, ed. Cary Nelson and Lawrence Grossberg, 35-57. Chicago: University of Illinois Press.

Halseth, G. 1999a. Resource town employment: Perceptions in small town British Columbia. *Tijdschrift voor Economische en Sociale Geografie* 90 (2): 196-210.

—. 1999b. "We came for the work": Situating employment migration in BC's small, resource-based communities. *Canadian Geographer–Géographe Canadien* 43 (4): 363-81.

Hammer, Juliane. 2005. *Palestinians born in exile: Diaspora and the search for a homeland.* Austin: University of Texas Press.

Hanzlik, E.J. 1922. Determination of the annual cut on a sustained yield basis for virgin American forests. *Journal of Forestry* 20 (10): 611-25.

Hardin, Garrett. 1968. The tragedy of the commons. *Science* 162: 1243-48.

Harding, Sarah. 2003-4. Defining traditional knowledge: Lessons from cultural property. *Cardozo Journal of International and Comparative Law* 11 (2): 511-18.

Hardt, Michael, and Antonio Negri. 2000. *Empire.* Cambridge, MA: Harvard University Press.

Harlow, Barbara. 1987. *Resistance literature.* New York: Methuen.

—. 1998. Palestine: Kan wa-ma kan? *Diaspora: Journal of Transnational Studies* 7 (3): 75-85.

Harris, R. Cole. 2002. *Making Native space: Colonialism, resistance, and reserves in British Columbia.* Vancouver: UBC Press.

Harvey, David. 1982. *The limits to capital.* Oxford: B. Blackwell.

—. 1989. *The urban experience.* Baltimore, MD: Johns Hopkins University Press.

—. 2001a. Globalization and the spatial fix. *Geographische Revue* 2 (1): 23-30.

—. 2001b. *Spaces of capital: Towards a critical geography.* New York: Routledge.

—. 2003. *The new imperialism.* Oxford: Oxford University Press.

—. 2005. *A brief history of neoliberalism.* Oxford: Oxford University Press.

—. 2007. In what ways is the "new imperialism" really new? *Historical Materialism* 15 (1): 57-70.

Hassan, Salah D. 2003. Nation validation: Modern Palestinian literature and the politics of appeasement. *Social Text* – 75 21 (2): 7-23.

Hayeur, Gaëtan. 2001. *Summary of knowledge acquired in northern environments from 1970 to 2000.* Montreal: Hydro-Québec.

Hayter, Roger. 2000. *Flexible crossroads: The restructuring of British Columbia's forest economy.* Vancouver: UBC Press.

—. 2003. The war in the woods: Post-Fordist restructuring, globalization, and the contested remapping of British Columbia's forest economy. *Annals of the Association of American Geographers* 93 (3): 706-29.

Hayter, Roger, and T. Barnes. 1990. Innis' staples theory, exports, and recession: British Columbia, 1981-86. *Economic Geography* 66 (2): 156-73.

—. 1997. Troubles in the rainforest: British Columbia's forest economy in transition. In *Troubles in the rainforest: British Columbia's forest economy in transition,* ed. T. Barnes and Roger Hayter, 1-11. Victoria, BC: Western Geographical Press.

—. 2001. Canada's resource economy. *Canadian Geographer* 45 (1): 36-41.

Heacock, Roger. 2004. Palestinians: The land and the law, an inverse relationship. *Journal of International Affairs* 57 (2): 151-65.

Heald, Paul J. 2003-4. The rhetoric of biopiracy. *Cardozo Journal of International and Comparative Law* 11 (2): 519-46.

Held, David. 1995. *Democracy and the global order: From the modern state to cosmopolitan governance.* Palo Alto, CA: Stanford University Press.

Helfer, Laurence. 2004. Regime shifting: The TRIPS agreement and new dynamics of international lawmaking. *Yale Journal of International Law* 29 (1): 1-83.

—. 2005. Using intellectual property rights to preserve the global genetic commons: The International Treaty on Plant Genetic Resources for Food and Agriculture. In *International public goods and transfer of technology under a globalized intellectual property regime,* ed. Keith E. Maskus and J.H. Reichman, 216-24. Cambridge: Cambridge University Press.

Helms, Mary W. 1971. *Asang: Adaptations to cultural contact in a Miskito community.* Gainesville: University of Florida Press.

Heong, Chee Yoke. 2004. Putting the brakes on intellectual property rights. *Asia Times,* 15 October. http://www.atimes.com/atimes/Global_Economy/FJ15Dj01.html.

Herlihy, Peter. 1993. Securing a homeland: The Tawahka Sumu of Mosquitia's rain forest. In *State of the peoples: A global human rights report on societies in danger,* ed. Mark S. Miller, 54-62. Boston: Beacon Press.

—. 1997. Indigenous peoples and biosphere reserve conservation in the Mosquitia rain forest corridor, Honduras. In *Conservation through cultural survival: Indigenous peoples and protected areas,* ed. Stan Stevens, 99-129. Washington, DC: Island Press.

Hesse, Carla. 2002. The rise of intellectual property, 700 B.C.–A.D. 2000. *Daedalus* 131 (2): 26-45.

Hiatt, J. 1998. Reply to Brown. *Current Anthropology* 39 (2): 209-10.

Higgins, Rosalyn. 1985. Conceptual thinking about the individual in international law. In *International law: A contemporary perspective,* ed. Richard Falk, Friedrich Kratochwil, and Saul Mendlovitz, 476-94. Boulder, CO: Westview Press.

Hirsch, Eric, and Michael O'Hanlon, eds. 1995. *The anthropology of landscape: Perspectives on place and space.* Oxford: Clarendon Press.

Hirst, Paul, and Grahame Thompson. 1999. *Globalization in question.* 2nd ed. Cambridge: Polity Press.

Hodgins, Bruce W., and Kerry A. Cannon, eds. 1995. *On the land: Confronting the challenges to Aboriginal self-determination in northern Quebec and Labrador.* Toronto: Betelgeuse Books.

Holder, Cindy. 2008. Culture as an activity and human right: An important advance for indigenous peoples and international law. *Alternatives* 33 (1): 7-28.

Home, Robert. 2003. An "irreversible conquest"? Colonial and postcolonial land law in Israel/Palestine. *Social and Legal Studies* 12 (3): 291-310.

Honduras. 1957. Tratado celebrado entre su Majestad Británica y el gobierno de Honduras, 1859. Creación del departamento de Gracias a Dios, sus antecedentes. Tegucigalpa: Talleres Tipo-Litográficos.

—. 1982. *Constitución de la República: Decreto no. 131 del 11 de enero.* Tegucigalpa: República de Honduras.

—. 1992. *Ley para la modernización y el desarrollo del sector agrícola.* Tegucigalpa: República de Honduras.

Hooker, Juliet. 2005. Indigenous inclusion/black exclusion: Race, ethnicity and multicultural citizenship in Latin America. *Journal of Latin American Studies* 37 (2): 285-310.

hooks, bell. 1990. Marginality as a site of resistance. In *Out there: Marginalization and contemporary cultures,* ed. Russell Ferguson, Martha Gever, Trinh T. Minh-ha, and Cornell West, 337-40. Cambridge, MA: MIT Press.

Hulme David, and Marshall Murphee. 1999. Communities, wildlife and the "new conservation" in Africa. *Journal of International Development* 11 (2): 277-86.

Hunt, Alan. 1993. *Explorations in law and society: Toward a constitutive theory of law.* New York: Routledge.

Igoe, Jim, Katja Neves, and Dan Brockington. 2010. A spectacular eco-tour around the historic bloc: Theorizing the current convergence of biodiversity conservation and capitalist expansion. *Antipode* 42 (3): 486-512.

Ikeda, Satoshi. 2004. Imperial subjects, national citizenship, and corporate subjects: Cycles of political participation/exclusion in the modern world-system. *Citizenship Studies* 8 (4): 333-47.

INA (Instituto Nacional Agrario). 1997. *Título de propiedad en dominio pleno por la reserva biosfera Río Plátano.* Tegucigalpa: INA.

Innis, Harold Adams. 1956. *Essays in Canadian economic history.* Toronto: University of Toronto Press.

Iriye, Akira. 2004. *Global community: The role of international organizations in the making of the contemporary world.* Berkeley: University of California Press.

ISAAA (International Service for the Acquisition of Agri-Biotech Applications). 2010. *ISAAA brief 41-2009: Executive summary.* http://www.isaaa.org/resources/publications/briefs/41/executivesummary/default.asp.

Japan Patent Office. 2001. Trilateral statistical report, Graph 2.1. Japan Patent Office. http://www.jpo.go.jp/torikumi_e/kokusai_e/tws/tsr2001/graphs/index.html (accessed 5 November 2003).

Jayussi, Salma Khadra. 1992. *Anthology of modern Palestinian literature.* New York: Columbia University Press.

Jenson, Jane, and Martin Papillon. 2000. Challenging the citizenship regime: The James Bay Cree and transnational action. *Politics and Society* 28 (2): 245-64.

Jessop, Bob. 2002. Liberalism, neoliberalism, and urban governance: A state-theoretical perspective. *Antipode* 34 (3): 452-72.

—. 2006. Spatial fixes, temporal fixes and spatio-temporal fixes. In *David Harvey: A critical reader,* ed. Noel Castree and D. Gregory, 142-66. Oxford: Blackwell Publishing.

Johns, Adrian. 2002. Pop music pirate hunters. *Daedalus* 131 (2): 67-77.

Johns, Fleur. 1994. The invisibility of the transnational corporation: An analysis of international law and legal theory. *Melbourne University Law Review* 19 (4): 893-923.

Johnson, Chalmers. 2004. *The sorrows of empire.* New York: Henry Holt.

Johnson, Jay T. 2008. Indigeneity's challenges to the white settler-state: Creating a thirdspace for dynamic citizenship. *Alternatives* 33 (1): 29-52.

Johnson, Larry. 1999. A letter from Chief Larry Johnson, Caldwell First Nation, to the Chatham/Kent Council. 13 January. http://www.geocities.com/Athens/Rhodes/6024/chiefs.htm (accessed 25 November 2001).

Kapczynski, Amy. 2002. Strict international patent laws hurt developing countries. *Yale Global Online,* 16 December. http://yaleglobal.yale.edu/content/strict-international-patent-laws-hurt-developing-countries.

Kay, Lily E. 2000. *Who wrote the book of life? A history of the genetic code.* Palo Alto, CA: Stanford University Press.

Keal, Paul. 2003. *European conquest and the rights of indigenous peoples: The moral backwardness of international society.* Cambridge: Cambridge University Press.

Keeling, David. 2004. Latin American development and the globalization imperative: New directions, familiar crises. *Journal of Latin American Geography* 3 (1): 1-21.

Kennedy, David. 1988. A new stream of international law scholarship. *Wisconsin International Law Journal* 7 (1): 1-49.

Keohane, Robert O. 1984. *After hegemony: Cooperation and discord in the world political economy.* Princeton, NJ: Princeton University Press.

Kevles, Daniel. 1998. *Diamond v. Chakrabarty* and beyond: The political economy of patenting life. In *Private science: Biotechnology and the rise of the molecular sciences,* ed. Arnold Thackray, 65-79. Philadelphia: University of Pennsylvania Press.

Khalidi, Rashid. 1997. *Palestinian identity: The construction of a national modern consciousness.* New York: Columbia University Press.

Khalidi, Walid. 1984. *Before their diaspora: A photographic history of the Palestinians, 1876-1948.* Washington, DC: Institute for Palestine Studies.

—, ed. 1992. *All that remains: The Palestinian villages occupied and depopulated by Israel in 1948.* Washington, DC: Institute for Palestine Studies.

Khasnabish, Alex. 2008. *Zapatismo beyond borders: New imaginations of political possibility.* Toronto: University of Toronto Press.

Kloppenburg, Jack R. 2004. *First the seed: The political economy of plant biotechnology, 1492-2000.* 2nd ed. Madison: University of Wisconsin Press.

Koivurova, Timo. 2008. From high hopes to disillusionment: Indigenous peoples' struggle to (re)gain their right to self-determination. *International Journal on Minority and Group Rights* 15 (1): 1-26.

Krueger, Karen Goodyear. 1981. Building a better bacterium: Genetic engineering and the patent law after *Diamond v. Chakrabarty. Columbia Law Review* 81 (1): 159-78.

La Prensa. 2003. ONU inspeccionará Biosfera del Río Plátano. 17 May. http://www.Laprensa.hn (accessed June 2003).

Landsman, Gail. 1985. Ganeinkeh: Symbol and politics in an Indian/white conflict. *American Anthropologist* 87 (4): 826-39.

—. 1987. Indian activism and the press: Coverage of the conflict at Ganeinkeh. *Anthropological Quarterly* 60 (2): 101-13.

Landsman, Gail, and Sara Ciborski. 1992. Representation and politics: Contesting histories of the Iroquois. *Cultural Anthropology* 7 (4): 425-47.

Larson, Erik, Zachary Johnson, and Monique Murphy. 2008. Emerging indigenous governance: Ainu rights at the intersection of global norms and domestic institutions. *Alternatives* 33 (1): 53-82.

Latham, Robert, and Saskia Sassen. 2005. Digital formations: Constructing an object of study. In *Digital formations: IT and new architectures in the global realm,* ed. Robert Latham and Saskia Sassen, 1-33. Princeton, NJ: Princeton University Press.

Latour, Bruno. 1993. *We have never been modern.* Brighton: Harvester Wheatsheaf.

—. 1999. *Pandora's hope: Essays on the reality of science studies.* Cambridge, MA: Harvard University Press.

Lavie, Smadar, and Ted Swedenburg. 1996. *Displacement, diaspora, and geographies of identity.* Durham, NC: Duke University Press.

Lawrence, Thomas. 1895. *The principles of international law.* London: Macmillan.

Lepage, Laurent, and François Blanchard. 1992. Analyse de contenu des audiences publiques "Grande-Baliene": Étude exploratoire. Unpublished report presented to the V.P. Communication et Relations publiques, Hydro-Québec.

Leskien, Dan, and Michael Flitner. 1997. *Intellectual property rights and plant genetic resources: Options for a sui generis system.* Issues in Genetic Resources, No. 6. Rome: International Plant Genetic Resources Institute.

Lewis, Frank D. 1996. Agricultural property and the 1948 Palestinian refugees: Assessing the loss. *Explorations in Economic History* 33 (2): 169-94.

Li, Tania. 2005. Engaging simplifications: Community-based natural resource management, market processes, and state agendas in upland Southeast Asia. In *Communities and conservation: Histories and politics of community-based natural resource management,* ed. J. Peter Brosius, Anna Lowenhaupt Tsing, and Charles Zerner, 427-57. New York: Altamira Press.

—. 2007. *The will to improve: Governmentality, development, and the practice of politics*. Durham, NC: Duke University Press.

Livanos Cattaui, Maria. 2005. Counterfeiting is out of control. *International Herald Tribune,* 13 May.

Liverman, Diana, and Silvina Vilas. 2006. Neoliberalism and the environment in Latin America. *Annual Review of Environment and Resources* 31: 327-63.

Ljungman, Seve. 1965. "Trends and harmonization of patent legislation in Europe." BIRPI Lectures, KMCEL WIPO, E231F13 BIRPI.C.

Locke, John. 1952 [1690]. *The second treatise of government*. New York: Macmillan.

—. 1988 [1690]. *Two treatises of government*. Ed. Peer Laslett. Cambridge: Cambridge University Press.

Lomborg, Bjørn. 2004. *Global crises, global solutions*. Cambridge: Cambridge University Press.

Long, Joanna. 2006. Border anxiety in Palestine-Israel. *Antipode* 38 (1): 107-27.

Loomis, Terrence M. 2000. Indigenous populations and sustainable development: Building on indigenous approaches to holistic, self-determined development. *World Development* 28 (5): 893-910.

Louwaars, N.P., R. Tripp, D. Eaton, V. Henson-Appollonio, R. Hu, M. Mendoza, F. Muhhuku, S. Pal, and J. Wekundah. 2005. *Impacts of strengthened intellectual property rights regimes on the plant breeding industry in developing countries*. Wageningen: Wageningen UR.

Lynch, Owen. 2005. Concepts and strategies for promoting legal recognition of community-based property rights: Insights from the Philippines and other nations. In *Communities and conservation: Histories and politics of community-based natural resource management,* ed. J. Peter Brosius, Anna Lowenhaupt Tsing, and Charles Zerner, 391-426. New York: Altamira Press.

Lysandrou, P. 2005. Globalisation as commodification. *Cambridge Journal of Economics* 29 (5): 769-97.

Mackey, Eva. 2002. *The house of difference: Cultural politics and national identity in Canada*. Toronto: University of Toronto Press.

—. 2005. "Universal" rights in national and local conflicts: "Backlash" and "benevolent resistance" to indigenous land rights. *Anthropology Today* 21 (2): 14-20.

Macklem, Patrick. 2000-1. Indigenous rights and multinational corporations at international law. *Hastings International and Comparative Law Review* 24: 475-84.

MacLean, Sandra, Fahimul Quadir, and Timothy Shaw. 2000. Structural adjustment and the response of civil society in Bangladesh and Zimbabwe: A comparative analysis. In *Globalization and the politics of resistance,* ed. Barry K. Gills, 295-312. Houndmills: Palgrave.

MacLeod, Christine. 1999. Negotiating the rewards of innovation: The shop floor inventor in Victorian Britain. *Business History* 41 (2): 17-36.

Macpherson, C.B, ed. 1978. *Property: Mainstream and critical positions*. Toronto: University of Toronto Press.

Magnusson, Warren, and K. Shaw, eds. 2003. *A Political space: Reading the global through Clayoquot Sound*. Minneapolis: University of Minnesota Press.

Malthus, Thomas, and G. Gilbert. 1993 [1798]. *An essay on the principle of population*. New York: Oxford University Press.

Mansfield, Becky. 2004a. Neoliberalism in the oceans: "Rationalization," property rights, and the commons question. *Geoforum* 35 (2): 313-26.

—. 2004b. Rules of privatization: Contradictions in neoliberal regulation of north Pacific fisheries. *Annals of the Association of American Geographers* 94 (3): 565-84.

—. 2007. Privatization: Property and the remaking of nature-society relations. *Antipode* 39 (3): 393-405.

Marchak, M. Patricia. 1983. *Green gold: The forest industry in British Columbia.* Vancouver: UBC Press.

—. 1988. Public policy, capital, and labour in the forest industry. In *Workers, capital, and the state in British Columbia,* ed. Rennie Warburton and David Coburn, 177-200. Vancouver: UBC Press.

Marchak, M. Patricia., Scott L. Aycock, and Deborah M. Herbert. 1999. *Falldown: Forest policy in British Columbia.* Vancouver: David Suzuki Foundation.

Marcot, Bruce G., and Jack. W. Thomas. 1997. *Of spotted owls, old growth, and new policies: A history since the interagency scientific committee report.* Portland, OR: United States Department of Agriculture, Forest Service, Pacific Northwest Forest Research Station, GTR-408 97-068.

Marcot, Bruce G., Michael J: Wisdom, Hiram W. Li, and Gonzalo C. Castillo. 1994. *Managing for featured, threatened, endangered, and sensitive species and unique habitats for ecosystem sustainability.* Portland, OR: United States Department of Agriculture, Forest Service, Pacific Northwest Forest Research Station, GTR-329 93-207.

Marks, Susan. 2003. Empire's law. *Indiana Journal of Global Legal Studies* 10 (3): 449-66.

Marshall, Dale. 2002. *Down the value chain: The politics and economics of raw log exports.* Vancouver: Canadian Centre for Policy Alternatives.

Martin, Emily. 1997. Managing Americans: Policy and changes in the meanings of work and the self. In *Anthropology of policy: Critical perspectives on governance and power,* ed. Chris Shore and Susan Wright, 239-59. London: Routledge.

Martínez, M. 2003. *Reporte preliminar: Análisis de las oportunidades y limitaciones de las comunidades indígenas y organizaciones comunitarias en la gestión de comanejo de las áreas protegidas en Honduras.* Tegucigalpa: Banco Mundial.

Marx, Karl. 1976. *Capital: A critique of political economy.* Vol. 1. Trans. Ben Fowkes. Harmondsworth: Penguin Books.

May, Christopher. 2000. *A global political economy of intellectual property rights: A new enclosure?* London: Routledge.

—. 2007. *The World Intellectual Property Organization: Resurgence and the development agenda.* London: Routledge.

McAfee, Kathleen. 2003. Neoliberalism on the molecular scale: Economic and genetic reductionism in biotechnology battles. *Geoforum* 34 (2): 203-19.

McClintock, Anne. 1995. *Imperial leather: Race, gender, and sexuality in the colonial contest.* New York: Routledge.

McEvoy, Arthur F. 1986. *The fisherman's problem: Ecology and law in the California fisheries, 1850-1980.* Cambridge: Cambridge University Press.

McKay, Fergus, and Emily Caruso. 2004. Indigenous lands or national parks? *Cultural Survival Quarterly* 28 (1): 14-16.

McLaren, John, A.R. Buck, and Nancy E. Wright, eds. 2005. *Despotic dominion: Property rights in British settler societies.* Vancouver: UBC Press.

McLean, Janet. 2003. The transnational corporation in history: Some lessons for today. *Indiana Law Journal* 79 (2): 363-77.

McManis, Charles. 2003-4. Intellectual property, genetic resources and traditional knowledge protection: Thinking globally, acting locally. *Cardozo Journal of International and Comparative Law* 11 (2): 547-83.

McManus, Phil. 2002. The potential and limits of progressive neo-pluralism: A comparative study of forest politics in coastal British Columbia and south east New South Wales during the 1990s. *Environment and Planning A* 34: 845-65.

McRae, Glenn. 2004. Grassroots transnationalism and life projects of Vermonter's in the Great Whale campaign. In *In the way of development: Indigenous peoples, life projects and globalization,* ed. Mario Blaser, Harvey Feit, and Glenn McRae, 111-29. London: ZED Books and IDRC.

McSweeney, Kendra. 2004. The dugout canoe trade in Central America's Mosquitia: Approaching rural livelihoods through systems of exchange. *Association of American Geographers* 94 (3): 638-61.

Medina, Laurie. 1997. Defining difference, forging unity: The co-construction of race, ethnicity and nation in Belize. *Ethnic and Racial Studies* 20 (4): 757-80.

Merson, John. 2001. Bio-prospecting and bio-piracy: Intellectual property rights and biodiversity in a colonial and post-colonial context. *Osiris* 15 (2): 282-96.

Miéville, China. 2005. *Between equal rights: A Marxist theory of international law.* Boston: Brill.

—. 2008. The commodity-form theory of international law. In *International law on the Left: Re-examining Marxist legacies,* ed. Susan Marks, 92-132. New York: Cambridge University Press.

Mignolo, Walter D. 2000. *Local histories/global designs: Coloniality, subaltern knowledges, and border thinking.* Princeton, NJ: Princeton University Press.

—. 2005. *The idea of Latin America.* Oxford: Blackwell Publishing.

Mitchell, Timothy. 1991. *Colonizing Egypt.* Berkeley: University of California Press.

Mohawk, John C. 2000. The Iroquois land claims: A promise of fairness. *Native Americas* 17 (1): 20-23.

Mollett, Sharlene. 2006a. Entanglements: Campesinos and indigenous tenure insecurities on the Honduran north coast. In *Development's displacements: Ecologies, economies and cultures at risk,* ed. Peter Vandergeest, Pablo Idahosa, and Pablo Bose. Vancouver: UBC Press.

—. 2006b. Race and natural resource conflicts in Honduras: The Miskito and Garifuna struggle for Lasa Pulan. *Latin American Research Review* 41 (1): 76-101.

—. 2010. Está listo? Gender, race and land registration in the Río Plátano biosphere reserve. *Gender, Place and Culture* 17 (3): 357-75.

—. 2011. Racial narratives: Miskito and *colono* land struggles in the Honduran Mosquitia. *Cultural Geographies* 18 (1): 1-20.

Monet, Don. 1992. *Colonialism on trial: Indigenous land rights and the Gitskan and Wet'suwet'en sovereignty case.* Philadelphia: New Society Publishers.

Monture-Angus, Patricia. 1998. *Journeying forward: Dreaming First Nations independence.* Halifax, NS: Fernwood Press.

Moore, Mike. 2003. Multilateral meltdown. *Foreign Policy* 135: 64-65.

Morantz, Toby. 1983. An ethnohistoric study of eastern James Bay Cree social organization, 1700–1850. Canadian Ethnology Service Paper No. 88, National Museums of Canada, Ottawa.

—. 2002. *The whiteman's gonna getcha: The colonial challenge to the Crees in Quebec.* Montreal and Kingston: McGill-Queen's University Press.

Morris, Benny. 1987. *Birth of the Palestinian refugee problem, 1947-1949.* New York: Cambridge University Press.

—. 1999. *Righteous victims: A history of the Zionist-Arab conflict, 1881-1999.* New York: Knopf Books.

Morton, Adam. 2000. Mexico, neoliberal restructuring and the EZLN: A neo-Gramscian analysis. In *Globalization and the politics of resistance,* ed. Barry K. Gills, 255-79. New York: St. Martin's Press.

Moses, Ted. 2002. A retrospective from Grand Chief Ted Moses. In *I dream of yesterday and tomorrow: A celebration of the James Bay Cree,* ed. Michael Gnarowski, 22-49. Kemptville, ON: Golden Dog Press.

Muehlebach, Andrea. 2003. What self in self-determination? Notes from the frontiers of transnational indigenous activism. *Identities* 10 (2): 241-68.

Mylavarapu, Swati, and Theodore Macdonald Jr. 2005. Inter-community conflicts: New considerations for resource disputes. *Cultural Survival Quarterly* 29 (1): http://209.200.101.189/publications/csq/csq-back.cfm (accessed 3 April 2006).

Nadasdy, Paul. 2002. "Property" and Aboriginal land claims in the Canadian subarctic: Some theoretical considerations. *American Anthropologist* 104 (1): 247-61.

Nair, K.R.G., and Ashok Kumar. 1997. Introduction. In *Intellectual property rights,* ed. K.R.G. Nair and Ashok Kumar. New Delhi: Allied Publishers.

Nash, Catherine. 2004. Postcolonial geographies: Spatial narratives of inequality and interconnection. In *Envisioning human geographies,* ed. Paul Cloke, Philip Crang, and Mark Goodwin, 104-27. London: Arnold.

Nedelsky, Jennifer. 1991. Law, boundaries, and the bounded self. In *Law and the order of culture,* ed. Robert Post, 162-89. Berkeley: University of California Press.

Negi, Chandra, and Sunil Nautiyal. 2003. Indigenous peoples, biological diversity and protected area management: Policy framework towards resolving conflicts. *International Journal of Sustainable Development and World Ecology* 10 (2): 169-79.

Nelson, Lita. 1998. The rise of intellectual property in the American university. *Science* 279: 1460-61.

Niezen, Ronald. 1993. Power and dignity: The social consequences of hydro-electric development for the James Bay Cree. *Canadian Review of Sociology and Anthropology* 30 (4): 510-29.

—. 2003. *The origins of indigenism: Human rights and the politics of identity.* Berkeley, CA: University of California Press.

NOON (Neighbours of the Onondaga Nation). 2005. Onondaga presses forward with land rights action targeting corporate polluters. Syracruse Peace Council. http://www.peacecouncil.net/NOON/AmendedAction.htm.

Novick, Peter. 1999. *The Holocaust in American life.* Boston: Houghton Mifflin.

Obi, Cyril. 2000. Globalization and local resistance: The case of Shell versus the Ogoni. In *Globalization and the politics of resistance,* ed. Barry K. Gills, 280-95. New York: St. Martin's Press.

Offen, Karl. 1999. The Miskito kingdom: Landscape and the emergence of a Miskito ethnic identity, northeastern Nicaragua and Honduras, 1600-1800. PhD diss., University of Texas at Austin.

Oguamanam, Chidi. 2004. Localizing intellectual property in the globalization epoch: The integration of indigenous knowledge. *Indiana Journal of Global Legal Studies* 11 (2): 1-24.

—. 2006. Regime tension in the intellectual property arena: Farmers' rights and post-TRIPS counter regime trends. *Dalhousie Law Journal* 29: 413-53.

Oilwatch and World Rainforest Movement. 2004. *Protected areas, protected against whom?* Montevideo: World Rainforest Movement. http://www.wrm.org.uy.

O'Keefe, Roger. 1998. The "right to take part in cultural life" under article 15 of the ICESCR. *International and Comparative Law Quarterly* 47 (4): 904-23.

Oldmixon, John. 1969 [1708]. *The British Empire in America.* New York: A.M. Kelley.

Onondaga Nation. 2005. *The Onondaga Nation, Plaintiff, v. The State of New York et al.* http://www.onondaganation.org/mediafiles/pdfs/lgl_declaratory.pdf.

—. 2009a. History — Timeline. Onondaga Nation: People of the hills. http://www.onondaganation.org/aboutus/timeline.html.

—. 2009b. Sovereignty. Onondaga Nation: People of the hills. http://www.onondaganation.org/gov/sovereignty.html.

Ostrom, Elinor. 1990. *Governing the commons: The evolution of institutions for collective action.* Cambridge: Cambridge University Press.

—. 2002. Property-rights regimes and common goods: A complex link. In *Common goods: Reinventing European and international governance,* ed. Adrienne Héritier, 29-57. Lanham, MD: Rowman and Littlefield Publishers.

Ostrom, Elinor, Joanna Burger, Christopher B. Field, Richard B. Norgaard, and David Policansky. 1999. Sustainability: Revisiting the commons — Local lessons, global challenges. *Science* 284 (5412): 278-82.

Ostry, Aleck. 1999. The links between industrial, community, and ecological sustainability: A forestry case study. *Ecosystem Health* 5 (3): 193-203.

O'Tuathail, Gearoid. 1998. Thinking critically about geopolitics. In *The geopolitics reader,* ed. Gearoid O'Tuathail, 1-12. London: Routledge.

Paarlberg, Robert. 2001. *The politics of precaution: Genetically modified crops in developing countries.* Baltimore, MD: Johns Hopkins University Press.

Pal, Les. 2009. Governing the electronic commons: Globalization, legitimacy, autonomy and the Internet. In *Unsettled legitimacy: Political community, power, and authority in a global era,* ed. Steven Bernstein and William D. Coleman, 280-99. Vancouver: UBC Press.

Palatella, John. 2007. Lines of resistance. *The Nation,* 1 February. http://www.thenation.com/doc/20070219/palattella.

Pappe, Ilan. 2004. *A history of modern Palestine: One land, two peoples.* Cambridge: Cambridge University Press.

Parry, Bronwyn. 2000. The fate of the collections: Social justice and the annexation of plant genetic resources. In *People, plants and justice: The politics of nature conservation,* ed. Charles Zerner, 374-400. New York: Columbia University Press.

—. 2004. Bodily transactions: Regulating a new space of flows in "bio-information." In *Property in question: Value transformation in the global economy,* ed. Katherine Verdery and Caroline Humphrey, 29-48. Oxford: Berg.

Pasha, Mustapha. 2000. Globalization, Islam, and resistance. In *Globalization and the politics of resistance,* ed. Barry K. Gills, 241-54. New York: St. Martin's Press.

Pashukanis, Evgeni. 1980. International law. In *Pashukanis: Selected writings on Marxism and law,* ed. Bierne Piers and Robert Sharlet, 168-90. London: Academic Press.

Pearce, David. W., and R. Keny Turner. 1990. *Economics of natural resources and the environment.* Baltimore: Johns Hopkins University Press.

Peluso, Nancy L. 1992. *Rich forests, poor people: Resource control and resistance in Java.* Berkeley: University of California Press.

—. 1995. Whose woods are these? Counter-mapping forest territories in Kalimantan, Indonesia. *Antipode* 27 (4): 383-406.

Perelman, Michael. 2000. *The invention of capitalism: Classical political economy and the secret history of primitive accumulation.* Durham, NC: Duke University Press.

—. 2007. Primitive accumulation from feudalism to neoliberalism. *Capitalism, Nature, Socialism* 18 (2): 44-61.

Perry, B. Thomas, Henry J. Vaux, and Nicholas Dennis. 1983. Changing conceptions of sustained-yield policy on the national forests. *Journal of Forestry* 81 (3): 150-54.

Pertusati, Linda. 1997. *In defense of Mohawk land: Ethnopolitical conflict in Native North America.* Albany: State University of New York Press.

Peteet, Julie. 2000. Refugees, resistance, and identity. In *Globalizations and social movements: Culture, power, and the transnational public sphere,* ed. John A. Guidry, Michael D. Kennedy, and Mayer N. Zald, 183-209. Ann Arbor: University of Michigan Press.

—. 2005. *Landscape of hope and despair: Palestinian refugee camps.* Philadelphia: University of Pennsylvania Press.

Peters, Evelyn J. 1999. Native people and the environmental regime in the James Bay and Northern Quebec Agreement. *Arctic* 52 (4): 395-410.

Pieterse, Jan. 2000. Globalization and emancipation: From local empowerment to global reform. In *Globalization and the politics of resistance,* ed. Barry K. Gills, 189-206. New York: St. Martin's Press.

Plahe, Jagjit Kaur, and Chris Nyland. 2003. The WTO and patenting of life forms: Policy options for developing countries. *Third World Quarterly* 24 (1): 29-45.

Pogge, Thomas W. 2005. Human rights and global health: A research program. *Metaphilosophy* 36 (1-2): 182-209.

Polanyi, Karl. 1944. *The great transformation: The political and economic origins of our time.* Boston: Beacon Press.

Preston, Richard. 1978. La relation sacrée entre les Cris et les Oies. *Recherches Amérindiennes au Québec* 8: 147-52.

—. 1981. East Main Cree. In *Eastern subarctic: Handbook of North American Indians,* ed. June Helm, 196-207. Washington, DC: Smithsonian Institution.

—. 1982. Towards a general statement on the Eastern Cree structure of knowledge. In *Papers of the Thirteenth Algonquian Conference,* ed. William Cowan, 299-306. Ottawa: Carleton University.

—. 1990. "Hunting where we please": Land and territories, ethics and treaties in the Mushkegowuk region, Ontario. Paper presented at Ontario Sociology and Anthropology Association conference, St. Catharines, Ontario, 19 October.

—. 1997. Getting to know the great community of persons. In *Papers of the 28th Conference on Algonquian Studies,* ed. David Pentland, 274-82. Winnipeg: University of Manitoba.

—. 2002 [1975]. *Cree narrative: Expressing the personal meanings of events.* Ottawa: National Museums of Canada.

—. 2010. Twentieth-century transformations of East Cree spirituality and autonomy. In *Indigenous peoples and autonomy: Insights for a global age,* ed. Mario Blaser, Ravi de Costa, Deborah McGregor, and William Coleman, 195-217. Vancouver: UBC Press.

Preston, Sarah. 1986. *Let the past go: A life history.* Narrated by Alice Jacob. Ottawa: National Museums of Canada.

Preston, Susan M. 1999. Meaning and representation: Landscape in the oral tradition of the Eastern James Bay Cree. Master's thesis, University of Guelph.

—. 2000. Exploring the Eastern Cree landscape: Oral tradition as cognitive map. In *Papers of the Thirty-First Algonquian Conference,* ed. John D. Nichols, 310-32. Winnipeg: University of Manitoba.

—. 2006a. Compassionate landscape: Eastern Cree expressions of relational anxiety in the face of development. Paper presented at the annual meeting of the Canadian Anthropology Society, Montreal, Quebec, 10 May.

—. 2006b. "Everything will be destroyed": Traditional values and opposition to hydro development in James Bay. Paper presented at the Society for Applied Anthropology, Vancouver, British Columbia, 30 March.

Prudham, Scott. 1998. Timber and town: Post-war federal forest policy, industrial organization, and rural change in Oregon's Illinois Valley. *Antipode* 30 (2): 177-96.

—. 2003. Taming trees: Capital, science, and nature in Pacific slope tree improvement. *Annals of the Association of American Geographers* 93 (3): 636-56.

—. 2005. *Knock on wood: Nature as commodity in Douglas-Fir country.* New York: Routledge.

—. 2007. The fictions of autonomous invention: Accumulation by dispossession, commodification, and life patents. *Antipode* 39 (3): 406-29.

—. 2008. Tall among the trees: Organizing against globalist forestry in rural British Columbia. *Journal of Rural Studies* 24 (2): 182-96.

—. 2009. Commodification. In *A companion to environmental geography,* ed. Noel Castree, David Demeritt, Bruce Rhoads, and Diana Liverman, 123-41. Oxford: Blackwell.

Prudham, Scott, and Rob Penfold. 2005. *Fractured lives: Results of the 2003 survey of Youbou sawmill workers.* Victoria, BC: Youbou TimberLess Society/Vancouver Island Public Interest Research Group. http://www.islandnet.com/~vipirg/publications/pubs/research_reports/0507_youbou.pdf.

Prudham, Scott, and Maureen G. Reed. 2001. Looking to Oregon: Comparative aspects of forest policy reform and sustainability in BC and the US Pacific Northwest. *BC Studies* 130 (Summer): 5-39.

Purich, Donald. 1991. The future of Native rights. In *Sweet promises: A reader on Indian-white relations in Canada,* ed. James R. Miller, 421-40. Toronto: University of Toronto Press.

Qu, Sanqiang. 2002. *Copyright in China.* Beijing: Foreign Languages Press.

Quebec. 2003. Technical sheet 9 — Cree Nation. Secrétariat aux affaires autochtones du Québec. http://www.mce.gouv.qc.ca/w/html/w2058010.html.

Rajala, Richard. 1998. *Clearcutting the Pacific rain forest: Production, science, and regulation.* Vancouver: UBC Press.

Rajan, S. Ravi. 2006. *Modernizing nature: Forestry and imperial eco-development, 1800-1950.* Oxford: Oxford University Press.

Ramanna, Anitha, and Melinda Smale. 2004. Rights and access to plant genetic resources under India's new law. *Development Policy Review* 22 (4): 423-42.

Rayner, Jeremy. 1996. Implementing sustainability in West Coast forests: Core and FEMAT as experiments in process. *Journal of Canadian Studies* 31 (1): 82-101.

Rayner, Jeremy, Michael Howlett, Jeremy Wilson, Ben W. Cashore, and George Hoburg. 2001. Privileging the subsector: Critical subsectors and sectoral relationships in forest policy-making. *Forest Policy and Economics* 2: 319-32.

Redclift, Michael R. 2006. *Frontiers: Histories of civil society and nature.* Cambridge, MA: MIT Press.

Reed, Maureen G. 1999. "Jobs talk": Retreating from the social sustainability of forestry communities. *Forestry Chronicle* 75 (5): 755-63.

Rempel, Terry. 1999. Dispossession and restitution in 1948 Jerusalem. In *Jerusalem 1948: The Arab neighbourhoods and their fate in the war,* ed. Salim Tamari, 189-235. Jerusalem: Institute for Jerusalem Studies/Badil Resource Centre.

Retort Collective. 2006. *Afflicted powers: Capital and spectacle in a new age of war.* London: Verso.

Revels, Craig. 2003. Concessions, conflict, and the rebirth of the Honduran mahogany trade. *Journal of Latin American Geography* 2 (1): 1-17.

Ribot, Jesse, and Nancy L. Peluso. 2003. A theory of access. *Rural Sociology* 68 (2): 153-81.

Richardson, Boyce. 1991. *Strangers devour the land.* Vancouver: Douglas and McIntyre.

Rittberger, Volker, and Martin Nettesheim, eds. 2008. *Authority in the global political economy.* Houndmills: Palgrave Macmillan.

Rivas, T. 1938. *Mensajes, memorias, acuerdos, decretos y comunicaciones oficiales para la Mosquitia Hondureña.* Tegucigalpa: Biblioteca de Juan Enrique Cardona.

Robbins, William G. 1982. *Lumberjacks and legislators: Political economy of the US lumber industry, 1890-1941.* College Station, TX: A&M University Press.

—. 1987. Lumber production and community stability: A view from the Pacific Northwest. *Journal of Forestry* 31 (4): 187-96.

—. 1988. *Hard times in paradise: Coos Bay, Oregon, 1850-1986.* Seattle: University of Washington Press.

Roht-Arriaza, Naomi. 1995-96. Of seeds and shamans: The appropriation of the scientific and technical knowledge of indigenous and local communities. *Michigan Journal of International Law* 17: 919-65.

Rose, Carol M. 1994. *Property and persuasion: Essays on the history, theory and rhetoric of ownership.* Boulder, CO: Westview.

—. 1998. Canons of property talk, or, Blackstone's anxiety. *Yale Law Journal* 108 (December): 601-21.

—. 2004. Economic claims and the challenges of new property. In *Property in question: Value transformations in the global economy,* ed. Katherine Verdery and Caroline Humphrey, 275-96. Oxford: Berg.

Rose, Gregory. 2004. The international treaty on plant genetic resources for food and agriculture: A new breed? In *Accessing biological resources: Complying with the convention on biological diversity,* ed. Natalie P. Stoianoff, 55-90. The Hague: Kluwer Law International.

Rose, Jacqueline. 2005. *The Question of Zion.* Princeton, NJ: Princeton University Press.

Rossiter, David. 2007. Lessons in possession: Colonial resource geographies in practice on Vancouver Island, 1859-1865. *Journal of Historical Geography* 33 (4): 770-90.

Rossiter, David, and Patricia K. Wood. 2005. Fantastic topographies: Neoliberal responses to Aboriginal land claims in British Columbia. *Canadian Geographer* 49 (4): 352-66.

Rudel, Thomas K. 1995. Do property rights make a difference? Open access, informal social controls, and deforestation in the Ecuadorian Amazon. *Human Organization* 54 (2): 187-94.

Rupert, Mark. 2000. *Ideologies of globalization: Contending visions of world order.* London: Routledge.

Russell, Peter H. 2005. *Recognizing Aboriginal title: The Mabo case and indigenous resistance to English-settler colonialism.* Toronto: University of Toronto Press.

Rynard, Paul. 2001. Ally or colonizer? The federal state, the Cree nation and the James Bay Agreement. *Journal of Canadian Studies* 36 (2): 8-48.

Saha, Suranjit. 2002. Theorising globalisation sustainable development. In *Globalisation and sustainable development in Latin America: Perspectives on the new economic order,* ed. Suranjit Saha and David Parker, 13-50. Northhampton: Edward Elgar Publishing.

Said, Edward. 1979. *Orientalism.* Toronto: Vintage Books.

—. 1984. Permission to narrate. *London Review of Books* 6 (3): 13-17.

—. 1993. *Culture and imperialism.* New York: Knopf/Random House.

—. 1994. *The politics of dispossession: The struggle for Palestinian self-determination, 1969-1994.* New York: Pantheon Books.

Salazar, Rene, Niels P. Louwaars, and Bert Visser. 2007. Protecting farmers' new varieties: New approaches to rights on collective innovations in plant genetic resources. *World Development* 35 (9): 1515-28.

Santos, Boaventura de Sousa. 2005. General introduction: Reinventing social emancipation — Toward new manifestos. In *Democratizing democracy: Beyond the liberal democratic canon,* ed. Boaventura de Sousa Santos, xvii-xxxiii. London: Verso.

—. 2007. Human rights as an emancipatory script? Cultural and political conditions. In *Another knowledge is possible: Beyond northern epistemologies,* ed. Boaventura de Sousa Santos, 3-40. London: Verso.

Sarat, Austin, and Thomas R. Kearns. 2001. *Human rights: Concepts, contests, contingencies.* Ann Arbor: University of Michigan Press.

Satterfield, Terre. 2002. *Anatomy of a conflict: Identity, knowledge, and emotion in old-growth forests.* Vancouver: UBC Press.

Schallau, C.H., and R.M. Alston. 1987. The commitment to community stability: A policy or shibboleth. *Environmental Law* 17 (3): 429-81.

Schama, Simon. 1995. *Landscape and memory.* New York: Vintage Books.

Schmidt, Johannes. 2000. Neoliberal globalization, social welfare and trade unions in Southeast Asia. In *Globalization and the politics of resistance,* ed. Barry K. Gills, 220-40. New York: St. Martin's Press.

Schneiderman, David. 2004. Habermas, market-friendly human rights, and the revisibility of economic globalization. *Citizenship Studies* 8 (4): 419-36.

—. 2010. A new global constitutional order? In *Research handbook on comparative constitutional law,* ed. Rosalind Dixon and Tom Ginsburg, 1-19. Northampton, MA: Edward Elgar Publishing.

Schoenberger, Erica. 2004. The spatial fix revisited. *Antipode* 36 (3): 427-33.

Scholte, Jan Aart. 2002. What is globalization? The definitional issue — again. Working Paper 109/02, University of Warwick, Centre for the Study of Globalization and Regionalization (CSGR).

—. 2005. *Globalization: A critical introduction.* 2nd ed. New York: Palgrave Macmillan.

Schroeder, Richard A. 1993. Shady practice: Gender and the political ecology of resource stabilization in Gambian garden/orchards. *Economic Geography* 69 (4): 349-65.

Schumpeter, Joseph Alois. 1947. *Capitalism, socialism, and democracy.* 2nd ed. New York: Harper and Brothers.

Scott, Anthony. 1955. The fishery: The objectives of sole ownership. *Journal of Political Economy* 63 (2): 116-24.

Scott, Colin. 1988. Property, practice and Aboriginal rights among Quebec Cree hunters. In *Hunters and gatherers 2: Property, power and ideology,* ed. Tim Ingold, David Riches, and James Woodburn, 35-51. Oxford: Berg.

—. 1996. Science for the West, myth for the rest? The case of James Bay Cree knowledge construction. In *Naked science: Anthropological inquiry into boundaries, power, and knowledge,* ed. Laura Nader, 69-86. New York: Routledge.

Scott, Colin, and James Morrison. 2005. Frontières et territoires: Mode de tenure des terres des Cris de l'Est dans la région frontalière Québec/Ontario — II — Reconstruction et renouveau. *Recherches Amérindiennes au Québec* 35 (1): 41-56.

Scott, James C. 1998. *Seeing like a state: How certain schemes to improve the human condition have failed.* New Haven, CT: Yale University Press.

Secretaría de Gobernación y Justicia and AFE-COHDEFOR. n.d. *El catastro y la regularización de la tenencia de la tierra en la Reserva del Hombre y la Biosfera del Río Plátano.* Tegucigalpa: Cooperación de la República de Honduras y la República Federal de Alemania.

Segev, Tom. 1993. *The seventh million.* New York: Hill and Wang.

Sell, Susan K. 2003. *Private power, public law: The globalization of intellectual property rights.* Cambridge: Cambridge University Press.

Seshia, Shaila. 2001. Plant variety protection and farmers' rights in India: Law-making and the cultivation of varietal control. *Economic and Political Weekly* 37 (27): 2741-47.

Shannon, M.A., and K.N. Johnson. 1994. Lessons from the FEMAT. *Journal of Forestry* 92 (14): 6-14.

Shinko, Rosemary E. 2004. Discourses of denial: Silencing the Palestinians, delegitimizing their claims. *Journal of International Affairs* 58 (1): 47-73.

Shiva, Vandana. 1997. *Biopiracy: The plunder of nature and knowledge.* Boston: South End Press.

—. 1998. The greening of global reach. In *The geopolitics reader,* ed. Gearóid O'Tuathail, Simon Dalby, and Paul Routledge, 231-35. London: Routledge.

—. 2002. *Protect or plunder? Understanding intellectual property rights.* New York: Zed Books.

—. 2004. TRIPS, human rights and the public domain. *Journal of World Intellectual Property* 7 (5): 665-73.

Simmel, Georg. 1971. *On individuality and social forms.* Chicago: University of Chicago Press.

Singh, Jaidev, and Heck van Houtum. 2002. Post-colonial nature conservation in southern Africa: Same emperors, new clothes? *GeoJournal* 58 (2): 253-63.

Slaughter, Anne-Marie. 2004. *A new world order.* Princeton, NJ: Princeton University Press.

Sletto, Bjorn. 2002. Boundary making and regional identities in a globalized environment: Rebordering the Nariva Swamp, Trinidad. *Environment and Planning D: Society and Space* 20: 183-208.

Sloan, Gordon M. 1945. *The forest resources of British Columbia.* Victoria: Public Inquiries Act of British Columbia.

—. 1957. *The forest resources of British Columbia.* Victoria: Public Inquiries Act of British Columbia.

Slyomovics, Susan. 1998. *The object of memory: Arab and Jew narrate the Palestinian village.* Philadelphia: University of Pennsylvania Press.

Smith, Jeffrey M. 2003. *Seeds of deception: Exposing industry and government lies about the safety of genetically modified foods.* Fairfield, IA: Yes! Books.

Smith, Neil. 2008 [1984]. *Uneven development: Nature, capital and the production of space.* Athens: University of Georgia Press.

Society of American Foresters. 1944. *Forest terminology.* Washington, DC: Society of American Foresters.

Somekh, Sasson. 1999. Reconciling two great loves: The first Jewish-Arab literary encounter in Israel. *Israel Studies* 4 (1): 1-21.

Speed, Shannon, and Jane F. Collier. 2000. Limiting indigenous autonomy in Chiapas, Mexico: The state government's use of human rights. *Human Rights Quarterly* 22 (4): 877-905.

Spivak, Gayatri. 1988. Can the subaltern speak? In *Marxism and the interpretation of culture,* ed. Cary Nelson and Lawrence Grossberg, 271-313. Basingstoke: Macmillan.

Srinivasan, C.S. 2003. Exploring the feasibility of farmers' rights. *Development Policy Review* 21 (4): 419-47.

Star, S.L., and J.R. Griesemer. 1989. Institutional ecology, "translations" and boundary objects: Amateurs and professionals in Berkeley's Museum of Vertebrate Zoology. *Social Studies of Science* 19 (3): 387-420.

Steger, Manfred. 2003. *Globalization: A very short introduction.* Oxford: Oxford University Press.

Sterling, Bruce. 2005. The sham economy. *Wired,* 13 March.

Stevens, Stan. 2005. Wilderness, social nature, and protected areas: IUCN's encounter with the indigenous world. Paper presented at the annual meeting of the Association of American Geographers, Denver, Colorado, 5-9 April.

Stevenson-Yang, Anne, and Ken De Woskin. 2005. China destroys the IP paradigm. *Far Eastern Economic Review* (March): 9-18.

Stevis, Dimitris, and Terry Boswell. 2000. From national resistance to international labour politics. In *Globalization and the politics of resistance,* ed. Barry K. Gills, 150-70. New York: St. Martin's Press.

Stoler, Ann L., and Fredrick Cooper. 1997. Between metropole and colony: Rethinking a research agenda. In *Tensions of empire: Colonial cultures in a bourgeois world,* ed. Fredrick Cooper and Ann L. Stoler, 1-56. Berkeley: University of California Press.

Stonich, Susan. 1993. *"I am destroying the land!" The political ecology of poverty and environmental destruction in Honduras.* Boulder, CO: Westview Press.

Story, Alan. 2002. Don't ignore copyright, the "sleeping giant" on the TRIPS and international educational agenda. In *Global intellectual property rights: Knowledge, access and development,* ed. Peter Drahos and Ruth Mayne, 100-22. Basingstoke: Palgrave.

Strange, Susan. 2003. The declining authority of states. In *The global transformations reader,* 2nd ed., ed. David Held and Anthony McGrew, 127-34. Cambridge: Polity Press.

Streeter, Stephen M., John C. Weaver, and William D. Coleman, eds. 2009. *Empires and autonomy: Moments in the history of globalization.* Vancouver: UBC Press.

Sundberg, Juanita. 2006. Conservation encounters: Transculturation in the "contact zones" of empire. *Cultural Geographies* 13 (2): 239-65.

Swaney, James A. 1990. Common property, reciprocity, and community. *Journal of Economic Issues* 24 (2): 451-62.

Swanson, F.J., and J.F. Franklin. 1992. New forestry principles from ecosystem analysis of Pacific Northwest forests. *Ecological Applications* 2 (3): 262-74.

Swedenburg, Ted. 1995. *Memories of revolt: The 1936-39 Rebellion and the struggle for a Palestinian national past.* Minneapolis: University of Minnesota Press.

Tanner, Adrian. 1979. *Bringing home animals: Religious ideology and mode of production of the Mistassini Cree hunters.* London: C. Hurst and Company.

TASBA. 2003. Memo to biosphere institutions regarding the land titling project. Brus Laguna, Honduras, 10 July.

Tawfik, Myra. 2007. No longer living in splendid isolation: The globalization of national courts and the internationalization of intellectual property law. *Queen's Law Journal* 32 (2): 573-601.

Taylor, Allyn. 1999. Globalization and biotechnology: UNESCO and an international strategy to advance human rights and public health. *American Journal of Law and Medicine* 25 (4): 479-541.

Taylor, Charles. 1991. *The malaise of modernity.* Toronto: House of Anansi Press.

Theological letter concerning the moral arguments. 1983. Presented to US Congress, Foundation on Economic Trends.

Thomas, Kenneth. 2000. Corporate welfare campaigns in North America. In *Globalization and the politics of resistance,* ed. Barry K. Gills, 207-19. New York: St. Martin's Press.

Thomas, Urs P. 2002. The CBD, the WTO, and the FAO: The emergence of phytogenetic governance. In *Governing global biodiversity: The evolution and implementation of the Convention on Biological Diversity,* ed. Philippe G. LePrestre, 177-206. Aldershot: Ashgate Publishing.

Thompson, Doug. 2004. "Useful laborers" and "savage hordes": Hispanic Central American views of Afro-indigenous peoples in the nineteenth century. *Transforming Anthropology* 12 (1 and 2): 21-29.

Thompson, E.P. 1975. *Whigs and hunters: The origin of the Black Act.* New York: Pantheon.

Tibawi, Abdul Latif. 1963. Visions of return: The Palestine Arab refugees in Arabic poetry and art. *Middle East Journal* 17 (5): 507-26.

Tollefson, Christopher. 1998. Introduction. In *The wealth of forests: Markets, regulation, and sustainable forestry,* ed. Christopher Tollefson, 3-15. Vancouver: UBC Press.

Trilateral Cooperation Statistical Report. 2007. http://www.trilateral.net/statistics/tsr/2007/activity.pdf.

Tsing, Anna Lowenhaupt. 2005. *Friction: An ethnography of global connection.* Princeton, NJ: Princeton University Press.

Tuan, Yi-Fu. 1979. Thought and landscape: The eye and the mind's eye. In *The interpretation of ordinary landscapes,* ed. Donald W. Meinig and John B. Jackson, 89-102. Oxford: Oxford University Press.

Tully, James. 2000. The struggle of indigenous peoples for and of freedom. In *Political theory and the rights of indigenous peoples,* ed. Duncan Ivson, Paul Patton, and Will Saunders, 36-59. London: Cambridge University Press.

Twain, Mark. 1994 [1889]. *A Connecticut Yankee at King Arthur's court.* New York: Bantam.

UN General Assembly. 1992. Rio Declaration on Environment and Development, Principle 1. In *Report of the United Nations Conference on Environment and Development, Rio de Janeiro, 3-14 June.* A/CONF.151/26. Vol. 1. Geneva: United Nations Department of Economic and Social Affairs. http://www.un.org/documents/ga/conf151/aconf15126-1annex1.htm.

UN Special Committee on Palestine. 1947. *Supplement to survey of Palestine; Notes compiled for the information of the United Nations Special Committee on Palestine.* Jerusalem: Palestine Government Printer.

Underkuffler, Laura. 1990. On property: An essay. *Yale Law Journal* 100 (2): 127-48.

UPOV (International Union for the Protection of New Varieties of Plants). 1987. *The first twenty-five years of the International Convention for the Protection of New Varieties of Plants: December 2, 1961–December 2, 1986.* Geneva: International Union for the Protection of New Varieties of Plants.

Vallejo Larios, Mario. 1997. Análisis legal, tenencia de tierras indígenas y colonizadoras en la Biosfera del Río Plátano. In *Análisis a los instrumentos e institucionales que regulan la tenencia de la tierra en la Biosfera del Río Plátano.* Tegucigalpa: AFE-COHDEFOR.

Vandergeest, Peter. 1996. Mapping nature: Territorialization of forest rights in Thailand. *Society and Natural Resources* 16 (1): 19-37.

Vandergeest, Peter, and Nancy L. Peluso. 1995. Territorialization and state power in Thailand. *Theory and Society* 24 (3): 385-426.

—. 2001. Genealogies of the political forest and customary rights in Indonesia, Malaysia, and Thailand. *Journal of Asian Studies* 60 (3): 761-812.

—. 2003. Racialization and citizenship in Thai forest politics. *Society and Natural Resources* 16 (1): 19-37

—. 2006a. Empires of forestry: Professional forestry and state power in Southeast Asia, Part 1. *Environment and History* 12 (1): 31-64.

—. 2006b. Empires of forestry: Professional forestry and state power in Southeast Asia, Part 2. *Environment and History* 12 (4): 359-93.

Vasudevan, Alex, Colin McFarlane, and Alex Jeffrey. 2008. Spaces of enclosure. *Geoforum* 39 (5): 1641-46.

Verdery, Katherine, and Caroline Humphrey, eds. 2004. *Property in question: Value transformations in the global economy.* Oxford: Berg.

Wade, Peter. 2001. Racial identity and nationalism: A theoretical view from Latin America. *Ethnic and Racial Studies* 24 (5): 845-65.

Wagner, B. 1988. An emerging corporate nobility? Industrial concentration of economic power on public timber tenures. *Forest Planning Canada* 4 (2): 18.

Waldram, James B. 1988. *As long as the rivers run: Hydroelectric development and Native communities in western Canada.* Winnipeg: University of Manitoba Press.

Wall Street Journal. 2005. Intellectual property and India. 11 April, A20.

Walton, William. 1906. Correspondence. "Fort George" in "Diocese of Moosonee." Diocese Reports, Anglican Church Records, Sudbury, Ontario.

Warwick, P.N. Tyler. 2001. *State lands and rural development in mandatory Palestine, 1920-1948.* Brighton: Sussex Academic Press.

Waterson, Roxana. 2007. Trajectories of memory: Documentary film and the transmission of testimony. *History and Anthropology* 18 (1): 51-73.

Watts, Michael. 1994. Development 2: The privatization of everything. *Progress in Human Geography* 18 (3): 371-84.

—. 2003. Development and governmentality. *Singapore Journal of Tropical Geography* 24 (1): 6-34.

Weaver, John C. 2003. *The great land rush and the making of the modern world, 1650-1900.* Montreal and Kingston: McGill-Queen's University Press.

Wells, Michael, and Katrina Brandon. 1992. *People and parks: Linking protected area management with local communities.* Washington, DC: World Bank.

West, Paige, James Igoe, and Dan Brockington. 2006. Parks and peoples: The social impact of protected areas. *Annual Review of Anthropology* 35: 251-77.

Westlake, John. 1894. *The principles of international law.* Oxford: Clarendon Press.

While, Aidan, Andrew E.G. Jonas, and David Gibbs. 2004. The environment and the entrepreneurial city: Searching for the urban "sustainability fix" in Manchester and Leeds. *International Journal of Urban and Regional Research* 28 (3): 549-69.

White, James B. 1986-87. Economics and law: Two cultures in tension. *Tennessee Law Review* 54 (2): 161-202.

Widenor, M. 1995. Diverging patterns: Labor in the Pacific Northwest wood products industry. *Industrial Relations* 34 (3): 441-63.

Williams, Brackette. 1991. *Stains on my name, war in my veins: Guyana and the politics of cultural struggle.* Durham, NC: Duke University Press.

Wilmsen, Edwin N. 1989. Introduction. In *We are here: Politics of Aboriginal land tenure,* ed. Edwin N. Wilmsen, 1-14. Berkeley, CA: University of California Press.

Wilson, Jeremy. 1988. Forest conservation in British Columbia, 1935-85: Reflections on a barren political debate. *BC Studies* 76 (Winter): 3-32.

—. 1998. *Talk and log: Wilderness politics in British Columbia, 1965-96.* Vancouver: UBC Press.

Wilson, Patrick Impero. 2002. Native peoples and the management of natural resources in the Pacific Northwest: A comparative assessment. *American Review of Canadian Studies* 32 (3): 397-414.

Wilson, Richard. 1997. *Human rights: Culture and context — Anthropological perspectives.* London: Pluto Press.

WIPO (World Intellectual Property Organization). 1972. *WIPO management report, 1971.* Geneva: WIPO.

—. 1976. WIPO activities in the field of economic cooperation among developing countries. Conference on Economic Cooperation among Developing Countries, Mexico City, 12-21 September, WIPO Archives KMCEL WIPO/77/ECDC/CMEX/1.

—. 1979. *INPADOC: General information.* Geneva: WIPO.

—. 1980. *WIPO model law on inventions for developing countries.* WIPO: Geneva.

—. 1981. Patent information and documentation seminar within the framework of the Industrial Property Organisation for English-Speaking Africa (ESARIPO), Salisbury, 8-11 December 1981. WIPO Archives KMCEL WIPO, E 2314f175 OMPI.ESARIPO/SEM.

—. 2003. *Intergovernmental organizations admitted as observers to the meetings of the assemblies of the member states, annex II: International non-governmental organizations.* Geneva: WIPO.

—. 2004. General information. http://www.wipo.int/.

—. 2007a. Report of the Provisional Committee on Proposals Related to a WIPO Development Agenda (PCDA). Doc. A/43/13 REV. http://www.wipo.int/meetings/en/doc_details.jsp?doc_id=85452.

—. 2007b. WIPO's development agenda. http://www.wipo.int/ip-development/en/agenda/recommendations.html.

—. 2009. Statistics on the PCT system. http://www.wipo.int/ipstats/en/statistics/pct/.

WIPO. Standing Committee on the Law of Patents. 2010. Fourteenth Session, 25-29 January. http://www.wipo.int/meetings/en/details.jsp?meeting_id=17461.

World Bank. 2002. *Building institutions for markets*. Oxford University Press.

—. 2007. *Inspection panel investigation report: Honduran land administration project*. Report 39933-HO, Washington, DC, 12 July.

World Health Organization (WHO). 2002. *Genomics and world health: Report of the Advisory Committee on Health Research*. Geneva: World Health Organization.

WTO (World Trade Organization). n.d. Intellectual property: Detection and enforcement. http://www.wto.org/english/thewto_e/whatis_e/tif_e/agrm7_e.htm.

Wright, Susan, and Chris Shore. 2001a. Audit culture and anthropology. *Journal of the Royal Anthropological Institute* 7 (4): 759-63.

—. 2001b. Changing institutional contexts: New managerialism and the rise of UK higher education. *Anthropology in Action* 8 (1): 14-21.

Yeatman, Anna. 2004. Right, the state and the conception of the person. *Citizenship Studies* 8 (4): 403-17.

Young, Iris Marion. 2001. Two concepts of self-determination. In *Human rights: Concepts, contests and contingencies*, ed. Austin Sarat and Thomas R. Kearns, 25-44. Ann Arbor: University of Michigan Press.

Zerilli, Linda M. 2005a. Response to Thiele. *Political Theory* 33 (5): 715-20.

—. 2005b. "We feel our freedom": Imagination and judgment in the thought of Hannah Arendt. *Political Theory* 33 (2): 158-88.

Zerner, Charles. 2000. Toward a broader vision of justice and nature conservation. In *People, plants and justice: The politics of nature conservation*, ed. Charles Zerner, 3-20. New York: Columbia University Press.

Zimmerer, Karl. 2006. Cultural ecology: At the interface with political ecology — The new geographies of environmental conservation and globalization. *Progress in Human Geography* 30 (1): 63-78.

Contributors

William D. Coleman is the Center for International Governance (CIGI) Chair in Globalization and Public Policy at the Balsillie School of International Affairs and professor of political science at the University of Waterloo. He has been the project director of the Major Collaborative Research Initiative, Globalization and Autonomy.

A. Claire Cutler is a professor of international relations and international law in the Political Science Department at the University of Victoria, British Columbia. Trained in both law and politics, she teaches courses on international law, international relations theories, and critical political economies of world order. Her most recent projects explore the privatization of international security and the nexus between law and capitalism.

Daniel Gorman is an assistant professor in the Departments of History and Political Science at the University of Waterloo, and he teaches in the Balsillie School of International Affairs. He is interested in the connection between the decline of imperialism and the rise of global governance over the past century.

Anna Greenspan is an independent researcher whose work focuses on the rise of Asia's giants. She is currently based in Shanghai, and both her writing and teaching concentrate on the dynamic rise of the city. She also works as an adjunct professor at New York University's Shanghai campus and maintains a website at wakinggiants.net.

Jasmin Habib is an associate professor in the Department of Anthropology and director of the master's program in public issues anthropology at the University of Waterloo. Her scholarly focus is on diaspora, refugee, and indigenous identities, practices, and relationships. In particular, she is interested in how such communities are represented through popular and political narratives of identity, violence, and the law.

Eva Mackey is an associate professor in the School of Canadian Studies at Carleton University. Author of *The House of Difference: Cultural Politics and National Identity in Canada* (University of Toronto Press, 2002), she is at work on "Unsettled Expectations," a manuscript that explores conflict over indigenous land rights in Ontario and New York as a lens through which to understand settler coloniality and its challenges.

Sharlene Mollett is an assistant professor in the Department of Geography at Dartmouth College. Her research is positioned at the intersection of political ecology and critical racial studies. Her writings interrogate the multiple ways race, racialization, and gender shape natural resource conflict and management in Central America, specifically Honduras and Panama.

Susan M. Preston's research and writing focus on culture-environment relationships. She is an adjunct scholar with McMaster University's Institute on Globalization and the Human Condition, where she completed a postdoctoral fellowship in conjunction with the Department of Anthropology. Her current research focuses on the development of ethically informed, integrated approaches to understanding the social, ecological, and economic values of nature and ecosystem services for human well-being.

Scott Prudham is an associate professor in the Department of Geography and the Centre for Environment at the University of Toronto. He is an editor of the journal *Geoforum* and vice-president (salary, benefits, and pensions) of the University of Toronto Faculty Association. His research is situated at the intersection of environmental politics, environmental change, and political economy. He is author of *Knock on Wood: Nature as Commodity in Douglas-Fir Country* (Routledge, 2005) and co-editor of the collection *Neoliberal Environments: False Promises and Unnatural Consequences* (Routledge, 2007).

Austina J. Reed holds a PhD in political science from McMaster University, where her work focused on global political economy and government programs for procuring, from Mexico and the Philippines, low-cost agricultural and domestic labour for Canada. She currently works as an independent researcher for the Government of Ontario.

Index